# Management for Professionals

The Springer series "Management for Professionals" comprises high-level business and management books for executives, MBA students, and practice-oriented business researchers. The topics cover all themes relevant to businesses and the business ecosystem. The authors are experienced business professionals and renowned professors who combine scientific backgrounds, best practices, and entrepreneurial vision to provide powerful insights into achieving business excellence.

The Series is SCOPUS-indexed.

Sabine Kirchem • Martin Stadelmann
Mario Pufahl • David Laux
Editors

# CRM Goes Digital

## Design and Use of Digital Customer Interface in Marketing, Sales and Service

Springer

*Editors*
Sabine Kirchem
DIGITALL Nature Germany GmbH
Karlsruhe, Germany

Mario Pufahl
DIGITALL Nature Germany GmbH
Düsseldorf, Germany

Martin Stadelmann
Zurich, Switzerland

David Laux
DIGITALL Nature Switzerland AG
Pfäffikon, Switzerland

ISSN 2192-8096 ISSN 2192-810X (electronic)
Management for Professionals
ISBN 978-3-658-45797-6 ISBN 978-3-658-45798-3 (eBook)
https://doi.org/10.1007/978-3-658-45798-3

Translation from the German language edition: “CRM goes digital” by Sabine Kirchem et al., © Springer Fachmedien Wiesbaden GmbH, ein Teil von Springer Nature 2020. Published by Springer Fachmedien Wiesbaden GmbH. All Rights Reserved.



This Springer imprint is published by the registered company Springer Fachmedien Wiesbaden GmbH, part of Springer Nature.
The registered company address is: Abraham-Lincoln-Str. 46, 65189 Wiesbaden, Germany

*Digitalization will not "pass," it is not just any technological trend. At most, the thought that it will pass will pass.*

*—Michael Pachmajer, Chairman of the Board of Trustees of the Cocreation Foundation and Co-Founder of d. quarks, a platform for entrepreneurial and social digital transformation*

# Preface

As editors of two best practice CRM books (2003 and 2008), among other publications, we have observed and accompanied the initial years of a very young discipline. A great deal has happened in customer management. Not only has management's awareness of and attention to the important "customer issue" have risen significantly, representing a "change from an IT-dominated perspective to a company-wide organizational and management philosophy." But the implementation of corresponding design approaches in corporate practice is now dominated by complete novelties: multi-, omni-channel, and mobile CRM concepts; customer experience and customer loyalty approaches; the use of artificial intelligence and the Internet of Things; social media management; marketing automation; and last but not least, the megatrend—almost taken for granted by many decision-makers and company designers—encompassing everything and known as "digital transformation."

This has provoked us to a publication project once again, in which we document how customer management has developed in recent years. We also examine potential for the future development of comprehensive and future-oriented customer management, entirely in the spirit of digital transformation that consistently exploits the benefits of core professional and technical trends in digital CRM (dCRM).

We are particularly pleased to offer this English-language edition, a further development of the German-language *CRM Goes Digital* of the same name, for an international audience.

As in our previous work, our co-authors come from renowned companies and include academics with a customer management focus and CRM consultants with many years of project experience and proven expertise in various specialisms. Together, we demonstrate current development trends and how we can expect their use and application in real innovations to progress in the coming years.

The framework set by our editors ensures that the content, concept, and terminology of the entire work are consistent.

With *CRM Goes Digital: Designing and Using Digital Customer Interfaces in Marketing, Sales and Service*, our title makes the challenging claim to represent a forward-looking, practice-oriented, and meanwhile conceptually sound book on digitalization.

Our conceptual framework is consistently based on the customer journey concept as established in corporate practice. To represent this journey simply, we have oriented ourselves using a method of process improvement: PDSA (plan, do, study, adjust). This is usually used in the Lean Business Management approach.

Within the digital transformation of CRM, we can equivalently speak of four fields that form a perpetual circle: plan, implement, use, and improve.

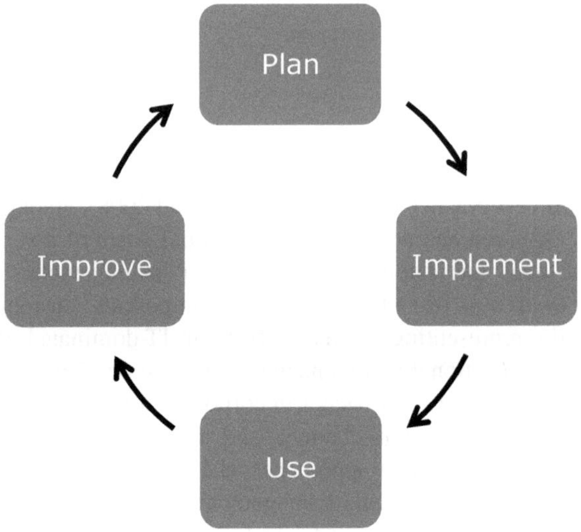


**Four Fields of Action (Kirchem 2022)**

This cycle begins with planning. To achieve a goal, the associated strategy must be formulated, success criteria defined, and an implementation plan formulated.

Following these activities, the "implement" step involves executing the components of the plan, such as integrating processes or setting up workflows.

Implemented CRM processes are then in use, usually by internal company users (inside), or prospects and customers (outside). This is when effective planning becomes apparent in signs of either progress and success, or problems and areas for improvement.

In the "improve" step, lessons learned are aligned with the strategy and used to continuously adjust or enhance processes.

A regular end-to-end review of these action areas and their interactions facilitates the transformation of customer-relevant business processes.

The reader will find all chapters of this book organized into one of these four phases. This division does not replace the CRM framework (Chapter "The CRM Competence Model: The Basis of Consistently Customer-Oriented Company Design"), which is based on the entire strategic consideration of the digitization of customer relationship management. But it serves to orient aid and primarily intends to simplify classifying and finding relevant topics, depending on the reader's transformation phase.

Contributions to this volume, in their totality and systematics, intend to serve the reader as inspiration. At the same time, they can act as a compass to navigate the thicket of design approaches propagated in various forms today.

The identification of successful, long-term approaches and their differentiation from regularly occurring CRM and IT fads or "flavors of the month" concerns authors throughout the book.

The contents of *CRM Goes Digital* include:

- Presentation and systematization of conceptual approaches
- Documentation of innovative approaches and tried-and-tested best practices
- Provision of "recipes" ("how-tos") for promising implementation of digital customer relationship management projects

With this work, we primarily address board members, executives, and users from customer-facing business units who, besides taking their first steps in digitization, are seeking deeper insight into the value-creating possibilities of current developments. Such readers will gain an idea of exactly how digital customer management can help achieve strategic and operational goals. In this context, the reports from the field are a particularly valuable contribution building bridges between today and the development of the future.

Our deepest thanks therefore go to the guest authors, who have given us all deep insights into their everyday customer management. Without them, this volume would not have been possible.

A book like this does not write itself, and we would like to take this opportunity to express our sincere thanks to all who have contributed to this book: from the content and concepts to the operational implementation and design. This especially includes our production editors Ramya Prakash and Prashanth Mahagaonkar, who supported us with great expertise and, above all, taught us the ins and outs of the international book market.

We would also like to thank Juliane Waack, who once again provided us with support through her special talent for languages, as well as our colleague Ana Varga, forever a rock to whom thanks are due for her consistency.

We wish all readers of *CRM Goes Digital* an entertaining, varied, and enriching read. We look forward to mutually enriching exchanges with you in future.

Karlsruhe, Germany — Sabine Kirchem
Zurich, Switzerland — Martin Stadelmann
Düsseldorf, Germany — Mario Pufahl
Pfäffikon, Switzerland — David Laux
October 2022

# Contents

# Part I

# Plan

# The CRM Competence Model: The Basis of Consistently Customer-Oriented Company Design

Martin Stadelmann

**Abstract**

In a multitude of strategic CRM implementation initiatives, the application of an integrative concept (often referred to as CRM framework) has proven decisive for successful analysis, conception, and realization of comprehensive and consistent customer management. The CRM competency model presented in this chapter is a holistic analysis and design approach for sustainably establishing competitively superior customer relationship management. It accounts for a comprehensive understanding of CRM in terms of content and meanwhile forms the basis for a tried-and-tested CRM project procedure and a uniform CRM terminology. The analysis and design framework addresses central aspects of CRM in four CRM context fields, seven CRM competence fields, and across three phases of the customer journey: the management of marketing (the "need"), sales (the "buy"), and service (the "use"). The application context of the CRM competency model is based on numerous best practices in customer relationship management, identified by research, education, business, and consulting practice.

## 1 The Status Quo of CRM: The Initial Situation and Requirements for Contemporary Customer Management

Since the turn of the millennium, due to the increasingly noticeable effects of digitalization and increasingly fluid customer behavior, companies of all sizes and in all industries have been intensively moving away from an inside-out, product- and organization-centric approach. In response to obvious disruptions, all functional

M. Stadelmann (✉)
Zurich, Switzerland


S. Kirchem et al. (eds.), *CRM Goes Digital*, Management for Professionals,
https://doi.org/10.1007/978-3-658-45798-3_1

corporate areas are being consistently realigned to specific and clearly identifiable customer needs, customer expectations, and customer experiences in the sense of an outside-in way of seeing and acting.

This reorientation of corporate thinking and action, guided by the maxim of customer centricity, finds expression in the now widespread customer journey management, the active shaping of the so-called "customer journey," understood as the sum of customer contacts and the customer experience, from the initial triggering of the need to the customer's first encounter with the product or service offering, its acquisition (the "buy"), its often long-term use (the "use"), and the termination or cancellation of the customer relationship or contractual relationship.

Strategic importance is increasingly ascribed—in line with associated customer management activities—to analyses and forecasts of customer behavior that derive insights into individual customers' situation- and lifecycle-specific service needs and requirements. Insights are operationalized, visualized, and thus made communicable through so-called "personas." Clearly, defined target groups (or customer segments) are similarly important.

Meanwhile, corporate design and investment decisions are increasingly based on the realization that companies can only acquire and secure the long-term loyalty of their customers through consistent and comprehensive needs orientation and increasingly proactive relationship building. The focus is no longer the battle for market share. Rather, the aim is to steadily expand business volume with each existing customer to fully exploit their overall potential ("share of wallet").

From the company's point of view, not every customer is a profitable customer. That is, not every customer has the same high customer value and correspondingly future-oriented value-creation potential for the company (so-called "customer lifetime value"). From both an efficiency and an effectiveness perspective, it is therefore crucial to intensify and consolidate business relationships, particularly with the customers that have the highest customer values or whose earning potential is currently the highest.

To identify attractive and loyal customer segments, evaluation and categorization is a first step. Based on customers' behavioral and transactional patterns, socio-demographic characteristics, and needs profiles, value- and potential-based customer segments can be formed, enabling the corresponding prioritization of customer care efforts and the corresponding design of customer care concepts. This enables companies to make targeted investments in their most profitable customers—for example, through special customer- or segment-specific service dimensions or differentiated conditions. The decisive factor is that the most up-to-date and detailed information on all customers is recorded and maintained.

On one hand, structural and process-related prerequisites must be created within which customer knowledge is placed on a "multipliable" basis; that is, knowledge can be used several times and in the context of different customer loyalty and support measures. On the other hand, data on existing and potential customers must be of high quality and topical relevance. Implementation has been achieved in many companies by setting up central customer databases with corresponding customer care functionalities. The widespread availability of high-performance and modern CRM systems and CRM IT platforms with process- and industry-specific characteristics is proof of this.

In addition to the technical anchoring of modern data management systems, the critical success factor of seamless, system-compliant data collection, which today is often still carried out by operational employees in service and sales, is particularly controlled by incentive and sanction systems. The accompanying change in the behavior of all employees through targeted change management is necessary for effective data management in corporate and CRM management.

At the same time, the company must strive to ensure that customer relationship management is understood and practiced as an integrating management and organizational principle across all hierarchical levels and all customer-related functional areas, especially marketing, sales, and customer service. The aim is to ensure that all processes and measures aimed at improving customer orientation and customer satisfaction are included.

The overriding objective must be to ensure that a company can:

- Establish long-term profitable customer relationships (customer acquisition).
- Intensify them over time (customer development).
- Maintain them in the long term (customer retention).

The basic idea of customer relationship management thus encompasses the systematic development and exploitation of customer potential, wherever possible and appropriate, using forward-looking, innovative, and end-to-end information and communications technologies.

To meet the requirements for customer-centric corporate design that result from this CRM definition, all activities and processes of the "customer-centric" corporate functions—marketing, sales, and customer care—must be designed to span all phases of the customer lifecycle and to continuously and consistently interlock. In doing so, it is important to:

(a) Make the interfaces between the internal corporate functions involved in customer care as smooth as possible for the customer.
(b) Design the customer's "journey" from one specific customer activity (customer lifecycle phase, if applicable) to the next and the associated changes in customer care approach to create a uniform and coherent customer experience, the so-called "customer experience (CX)."

In addition, customer management activities must be embedded in a corporate management and organization that is consistently aligned with the customer perspectives, expectations, and requirements (outside-in) for the respective products and services.

On one hand, it is important to strive for an organizational structure with short and direct communication channels from company to customer and vice versa. On the other hand, the central tasks of customer management must be clearly assigned to responsible organizational units to ensure ownership and responsibility. This is the only way to ensure that "customer promises" are kept.

Successful implementation of a departmental or company-wide CRM project depends on selecting an approach in the early strategic and technical conception phase of a CRM initiative that accounts for all aspects and dimensions of customer management design in its goal formulation and resulting CRM roadmap. The approach should include the creation of consistent end-to-end customer processes.

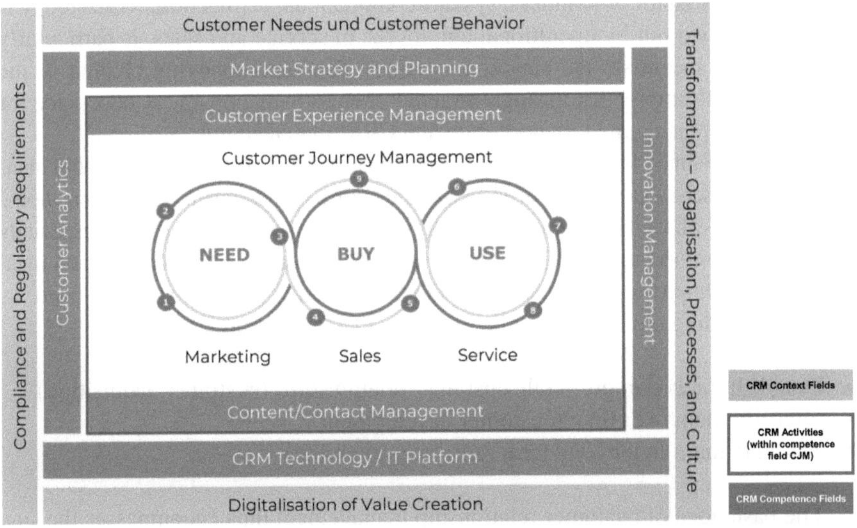


**Fig. 1** CRM competency model—the basis for a consistently customer-oriented company structure

## 1.1 The CRM Competence Model: A Model for the Analysis and Design of Customer Management

In a multiplicity of strategic CRM conversion initiatives of considerable nationally and internationally active enterprises, the availability of an underlying integrative concept—and regular reference to it—for the analysis and conception of comprehensive and continuous customer management has proved a crucial factor in success.

The CRM competence model presented here is a holistic analysis and design approach for the sustainable establishment of competitively superior customer relationship management. It accounts for a comprehensive understanding of CRM in terms of content. At the same time, it forms the basis for a tried-and-tested CRM project procedure and for a uniform CRM terminology.

The holistic analysis and design framework addresses both exogenous and endogenous CRM-relevant aspects in four CRM context fields and seven CRM competency fields across the customer journey phases of marketing, sales, and service. In addition, the application context of the CRM competency model is based on work from over 1000 authors on best practices in customer relationship management identified in academic research, corporate practice, and management consulting (Fig. 1).

## 1.2 Four CRM Context Fields: The Frame-Setting Orientation Lines of Future-Oriented Customer Management

Four CRM context fields act as frame-setting orientation lines to address the exogenous aspects of sustainable customer relationship management. Taken together, they encompass the fundamental framework conditions with which all companies are factually confronted and to which they must specifically respond, wherever they directly or indirectly affect them.

To prepare appropriately for the necessary design requirements resulting from each CRM context field, knowledge of the field and its associated entrepreneurial risks is indispensable.

In the following, we identify the core contents of the four CRM context fields, and name the key success factors for consideration in each case:

- Digitization of value creation
- Customer needs and customer behavior
- Transformation of organization, processes, and culture
- Compliance and regulatory requirements

### 1.2.1 The Digitization of Value Creation

Trends in digitization—from purchasing, to education, to healthcare—have affected almost every area of life, so corresponding developments have also found their way into customer management. These include the use of artificial intelligence, automated processing and decision-making processes, voice robots, and so-called chatbots, as well as automated communication in digital channels. Massive value creation, whether through revenue or costs, is promised.

At the same time, a certain disillusionment is spreading: according to the 2018 study "Trends & Digitalization in CRM 2018" (Zukunft.Kunde 2018), CRM, IT, and corporate strategy are only moderately (41%) or even poorly (31%) aligned in many companies. As a consequence, respondents indicated that their companies were only moderately (50%) or even poorly (8%) prepared for the challenges of digital customer management.

The largest obstacles to effective use of CRM systems were the lack of integration of CRM tools into the existing IT application landscape (51%), inadequate mapping of sales processes (45%), and unsatisfactory user-friendliness of existing tools (41%).

Respondents identified various causes for this: digitalization was much faster than the changes required in their own company (69%); employees lacked the necessary technical skills (67%); and the organization was either not designed for digitalization (45%) or too rigidly structured (44%).

To lend additional weight to these findings, it should be noted that "digitization" has so far almost exclusively described mapping previously analogue processes with digital aids, for example, making the telephone directory electronically available and thus now electronically searchable. Fundamentally "new" routines or processes were not created—in the sense of "first-order digitization"—in most cases.

In this book, however, "digitization" is understood to mean the possibility of realizing processes that could not or cannot be depicted with traditional digital aids, like objects in an originally analogue form that could now be available digitally, for example, texts, sound/speech recordings, or films.

As an illustrative example of digitization, take the mobile calculation of a journey and arrival time, defined ad hoc by a user of a vehicle rented at a train station. This accounts for current traffic reports, with simultaneous recommendations for alternative routes; and it can meanwhile make reservations in the desired hotel and a nearby restaurant based on the menus of the last three restaurants visited at the point of departure. A customer living nearby can be invited to dinner by email, and so on. This is "second-order digitization," which not only promises value creation through more efficient process design, but also value creation through more effective (i.e., innovative) process design.

The following core professional and technical trends in digitization. When they are coordinated and used in line with strategy, they are capable of creating qualitative and quantitative added value and simultaneously eliminating coordinated obstacles named above:

- Multichannel management
- Mobile business (mobility)
- Social media management
- Big Data/Customer Insight
- Cloud computing/virtualization
- Internet of Things
- Artificial Intelligence

**Key Takeaways**
Success factors in dealing with the context field of digitization of value creation:

- Identifying and evaluating trends in digitization that are relevant to the industry and customer needs (trend scouting).
- Embedding identified digitization trends in the pursued market strategy and integrating them with agreed market planning, particularly the defined CRM roadmap.
- Defining business models (variants) for differentiation from the competition.
- Elaborating sustainable, positive revenue models (cost/benefit calculations, business cases) to secure long-term revenues.

### 1.2.2 Customer Needs and Customer Behavior

Digital technologies and innovations have turned today's marketing and customer relationship management upside down. In a world in which the customer experience is shaped by disruptive "game changers" such as Amazon, Facebook, Uber, and Airbnb, companies in almost all industries are confronted with fundamentally different customer requirements. Today's customers are used to tailored products, services, and pricing models, and they expect the same from companies in industries that have only just entered the phase of digital transformation and are accordingly still stuck with old ideas and customer relationship structures.

Technology, automation, and globalization are dramatically changing what customers expect from companies and the products and services they provide. Customers compare service levels across industries and therefore expect the highest standards of personalization, choice, speed of delivery, and quality in every interaction.

The buzzword "Age of the customer" describes this paradigm shift, which is not only changing customer expectations, but also customer behavior, especially customer loyalty. In the digital age, customers have increasingly more control and are less patient and loyal. Simply put, customers expect consistent and high-quality personal and digital experiences. They do not care if "producing" this customer experience is difficult and costly. They want immediate value at the best price, and will look for another provider if their expectations are not served.

Digital technologies and innovations empower customers to make complex purchasing decisions autonomously. Marketing and sales strategies must reflect this. In the age of the customer, companies that not only meet rapidly changing customer expectations but are also able to anticipate customers' future needs will be equipped to survive the digital transformation. Only consistent customer orientation will ensure value creation and customer loyalty in the future.

Today, the customer journey usually begins with an autonomously guided information search. Customers have had enough of traditional communication messages, marketing, and advertising; they are more skeptical. They trust the content on company websites less and less but trust the members of their own community all the more. They conduct more research and use digital communication channels to get tasks done. At the same time, however, the time people can spend seeking, absorbing and, perhaps most importantly, verifying information is dwindling. The combination of increasing access to information and dwindling attention spans requires a clear structuring of information offerings (content) from the company side. Information alone is no longer enough. It must be easily accessible and comprehensibly adapted to the usage behavior of customers.

And customers expect fast and reliable solutions to their questions and problems at first contact (so-called "first contact resolution"). Technologically, companies can already rely on systems that respond to customer inquiries in an automated and structured way, drawing on knowledge databases and documented feedback from similar customer inquiries. This enables service staff to provide the highest level of personalized customer service.

The best customer service models consider different types of customers and strive to cover a wide variety of customer needs with their CRM. While some customers prefer to address their questions to a service representative in person, others prefer to address their service needs via email and chat while browsing online. A high-functioning customer service team is equipped to handle any customer preference.

Digital thinking, "mobile first" and chat, Big Data, and self-service mean very little without a strong and dedicated team of customer service enthusiasts. The best customer service representatives are those who "step into the customer's shoes" and take ownership of the customer's problems. Customer service is as much about empathy and care as it is about technology and data.

Accordingly, the "Customer Needs and Behavior" context area focuses on:

- Developing targeted measures to establish profitable customer relationships (customer acquisition), to intensify them over time (customer development), maintain them over the long term (customer retention), and, if necessary, win back lost or migrated customers (customer recovery).
- The documentation and standardization—including defining quality and measurement criteria—of all CRM processes is required for this purpose.

- Measuring process execution in a systematic control cycle—which includes target definition, deviation analysis, defining improvement measures, and success control—and measuring customer and employee acceptance of CRM processes.
- Designing a transparent organizational structure geared to customer needs with direct communication channels between management, employees, partners, suppliers, and customers.

**Key Takeaways**
Success factors in dealing with the context field of customer needs and customer behavior:

- Recording and evaluating trends in digitization that are relevant to the industry and customer needs (trend scouting).
- Developing cross-channel and consistent product and service offerings along the entire customer lifecycle.
- Establishing a self-contained customer feedback loop to capture customer reactions, at all touchpoints, in real time, along with analytical links and available relational and transactional data on customers to develop and establish different customer (service) segments, each with different service qualities.

### 1.2.3 Transformation: Organization, Processes, and Culture

Because employees continue to provide the majority of all customer relationship measures and activities today and will for the foreseeable future, they represent the most important interface between a company and its customers. In performing their tasks and responsibilities within defined customer management activities (customer journeys), employees must be supported by management, including through targeted training and continuing education.

Due to the empirically proven and frequently cited positive correlations between customer satisfaction, customer loyalty, and effects on corporate success on one hand, and employee satisfaction and loyalty on the other hand, the design requirements of the CRM context field of transformation—organization, processes, and culture—are of central importance in the context of a CRM-focused corporate orientation.

Identifying externally and internally induced change processes and their effects on respective companies and customers, and aligning future entrepreneurial thinking and action accordingly, the CRM context field of transformation—organization, processes, and culture—postulates the following:

- The identification of CRM tasks and responsibilities that are decisive for customer orientation and their assignment to corresponding management roles (Chief Customer Officer, Key Account Manager, Head of Marketing, Head of Customer Service, etc.) (Stadelmann 2004, p. 3).

- The creation of a customer-oriented, less complex organizational structure with direct communication channels between management, front-line staff, and customers.
- The perception of clearly visible role model functions in customer relationship management (management leadership).
- Ensuring the highest possible level of employee satisfaction and loyalty, or at least the lowest possible level of employee turnover.
- Formulating and defining clear employee goals in line with the company's overarching CRM goals (CRM goal system, goal hierarchy).
- Promoting customer-oriented attitudes and behaviors through the appropriate design of management tools and incentive systems.
- Ensuring the qualifications and competencies required for CRM by recruiting and training ("enabling") all employees with customer management tasks.
- Selecting and managing suppliers with a highly congruent understanding of how to perform customer management activities.

**Key Takeaways**
Success factors in dealing with the context field of transformation—organization, processes, and culture:

- Targeted focus on skills, competencies, motivation, and satisfaction of all employees.
- Promotion of customer-oriented attitudes and behaviors among all employees.
- Company-wide anchoring of customer orientation as the overriding maxim for action.
- Creation of organizational framework conditions for performing the tasks relevant to customer orientation (roles, responsibilities, communication channels).

### 1.2.4 Compliance and Regulatory Requirements

Ongoing digitization in companies is causing changes on many levels. On one hand, there is a noticeable acceleration of business processes. Response time in communication is becoming shorter, the risk of errors is increasing, as is the risk of compliance violations; on the other hand, the amount of internal information is increasing significantly.

At the same time, global digital networking is leading to a new flood of data that must be captured by the risk management system. Both acceleration and information growth threaten the proper functioning of the compliance management system. It is not uncommon to react by increasing internal regulatory requirements, but this endangers profitability through additional costs for processes, it slows down day-to-day business, and it prevents innovation by discouraging motivated employees. It is therefore "decisive for war" that not only the business processes in the company adapt to the effects of digitalization, but also the compliance management systems themselves. Intelligent technologies for monitoring legal requirements are already available today. In the age of Big Data, large databases can be analyzed in seconds, not only for the purpose of business optimization but also for the purpose of compliance. Fraudulent actions by employees can be detected using forensic data analysis. Vulnerabilities are automatically fixed by self-learning algorithms and analysis is visualized on a dashboard in real time.

The General Data Protection Regulation (abbreviated to "GDPR"), which came into force across Europe on May 25, 2018, has fundamentally changed the framework conditions for marketing and sales for the vast majority of companies. GDPR regulates the documentation and processing of personal data in companies. Any contact with customers or disclosure of information to third parties must be listed and justified in detail when it is introduced. In cases of non-compliance, companies face heavy fines.

According to GDPR, companies must, for example, maintain a procedure directory, which documents any contact with customers. However, only information that is directly necessary for a contract or for the use of a service may be stored or processed. Nevertheless, there must always be consent to use the data. Precise logging of the use is also necessary. Customers have the right to revoke their consent at any time. Keeping sensitive information as soon as it loses its effective use for companies is now illegal; with the termination of a contract, data protection requires the complete deletion of the documentation at hand.

To comply with GDPR, and at the same time benefit from innovations in sales, it is appropriate to digitize and effectively adapt sales processes. Intelligent software programs include the possibility of time-limited use of data and whitelisting contacts. Complex functions for storing or processing information, such as documenting proofs of origin with sources, the validity of information, the permission to use it, and recording all contact paths, are becoming indispensable for daily marketing and sales work. Digital distribution has thus replaced paper-based distribution. This eliminates error-prone media disruptions and time-consuming administrative work, leaving more time for promising leads.

**Key Takeaways**

Success factors in dealing with the context field of compliance and regulatory requirements:

- Risk and compliance management must be digitally transformed, just like other central corporate areas—this is the only way to prevent it from becoming a bottleneck in corporate development.
- Consistent technical implementation of modern instruments for data protection, including their safeguarding through consistent cultural change in the company's handling of data.
- Creation of an organizational framework to ensure compliance with data protection requirements and other regulatory requirements within the company (roles, responsibilities, communication channels).
- Use of stricter data protection requirements to transform marketing and sales in the direction of personalization and transaction management.

## 1.3 Seven CRM Competency Fields: Frameworks for Future-Oriented Customer Management

The seven CRM competence fields are the constituent elements of the CRM competence model. The customer management activities, which are represented in the model by the "customer journey," form the core of the model. These are presented and explained in detail below.

### 1.3.1 Customer Analytics

The starting point for customer management, aligned with the overarching corporate and market strategy and its corporate objectives, is a company's understanding of the behaviors, attitudes, and values of its customers and customer groups. The resulting understanding of customer needs and customer requirements is derived from analysis of internally available data (i.e., analytical CRM) in targeted combination with external sources of information. At the same time, more far-reaching questions become the focus of management interest, which in turn determine the company's market research activities and market monitoring (e.g., competitor analyses).

As soon as a comprehensive understanding of the market situation and the behavior and needs of both potential and existing customers has been achieved, the planning of the costs of effective acquisition and retention of customers and the optimization of support for the active customer base can be tackled. The CRM competence field of Customer Analytics is therefore fundamentally concerned with:

- The strategic input to or from the planning of customer management.
- The comprehensive analysis of customer values and the determination of existing value-creation potential for the company, based on this analysis.
- The segmentation of customers and potential customers.
- The management of knowledge about customers, their needs, their behavior, and their value-creation potential for the company.

The resulting findings regarding the performance of employees entrusted with the delivery of customer relationship management, customer processes, associated costs and revenues, channel performance, and customer behaviors must underpin the vision and objectives of customer management. They are used to assess the success or failure of CRM activities and measures. In this context, any feedback on successes and failures is a basic prerequisite for improving and redesigning future customer management plans and activities.

In terms of effective implementation, it is essential to take CRM-relevant metrics into account in the company's controlling instruments and to set up corresponding closed management and control loops.

From a controlling perspective, the CRM competence field Customer Analytics therefore additionally focuses on:

- The definition and systematic measurement of key performance indicators (KPIs) for customer relationship and customer value management.

- The identification and measurement of customer behavior, value creation, and loyalty.
- Measuring the effectiveness of campaigns.
- Measuring the effectiveness of channels.
- Measuring the effectiveness of all employees with tasks in marketing, sales, and customer care.

A comparatively new area of expertise in customer analytics is the prediction of customer behavior or the utilization of static models of customer behavior to positively shape customer relationships. The buzzwords here are "trigger-based marketing" and "event-based marketing." Here, the (in the best case) historicized knowledge about the customer and their behavior in the contractual relationship (e.g., claims frequency and payment quality) is used to develop mathematical models, on the basis of which certain actions are triggered automatically. The near-classic examples are models for predicting the probability of cancellation or those in the area of additional sales ("cross-selling and upselling").

Digitization is opening up unimagined new possibilities for customer analytics, not only to make traditional models much more intelligent and customer-specific, but also to open up almost every area of the customer's life for which data is available, using prediction models for marketing, sales, and inventory management and making them accessible for customer relationship management. On the systems side, the entire subject area of artificial intelligence (AI) corresponds to the "predictive marketing" just described, the prediction of customer behavior.

### 1.3.2 Market Strategy and Planning

Competitive strategic orientation has significant consequences for the corporate design of customer management. Consequently, within the framework of the CRM context field of market strategy and planning, all inputs from corporate strategy and corporate planning that are relevant for customer management must be systematically recorded, considered in the concrete design of the market approach, and communicated at the appropriate level, internally and externally, for example, to sales partners. This is the only way to ensure uniform service provision and, based on this, consistent customer experience.

Within the context of market strategy and planning, it is important to compare one's own customer management with that of competitors ("benchmarking"): Customers experience the approaches of different companies, and their expectations of how to deal with them as customers and thus as value creators arise on the basis of these experiences. In this respect, success relies on insights into the customer management practices of companies in one's own industry and selected other industries that adopt similar strategic positioning.

In addition, factors external to the company that influence customer management activities—be they political-legal, societal, economic, technological, or social—must be examined. The selection of CRM context fields attempts to take account of this circumstance within the CRM competence model with its holistic perspective.

Finally, it is important to account for existing cooperation on the company side and social networks on the customer side (for example, in communities) through an appropriately aligned, comprehensive concept.

**Key Takeaways**
Success factors of the CRM competence field market strategy and planning:

- Recording, consideration, and systematization of all relevant inputs—especially corporate strategy, containing financial, HR, and product strategy—in the market strategy.
- Creation, implementation, operationalization, and monitoring (performance measurement) and ongoing adaptation of market planning in line with the strategy.
- Creation and use of market environment and competitor analyses.
- Identification and use of selected social network cooperation and on the company and customer sides (communities and social media).

### 1.3.3 Customer Experience Management

Customers are especially perceptive of customer management activities during so-called "game-changing" customer contact situations, or "moments of truth." It is critical to understand how associated experiences influence not only immediate reactions but also medium- and long-term attitudes and behaviors of customers.

Customer experience management is therefore understood as the creation of positive customer experiences that lead, consciously or unconsciously, to the development of an emotional bond between the customer and the company or its market service. The primary goal of customer experience management is to turn satisfied customers into loyal customers and subsequently into "ambassadors" for the product or the company. The aim is not only to achieve direct effects such as increased sales, willingness to buy, or usage intensity but also indirect effects such as recommendations or cooperation in customer forums. Ideally, this is done at every customer contact point (touchpoint).

This can only succeed if the customer perspective is consistently adopted and the company itself is viewed from precisely this perspective (outside-in), and assessed in terms of its CRM performance, in direct and, if possible, concrete comparison with competitors.

Therefore, the CRM competence field of Customer Experience Management focuses on:

- Understanding customer attitudes and satisfaction.
- The relationship between customer satisfaction and loyalty.
- Understanding customer engagement.
- Understanding how the customer feels.
- Identifying and applying cross-company CRM-relevant benchmarks.

**Key Takeaways**
Success factors of the CRM competence field Customer Experience Management:

- Comprehensive analyses of customer needs, satisfaction, and loyalty.
- Creation of customer enthusiasm.
- Investigation of short-term customer reactions and medium- to long-term customer behavior.

### 1.3.4 Innovation Management

After changing and/or new customer needs have been identified—for example, through a market research "needs radar," focus groups, or a sounding board of employees with customer contact—on the basis of customer needs analyses or analysis of customer behavior, customer-oriented companies must respond in a clearly recognizable manner through the design of their products and services.

The goal is the continuous renewal of an innovative product and service offering for each identified market or customer segment. This offering must be effectively communicated and made understandable both to customers and to employees responsible for its production, for sales, and for connected services.

Ideally, innovation activities will succeed in emotionalizing both products and accompanying service processes, thus creating novel and, if possible, inspiring customer experiences.

By coordinating and prioritizing CRM services and CRM content expected by customers, carried out through the CRM competence fields of Customer Analytics, Customer Needs, and Customer Behavior, the task in the CRM competence field Innovation Management is:

- Innovatively adapt existing products and services and necessary processes of service provision (delivery, fulfillment) to changing segment-specific customer requirements and expectations.
- Permanently redesigning existing products and services in response to changing needs situations.
- Develop innovative products and services that delight customers and convince them of the comprehensive benefits of a long-term customer relationship.

**Key Takeaways**

Success factors of the CRM competence field innovation management:

- Developing innovative products and services with obvious differentiation from direct competitors.
- Creating genuine customer enthusiasm (customer experience).
- Realization of sustainable customer retention effects (loyalization).

### 1.3.5 Content and Contact Management

All customer contact-related activities must be defined in terms of both the content used (such as core messages, terms and conditions, and value propositions) and the details of their processes, designed for preferred customer contact points and managed through appropriate controlling mechanisms.

Digitization opens up new opportunities for content management in the area of personalization. In the past, personalization meant addressing customers with their correct first and last names, which is not even a given today, but otherwise triggering standard communication according to the "one-content-fits-all" principle. Today, customers expect a company to know and serve them through their preferred communication channels and to coordinate the content and timing of its communication. Modern marketing automation solutions now offer companies highly developed options to actually address customers on a person-by-person basis, especially digitally, and to develop such contact for business purposes. Content and contact management therefore considerably expand the possibilities of lead management (especially in the lead-nurturing phases).

The central instrument for a consistent design of the associated requirements is well-thought-out and coherent channel management. This reconciles customer requirements for transaction and interaction with the channels provided by the company and preferred for each CRM activity (lead channels). In this way, it ensures a customer experience which is, from the customer's point of view, centralizes the creation of a convenient application environment (customer convenience).

Continuous and step-by-step process improvements are stimulated and made possible through correspondingly consistent handling of contact management.

The CRM competence field content/contact management addresses:

- The identification, documentation, and standardization of all customer management processes, including definition of quality and measurement criteria.
- The measurement of process execution and the mapping of measurement activities in a systematic controlling cycle, including target definition, deviation analysis, definition of improvement measures, and success monitoring.
- Measuring customer acceptance of CRM processes, for example, by conducting customer panels, and user acceptance and usability tests.
- Developing customer-relevant communication offers, whether for the primary use of the marketed service or product or within the loyalty program or business initiation (lead nurturing).
- Ensuring internal acceptance of CRM processes.
- Planning and implementing measures for continuous process improvement.

**Key Takeaways**

Success factors of the CRM competence field content/contact management:

- Ensuring consistency and continuity of customer care.
- Covering all phases of the customer lifecycle and all customer touchpoints, contact channels, and media.
- Production, provision, and personalization of relevant content throughout the customer lifecycle (including business initiation).

### 1.3.6 CRM Technology, IT Platform

Customer-specific data (e.g., demographic info, income, assets, and lifestyle) and data on the respective customer behavior (e.g., interactions, transactions, contact history, services purchased, use of consulting services, and receipt of information material) must already be recorded in a basic customer management form, available for evaluation, and consistently used to support planning and execution of customer management activities. As a consequence, this requires data management that meets the demands of data quality (freedom from errors, freedom from redundancy, and up-to-date).

In addition to consistent information management, the systematization and standardization of CRM activities require consistent support through software applications. CRM technologies/IT platforms are required to form the technical infrastructure for customer relationship management on both the data and functional sides.

In addition, the systematization and standardization of CRM functions and customer management activities, particularly in B2C business—individual customers or mass customer business with high data and transaction volumes—requires appropriate design. This includes mapping within simple web applications, and ideally automatic handling of complex business processes by powerful software applications (e.g., intelligent agents and bots).

The main requirement of the use of technology is to provide all employees involved in the value-creation process with an overall view of the respective customer across all phases of customer management. This means providing a 360-degree customer view encompassing the type and duration of the customer/business relationship, the products purchased by the customer, the services obtained, the relevant contacts in each case, the information exchanged, and the channels used in the interaction.

The data-side integration and ongoing consistency maintenance of existing (often heterogeneous) transaction-oriented pre-systems, the systematic conception and function-specific use of analytical applications, and the functional consolidation of all possible contact channels (e.g., telephone/call center, vending machine, counter, web page, email, fax, and letter) are the fundamental prerequisites for this.

Due to the data volumes and heterogeneity handled within an appropriately designed, end-to-end CRM IT architecture, the use of powerful and mutually aligned information technology or corresponding components is essential. This must be accompanied by an awareness that IT is no longer used primarily to reduce costs by increasing efficiency, but rather to create feasible, novel, and innovative business routines to increase the effectiveness of all customer management processes and activities.

Therefore, the CRM competence field CRM technology, IT platform deals with:

- The sources and understanding of the meaningfulness of customer data and customer information.
- The matching of information needs and information availability (so-called information planning).
- Systematic quality management for customer and prospect data.
- The functions and data accessibility of existing customer management systems in the sense of a CRM business architecture.
- The design of a purpose-oriented CRM IT architecture and the provision of new systems and applications to support customer management activities.

- Identifying the CRM potential of new technologies.
- Identifying and defining future requirements for CRM system development.

The sum of their effects on the feasibility of innovative processes in customer relationship management (CRM) constitutes the technological foundation for the conception and implementation of all digitization projects. In this context, innovative CRM business processes are created and provided to customers in line with requirements and expectations. Only in this way does digitization become a design factor so that future-oriented companies can achieve sustainable differentiation from the competition and attain customer loyalty and value creation.

**Key Takeaways**
Success factors of the CRM competence field CRM technology, IT platform:

- Understanding the sources and significance of customer data and information.
- Targeted and consistent use of information and communication technology tools.
- Ensuring data quality and data use that meet customer requirements, including data security and data protection requirements.
- Creation of the technological and professional basis for digitization as a competitively differentiating design factor.

### 1.3.7 Customer Journey Management: Customer Activities in the Marketing, Sales, and Service Phases

Discussion of corporate applications since the mid-2010s has intended to consistently map the development of offerings along the entire customer lifecycle from the customer's perspective ("the external perspective") rather than the company's perspective ("the internal perspective"). In this context, the concept of customer journey management has understood the customer lifecycle as a customer journey and, with this understanding, as a sequence of business phases (so-called "journeys") from the prospective customer to the service provider. Journeys run from "prospective customer" to "new customer," go further to "regular or key customer," and if necessary include "the endangered, migrated customer" (who is thus to be won back), up to finally the "won back" customer.

Customer activity design is appealing when the highest value is attached to the experience of the respective customers or customer groups. Central to the design is the adoption of a holistic customer-centric view by the company, from definition of strategy by company management, to the framework-setting conditions of the corporate culture, to implementation by entrepreneurially thinking and acting employees in daily operational customer contact.

However, because of its special nature as an upstream "fork in the road," companies can only shape it very indirectly; successful customer journey management must therefore also include social media and influencer marketing.

The Customer Journey Management competence area forms the core of the CRM competence model and focuses on the consistent and uniform design of customer management activities along the customer journey. This must be carried out in line with the goals and plans developed by Customer Analytics.

The competence field of Customer Journey Management thus comprises:

- Identification and addressing target groups, especially through campaigns.
- Handling, processing, and responding to customer inquiries.
- The execution of customer advisory activities, the formulation of needs-based recommendations, and the creation of customer-specific offers (quotations).
- The specific recognition and support of new customers (customer welcome, welcoming).
- The collection and dissemination of information among customers.
- The ongoing identification and differentiated support of key and regular customers.
- The development and implementation of cross- and up-selling concepts and measures.
- The development and application of instruments and measures to promote customer loyalty (loyalty programs, customer clubs, communities).
- Feedback and complaint management, as well as the identification and management of dissatisfaction.
- The identification of those at risk of churn (i.e., an "early warning system").
- The friendly farewell of lost customers (farewell, "beautiful exit"), which creates the prerequisite for a later resumption of the business relationship.
- The definition of approaches and processes to win back customers who have left (customer winback).

**Key Takeaways**

Success factors of the CRM competence field Customer Journey Management:

- Defining the "customer journey" with the phases Need (i.e., Marketing), Buy (i.e., Sales), and Use (i.e., Service).
- Defining the customer groups or customer types to be focused on in the respective corporate context, ideally in the form of so-called "personas."
- Defining and allocating preferred channels (multi–/omnichannel) from the company's and the customer's point of view for the perception of the interaction and the transaction between the business partners involved.
- Ensuring future viability ("future proof") by focusing channel management on the defined channels.

## 1.4 Application of the CRM Competence Model: Procedure for Implementing Customer-Oriented Business Models

The implementation of a consistently customer-oriented business model which follows the design requirements described in the CRM competence areas presents decision makers with the challenge of identifying the functional areas of their company with prospects for the most results-effective improvement in customer relationship management. This is all the more challenging when human, financial, and material resources are scarce and only available on the basis of evidence of direct result effectiveness (business case).

The corresponding requirements of top management can be met by using a systematic strengths/weaknesses analysis to define packages of measures across all CRM competence areas of the company (or of the business unit under consideration), each of which has a common content focus: for example, development of a company-specific customer typology or customer segmentation; the realization of a company-wide model for calculating customer value; the provision of a central CRM data warehouse for implementing the overall customer view (e.g., as part of a data warehouse project); process optimization in marketing (e.g., in a marketing automation project); the design and implementation of a comprehensive customer need analysis; or the introduction of an end-to-end CRM target system.

The definition of customer journeys to be worked out and consistently applied by individual companies in the context of customer relationship management has proven an ideal pivotal point for the demand for common content focus. For this reason, the authors selected the customer journey as the focal point of the CRM competency model presented, to which all other competency fields consistently refer.

The packages of measures to be defined during implementation must be prioritized in accordance with the corporate strategy and the CRM strategy derived from it. In particular, the prioritization dimensions "Expected business benefit" and "Estimated implementation effort" should be applied. Subsequently, the packages of measures rated "high" in the benefit dimension must be transferred to implementation against the background of the available resources and according to urgency. In this context, it goes without saying that the packages of measures classified as "quick wins" are of particular importance. At the same time, however, these must not be confused with "quick fixes" (i.e., emergency solutions): Even the packages of measures in the "quick wins" category must fully account for the requirements formulated at the outset for the consistency of a comprehensive CRM concept in terms of content. They must also do justice to the core CRM idea of management and organizational principles integrated throughout the company.

Despite the application of these or similar systematic procedures in the early phases of CRM projects, however, even customer management projects and initiatives initiated today come to a standstill or fail to achieve expected success. The most frequent causes of failure are, on one hand, the technology-centric nature of the approach, in which decisions on software packages and technologies are made before a jointly supported vision and consensus on the strategic objectives of customer management have been reached within the company. On the other hand, a lack of understanding and commitment from senior management and an associated lack of systematic (i.e., aligned with corporate strategy) planning and design of instruments repeatedly lead to failures in the implementation of CRM programs.

As a consequence of these failures, decision-makers are realizing that successful CRM involves more than just the optimized use of information technology: from customer segmentation and the target group-specific alignment of the product and service offering to the systematic establishment and expansion of a customer relationship, completely different areas of the company are involved. It is necessary to perform completely different functions and tasks that must be coordinated. This is also why the conception of company-wide CRM programs is associated with a high degree of complexity.

But does a comprehensively designed customer management system actually pay off? Does it have a positive effect on the company's success? Is there a direct correlation between CRM performance and business performance? Do investments in comprehensive, systematic, and company-wide customer relationship management justify themselves? Likewise when establishing a progressive, proactive, and customer-focused product and brand image that attracts and retains valuable, partner-minded customers over the long term; does it pay off?

This question can be answered with a resounding yes: A large number of surveys conducted in this context—especially those by Professor Neil Woodcock of DeMontfort University, Leicester, UK (Woodcock and Broomfield 2017)—show that CRM has long since ceased to be a buzzword or IT trend. Woodcock's research shows that companies that succeed in consistently aligning their entire organization with the requirements and needs of their potential and existing customers (an entirely "outside-in" process) are more successful in maintaining their position in increasingly competitive markets while securing business success in the long term, than those that neglect this focus.

## References

Stadelmann M (2004) Chief Customer Officer—Motor einer kundenorientierten Unternehmung, in: Alpha Stellenmarkt (Beilage der Sonntagszeitung), Edition 10./11. January 2004, S. 3

Woodcock N, Broomfield N (2017) The business performance impact of a being customer centric. A presentation to Worldwide Federation of Advertisers, Autumn 2017

Zukunft.Kunde (2018) Trends und Digitalisierung im CRM 2018: Es gibt noch viel zu tun. https://www.zukunftkunde.de/trends-und-digitalisierung-im-crm-2018-es-gibt-noch-viel-zu-tun/. Accessed: 20 Feb 2019

**Martin Stadelmann** is an expert in advanced customer management and has been accompanying companies in multiple industries toward holistic CRM for almost 20 years. This combines professional requirements and possibilities of technical implementation to realize the most comprehensive customer experience possible, under consistent orchestration of the "customer functions" marketing, sales, and customer service.

Dr. Stadelmann is a lecturer at the University of St. Gallen, as well as cofounder (2002) of the executive study program "Master of Advanced Studies in CRM" at the Zurich University of Applied Sciences (ZHAW), where he is active as a lecturer in numerous core topics for CRM courses. He is a sought-after speaker on topics of "Customer-Oriented Management" and the author of numerous CRM publications. In 2004, he launched the "Swiss CRM Expert Forum," where he has since served a number of leading Swiss companies as a coach and source of inspiration.

# People and Organization in the CRM Competence Model: New Approaches to Organizational Development on the Way to a Customer-Centric Company

Frank Klinkhammer

**Abstract**

Customer orientation requires non-universal CRM systems and processes, a coherent corporate culture, and employees with a customer focus. Employees want self-determination, a sense of purpose, and further development, while shareholders demand sustainable profit growth. This requires balancing planning security and adaptability on a time scale that is shorter than ever. Traditional methods and ways of thinking about change are slow and ineffective and therefore being overtaken by new organizing methods. Organizations must constantly adapt, integrate internal and external ideas and influences, and provide frameworks for adaptable, responsible, and motivated people. Self-organization and decision-making authority replace rigid hierarchies and leadership models. The responsive organizations presented here demonstrate these characteristics and can be the basis for end-to-end customer-centric enterprises.

## 1 The Transformation of the Organization: Change or Transformation?

Customer centricity is not a new requirement for an organization whose purpose is to satisfy customer needs. Many familiar challenges have already been addressed in the past, sometimes in a different context. However, the main innovation is the shortening of the time axis on which change occurs. The significant technological, social, and societal advances of the last two decades have made this possible. This innovation is enduring, and the evident impact is not linear, but rather exponential.

F. Klinkhammer (✉)
OOTW AG, Schindellegi, Switzerland
e-mail: frank.klinkhammer@ootw.one





S. Kirchem et al. (eds.), *CRM Goes Digital*, Management for Professionals,
https://doi.org/10.1007/978-3-658-45798-3_2

Triggering the changes in our organizations are powerful technological, social, and societal trends. We are on the threshold of a new era in which different principles will organize collaboration and in which processes will take on completely different dimensions. People have changed from an extrinsically motivated with a long-lasting commitment to their employer and traditional career planning. They are now experts that are their own entrepreneurs in the "gig economy" who—by interacting with AI algorithms—contribute to company success on a self-organized project basis.

▶ **Gig Economy** The gig economy refers to a section of the labor market in which clearly defined assignments are awarded to independent freelancers on a short-term basis. An Internet platform often serves as an intermediary between client and contractor, with the platform operator receiving a commission.

The culmination of these trends will also fundamentally impact the implementation of consistently customer-oriented corporate design. This requires a substantially different approach, a new understanding of change processes, and a future-oriented interpretation of leadership. In other words: We must learn new things, discard old behaviors, honor our experiences, but also accept that the successful change management methods of the past will not serve our purposes in the future.

We are facing a demanding paradigm shift. Our existing organizational formats are optimized for control, reliability, and efficiency. Planning and control are essential features, and the mantra of centralized control continues to echo through boardrooms.

Recognizing familiar patterns, we respond with familiar measures, define new processes that are now "designed" to be customer-centric, and build organizations on the drawing board that reflect our vision of the perfect future solution. We thus take our time and deal with ourselves first and foremost. In the future, this approach will no longer work. Our knowledge of the customer's needs is incomplete and is a poor basis for design. Market feedback will be much faster and more direct than we are used to. We can afford fewer mistakes, even though we have to be faster. This contradiction is difficult to resolve with traditional management approaches.

The plan to actively shape the customer journey can only be successful with a sufficiently agile approach that reflects the complexity of the situation. The customer journey takes place in an ecosystem with any number of participants. Sometimes parameters can be modified to reduce complexity and situational analysis through simplified and known models can be so accurate that clearly derived and implemented measures are executed through known methods. Often, however, reducing complexity is simply impossible, or doing so would obstruct the company's future opportunities.

What we need is an organization that, despite a complex context, is agile and responsive in finding customer-centric solutions and developing them in an evolutionary manner. This characteristic goes far beyond traditional process design;

rather, this means continuous redesign occurring iteratively at many points in the organization.

## 2 Responsive Organizing and a Responsive Organization

Instead of organizations structured as hierarchical levels that allow "top-down" execution to all levels and offer only limited "bottom-up" communication and influence, we envision a network of self-organized units with very high-level and decentralized decision-making authority.

A responsive organization is a self-organized network of people, business units or AI algorithms working toward a customer-centric purpose, using transparent information to act with high-level autonomy. The organization learns continuously, evolves in small iterations, and can conduct experiments with rapid feedback loops in unplanned situations.

While in German we talk about a "responsive organization," in English We use the term "responsive organizing" to emphasize the continuous change organizations must undergo in the future. Responsive organizing does not involve designing a blueprint for organizational structure. Rather, it means enabling the organization and its people to continuously transform according to the needs of the changing ecosystem in which they operate. Only then can a responsive organization be the foundation for the customer-centric enterprise.

Self-organized systems are rarely anarchic or chaotic. The basis for functioning self-organization is adherence to existing rules. Just as nature is based on scientific principles, organizations and people need principles and rules of interaction to exist. A responsive organization is built on the following principles and elements:

- Purpose and values
- Roles, responsibilities, and competencies
- Strategy, goals, and metrics
- Transparency
- Separation of operational and structural work
- Experiments and defined processes
- Self-organization and continuous learning
- Trust and security

### 2.1 Purpose and Values

Purpose answers the question of why the organization exists. The purpose of a customer-centric company is always considered from the outside. How do the company's customers benefit if the purpose is achieved? If the company benefits people by satisfying a need, it is relevant to existing and potential customers. Purpose can be similar to a strong vision, but does not have to be. In the past, vision was often formulated from an internal perspective, but this is no longer purposeful. A responsive organization sensibly differentiates vision and purpose.

Since a responsive organization consists of self-organized units, each unit can have its own purpose. A hierarchy of purpose across the unit maintains a common direction, but there may be some deviation among individual parts of the organization. This makes sense, since the overall organization's purpose will be much broader than that of individual units, where the formulation can be much more specific.

Although as many people as possible should be involved in defining the purpose of the organization, the purpose must ultimately be independent of the organization's people. The organization should not exist to meet the needs of individuals within the organization, but to meet the needs of people outside the organization: the customers. People occupy roles in the organization and interact with each other to fulfill the purpose. The social interaction of people in the organization makes up the culture of the company. Here, in addition to purpose, we need a shared value system.

Values express the beliefs, convictions, and foundations we adhere to. They determine behavior and thus organizational culture. A coherent and consistent value system is recognized externally and makes the company unique. As with purpose, the definition of values should involve as many people in the organization as possible.

The rules of conduct concretize values and should serve all employees in day-to-day decisions. Meanwhile, they serve partners and customers as a framework for expectations.

## 2.2 Roles, Responsibilities, and Competencies

How decisions are made is an essential organizational characteristic. Decision-making is an expression of culture and indicates whether the purpose statement is reflected in the organization's behavior.

In a responsive organization, activities are allocated to clear roles with distributed decision-making authority and power. Roles can be grouped into superordinate units, usually referred to as circles or cells. Whether a superstructure is formed is decided by those in the roles involved and not dictated by a central function. A role always includes clear responsibilities: What can others expect from this role or circle? With this comes necessary authority and decision-making power.

Similarly, a role includes clear duties. Each role must contribute to the company or unit's goals. Responsibilities should be understood in terms of positive, not negative delineation, which describes the activities expected of the role. The role prioritizes these responsibilities and their attendant activities. However, the role could and can assume other activities if that is important to the company or unit in question. The principle is that anything can (and must) be done, as long as it is not prohibited. And it is amazing how few things need to be prohibited.

Furthermore, people can have multiple roles in an organization. This is much more reflective of reality than a traditional organizational chart. Since the competence of a role is always in context, it is not attached to a person. Consequently, an employee with a leadership role in one area may have a delivery role in another, and may not derive any particular rights from their leadership role in the other area. This is important so that new ideas and approaches can emerge and be implemented.

The responsive organization does have a hierarchy, but the hierarchies are based on roles and not on people. This is important so that new ideas and approaches can emerge and be implemented but requires a new understanding and behavior from all involved.

## 2.3 Separating Operational and Controlling Tasks

When a traditional organization changes, a target state for the organization is designed, steps for the change process are defined and rolled out to the company. The new organizational structure is initially fixed and thus must be as perfect as possible. Problems then always appear as problems of the organization's people, who do not adhere to the planned structure. This causes friction and unnecessary effort. People manage their daily work and deal with the organization, mostly without the possibility of structured influence. This opportunity rarely exists because the change approach does not assume the need for subsequent organizational adaptation.

A responsive organization is flexible and adaptable. For this to be feasible, the organization needs a framework for change: there must be defined rules for organizational change, and operational work and organizational control (governance) must be separated. While we deal with operational issues ("working *in* the organization"), we focus on executing tasks. Discussions about structural topics are not useful because they distract from actual work.

If coordination meetings are necessary, the number of participants and the topics are handled very restrictively. Since each role has decision-making authority, necessary coordination is minimal, compared to traditional processes. These meetings only concern the organization of work; the actual work takes place outside. If meetings are necessary to jointly develop work results, the relevant roles meet separately.

Periodically, the employees deal with the organization ("working *on* the organization"). The aim is to process improvements to structure and processes. Defined rules apply, ensuring suggestions are treated equally and only rejected if they would cause harm. The group thus decides through the consensus principle, fulfilling the requirement for adaptability and security. Consent should not be confused with consensus in implementation. This is not about getting agreement from every participant. The question is not, "Are we all in favor of the proposal?" but rather "Can anyone provide evidence that the proposal will harm us?"

## 2.4 Strategy, Goals, and Metrics

Responsive organizations, like all organizations, require governance at all levels. However, it is not the manager who steers; the steering is rather done by the organization itself, that is, by multiple roles or the team. This requires clearly defined goals that are transparent to all stakeholders and for goal achievement to be continuously measured, with information available to every member of the organization.

Goals are derived from the purpose through strategy processes. Strategy processes run more frequently than in the past, with shorter time frames, gaining much more flexibility.

Metrics in a responsive organization are imperative: Without metrics, where we stand is unclear and we fail to improve. The saying, "What gets measured, gets done" also applies to responsive organizations. What differs is how metrics are interpreted: In responsive organizations, the first step is a value-free view of data and metrics. Latterly, the responsible role or team interprets the data depending on the situation.

A response is thus not automatically tied to each metric, but deviations are assessed in context and available knowledge determines an appropriate response. This interpretation of metrics and target values may contradict traditional management methods, but it has proven its worth in volatile and unpredictable areas.

## 2.5 Transparency

Transparency is a necessary prerequisite for a responsive organization. Data and information must be available everywhere and at all times. The technical and organizational conditions must be created to achieve this.

The aggregation of information across several management levels, as in many companies today, hinders a responsive organization and should be avoided. Organizations should move away from the prevailing "need-to-know" mentality and toward a "default-to-share" mentality. This means we need not control information flow centrally, but rely on people in the roles they fill in our company to access necessary information in a self-organized manner. Legal requirements are still met, sensitive data must be protected. For all other information, there is no reason to restrict access.

## 2.6 Experiments and Defined Processes

A responsive organization aims to make better decisions faster, especially on new topics. Well-known situations that provide a basis for reliable planning are not understood as experiments. Defined processes are used when the future state, is deterministic, that is, it can be mapped with clear process steps. Experiments are necessary when the future is uncertain and insufficient information is available.

In these situations, traditional companies tend to want to create a supposed certainty through increased planning, clarification, and risk management. This reduces implementation speed. Fast units know not to intensify analysis in unknown situations, which is why experimenting by repeating, changing, or further developing initial steps depending on results reaches the goal more quickly and with less effort.

## 2.7 Self-Organized and Continuous Learning

A responsive organization has a fixed set of rules that help individual units and people work in a self-organized way toward the company's purpose. Continuous learning, proposed as a "learning organization" concept in the 1990s (Senge 2006), is becoming more important than ever in the digital age, as many stabilizing frameworks for individuals and companies are eliminated and thus more responsibility can and must be assumed at all levels. In this context, continuous learning—and thus the experimentation described above—is fundamental.

Classical education and training measures to impart knowledge and skills also occur in a responsive organization. However, there is more to learning than this, as feedback and exchange provide supplementary continuous improvement, for which space and time are set aside. Content and form develop in a self-organized manner according to the acute needs and individual development plans of employees.

## 2.8 Trust and Security

A responsive organization creates transparency about the performance and priorities of individual roles and units. When this is reliable, information is trusted and so are the people in their roles. Trust means there is no reason to control individual activities in a dedicated way because the unit is progressing towards the goals. Trust in people is as necessary as trust in the system, which is the basis for open communication that uses all relevant ideas and impulses for the organization. Ideas and contributions are valued, regardless of hierarchy.

Trust and security are bidirectional properties that everyone needs to both show and feel. Google's "Aristotle" project examined this in seeking reasons for team success. The project found that professional skills in the team's composition play a role, but that individual personality traits are significantly less important than how team members communicate with each other (Duhigg 2016). The scientific basis is the concept of "psychological safety" (Edmondson and Schein 2014), which is a cornerstone of social interaction in a responsive organization.

# 3 Holacracy: Rules for a Responsive Organization

Many companies from different industries have implemented progressive management approaches that are both radical and successful (Laloux 2014). The success frequently builds on a conviction among senior managers or founders that company management can and should differ from traditional management methods. This results in a willingness to experiment and investing the time to learn and develop a new way of working.

Much can be learned from these examples, but no approach is easily transferable as these companies have long-developed their own methods. Developing a method that is transferable to other organizations was not their prime goal. Time is also short for those who are not there yet. Today, faster changes and adaptations are needed: Becoming a responsive organization requires a kick-starter, like, a method with an already defined set of rules. In this case, principles do not need to be developed, and transformation can begin immediately. Instead of defining rules, content can be developed and the interpretation and adaptation of principles to the company's situation is part of the transformation.

The most advanced method for implementing a responsive organization is Holacracy. This was developed under the brand name Holacracy® by Brian Robertson and his team in the USA, building on various agile management approaches. Its basic set of rules is freely available as a "Constitution" in the public domain, and can be adapted according to individual requirements. Here are the key features:

- The rulebook applies to all employees in the organization, or to all employees in the organizational unit implementing Holacracy. The rulebook describes universal rights and responsibilities, and processes for changing organizational structures and rules.
- Work is organized into roles and circles. The traditional manager role is divided into four roles. One provides technical direction to the circle; a second facilitates the process; a third provides documentation and rule interpretation; and the fourth provides escalation communication. At first glance, this looks like overhead, but in practice it eases the manager role through clear responsibilities and it thus accelerates processes.
- Meeting formats are clearly defined. Operational and governance are strictly separated and dealt with according to fixed rules.
- Operational work focuses on metrics and strategic goals, which form the basis for team coordination. There is complete transparency, and each role is required to act proactively.
- Holacracy is predominantly used in the tech environment in smaller companies. Among larger companies, Zappos is often cited, with just over 1500 employees; in Europe, Netcentric and Mercedes-Benz.io are among the largest users of the approach, with more than 400 and 200 employees, respectively.
- The method is repeatedly criticized for the technocratic approach on which it is based. This criticism is partly justified, but also arises from exaggerated expectations.
- Holacracy includes rules for the interaction of roles, but not for the interaction of people. Communication occurs at many levels. The clarity Holacracy adds to work processes must still be supplemented with a coherent value system and culture of togetherness. Then a coherent responsive organization is possible.

## 4 Introducing the Responsive Organization: Procedures and Criteria for Success

The transformation to a responsive organization requires consistent customer centricity and an iterative introduction. As with any change, honestly assessing the current situation is the first step. Considering the organization separately from its people has proven advantages in enabling analysis of change needs, potential, and required effort at the two separate levels.

Conducting a pilot is an advisable next step. The pilot needs sufficient scope and duration to gain a fair impression of a larger rollout's feasibility for all people and organizational levels. Meanwhile, the organization builds an idea of what transformation will involve: What support do the people in the organization need? What measures should be used to change the organization and how? What set of rules, with which elements and methods, should be used in the rollout?

Transformation ambassadors are identified and trained during the pilot. A good mix across all hierarchy levels is recommended. This enables the company to demonstrate a sustainable will to change and trust in its employees during the process.

The pilot should conclude with a detailed review with all participants, who develop joint recommendations for further action at the levels of organization (rules and regulations), people, and culture.

Change processes naturally introduce new situations and challenges for all members of the organization. Dealing with these challenges requires a stable set of rules—which can be created through the pilot—and an open approach to change and shared learning. These are the keys to successful transformation.

In becoming a responsive organization, learning mechanics and methods are therefore as necessary as taking a holistic view of the change process. A holistic view includes elements enabling long-term stability and supporting mindset change.

The rollout phase is crucial to the success of the transformation. Inspiring employees and transferring the energy generated in the pilot to everyone else is key. The internal ambassadors of the transformation, usually the pilot participants, play a major role and must have clear roles during the rollout.

Since a transformation to a responsive organization is not a normal change process but an evolutionary development, a structured communication plan, and regular communication are absolutely essential.

The transformation to a responsive organization is most successful when all stakeholders are willing to critically question their beliefs and the way work is organized and decisions are made. Moreover, they must be willing to change them. This process requires time. It is not enough to approach change at the rational level of beliefs and convictions; rather, change must be initiated at the behavioral level of habits.

The transformation to a responsive organization does not necessarily lead to a successful company; it can only lay the foundation. The actual entrepreneurial work, the shaping and the steering, should then be ongoing. This is the essence of a responsive organization.

Avoiding classic "manager traps" is vital: For example, the expectation that simply introducing a responsive organization is a solution in itself. A responsive organization is a good basis for a customer-centric company and provides a framework for better preparation for future challenges. It is a worthy experiment!

## References

Duhigg C (2016) Smarter faster better: the secrets of being productive. Random House, London

Edmondson A, Schein EH (2014) Teaming: how organizations learn, innovate, and compete in the knowledge economy: what leaders must do to Foster organizational learning. Jossey-Bass Pfeiffer, San Francisco

Laloux F (2014) Reinventing organizations: a guide to creating organizations inspired by the next stage of human consciousness. Brüssel, Nelson Parker

Senge PM (2006) The fifth discipline: the art & practice of the learning organization. Random House Business, London

**Frank Klinkhammer** started his second career in the IT industry in the mid-1990s after conducting research and receiving his PhD in physical chemistry, with stints in traditionally structured companies and successful startups in the consulting industry.

He was co-founder, and for 4 years, CEO of the Swiss start-up Netcentric, which grew to more than 270 employees during this time, and he was also the initiator of the largest Holacracy implementation in Europe. Today, he shares his knowledge as an advisor, board member, and investor with other organizations on their way to responsive structures.

# The Exploded View as a Frame of Reference for More Successful CRM

Hans Albrecht Bartels and Jonathan Möller

**Abstract**

Companies depend on continuously, and increasingly rapidly, aligning customer-oriented services and related organizational structures, processes, systems, and data with market requirements. Typical challenges in the CRM environment show that selective measures and isolated projects are only somewhat suitable for achieving sustainable improvements. It is essential to build up a common basic understanding of the interrelationships. Only by taking a holistic view and using different perspectives is it possible to localize the relevant fields of action on the company and customer sides. This chapter outlines the path from the company analysis to the final project roadmap. It uses the "Exploded View" model, which was developed by the consulting firm foryouandyourcustomers and has been used successfully in numerous customer projects.

## 1 Digital Transformation As a Trigger for Improving the Customer Relationship

Companies are strongly challenged by the digital transformation and the highly dynamic market environment. Changing social and technological conditions make it necessary to not only continuously review and adapt services and their associated value-creation processes, but also to completely rethink them. Changes no longer result from periodic strategy formulation, planning, and implementation, but occur almost independently of time-based cycles.

Companies must therefore demonstrate ever-greater agility if they want to meet the demands of fast-moving markets.

H. A. Bartels (✉) · J. Möller
foryouandyourcustomers AG, Uster, Switzerland
e-mail: hab@foryouandyourcustomers.com; jom@foryouandyourcustomers.com



S. Kirchem et al. (eds.), *CRM Goes Digital*, Management for Professionals,
https://doi.org/10.1007/978-3-658-45798-3_3

In practice, this agility requires clarity and orientation from the organization. Managers must react more consciously and at shorter notice. This is inextricably linked to a consistent customer focus and a corresponding corporate structure. In itself, this is nothing new. Successful entrepreneurship has always been based on the art of developing customer relationships, recognizing needs, and aligning existing performance processes. CRM initiatives are therefore usually based on three core questions:

- Which market segments should be my company's focus in the future?
- Who are the customers in these segments and how can added value be generated for customer groups that differentiate my company from the range of services offered by my competitors?
- How can I as a company ensure the efficiency and profitability of service provision through flexibility, innovative strength, and by optimizing the supply chain and the associated process and organizational structure?

What is new, however, is that the type and number of interaction points with the customer have increased dramatically. Technological advances are enabling integrated and personalized customer experiences through innovative omnichannel approaches. The traditional supply chain is being supplemented by a high-performance digital supply chain that links customers and companies ever more closely, but also more transparently, and translates customer needs for implementation by the company in close to real time.

The resulting intensification of the customer relationship leads to an ever-increasing overlapping of the external customer perspective and the internal company perspective. As a result, it is much more difficult to implement customer-oriented functionality in isolation from adapting the necessary internal structures and processes. The effect is also retroactive because existing implementation errors become mercilessly visible in this environment.

In a description of how to measure the success of CRM initiatives, various "implementation traps" that lead—not exhaustively—to failure in the introduction of CRM measures:

- Transparency trap: Transparency and measurability are missing at the interaction points and in the linked process chains.
- Strategy trap: A corporate strategy is missing or not aligned; that is, it is not in line with actual customer performance.
- Technology trap: CRM software or technology is implemented without the underlying processes being adapted.
- Implementation trap: Measures are implemented without sufficient customer knowledge, without coordination of the planned added value, and without consideration of data quality.
- Time-to-market trap: It takes too long to deliver the right benefits to customers.

- Acceptance trap: New processes and new functions are introduced without ensuring that added value is felt by all those affected on the customer or company side.

Companies should therefore increasingly address customer- and company-related challenges. Existing services, traditional interaction channels, processes, functions, and roles must be scrutinized just as much as existing system solutions.

This applies to all CRM initiatives, be they investments in technology and software, the implementation of new campaigns to increase marketing efficiency, or the provision of new touchpoints along the customer journey. It is always necessary to take different perspectives on the customer, the market, and the company, to visualize interrelationships, and to develop a common understanding of the need for improvement measures.

Although this comprehensive approach is necessary in order to implement corresponding improvements sustainably, many companies are still overburdened by implementation and tend toward rather manageable quick fixes. However, without an underlying overall understanding of the interdependencies, many implementations are doomed to failure.

In a large number of implemented projects, foryouandyourcustomers has recognized the need for support and developed the "Exploded View" model. Over recent years, the Exploded View has been used in numerous companies across industries, in both B2B and B2C environments. The approach has been continuously refined and has proven itself in practice.

## 2 The Exploded View Model

The Exploded View is comparable to an architect's exploded view. It depicts the company, the market, and the associated customers on a total of six layers (Fig. 1):

1. Customer layer: The customer layer is the top level of the model and contains the company's target groups. It includes customers, potential customers, interested parties, and business partners who can obtain services from the company in some form. This layer therefore includes people (B2C) and/or companies and the people who act within them (B2B).
2. Experience layer: The experience layer represents the sum of all channels and thus the perceptible "surface" of the company. The company can control some channels because it owns them (Owned Channels), while others can be influenced indirectly (Paid and Earned Channels) or not at all (Rival and Other Channels). The interaction of the channels in the context of customer use shapes the customer journey and enables a range of customer experiences that are decisive for the purchase.
3. Organization layer: The organization layer comprises all employees of a company, the associated organizational structure, and roles and functions. It is thus responsible for the characteristics and quality of customer interactions in the

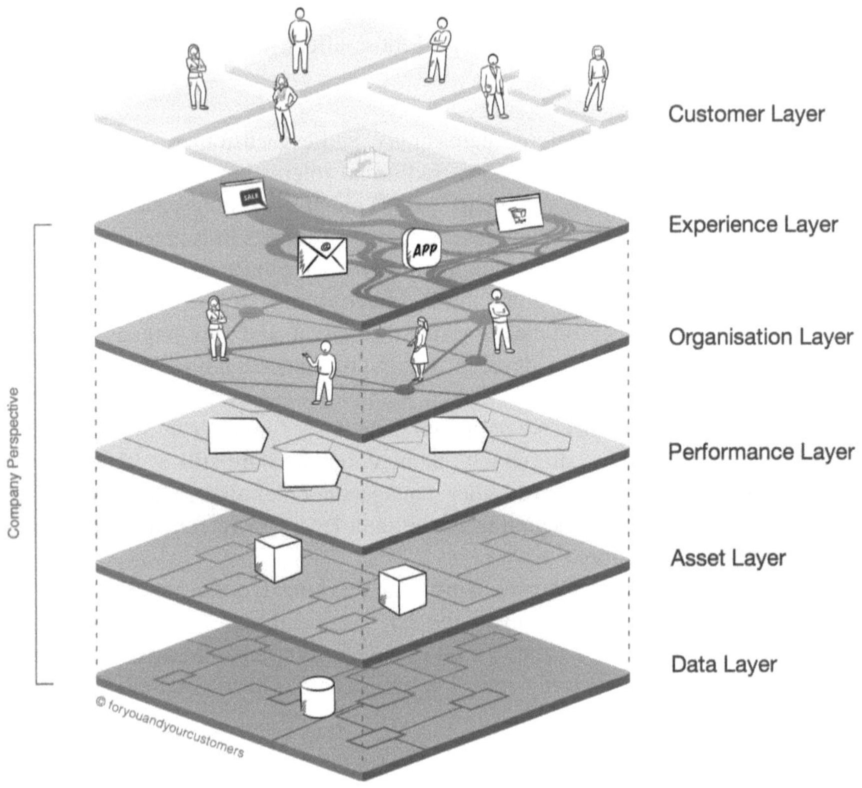


**Fig. 1** The exploded view model

company-specific channels of the Experience Layer. The company's services are transported to the Experience Layer via the Organization Layer.

4. Performance layer: The performance layer contains all services and associated customer processes. It forms the basis for covering all existing and future customer needs. Clever structuring of services and processes enables freedom from redundancy, automation, and thus an efficient company.
5. Asset layer: The asset layer consists of all assets in the company, such as IT systems, real estate (e.g., sales areas), warehouses, logistics, production, but also IP/know-how, infrastructure, and capital. The asset layer is the foundation of the company. In the context of digitalization, existing and planned IT systems play a particularly essential role. The provision of services, collaboration within the company, or the creation of shopping experiences for customers are hardly possible today without systems.
6. Data layer: the data layer contains the sum of all data and data structures of a company. Data is the foundation of any company. In order to use data, the data must be understood and processed into information. To do this, it is necessary to evaluate it, connect it, and put it into a meaningful context.

Working with the six levels of the Exploded View provides all stakeholders with a comprehensible overview of the company and simplifies collaboration. The levels can be grouped into different perspectives and applied. Each perspective enables a different view of elements and mechanisms of digitalization. In its approach, foryouandyourcustomers primarily distinguishes four perspectives (Brunner 2008):

1. The customer perspective, to understand the customer and their experience.
2. The market perspective, to overview the interaction of customers and competitors in the context of information and decision-making processes.
3. The company perspective, in order to develop processes and localize necessary adjustments in one's own company.
4. The employee perspective, in order to build a smoothly functioning, cooperative, and customer-focused organization.

Adopting the respective perspective achieves a more complete and integrated picture of customers, the market, the company, and its top performers. A common language and understanding of requirements and the necessary adjustments are developed. The Exploded View thus provides a framework and structure for a business analysis.

## 3 The Use of the Exploded View to Develop Improvement Potential

In the application, the levels of the Exploded View form a reference system onto which problem areas and possible improvement measures can be mapped as a result of a requirements analysis. The basis for this is often already existing challenges. Depending on the perspective selected, different layers are in the foreground, but attention should always be paid to a holistic view.

Table 1 deals with typical challenges in the CRM environment, which are made visible and workable by applying the Exploded View with the help of various tools:

This list is exemplary and not exhaustive. Numerous challenges only become visible through a holistic view of the company and can only then be discussed and concretized. This provides the necessary overview and orientation for faster action.

## 4 From Company Analysis to Continuous Improvement

A company analysis with the help of the Exploded View leads to indicators and approaches that span different levels. The traditional view and approach is horizontal, and this approach is now extended by a vertical view (Fig. 2).

An initial consolidation connects the different levels and provides the required overall view. Customers, organization, and infrastructure are thus equally in focus for the observation. At the same time, the foundations are laid for a future, repetitive review of the company's performance across all levels.

**Table 1** Typical challenges in the CRM environment (authors' creation)

| | |
|---|---|
| *Challenge:* | *1. Lack of Customer Knowledge* |
| *Perspective/ layer:* | Customer perspective/customer layer |
| *Indicators:* | Numerous contradictory customer images in the company. Current and future core needs of customers are not known<br>The processing of customers and the allocation of resources in market development are unstructured<br>There is no target system and the results of market cultivation are not tracked according to their customer impact<br>Customer status, potential, and risk of churn are unknown. Investments and measures for customer management are not controlled. Processes are suboptimally aligned with the creation of the required benefits and services |
| *Analysis approach:* | *Requirements analysis:*<br>Analysis of the customer base and its development, taking into account existing and potential customers<br>Review of existing customer-oriented target systems and revision of segment-oriented target setting<br>Analysis of the market situation and the service chain (B2B) from which customers can obtain their services<br>Potential analysis and introduction of scoring procedures to evaluate the segments<br>*Requirements implementation:*<br>Cleansing and expansion of existing customer attributes through consolidation and development of data along the entire customer journey<br>Introduction of behavior-, customer value-, and potential-based customer segmentations<br>Establishment of a segment-specific scoring system to measure performance relevance<br>Optimization and establishment of a customer strategy<br>Identification of customer roles (e.g., buyer, decision maker, and user) in customer contacts<br>Development of ideal-typical personas to sharpen the customer image and support content development<br>Implementation of training measures within the company and with partners |
| *Tools:* | Customer segmentation<br>Customer journeys<br>Personas<br>Overview of target and segment-specific metrics (KPIs)<br>(Transaction data-based) potential analyses<br>Customer needs assessment (tasks to be done/customer tasks) |
| *Challenge:* | *2. Limited customer experience in the customer journey* |

(continued)

**Table 1** (continued)

| | |
|---|---|
| *Perspective/ layer:* | Customer perspective/experience layer |
| *Indicators:* | Negative revenue and sales development overall or among specific target groups<br>Low channel usage, customer complaints, abandonment of purchase processes, customer churn, low repurchase rate<br>Low performance of channel-specific measures and unsatisfactory performance relevance at touchpoints (the customer is disappointed)<br>Allocation of relevant channels to customer groups is not possible<br>Lack of content strategy leads to inappropriate content and wrong tone |
| *Analysis approach:* | *Requirements analysis:*<br>Build channel overview and determine channel relevance and usage<br>Determination of channel profile per channel with clear assignment of purpose, target group, and responsibility<br>Creation of personas and recording of segment-typical customer journey(s). Clarification of customer-specific usage (tasks) and expectations. Inclusion of all channels and touchpoints, regardless of how they can be influenced<br>Analysis of search results for online channels in the evaluation phase of the customer journey<br>Visualization of the customer journey, the phases, the pain points, and possible improvement measures<br>*Requirements implementation:*<br>Development of an optimized customer journey by building, replacing, and adding to the technical foundations and channel content<br>Implementation of channel-specific measures to activate channel frequency and usage behavior<br>Establishment of suitable measurement methods and development of the necessary data sources<br>Formulation and implementation of a content strategy |
| *Tools:* | Personas<br>Customer journeys<br>Channel inventory (channel map)<br>Channel evaluation (Channel cards, Channel survey)<br>Customer journey analyses (Channel opera)<br>Tasks to be done/customer tasks<br>Content strategy |
| *Challenge:* | *3. Acceptance problems* |
| *Perspective/ layer:* | Company perspective, organization layer, and performance layer |
| *Indicators:* | *Customer side:* Limited use of channels, touchpoints, and performance content<br>*Company side:* The implemented CRM functionality is only used to a limited extent; know-how and important information are not passed on; but are retained as "personal assets"<br>Processes are not clearly defined or overlap. The "time to market" is too high compared to the competition. Standards are lacking, including in handling customer concerns; data quality is poor; key customer information is incorrect or not captured; customer goals are missing and not measured and development is not tracked; internal training is lacking |

(continued)

**Table 1** (continued)

| | |
|---|---|
| *Company analysis approach:* | *Requirements analysis:*<br>Capture existing customer-facing processes<br>Analysis of the company's internal target systems (structure, ability to influence targets, incentive systems)<br>Description of required assets (quality, condition).<br>Analysis of responsibilities and accountabilities with reference to customers<br>Recording and evaluation of the "Employee Journey" in all relevant areas of the company. The goal is to identify problems from the employee's point of view in (CRM) system usage, information procurement, customer support, and service provision<br>Examination of internal information supply and data quality<br>*Requirements implementation:*<br>Establishment of "to-be" processes<br>Redefinition of responsibilities and competencies in customer traffic and assigned processes<br>Establishment of scenarios for the further development of the organization with a focus on digital transformation and the skills required |
| *Tools:* | Organizational overview<br>Roles<br>Employee journey<br>Process description<br>Process map/process management system<br>Q messages<br>Information model |
| *Challenge:* | *4. Efficiency problems/time to market* |
| *Perspective/ layer:* | Employee perspective, organization layer, and performance layer |
| *Indicators:* | Complex processes for service creation and service provision, especially in conjunction with partner companies and suppliers<br>Reaction to customer inquiries and provision of services takes too long; responsibilities in the organization (related to customer groups, channels, and content) are not defined<br>Unclear competencies lead to lengthy clarifications between departments, with the result that different organizational areas/employees process the same customer without coordination<br>The software used is not ergonomic and is insufficiently adapted to the requirements of the processes. Essential functions with automation potential are performed manually. Significant data and function redundancy |

(continued)

**Table 1** (continued)

| | |
|---|---|
| *Company analysis approach:* | *Requirements analysis:*<br>Organizational analysis (and here specifically the examination of responsibilities and competencies)<br>Analysis of the information structure<br>Analysis of existing system support and underlying system architecture<br>Measurement of turnaround time for critical customer processes<br>Clarification of training levels and staff qualifications<br>*Requirements implementation:*<br>Redesign of customer-specific processes, automation, and customization of system support<br>Optimization of information management and information supply in customer processes<br>Implementation of target and incentive systems |
| *Tools:* | Overview of services<br>Employee journey<br>Performance profiles that provide information about tools, responsibilities (RACI), input/output, and KPIs<br>Target processes include necessary indicative timelines |
| *Challenge:* | *5. Introduction/replacement of existing customer systems* |
| *Perspective/ layer:* | Enterprise perspective, performance layer, and asset layer |
| *Indicators:* | *Trigger:* Fundamental realignment of the system landscape in the context of digitization, introduction of new channels and functions, obsolete or missing functionality, poor performance, low scalability, high licensing costs, limited adaptability and release capability, limited support for modern data and interface standards, centralization of data management (consolidation of fragmented datasets and maintenance functions), obsolete DB standard, interface problems due to architectural incompatibility, loss of know-how (employee competence) |
| *Company analysis approach:* | *Requirements analysis*<br>Creation of a functional and usage overview<br>Analysis of information management and information supply in customer processes<br>Delimitation of user stories<br>Definition of requirements to support system evaluation and agile implementation/development<br>*Requirements implementation:*<br>Basic decision on data hosting<br>Specification of data volume and sizing requirements |
| *Tools:* | System and service architecture, listing systems with their roles and interconnectivity<br>System roadmap, derived from the system strategy<br>Data strategy |
| *Challenge:* | *6. Data quality* |
| *Perspective/ layer:* | Customer perspective, data layer, and asset layer |

(continued)

**Table 1** (continued)

| | |
|---|---|
| *Indicators:* | Complex maintenance processes, missing and/or erroneous data, data redundancy, data fragmentation due to different data statuses in distributed databases, insufficient data availability, time dependency in data provision or incorrect granularity (no real time), orphaned data elements without functional context, datasets without assigned data responsibility, functional requirements can no longer be met with existing data, insufficient data protection, insufficient data exploitation and use by analytical methods and models (e.g., mining, predictive models, and AI) |
| *Company analysis approach:* | *Requirements analysis:*<br>Analysis of data sources, processing, and storage<br>Creation of an interface overview<br>Data description of important data elements (data dictionary) |
| *Tools:* | Information model that semantically maps and describes all entities of the enterprise<br>Data index as an overview of which data sources exist in which state in the company<br>Data models of business critical entities |

For project work, the application of the Exploded View results in a clear procedure:

- Requirements analysis, top-down: Requirements are collected from the top level down in the enterprise analysis. From the customer's understanding and the Customer Layer, the requirements for the channels on the Experience Layer and the following levels can be derived. The requirements for the organization and below can then be derived from the insights into the channels on the Experience Layer, and so on.
- Requirements implementation, bottom-up: Implementation starts at the lowest level and gradually includes the levels above. It is advisable to start the implementation of the Data Layer with the implementation of the information model; the data and especially the data structures are the basis for any project. The implementation of the systems on the Asset Layer follows this. Once the systems are ready, the services can be established on the Performance Layer, and operational implementation follows incrementally up through each additional layer. In this way, implementation through all layers ultimately reaches the customer and creates the desired benefits.
- This approach avoids typical problems that are too often committed in a classical approach:
  - Customer-specific functionality is often expanded under pressure from technological innovation, without the underlying organization being adequately adapted to the new service processes.
  - The situation is similar to the data and information flows required for specific functionality on the customer side. Often, the foundations of the company are insufficient to support a higher level of functional maturity.

The overall result is the analysis and planning process shown in Fig. 3.

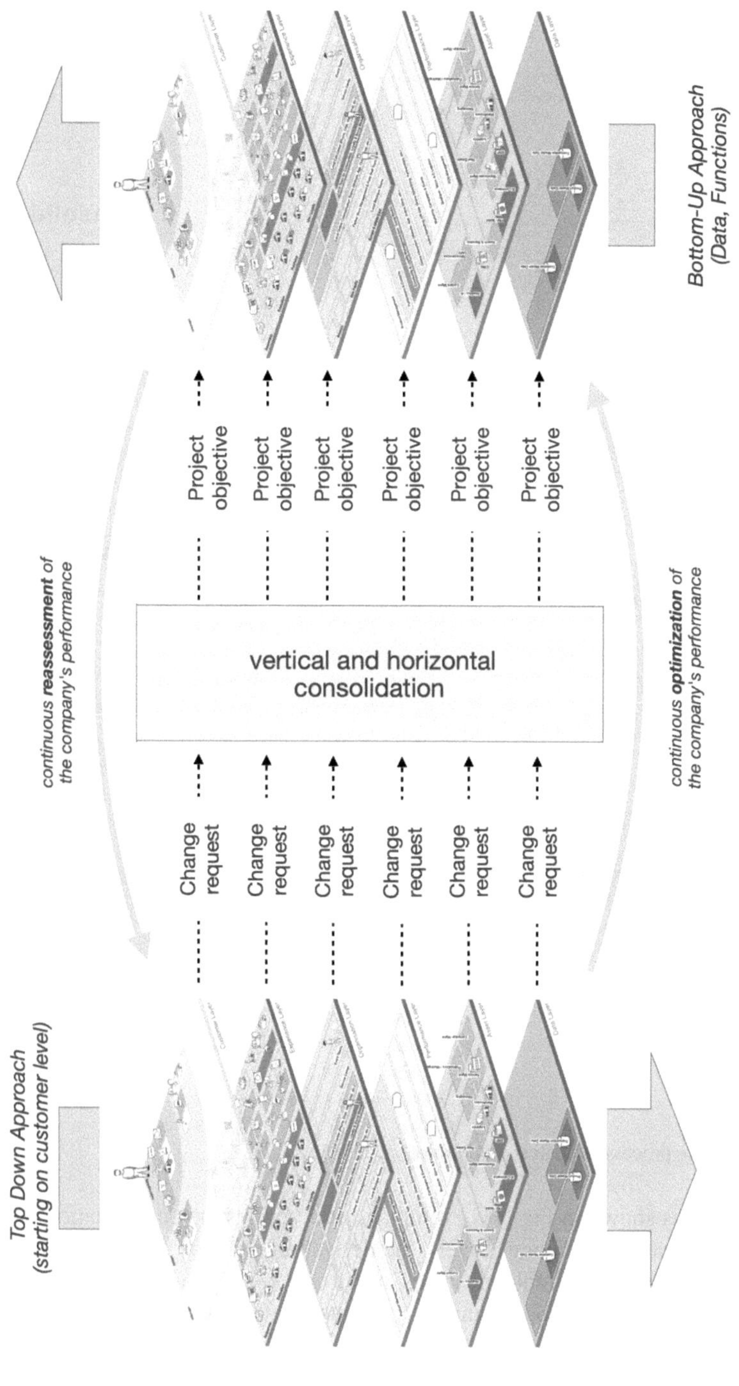


**Fig. 2** Horizontal derivation and vertical consolidation of change requirements

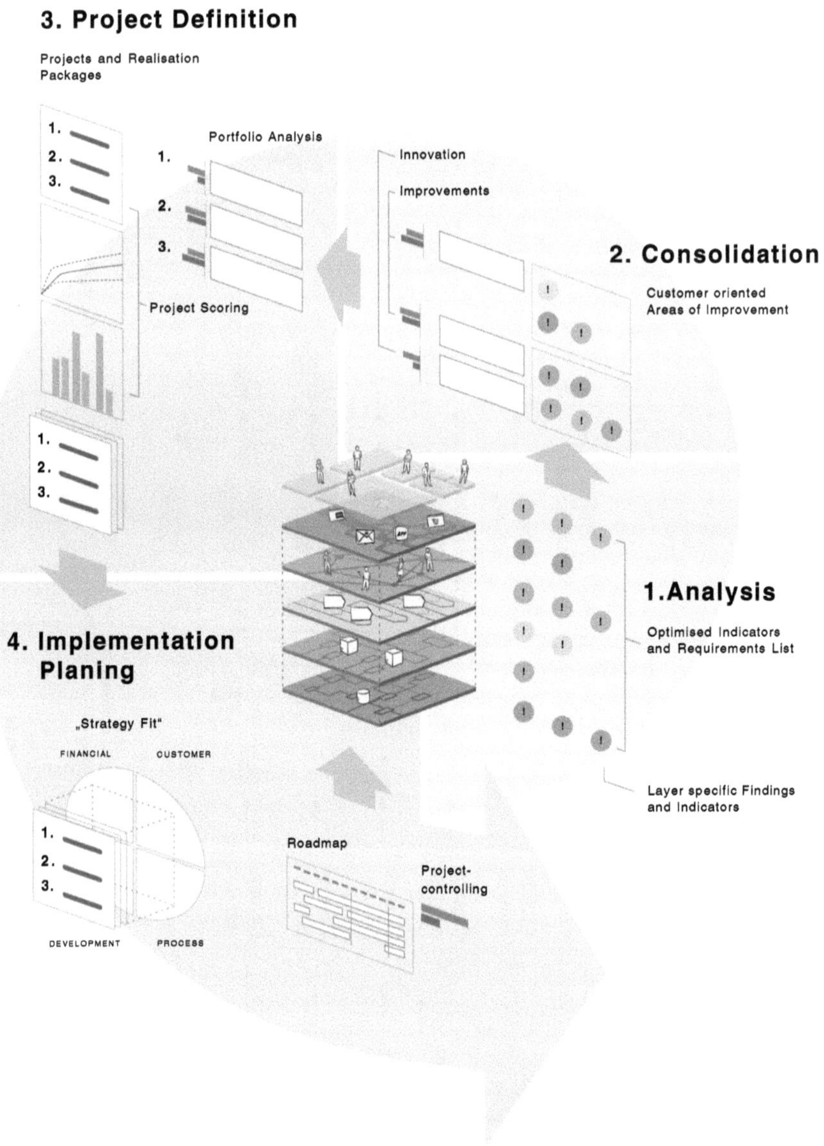


**Fig. 3** Iterative process of analysis and project planning

The process shown in Fig. 3 is exemplary. It describes the consolidation of indicators across various corporate levels, the derivation of fields of action, the definition and evaluation of suitable measures and projects, the strategy comparison, and the concrete implementation planning within the framework of a roadmap. The process is divided into four phases:

1. Analysis: The starting point is the company analysis using the selected perspective(s). The level-specific indicators and requirements developed through the analysis are vertically merged, documented, and consolidated. Assuming the original number of indicators, the number of individual elements decreases in this step, since identical requirements can be generated from different perspectives and levels of the Exploded View. The result is a cleansed list of indicators and requirements that describes overall change requirements.
2. Second consolidation: In the second phase, indicators and requirements with identical orientation and subject matter are grouped into customer-oriented action areas. It is helpful if concrete "business questions" have been assigned to the indicators beforehand. The fields of action thus always describe a concrete change concern with a direct or indirect impact on the customer. All known suggestions for improvement are then assigned to the respective field of action. If no solution approach is apparent, supplementary approaches must be introduced into the process (solution enrichment). Once all the information has been assigned, the solutions are classified as:
   (a) Improvements to existing services, channels, functions, or processes
   (b) Innovations (further development)
3. The phase ends with a potential assessment of all individual measures per type, in which both the customer value ("Value for the Customer") and the development and implementation complexity ("Ease of Implementation") are determined.
4. Project definition: The evaluation criteria for individual measures are incorporated into a portfolio analysis. The result is a categorization of the measures, which enables a filtering of measures and a later prioritization of implementation packages. All measures selected in this step are then combined into a project or implementation package. The basis for the combination is not only the object of change but also the resource requirements and the implementation period. IT projects and organizational projects are separated. This is followed by a project evaluation. Various scenarios (ROI approach, implementation costs) are calculated and, in some cases, a concrete business case is calculated.
5. Implementation planning: project profitability (scenarios) and business cases are part of the approval process. Approved projects are assigned to various strategic goals and initiatives via a "strategy fit." Targets and timeframes (staging) are taken from the strategy fit. These specifications enable projects to be scheduled and a concrete implementation plan (roadmap) to be drawn up. Finally, based on the target definition, performance measurements for projects and initiatives are built and tracked.

In summary, the Exploded View model approach offers the opportunity to develop measures as a result of a comprehensive company analysis. The different perspectives and levels ensure that all relevant influencing factors, whether on the customer or company side, are sufficiently considered and incorporated into the change process. Complicated interrelationships can be made understandable through the simplifying model approach, so that ultimately a common language results within the company and with the customers. This understanding results in sustainable cooperation and the company develops successfully for owners, employees, and customers.

## Reference

Brunner J (2008) Erfolgsmessung von CRM Initiativen im customer relationship management. In: Stadelmann M, Wolter S, Troesch SR (eds) Customer-relationship-Management: neue CRM-best-practice-Fallstudien und -Konzepte zu Prozessen, Organisation, Mitarbeiterführung und Technologie. Verlag Industrielle Organisation, Zürich, pp 171–186

**Hans Albrecht Bartels** works as a CRM consultant at foryouandyourcustomers. His concepts focus on connecting customer needs and value-creation processes in companies by using different data sources along the customer journey. He draws on more than 20 years of experience in the CRM environment.

In his previous roles at a large Swiss retail group, he was responsible for setup and enterprise-wide customer data usage. He managed customer data analytics, developed segmentation concepts, and implemented extensive systems for the use of customer data in marketing and category management.

**To date, Jonathan Möller** has founded and built eight companies. His work focuses on the use of technology for economic innovation and the integral development of people and organizations. Seven years ago, he founded foryouandyourcustomers with companions and friends. It has become an extraordinary company with an exemplary effect due to its family cell structure.

Jonathan Möller advises organizations on digital transformation and has put his extensive experience into his book *Multichannel Guide* (2016). With his wife and three children, he currently lives in Grüt, Switzerland and Melbourne, Australia.

# Performance Management: Leadership in the Digital Transformation

Jürgen Brunner Candrian

**Abstract**

Companies that can match the increasing pace of innovation and address change with a strong customer-centric strategy can continue to be successful in the future, but only if they successfully implement defined strategies and strategic initiatives. The importance of performance management for successful strategy implementation is not a new insight, but it requires new approaches that enable targeted and modern employee management with an agile management system. If performance management is to retain its important role in successful strategy implementation in the future, currently established management and controlling processes must adapt to become more flexible. Agile leadership systems combined with a continuous leadership process form an important coherence to transformational leadership, which is central to managing digital change.

## 1 Leadership in the Digital Transformation

For several years, companies have been more preoccupied with digitalization than any other topic. Successful digital transformation will only succeed if presently mature digital technologies, data explosion, and changing customer behavior are incorporated into strategies and processes, and if disruptive trends in market developments can be anticipated. Companies that can keep up with the increasing pace of innovation and address strategic changes with a strong customer-centric strategy can continue to be successful in the future, but only if they successfully implement defined strategies and strategic initiatives. The best strategy is useless if not lived

J. Brunner Candrian (✉)
UBS Switzerland AG, Zurich, Switzerland
e-mail: juergen.brunner@ubs.com



S. Kirchem et al. (eds.), *CRM Goes Digital*, Management for Professionals,
https://doi.org/10.1007/978-3-658-45798-3_4

out through if convinced employees. Only through a paradigm shift in management is it possible to centralize the commitment, ideas, and motivation of employees.

The importance of performance management for successful strategy implementation is not a new insight. Although proven and successful approaches in this area should not be dispensed with, the future calls for a differentiated approach. The management and controlling systems established today could represent a barrier to successful change. Often static measurements of success must be replaced by agile approaches, creating an important coherence with transformational leadership, which is an important prerequisite for committed, motivated employees.

The transformation brought about by digitalization requires agile methods and a new understanding of leadership. But the challenge of successful implementation remains. Too often, the necessary cultural change is not sufficiently prioritized or change management is under-resourced. Senior management often takes more pleasure in the new digital features and tends to lose sight of the necessary "digital skills" of employees. The desired results can then often not be realized because the drivers of the transformation were not sufficiently known and the underlying new tasks, new skills, and new competencies were insufficiently defined (Narasimhan and Barsoux 2018). Wisdom originally known from the philosopher Heraclitus, "The only constant in life is change," is rarely understood as a necessary core competency for managing change. This is all the more surprising given that the dynamics of change in various industries will continue to increase in the coming years. Performance management must systematically support this change and can thus make an important contribution to the successful management of digital change.

## 2 Management of Digital Interfaces As a Challenge

Changing customer behavior, new technologies, and new competitors are causing business models and existing value chains to change. But are companies prepared for this? An exemplary survey of the financial industry (Efma-Infosys 2017) shows that despite the approaching disruption, half the banks surveyed state lack a clearly defined innovation strategy. Are important technological developments being missed or are they trying to ensure survival by means of a conscious "follower strategy"? In many places, a "winner-takes-all" strategy is rather propagated as a successful response to digitalization (Bughin et al. 2018). Predicting success is up to others.

With the exponential development of technological progress, the establishment of a strategic management process is becoming increasingly important to prepare for the changes in good time. The first step is to regularly review existing technologies (e.g., using a disruption map) and use scenario thinking to assess possible effects on the business model. How will customer behavior change? Which digital processes will be relevant in the future? What positioning at the customer interface is the company aiming for? What is the significance of innovative digital platforms or marketplaces? What skills will customer advisors need in the future?

**Fig. 1** Drivers of change and future success monitoring (example)

Many companies have now taken remarkable steps and innovations. For example, through "innovation labs" that quickly enable innovative product solutions or the digitization of individual business processes. They are now an important implementation model for digital transformation for many companies. Nevertheless, they have not yet overcome the challenges of the past, like process breaks, legacy systems, isolated solutions, complex processes, and rigid product structures.

If companies have not yet addressed the problems of the past, time is running out to determine a strategy and process fit for digitization. What now looks like a feasible but costly "overhaul" could become an immense challenge, at least when preparing and training employees. A look at the drivers of change (Fig. 1), current developments and future success factors can serve as a "strategy check."

**Key Takeaways**

There are three customer-related challenges at the digital interface:

1. Digital customer experience: Customers want a seamless, end-to-end customer experience. In the future, this will balance humans and machines. Furthermore, the customer is becoming more demanding of things like convenience, added service value, and ethical standards. In many cases, this necessitates new digital innovations, but it may also entail a change in distribution. For example, from the financial industry, the branch becomes the center of complex advisory services and worlds of experience (keyword: "pop-up").
2. Breaking up value chains: The importance of data and analytics will not only increase at the customer interface but also for the optimization of internal processes. Digitalization is forcing the integration of processes. For example, from the financial industry, customers actively inform themselves, increasingly use online comparison portals, and want simple, direct product conclusions. This changes sales processes and value creation, especially for customer consulting.
3. Management of change processes: Technological innovations will lead to increased collaboration between humans and machines. The future requirements profile for employees—also at the customer interface—will change significantly. For example, from the financial industry, new job profiles and competencies will become necessary, for example, through artificial intelligence in call centers.

## 3 The Importance of Performance Management

In order to successfully master the aforementioned challenges at the digital interface, it is essential to drive strategy implementation forward while avoiding the so-called "implementation trap": Why do companies fail to achieve the implementation effect despite having formulated goals? The importance of performance management for successful strategy implementation is undisputed. A systematic breakdown of objectives and multidimensional performance measurement and control at various corporate levels (business unit, processes, teams) has been established in many cases.

The secret of implementation success lies, on one hand, in the alignment of strategic priorities and the portfolio of strategic initiatives, and on the other hand, in defined decision-making and control processes. The former ensures the alignment of prioritized initiatives and projects with strategy and the definition of readiness for change or implementation in terms of resources and capabilities. In addition, project responsibility must be defined at the executive level and the business case—the cost/benefit analysis of various decision options using quantitative and qualitative evaluation methods, like the net present value method, for example—must be developed and approved by the most senior decision-making body. Quarterly reporting of initiatives at the decision-making level by an independent function (e.g., a CFO) closes the loop.

Performance management provides a structured approach for operationalizing strategy. With the help of key results and key performance indicators, strategies become concrete and measurable. By integrating them into continuous management and controlling processes, information on the achievement of strategic goals is communicated to the organization. This is particularly important in view of the major changes and flexibility required in the implementation of digital strategies. Through operationalization by means of key results and strategic initiatives and their systematic measurement, the entire company can be aligned with overarching goals. The effects of the strategy on the company become transparent and tangible at all levels. By means of a closed management and control loop, feedback loops and learning effects are additionally initiated.

A look at existing approaches that support successful strategy implementation offers a variety of approaches with different purposes. Performance management approaches such as cockpit controlling, balanced scorecard, or shareholder value approaches tend to represent the traditional options today. New concepts such as OKR (Objectives and Key Results) offer a management system for goal-oriented and modern employee management (Ewenstein et al. 2016). Approaches at the operational level today include, for example, the Net Promoter Score (NPS) and classic benchmarking. These offer important impulses, but have no claim to function as a holistic approach to performance management.

Various performance management approaches can represent important tools to concretize corporate strategy and identify key qualitative and quantitative results. Only 10–15 years ago, the transfer of these concepts to qualitative issues was only somewhat possible due to the difficulty of measuring them. Key performance indicators and systems were often limited to financial aspects. Performance measurements were often only as good as the underlying data, with the problem of multiple ineffective control variables. Even today, the IT landscape is often fragmented and heterogeneous. This often only allows consistent measurement of business processes in digital channels and processes. Unfortunately, when people talk about data diversity (big data), this usually does not mean that the key performance indicators critical to success are available across all business processes.

## 4 Developments in Performance Management

The development of performance management into a discipline in its own right, as opposed to simply a further development of the classic concept of controlling, has enabled a link to strategic management (see the concepts of the balanced scorecard, value-based management, and the St. Gallen performance management model (Cf. Brunner et al. 1999; Möller et al. 2015). The multidimensional measurement of performance established today enables an open view of measurement in management and controlling processes. The paradigm shift toward transformational leadership accounts for the result and behavior orientation.

In many large companies, there is now—in contrast to the past—an understanding that quantitative aspects of corporate management should not dominate the discussion, but that forward looking and multidimensional variables now contribute much more heavily to decision-making (Cf. Brecher et al. 2016; Rigby and Bilodeau 2018; Schmidt 2018). However, the implementation of these quantities in management and controlling is not established everywhere. In particular, when linking to incentive and reward systems (performance-related pay), there is often a reduction in financial aspects. "Management by objectives" and performance-based pay are very common in this context, especially in the financial industry. However, individual banks have started to successfully apply new agile approaches (Escher 2017).

The necessary multidimensionality of strategic management can be well represented by means of the Balanced Scorecard (BSC) (e.g., key figures on time, quality, and costs). The BSC also fulfills the desire for a flexible and networked representation of different key figures. The BSC is proven as a method for identifying, measuring, and presenting multidimensional performance indicators in many companies. A challenge for successful implementation in practice is connecting the cause-effect analysis across different levels and consistently integrating it into management processes. Alongside the BSC, value-based management has established itself as modern corporate management (value enhancement, measured in terms of economic added value). However, value-based concepts are only of limited use for the demands of a modern management system, including for employees.

New concepts such as OKR (Objectives and Key Results) explicitly address this aspect by making objectives and key results integral to management and controlling processes. Furthermore, great emphasis is placed on results and behavior. The process of alignment and the involvement and motivation of managers and employees in management and controlling processes is becoming increasingly important.

**Key Takeaways**
Three requirements for today's performance management approaches can be identified:

1. Concretizing corporate strategy through key results and multidimensional, measurable key performance indicators.
2. Changes in the dynamics of planning and control through continuous performance measurement (including real-time planning and control) and an increasing focus on outcome and behavior control.
3. Changes in target agreement and feedback systems, which place higher demands on performance appraisal due to changes in performance cycles (including frequency and quality of feedback, and links to incentive and reward systems).

What previous approaches have in common is the managerial adage "What gets measured gets done," propagated by Peter Drucker and Tom Peters, among others. The message is clear: performance measurement provides an important indication of whether the defined strategy is being implemented. But what does this mean exactly? How does the measurement of goals and their reporting influence the behavior of employees with regard to strategy implementation? Do performance measurement and the bonus payments aligned with it have a motivating effect per se? A recent study (Fehr 2018) shows no correlation between performance and bonuses in about 60% of companies. Another study (Brecher et al. 2016) shows that 94% of executives believe that performance management improves business performance. Nevertheless, 89% of employees answered that their performance would be significantly better if performance management was changed. So companies clearly need to act.

The need to rethink the existing, traditional "command and control" systems is obvious. But why change anything when things are going well? If the business model changes, the behavior of the employees must also change. However, existing performance management sometimes even prevents changes if behavior and results relating to the new business model are not considered in incentive and reward systems. Until the new business model is established and implemented in all areas, employees face a dilemma. Classic performance measurement on one hand; successful change on the other. Static approaches are too inflexible here to map increasingly time-critical impulses and provide meaningful behavioral guidance.

The necessary paradigm shift in management from reactive-analytical to proactive forecasting, as well as new management cycles in the direction of agile, real-time, automated, and data-based analysis, allows performance management to blossom anew and become the heart of change. However, if the new impulses meet management processes and philosophies that do not correspond to this new approach, we will have built a sports car with a lot of horsepower, but have no drivers to steer it. Let us take sales management as an example: Today, we have a lot of data at our disposal, covering things like customer needs, which topics sales representatives have addressed, and which products are closed, and who has delivered better sales figures (benchmarking). Does the magic of successful sales management consist only in defining the right key performance indicators and measuring and reporting them? A modern management philosophy goes much further and includes empowerment and coaching as important elements.

## 5 Performance Management As a Core Element of Leadership

Professional concepts often remain theoretical because they do not convince employees. New approaches for defining leadership and controlling processes are provided by concepts like Objectives & Key Results - OKR (used by companies such as Adobe, Google, and Microsoft). Goal-oriented employee management places the process and dialogue at the center. However, it also combines established elements (qualitative objectives and quantified key results and key performance indicators) with a continuous leadership process, starting from the corporate level down to the individual team. In this way, OKR forms a framework that breaks down concise annual goals into key results that can be achieved in a few months and can be permanently adjusted to respond immediately to changes. OKRs are transparent within the company and are adjusted at various levels. Guard rails are defined with a results corridor. Negative target achievement is not sanctioned but is seen as a data point and valuable experience. There is no direct link between results and the bonus system or employee ratings. Rather, a streamlined, informal process of continuous feedback is established that collectively defines priorities and key outcomes and facilitates feedback at face-to-face level. Feedback focuses on the future and the development of the employee's strengths (dialogue, feedback, appreciation) and thus their contribution to success (Doerr 2018).

**Key Takeaways**
The benefits of the new agile performance management process:

- Company goals are broken down transparently at various levels and made measurable (measurability).
- High dynamics in management processes and responsiveness through regular reflection on results (learning processes).
- Coordination processes are characterized by self-organization, team spirit, and cooperation (promotion of motivation and personal responsibility).
- Strengths-based feedback culture through regular discussions between supervisors and employees, characterized by a focus on employee strengths and positive appreciation of performance (increasing commitment).

At the core of the performance management process is two levels: on one hand, the target level, which is managed through OKR; and on the other hand, the implementation level, which ensures results through initiatives. Initiatives are becoming increasingly important, particularly for transformation processes managed outside

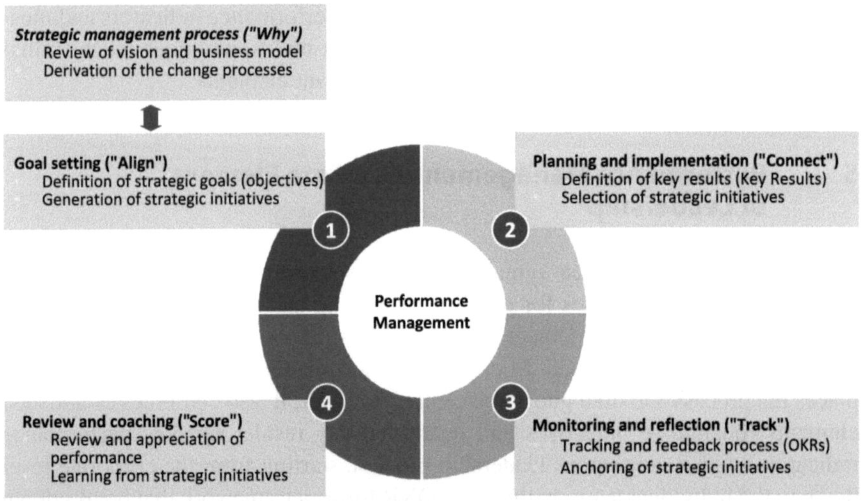


**Fig. 2** Continuous performance management cycle

the line organization. The performance management process (Fig. 2) consists of four phases and the strategic management process.

## 5.1 Practical Example: Customer-Centric Strategic Map

Communicating strategy using a strategy map and operationalizing it through key results at different levels plays an important role, especially at the customer interface (Brunner 2008; Brunner et al. 2001). At the outset, there is the question of what added value is provided for the customer. The subsequent step is the consistent alignment of all support activities to customers and their specific needs, both in terms of the products and services used and in how business is conducted. Accordingly, this requires close links with CRM, which aligns decision-making and action in customer management with value-adding activities. Increasing networking and new business models also lead to organizational change and thus to new functions at the customer interface. One example is provided by customer success management, which looks after the customer experience and is responsible for ensuring that the customer derives maximum benefit from the product. Customer success management has post-sales responsibility for the customer relationship, measured by product usage, customer loyalty, and customer satisfaction (e.g., NPS), among other things (Porter and Heppelmann 2018).

At the customer interface, the employee must know exactly what to do and what is important: What are the goals? What are the success factors? What is the measure of success? The Strategy Map (Kaplan and Norton 2004) combined with the concept of OKR provides the right answer and offers a strategic communication tool for all levels.

A strategy map results from strategy development and shows the main strategic goals and their interrelationships. Objectives must never be viewed in isolation, but rather in their interconnectedness with other objectives and with the paths to achieving them. The following example serves as a grid for a customer-centric strategy in the context of digitization, in order to align it consistently with all important dimensions.

The identified cause/effect relationships enable a better understanding of the customer-centric strategy for all employees. The defined success factors are concretized at each level with the corresponding key results and made measurable with key indicators.

## 5.2 Practical Example: Performance Management at the Customer Interface

From the sales representative's perspective, the challenge is to reconcile the new digitization strategy and the existing business with the applicable metrics. How much change behavior is possible without meeting previous success criteria? In many cases, today's performance measurements leave little room for flexibility and are usually revised only once a year. This naturally provides little support for a change in the business model, and the impetus is limited.

Using OKR (Doerr 2018), concise annual targets can be concretized with key results that can be realized in a few months and are permanently adjustable. This approach is suitable to react to changes. Here, too, as with the strategy map, the goals must be considered in their context. Figure 3 illustrates an example that links strategic goals across different levels.

Simple answers for the design of sales processes cannot be found in times of digital transformation. Tension almost always arises over the importance of the previous business experts versus the new ones. If this is not clearly communicated, uncertainty arises among employees as to where the future of the company lies and what role they will play in it. Employee management is especially challenged when the new strategy creates "cannibalization effects" toward the existing business.

The previous success factors of a successful sales organization—clear sales strategy, focused sales management, structured sales process, and efficient sales organization—are overlaid by the need for high-level agility in sales management. Classic, static measurement systems are not very compatible. A clear target and the freedom to follow the path toward it represent necessary leadership practice in a rapidly changing world. The corporate culture and trust within the company thus become decisive for successful change in sales.

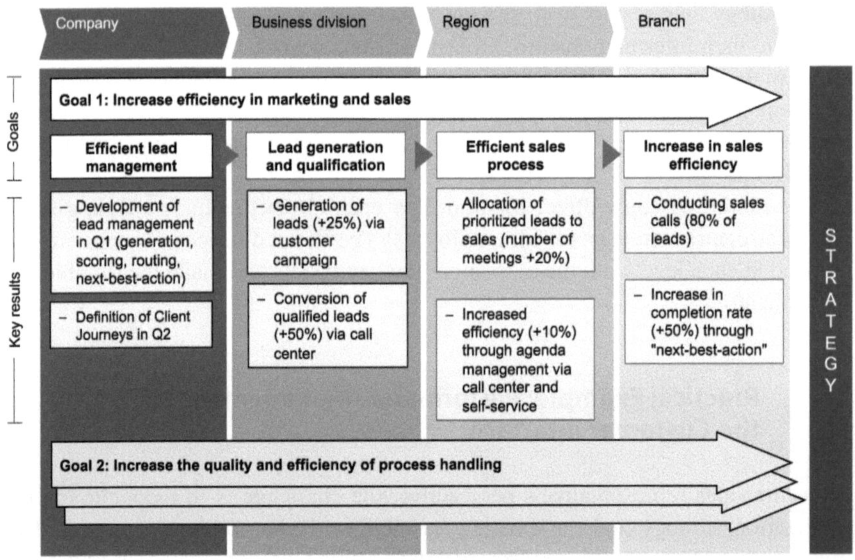


**Fig. 3** Practical example of Objectives and Key Results (OKR)

## 6 Procedure for Developing Continuous Performance Management

In battling for the customer interface, one should first analyze existing business models and drivers of change. The analysis of future value chains and the definition of client touchpoint management along various client journeys conclude with new requirements through digital products, services, and channels. The success factors valid today at the customer interface will not necessarily remain relevant in the future. This necessitates extensive change to continuously adapt the company's reality to changing customer needs.

The increasingly rapid transformation process poses greater challenges for employees because they are in a constant state of flux, through new technologies, new job requirements, new forms of collaboration, and new leadership culture. Only those who accompany the challenges through an agile organizational format and cultural change will be successful and retain their employees in the long term. However, it is a mistake to believe that agility is easily achieved. Agility challenges not only the organization, but also its leaders. But there is no alternative to this lengthy journey. Without the commitment, ideas, and motivation of employees, the digital transformation will not succeed. Appropriate preparation for change processes is crucial for success. "Redefining leadership for a digital age" (Neubauer et al. 2017) shows that successful leaders must have four competencies: Humility, actively soliciting feedback, high adaptability, and visionary thinking.

**Key Takeaways**

Four success factors determine successful performance management:

1. The definition of the strategic management process: regular review and, if necessary, transformation of the existing business model, and deriving the vision and strategy ("why") of disruptive innovations and other necessary changes. Definition of key outcomes (OKR) at all levels ("align"). Development of aligned, balanced strategic initiatives including change processes (e.g., leadership development and competencies).
2. Communicating and aligning strategic and operational priorities: align key outcomes across all levels ("connect"). Increasing the strategic orientation of managers and employees through clear commitment to key results (including strategic and operational priorities). Align key results with strategic initiatives (e.g., empower and develop sales).
3. Establishing a continuous performance management process: Regularly aligning defined and achieved key results across all organizational levels with critical processes ("track"). Focusing on variables critical to the company's success through realizing the influence of key performance indicators on strategic success factors (identifying and communicating cause-and-effect relationships).
4. Developing leadership processes and culture: Strengths-based feedback culture, exemplifying a positive understanding of leadership, establishing feedback mechanisms to employees ("score") based on transparent and consistent leadership processes. Developing leadership competencies such as humility, actively requesting feedback, high adaptability, and visionary thinking.

## 7 Challenges for Corporate Practice

Challenges for successfully implementing modern performance management in corporate practice lie particularly in leadership quality. The digital transformation requires a paradigm shift in leadership. New approaches such as OKR place high demands on the critical faculties and reflective abilities of employees, but also of managers. Many managers see themselves less as mentors or advisors to their employees. However, the required skills and behavior for successful change must be exemplified by management. Managers occupying key positions today have made their careers from other factors and situations. This makes the willingness to change and the example set by senior management a critical success factor.

Further process-related challenges can be added to these behavioral priorities. These include establishing strategic management and communication, which has already been established in many companies through the Balanced Scorecard, for example. This process, supplemented with OKR processes and quarterly review processes, is time- and resource-intensive, especially since key results are now reviewed quarterly and revised if necessary. Agile processes require the necessary adaptation to customer needs and market dynamics. The internal system must thus adapt to external complexity.

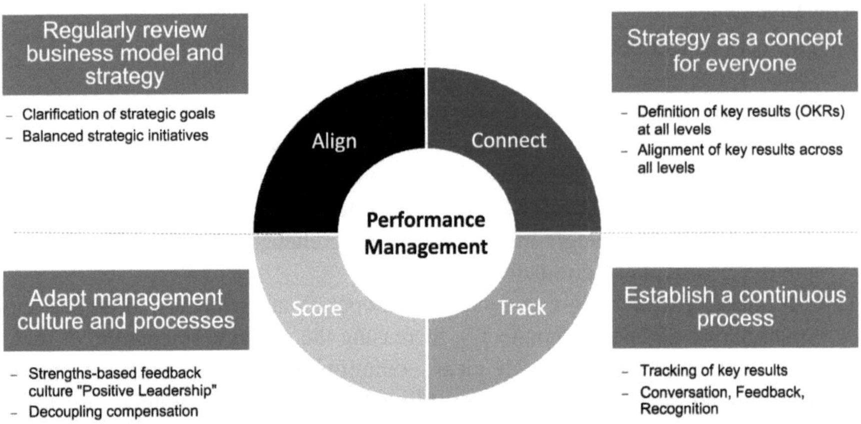


**Fig. 4** Success factors for performance management

However, existing concepts and methods in performance management need not be thrown overboard. Examples include benchmarking and performance measurement systems in the area of quality and processes, or the balanced scorecard approaches already mentioned. The trick is to combine traditional approaches with new agile approaches. A balance of continuity and change is the key to managing digital change.

The business case should act as the central link between strategy formulation and implementation. The business case should make necessary strategic initiatives transparent and measurable. Too often, new agile project management methods (e.g., Scrum and Minimum Viable Product) or lean start-up ideas are brought into the field without analyzing and discussing detailed cost/benefit aspects. A business case developed in the interplay of top-down and bottom-up discussions increases the quality of the project and thus the success rate, due to the broad coordination. Ideally, the business case is developed by "high-performance teams" within a clearly defined period of time with clearly defined role-holders and with the support of internal and external experts. The project idea formulated at the beginning should always be accompanied by a member of the management as a "sponsor" or as responsible for it. Experience with the development and review of business cases is often available in large companies, but elsewhere it is usually only rudimentary, which often makes objective assessment by third parties necessary to further success, measured against the original assumptions (outside view).

The important steps in the process and the challenges for corporate practice are summarized again in Fig. 4.

## References

Brecher D, Eerenstein J, Farley CS, Good TP (2016) Is performance management performing? Accenture Strategy, Washington DC

Brunner J (2008) Erfolgsmessung von CRM-Initiativen mittels business case und performance management. In: Stadelmann M, Wolter S, Troesch M (eds) Customer relationship management. Industrielle Organisation, Zürich, pp 171–185
Brunner J, Becker D, Bühler M, Hildebrandt J, Zaich R (1999) Value based performance management. Wertsteigernde Unternehmensführung: Strategien, Instrumente, Praxisbeispiele. Gabler Verlag, Wiesbaden
Brunner J, Becker D, Wolfisberg S (2001) Value Scorecard—Ansatz zur wertorientierten Konzernsteuerung. In: Klingebiel N (ed) Performance Measurement & Balanced Scorecard. München, Vahlen, pp 91–109
Bughin J, Catlin T, Hirt M, Willmott P (2018) Why digital strategies fail, McKinsey Quarterly, https://www.mckinsey.com/business-functions/digital-mckinsey/our-insights/why-digital-strategies-fail. Accessed: 07 Feb 2019
Doerr J (2018) Measure what matters: OKRs. The simple idea that drives 10x growth. Portfolio Penguin, London
Efma-Infosys Finacle (2017) Digital Banking Report Survey. https://www.efma.com/study/detail/26476. Accessed: 07 Feb 2019
Escher CS (2017) Weg vom Prozess—hin zum Dialog, Handelszeitung. https://www.handelszeitung.ch/schweizer-bank/mitarbeiterbeurteilung-weg-vom-prozess-hin-zum-dialog. Accessed: 07 Feb 2019
Ewenstein B, Hancock B, Komm A (2016) Ahead of the curve: The future of performance management, McKinsey Quarterly. https://www.mckinsey.com/business-functions/organization/our-insights/ahead-of-the-curve-the-future-of-performance-management. Accessed: 07 Feb 2019
Fehr E (2018) Bonus-Kriterien sind oft leicht manipulierbar, Wirtschaftswoche. https://www.wiwo.de/erfolg/beruf/oekonom-ernst-fehr-bonus-kriterien-sind-oft-leicht-manipulierbar/21074844.html. Accessed: 07 Feb 2019
Kaplan R, Norton D (2004) Strategy maps: converting intangible assets into tangible outcomes. Harvard Business School Press, Boston
Möller K, Wirnsperger F, Gackstatter T (2015) Performance Management—Konzept, Erfahrungen und Ausgestaltung einer neuen Disziplin, Controlling 2/2015, S. 74–80. https://aca.unisg.ch/-/media/dateien/instituteundcenters/aca/moeller/controlling-02-2015-beitrag-m%C3%B6ller-wirnsperger-gackstatter.pdf. Accessed: 07 Feb 2019
Narasimhan A, Barsoux JL (2018) Warum Change-Management scheitert, HBR, 6/2018, S. 18–27
Neubauer R, Tarling A, Wade M (2017) Redefining leadership for a digital age, IMD. https://www.imd.org/globalassets/dbt/docs/redefining-leadership. Accessed: 07 Feb 2019
Porter ME, Heppelmann JE (2018) Wie smarte Produkte Unternehmen verändern, HBR, 3/2018, S. 6–23. http://www.ptc-de.com/~/media/DE/Files/PDFs/IoT/de_HBR-How-Smart-Connected-Products-Are-Transforming-Companies2.pdf?la=en. Accessed: 07 Feb 2019
Rigby D, Bilodeau B (2018) Management tools & trends, bain & company. https://www.bain.com/insights/management-tools-and-trends-2017/. Accessed: 07 Feb 2019
Schmidt T (2018) Performance management im Wandel. Gabler Verlag, Wiesbaden

**Jürgen Brunner Candrian** works in the Swiss financial industry. He studied and obtained his doctorate at the University of St. Gallen. He was a research assistant at the Institute for Small and Medium-Sized Enterprises (KMU-HSG) and worked for 10 years in management consulting at Arthur Andersen and Mummert Consulting. He joined UBS in 2004. Initially, he was in the CFO area of Global Wealth Management and Business Banking and was later responsible for Strategic Portfolio Management within UBS Switzerland AG. In 2010, he became Chief of Staff of Personal Banking, where he is responsible for strategy implementation and strategic projects, including leadership culture, sales management, positive leadership behavior and Objectives & Key Results (OKR). He has also been a lecturer at the ZHAW School of Management and Law between 2004–2019.

# On the Way to Digital CRM (dCRM): The Transformation of Customer Management

Martin Stadelmann, Patrick Schäfer, Peter Tüscher, and Juliane Waack

**Abstract**

In the move from the "traditional" handling of prospects and customers to the modern understanding of Digital CRM (dCRM), numerous professional and technical core trends are emerging and being embedded within the design of customer management, with increasingly recognizable effects. This analysis highlights seven core trends that every company should address to become a data-driven business. Not every trend is equally relevant to every company's individual requirements. However, the practical examples listed here are worth exploring from a wider perspective: they provide individual companies with digital transformation ideas, and help to envision the ideas as use cases.

M. Stadelmann (✉)
Zurich, Switzerland

P. Schäfer
DIGITALL Nature Switzerland AG, Zurich, Switzerland
e-mail: Patrick.Schaefer@digitall.com

P. Tüscher
AGROLA AG Freiraum Consulting GmbH, Zurich, Switzerland

J. Waack
Billwerk+ Germany GmbH, Berlin, Germany
e-mail: juliane.waack@billwerk.com



S. Kirchem et al. (eds.), *CRM Goes Digital*, Management for Professionals,
https://doi.org/10.1007/978-3-658-45798-3_5

# 1 The Status Quo of CRM: The Initial Situation and the Requirements for Contemporary Customer Management

When anticipating the future of Customer Relationship Management (CRM), we need to look at recent years; only then will we understand the following:

- How customer relationship management (CRM) has evolved to its current status.
- Which market players have led the way and why.
- Which requirements, elements, and definitions have been added over time.

A future-oriented CRM based on these points shows clearly, in which direction development will be heading and why.

## 1.1 Back to the Future: What Has Actually Happened in the Last 30 Years?

CRM's history began in the 1980s and developed from marketing. Growing technological possibilities at the time birthed database marketing, which led to the first systems that collected and analyzed customer information, and then designed customer communication based on it. The basic idea of CRM we know today—optimizing the personalized approach with the help of powerful databases—was thus born. With developments in computing, ideas could be implemented over time that had long been possible only with extended manual effort.

In the 1990s, contact management software was one of the first building blocks of the CRM systems used today. "Sales automation" made automating the marketing databases created in the 1980s and linking them to contact management software possible, enabling inventory controls and tracking of customer transactions and interactions. The optimization of personalized targeting using databases was thus complemented with automation.

With the founding of Siebel by Tom Siebel in 1993, the first global player in sales force automation emerged. Two years later, the software was given its name, which is still valid today: Alongside suggestions like Enterprise Customer Management and Customer Information System, "Customer Relationship Management" established itself. This term, which added the dialogue or relationship level to the technological concept, gave the development and concept of CRM the orientation it has today.

This name gave rise to an industry that grew and developed continuously over the following decades. The increasing spread of the internet—privately and professionally—particularly ensured that CRM systems would be used across different locations. This provoked completely new collaboration opportunities and business models. For example, in 1993, Siebel was one of the first companies to push the market toward mobile solutions with "Siebel Handheld."

Even before 2000, one of the still untouchable Siebel's biggest competitors was founded almost unnoticed. Salesforce, which at the time offered "Software as a Service" (SaaS), was initially aimed at small and medium-sized companies. At the time, Siebel probably never dreamed that Salesforce, under the leadership of Mark Benioff, would grow into a serious competitor within just a few years. But Salesforce was not the only company to challenge Siebel's place under the sun. Other players were establishing themselves in the market. SAP and Baan, for example, ensured that CRM software providers consistently expanded their systems from pure sales toward the specialist areas of marketing and service, and linked them to the ERP systems (enterprise resource planning) they were also promoting.

In this era, fueled by the establishment of the Internet, cell phones, and the mobile (and even handheld) computer over recent decades, CRM systems—and the terms surrounding customer relationship management—began evolving in various directions.

With his book *CRM at the Speed of Light*, Paul Greenberg revisited the concept of CRM systems after the dotcom bubble burst in the early 2000s, which had caused CRM companies in particular enormous losses (Greenberg 2009). Against the backdrop of multiplying terms like customer experience, customer engagement, and customer service, he explained his thoughts in an interview at ExCom 2016: "If CRM were what we wanted CRM to be back then, there would be no difference between CRM and customer engagement. It would encompass everything. We used to look at it philosophically and strategically, but in the end it has become a topic that is about technologies and systems; in short, it's about enablement" (Small Business Trends 2016).

CRM, then, according to Greenberg, is the enablement foundation for marketing, sales, and service to create positive customer experiences. At the end of the day, these experiences are feelings that develop based on how a company interacts with customers over time and how companies engage in that dialogue. With ever-increasing opportunities for interaction, it is no surprise that CRM systems have evolved in various directions over recent decades. Different approaches, philosophies, and customer perceptions demand different tools to enable successful customer management.

Another major change was announced when Salesforce caused a surprise with the first cloud-based CRM system. In the following years, they showed that the cloud was potentially more flexible than any onsite system in a complex and uncertain world. The CRM concept of optimizing personalized and individualized targeting using databases and automation grew again.

In recent years, the integration of modern communication channels has been reflected in the development of CRM. Under the term "social CRM," social networks play an increasing role in the design of innovative business models, from first contact with customers (leads) to the provision of service and support.

From the simple customer database to the integrated CRM platform that covers sales processes and the customer-relevant functions of marketing and service, to a full view of the customer (closed loop), CRM has come a long way in barely 30 years. It has thus undergone significant change processes regarding customer centricity, which places the customer's specific behavior and individual requirements at the center of every application context.

## 1.2 Where Are We Today? The Status Quo of Customer Management

In addition to technological innovations, CRM has steadily evolved as a philosophy and company-wide differentiation strategy. For a long time the product was the focus of sales and marketing; today it is the customer, through customer centricity and the customer journey.

The digital transformation does not mean the classic sales channels—telephone, branch, visits, events—have been replaced by digital channels, but they have been supplemented. Today, the single-channel approach to customer contact falls short and is no longer effective. Instead, the omni-channel experience is what counts; that is, the offer of different channels that customers can freely select and combine without experiencing any loss of information between channels.

In particular, the linking of automation and data analysis today enables personalization of the individual customer experience. The long-held "one message for all" methodology misses the point of mature customer interest and creates a significant competitive disadvantage in the context of online information diversity. Instead of sending out broadly standardized messages in a generalized approach and hoping they will be received by prospects and customers, marketing and sales are called upon to respond to individual customer needs. Through a personalized approach, this conveys the right message, to the right customer, at the right time, through the right medium: this is fully integrated, constantly coordinated, and seamless across content and channels.

However, in view of digitalization-related changes, which are supposedly shaping the future of CRM, the following fact should not be forgotten: Digitalization itself is not a new phenomenon. Shifts toward new business models—with the selective aid of digital solutions—have been ongoing for decades and can be traced back to the invention of the steam engine. Developments understood in modern terms as "digitalization" refer to highly innovative and interlinked digital technologies that trigger new trends and create new potential.

The breadth represented by the term "digitalization" is reflected by Prof. Dr. Oliver Bendel of the University of Applied Sciences and Arts Northwestern Switzerland FHNW: "The term digitalization has several meanings. It can mean the digital transformation and representation or execution of information and communication or the digital modification of instruments, devices and vehicles, as well as the digital revolution, also known as the third revolution or digital turnaround" (Gabler Wirtschaftslexikon 2018).

When customer management "goes digital," it does not mean digital had no prior existence. Rather, customer management can now reach new heights by applying digital capabilities; for example, by using cloud-based systems, automating processes, or opening up individualized interaction and analysis options.

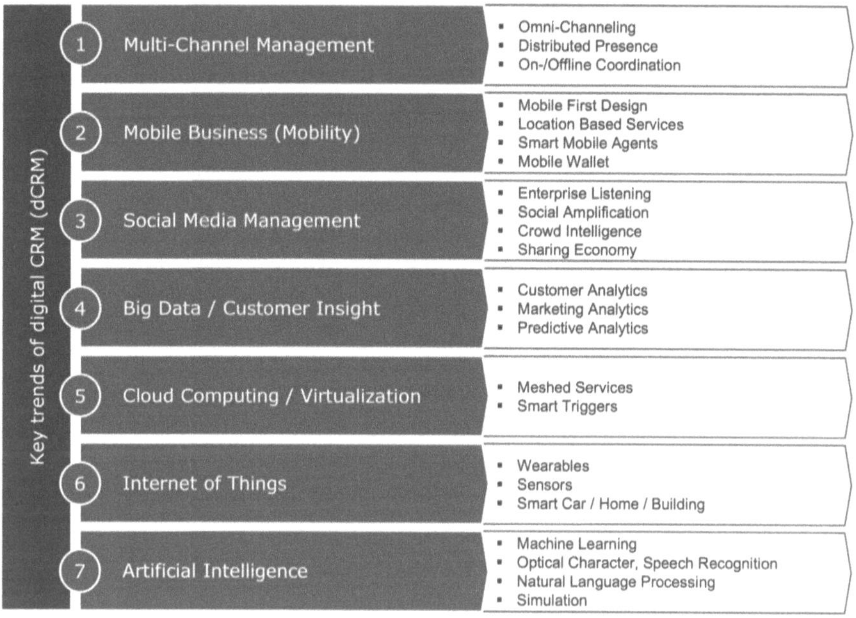


**Fig. 1** Core business and technical trends in Digital CRM

## 2 Core Trends in Digital CRM (dCRM) and Their Application Potential for Modern Customer Management

In the evolution of Digital CRM (dCRM), numerous specialist and technical core trends are emerging and finding increasingly profound integrations with customer management (see Fig. 1). This analysis highlights seven core trends that every company should address to become a data-driven business. Not every trend is equally relevant to every company's individual requirements. However, the practical examples listed here are worth exploring to find possible ideas for one's own digital transformation.

### 2.1 Multi-Channel Management

Multi-channel management, a term from distribution policy, represents the coordination of different communication (information flow) and sales (performance flow) channels. Its goal is to address and serve different customer groups on different channels. It is based on the seamless linking of channel functions and data, in order to create positive interaction (seamless integration). In marketing, this is referred to as "cross" or "omni-channel management"; that is, linking individual channels instead of maintaining parallel channels without interaction or switching possibilities.

In recent decades, the number of channels through which companies can reach existing and potential customers has steadily increased, especially in the digital space. The goal of the multi-channel approach is obvious: customers are individuals, and accordingly they behave differently when seeking information, and making selections and purchases. Due to the proliferation of analog and digital channels, companies need to identify which channels their target customers use for information, selection, and purchasing, and specifically make them available.

Ideally, the individual strengths of individual channels are combined to optimize the overall customer experience. Customer centricity plays a key role here. Companies must respond to how their customers use the channels they offer and align them accordingly. A clear example is the use of Twitter as a service channel.

Originally, companies used Twitter as a one-way tool for marketing communications. However, the platform's dialogue function means customers have increasingly communicated service concerns to the company profiles. Since these problems and complaints were immediately visible to all other customers, PR and marketing reasons alone meant they could not be ignored. Companies such as Adobe, DHL, and even Zappos have therefore adapted their Twitter strategy to customer needs and tasked service staff with monitoring social channels, managing the resulting insights systematically and professionally, responding promptly to customer concerns, and answering through the chosen channel, if possible, so the customer does not experience a channel break.

**Corporate Example: Adobe**

Design software company Adobe is a good example of a company using Twitter to help customers. Users can tweet specific questions about various software and receive direct assistance from @AdobeCare. Instead of scrolling through YouTube channels for particular problems, the user receives a direct, targeted answer, which is visible to other users on the channel. Experience shows it is too inconvenient for customers to contact customer service by telephone with such problems. The use of Twitter is thus a smart move because it prevents customers with problems from being left to their own devices in frustration and, in the worst case, switching to a competitor. Furthermore, this type of service contributes to brand loyalty, as customers feel their problems are taken seriously.

In addition, Adobe is present on all major social media platforms, works with online communities, and of course offers helpful self-service videos on YouTube.

Systematic multi-channel management enables companies to distribute specific services to individual channels such that they reach the right target groups while creating a comprehensive brand experience. A better competitive position is the result. Customers can be managed in a more targeted manner via different channels, customer wishes can be identified and fulfilled more quickly, and positive interaction is created. The successes of digital channels in particular can be measured with analytical tools, and gaps in the customer experience can be identified and dealt with more quickly.

Ultimately, increased accessibility and visibility on various channels increase customer loyalty. Communication does not necessarily stop when customers end their presence on a channel, that is, when they leave the store or hang up the phone. Through exciting, relevant or even playful customer engagement (for example, competition or gamification), a targeted continuity of interaction can be achieved.

For customers, this result in the flexibility to contact companies outside of working days and regular working hours, to obtain information, make purchases, and receive technical support. If the information, tone, and interaction options adapt to the respective channel, customer relationships can be strengthened through their "favorite channels." This in turn adds value to the customer experience.

In particular, 24/7 access to information, whether for product research, identifying purchase options, service offerings, or company information, enables customers to shape their own buying experience. The more channels are available, the more flexibly the customer can decide how and when they want to contact the company.

## 2.2 Mobile Business (Mobility)

Mobile business is another subsection of classic e-commerce in which e-business and mobility are linked. Thanks to the widespread use of mobile devices and the ready availability of corresponding networks and services, e-business is increasingly merging into mobile business. Mobile business takes advantage of the functionality and performance of mobile devices such as smartphones, notebooks, tablets, and even wearables, and uses them in mobile work and customer interaction processes.

The main focus is customer interaction and customer relationship management. Mobile CRM encompasses all the marketing, sales, and service measures for which a company uses mobile devices to record and support the behavior of prospects, customers, and—increasingly—partners, for commercial purposes. This applies throughout the entire customer lifecycle, from customer information and communication to interaction and transaction.

This gives companies the opportunity to reach customers on the move and to communicate appropriately, regarding their location and context. This is particularly successful when companies use platforms that customer's access to obtain location-based information, offers, and discounts (e.g., Foursquare and TripAdvisor). The technological basis for this is so-called geo-positioning (geolocation), which determines the exact location of a device or its user.

**Example from Corporate Practice: Foursquare**
Foursquare is a location-based social network. Customers download the Foursquare app to their smartphones to "check-in" to stores, museums, restaurants, etc. Points and awards (so-called "badges") are collected with each check-in (gamification).

Users can rate and comment on visited locations and act as "ambassadors" or critics. They can exchange information and find out about restaurants and stores for planned visits. Businesses gain reach, new customer groups, and thus more deals when reviews are positive. Even negative reviews can be used to publicly demonstrate service competencies and work on deficiencies in the customer experience.

Companies use mobile opportunities, among other things, to increase their revenue by reaching users or customers on additional channels (see also multi-channel management) in a local context. Customers hear of relevant opportunities in their immediate vicinity or near their destination. In this way, frequency at the point of interest or point of sale (POS) can be increased; for example, by targeting customers with cross-selling and upselling offers.

Ideally, customers can be motivated to buy directly on site with relevant decision-making aids, which can also reduce marketing costs. It is advantageous for decision-making aids to come from vendor-neutral platforms, as customers rate these as more trustworthy than information directly from a company website or an advertising campaign. In 2017, software provider Bright Local surveyed more than 1000 US customers about their buying behavior and found that 85% trusted online reviews as much as recommendations from friends and acquaintances. Customer reviews are now one of the main sources of product and service research (BrightLocal 2018).

Various studies show customers are increasingly turning to smartphones to research and compare products in brick-and-mortar stores. It is therefore worth creating the conditions to influence purchase decisions directly in the local context, through your own or vendor-neutral platforms, optimized for mobile access. According to a 2017 study published by Salsify, a provider active in the field of digital product experience, 77% of all American shoppers reach for their smartphones in stores to research products and compare prices (PR Newswire 2017).

For companies, the advantages of mobile business therefore lie in tapping into new customer groups, reaching and influencing potential customers at the moment of the purchase decision, and demonstrating an early presence on platforms that are constantly growing in content relevance, due to increasing user numbers.

Customers, on the other hand, have the advantage of mobile access to products, services, and information, even enabling considered decisions spontaneously in stores and beyond.

App-driven notifications also enable companies to suggest individual special offers (using mobile analytics in conjunction with real-time analytics) directly on site, which of course benefits customers. In addition, social rating platforms offer customers supplier-neutral suggestions and information to help them navigate spontaneously when shopping or on vacation, for example.

Mobile ticketing and mobile tagging (using QR codes) are already well-established mobile business applications. Mobile payment functions are probably one of the most important areas in the field at present.

## 2.3 Social Media Management

Social media plays an increasingly important role in the information age. In focus, here are recommendations from friends and acquaintances, and provider-neutral platforms. The following section discusses the possibilities of comprehensive social media management in greater depth.

Social media monitoring means searching social networks for mentions and information about one's own company. With the help of keywords, current industry, and customer opinions can be recorded in real time. Automated social media monitoring, through platforms like Hootsuite, can also distinguish between positive and negative mentions.

Social platforms primarily serve companies in the CRM area to generate and increase knowledge. Needs, expectations, and requirements are expressed on the platforms and can be evaluated through social media monitoring and used to optimize marketing, sales, and services.

In the B2B sector, professional social networks like LinkedIn and Xing are also used to identify potential new customers and strengthen relationships with partners and existing customers in the long term. Interaction offers both parties the option of communicating in a non-pressured, self-determined manner.

Social media management thus helps companies collect and analyze customer requirements and needs through attentive monitoring and analytics tools.

In addition, customer loyalty can be strengthened through targeted, public interactions and authentic communication. If this communication stands out from the competition through appropriate use of humor or service power, this can strengthen brand and company awareness. Ideally, it builds up and positively develops brand image.

**Example from Corporate Practice: Old Spice Ltd**

The men's perfume brand Old Spice was founded in 1937 and marketed at the time primarily as a gift option for women to give men at Christmas. Around the turn of the century, however, the company aimed to open up new customer groups and appeal to younger generations, using its classic image.

A marketing campaign in 2010 affected the change. The commercial featured model and actor Isaiah Mustafa as a dream man with exaggerated masculinity, declaring "The man your man could smell like." It became a viral hit on YouTube, Twitter, and Facebook. Old Spice used this success for repeated viral effects and thus achieved enormous reach with similar concepts in the following years.

Part of Old Spice's success was that its commercials were perfectly produced for sharing and liking on social networks. Instead of producing one long commercial, they released numerous segments, no longer than half a minute, and used humor to convey the brand message. Old Spice also linked social media channels by having Mustafa answer 180 Twitter queries and comments via video and posting them on YouTube. This generated a personal experience with customers on a relatively small budget. As a result, the company's sales increased by 107% (Maynard 2010).

Social media offers the advantage of communicating short, concise information immediately. This enables reputation campaigns, PR, and crisis measures to be executed more quickly and directly. The feedback functions of most networks enable companies to analyze customer perceptions in real time and use them to optimize their own products and services. Last but not least, tweets, likes, and links increase a company's own website traffic.

The main benefit of social media management for companies is that knowledge of customer needs, criticism, and behavior can be gathered and used immediately. The low-threshold interaction options enable customer loyalty to be strengthened and ensure that satisfied customers act as brand ambassadors, which also supports the acquisition of new customers. This is not least due to existing customers' memberships of their respective social networks.

Customers can be alerted more quickly to information, updates, and news through social networks and company profiles, obtain more detailed information, and enjoy clear contact. A well-managed social media profile lets customers take advantage of service opportunities in a timely manner, regardless of location (for example, in the event of flight delays or when enquiring about opening hours). And the fact that customers can engage directly with the company helps strengthen the relationship.

## 2.4 Big Data/Customer Insight

Whereas companies used to have to fill entire warehouses with gigantic computers in order to process a few megabytes of data, modern technology, and cloud computing today means very large volumes of data, especially unstructured data, can be processed reasonably quickly. Big Data refers to data that is too voluminous, too complex, too fast-moving, or too weakly structured to be meaningfully processed manually. It must therefore be processed by machines to gain commercially useful information through complex analyses. Due to the increasing digitalization of customer contact and the data it generates—particularly also the data-describing metadata—the use of Big Data technologies in marketing, sales, and service is becoming increasingly important.

In addition to Big Data, there is also increasing talk of "Smart Data," that is, the targeted collection and analysis of data. This intends to prevent unnecessary data from being collected "on the off chance" without stringent regulation of what it should ultimately be used for. Particularly in view of the stricter European data protection legislation (GDPR), the smart data approach will gain additional importance.

Today, Big Data analyses are primarily used to make timely statements about customer behavior and consumer trends. The aim is to obtain in-depth knowledge about customers (customer insights) to inform appropriate measures to acquire new customers and retain existing customers. Combined with suitable individualization and automation, very large customer groups can thus be individually served based on their behavior (e.g., through marketing automation). Extended to corporate data and supported by clear business rules, these analyses can assist data-based business decisions.

**Example from Corporate Practice: YouTube**

YouTube, Netflix, and Spotify are prime examples of companies that use Big Data in a very targeted way. Any users of these media services will be familiar with the recommendations for videos, movies, and music that reflect already-consumed content. And anyone who has followed these suggestions will know they become increasingly accurate. There is strong competition in the media and entertainment industry, so offering users optimal experience and clear added value is important. Recommendations provide both.

Thanks to Big Data, massive amounts of structured data (e.g., video titles from search, preferred genres for music) and unstructured data (e.g., patterns by which users watch videos or listen to music) can be processed. For example, YouTube, Netflix, and Spotify can analyze billions of clicks and consider the data of the content viewed, both for users and from all similar users, to find ideal recommendations. Over time, machine learning and predictive analytics make the recommendations increasingly accurate.

There are far-reaching benefits for companies that use Big Data analytics. Marketing measures can be individualized in real time to match customer requirements and behavior. This positively impacts customer loyalty and the profitability of customer relationships. Data on customer behavior can generate forecasts and brand trends, making marketing activities more accurate.

The goals of Big Data or Customer Insight span the entire enterprise:

- Creating strategic competitive advantage through the use of predictive analytics.
- Creating more reliable sales forecasts.
- More accurate forecasts of advertising effectiveness by analyzing previous campaigns and customer responses.
- Increase sales (e.g., through more targeted customer communications).
- Increased productivity and cost reduction; for example, through methods like the uplift model, under which campaigns are directed only to customers most likely to respond to sales campaigns (positive in terms of purchase motivation).
- Improved monitoring of brand perception (social media monitoring).
- Optimization of pricing through automated price adjustment, depending on demand and/or customer behavior.
- Creation of new business areas through the use of business intelligence.

Customers are also enormously advantaged by analytics. The customer experience is more individualized, consumers receive relevant offers at the right time, and at appropriate prices based on their behavior or the behavior of similar customers. This increases customer satisfaction and thus the feeling of being perceived and treated as an individual.

## 2.5 Cloud Computing/Virtualization

When defining cloud computing, experts refer to the US standardization body NIST's definition (National Institute of Standards and Technology): "Cloud computing is a model that allows on-demand, anytime, anywhere convenient access over a network to a shared pool of configurable computing resources (e.g., networks, servers, storage systems, applications, and services) that can be made available quickly and with minimal management effort or service-provider interaction" (CSRC 2011). Cloud computing thus enables organizations to store their data on a non-locally installed computer or network or to access applications and services that reside in the metaphorical "cloud." The cloud-based applications, services, or data can therefore be accessed and used from anywhere. For the user, cloud computing reduces IT costs, since cost-intensive investments in hardware and networks, in particular, are eliminated.

Cloud computing therefore includes technologies and business models in which IT resources can be made available dynamically, based on qualitative and quantitative requirements. Common service models are SaaS (Software as a Service), PaaS (Platform as a Service), and IaaS (Infrastructure as a Service). Usage is billed according to effective utilization of the purchased service.

Virtualization goes hand in hand with cloud computing. Here, individual physical computers or servers are divided into several virtual computers. This improves scalability and system utilization with potentially fewer servers and lower costs for infrastructure and maintenance. Known forms of virtualization are:

- Desktop virtualization, which allows a centralized server to deliver and manage individualized desktops.
- Network virtualization, which splits network bandwidth into multiple independent channels, allocated to specific servers, devices, or applications.
- Software virtualization, which separates applications from hardware and operating systems.
- Storage virtualization, which combines multiple network storage resources into a larger whole that can be accessed by multiple users.

Cloud computing and virtualization place high demands on the performance, stability, and availability of network infrastructure. In this context, one hears of "meshed services." Networks with this technology, in which each network node is connected to at least one other node, are regarded as very secure and reliable, because if a device or connection fails, data communication is still ensured by redirection.

The number of cloud-based applications is now immense. Not least among these are CRM and marketing applications. Scott Brinker shows an impressive picture of the rapid development of marketing tools by means of a map in his blog, chiefmartec.com. While only about 150 tools filled the map in 2011, there were already 8000 tools at the beginning of 2020. The thematic clusters of the map show very clearly which marketing technology topics have developed over time (Chef Marketing Technologist Blog 2018).

Today, marketing technology products are often bundled in a marketing cloud to form an integrated marketing service portfolio. This allows companies to implement inbound and outbound marketing in an increasingly complex world of tools using a cloud service model that provides analytics, automation, and orchestration of customer interactions based on insight data.

Not to be confused with a marketing cloud is cloud marketing. Cloud marketing deliberately focuses on decoupling marketing activities from the business. Marketing content is distributed in collaboration with various sales partners. The required marketing tools and content are made available to the sales partners on a corresponding platform.

**Example from Corporate Practice: TripAdvisor**

TripAdvisor is a travel website that offers users individual testimonials from third parties in order to plan their own vacations. This includes testimonials and reviews from travelers; links to reports from newspapers, magazines, and travel guides; and travel forums. These reports lead to accommodation, airlines, restaurants, sights, and stores. According to its own data, 463 million visitors a month use more than 859 million reviews and opinions to gain inspiration and decision-making for their travels (TripAdvisor 2018).

In this cloud marketing example, TripAdvisor deliberately uses the decoupling of marketing activities from the service-providing companies. Companies in the tourism industry are particularly characterized by advertising messages that do not always coincide with customer perceptions. Thus, it makes sense for a credible sales partner, namely the customers themselves, to advertise their products and services. This user-generated content creates credible advertising for the service providers. At the same time, it increases the relevance and reach of TripAdvisor's business model.

Other cloud computing applications have also become a natural part of everyday life. Widely used examples are Apple's iCloud, cloud storage services such as DropBox, Microsoft OneDrive, and Google Drive, all webmail services, Skype's voice-over-IP service, and social media platforms like Instagram, Facebook, Twitter, and the like.

The key success factor in cloud-based applications is access to information. This is no longer limited to a local computer. Through the cloud, data and information can be viewed and edited any time, and date synchronizes promptly so all users access the latest data at all times (mobility). This makes users more flexible and gives customers better access to services.

## 2.6 Internet of Things

The Internet of Things, or IoT for short, refers to the increasing networking between "intelligent" objects. Various objects, everyday objects, or machines are equipped with processors and sensors. Each intelligent object has its own internet address to be identified and uniquely addressed. Through these prerequisites, smart devices can communicate with each other, act independently, and adapt and react to specific scenarios.

The IoT thus connects "things" such as production machines, household appliances, medical devices, control motors, cars, fitness wristbands, and much more. They connect to each other and to information technology applications like apps to enable a variety of services using the transmitted data.

When devices, sensors, actuators—that is, drive elements that convert electrical signals into mechanical movement or other physical quantities—and applications are connected, the term "M2M communication" (machine-to-machine) is used, since the endpoints are not people, but machines and algorithms.

The terms IoT and M2M (machine-to-machine) are often mentioned in the same breath. However, IoT goes further than M2M. The explanatory approaches of the market research company Machina Research demonstrate this. Machina Research specializes in IoT and has been part of the Gartner Group since 2016. According to Machina Research, M2M refers to the connection of a device via a network to a back-end system. This solves a single, specific task, such as reading an electricity meter or triggering an alarm. An M2M solution is primarily based on data from one source, and is thus also easily provided from a single source.

In IoT applications, data is usually collected from a variety of sensors, devices, systems, services, and other assets. Data sources include networked devices and M2M applications, enterprise IT systems, public data feeds, social media, and other IoT applications. This data is aggregated, analyzed, and further processed in complex applications. The IoT is thus a complex construct that requires the interaction of multiple service providers.

The above definition shows that IoT is more than just networked devices. The data generated, which must be stored, analyzed, and processed, is also central. The network of things provides a huge amount of sensor data, from simple temperature measurements to aggregated status data from highly complex production processes. Through algorithms and analysis tools, this data is turned into useful, value-creating applications for companies and end customers.

Last but not least, the networking infrastructure elements such as management and integration platforms complete the Internet of Things. These elements, which are logically based on cloud technology, ensure secure, logically orchestrated connections between devices, applications, and users.

**Example from Corporate Practice: Amazon**

Amazon's Dash button, developed in 2014, is probably best known. A small button, the click of which activates the Amazon order for a pre-determined product. This Wi-Fi-enabled button has steadily evolved as a technology and service in recent years.

Under the name "Dash Replenishment Service," various projects now combine the concept of the dash button—that is, automated ordering at the touch of a button—with smart household appliances, which are supplied through integrations in the device. The networked devices are equipped with sensors that monitor the consumption of a product and also the consumption rhythm. For example, Brother printers measure the fill level of printer cartridges and reorder suitable ones as needed.

The advantage for Amazon is obvious: the devices always place their orders through the online giant's platform. What is more, the subscription-like service generates calculable sales on one hand, and on the other, customers need not face regular purchase decisions that risk them changing their minds. Manufacturers also benefit from the concept, as devices only ever buy original accessories.

In 2018, Amazon also linked its Alexa voice assistant to home appliances. Thus, the company exhibits a microwave with an Alexa button. If you press the button, you can give the device voice commands. When prompted, Alexa heats up a cup of coffee and knows that 1 min and 43 s is the right duration.

The IoT trend is fueled by technological developments. Enormous access to computing power is available through global, highly available data networks, regardless of location and time. Meanwhile, the costs for computing power, storage, sensors, and communication services have fallen massively. Combined with steady progress in software development, this opens up increasingly complex IoT application areas.

What is also conducive to IoT is the charming fact that IoT solutions benefit both solution providers and end customers. Customers benefit from innovative new products and value-added services, which also positively impact customer experience. Companies can increase their efficiency and reduce their costs. Through innovative approaches, they strengthen their market position and can even open up new markets.

IoT application areas are manifold. Currently, prominent areas are:

- Connected home and work—this includes applications such as smart home, with the networking and control of household appliances, smart metering with intelligent electricity meters, and building automation and security technology.
- Connected mobility or "connected car"—this includes applications around connected vehicles, self-driving vehicles, and usage-based insurance or charging models that define tariffs based on actual vehicle or infrastructure usage.
- Connected cities or "smart cities"—application areas include public transportation, street lighting, video surveillance, and traffic management.
- Industrial applications—solutions across the entire value chains of production, logistics, and retail.
- Healthcare—this includes applications like wearables for medical self-monitoring, through to entire clinical environments with the integration of complex medical technology.

In marketing, the Internet of Things can be used intensively, particularly in upselling and cross-selling. Smart devices can identify needs in real time and offer purchase advice, be it reordering printer cartridges, detergents, or coffee capsules.

For users, IoT makes everyday life easier and optimizes control over household appliances. Lighting systems, security systems, and other devices can be checked and adjusted on the go. Uncertainties in operation are removed by smart devices, and even repetitive activities can be automated to be performed regularly without manual input.

For companies, IoT creates various opportunities to place their products with new customer groups. Collaborations with other providers can increase reach and add value for customers. In addition, a unique selling proposition can be achieved if the additional functions, or even the app, are more attractive to customers compared to other providers.

## 2.7 Artificial Intelligence

The definitions of Artificial Intelligence (AI) are manifold, if only because of the complex concept of intelligence. What constitutes intelligence is already controversial in the case of humans. It is even more so with machines. In general, however, artificial intelligence refers to attempts to emulate human-like decision-making structures, that is, to enable a computer to process demanding problems independently.

The aim is for computers to take over tasks previously the preserve of humans. These include recognizing written and spoken language; learning; and recognizing facial expressions. The enticing thing is that an AI solution can "think" faster and process more information than the human brain. Exemplary use cases in medical diagnoses show it can be done with a lower error rate than diagnoses made by doctors.

Ongoing digitalization is continuously generating enormous amounts of data. Here, the ability to process large volumes of data quickly and accurately is driving AI's increasing importance. According to IDC, the volume of data generated globally each year will grow to 175 zettabytes (1021 bytes) by 2025 (IDC 2018). By comparison, the figure was 23 zettabytes in 2017.

Meaningfully using such enormous volumes of data necessitates appropriate tools. Here, artificial intelligence positions companies to take completely new paths in product development, in the digital transformation of their IT and specialist departments, and also in customer interactions and customer experience when evaluating and using this flood of data. AI-based recommendations and forecasts assist users across a wide range of applications and in countless application scenarios, enabling faster and more informed decisions.

Many AI applications are based on neural networks. Similar to the human brain, tiny functional units—the artificial neurons—are networked and then "trained," in robotics, for example, with sensorimotor data. This learning data enables the system to recognize patterns and regularities. Based on these insights, AI generates constantly growing knowledge. Although training takes time, it enables the system to learn on its own. This is why we speak of "self-learning systems" or "machine learning."

The examples of applications for intelligent systems are already diverse. The poster children for the use of AI in marketing are undoubtedly Google and Facebook.

With the help of artificial intelligence, they analyze their customers' every click. This enables them to reliably predict the behavior of a target group and to highly personalize products and service offerings. Customers feel they are being addressed individually, which develops a positive feeling and leads to higher customer satisfaction in the long term.

**Example from Corporate Practice: Tesco**

Tesco, a leading supermarket chain in the UK, has transformed its entire data process in recent years to evaluate analog and digital customer behavior and use it for optimization. In 2017, the company initiated a solution with voice assistant Google Home to allow users to add products to an individual digital shopping cart at any time. What makes Tesco's solution special is that the system remembers what the user usually buys and can thus make suggestions if a certain product is missing. Users can then specify a fixed date when the order should be dispatched.

On the employee side, meanwhile, Tesco is using AI to optimize the routes in-store that employees take to gather user orders from warehouses and shelves. This can reduce overall order times and allow more orders to be taken. Similar technology is also used to determine optimal shipping routes.

Intelligent chatbots are currently a hot topic: Customers contact virtual customer advisors directly with questions at any time. Written dialogue is clearly shifting to spoken dialogue, whereby users formulate concerns in their own words. Popular examples are voice assistants such as Apple's Siri or Amazon's Alexa, which provide information in response to voice commands, but also perform actions. Google also has a solution on the market with Assistant, which sounds very human and can make appointments with people by phone.

**Example from Corporate Practice: Ryan Air**

The low-cost airline Ryan Air uses chatbots when fielding numerous flight change or cancellation requests, for example, due to strikes. In such cases, the high number of requests is difficult to handle by human service staff. This is where the use of chatbot technology helps to filter requests by level of standardization and answer frequently arising questions, all without the interaction of a costly service agent.

When the chatbot detects that a customer is upset or that its basic knowledge is not sufficient to answer the customer query to a satisfactory degree, it refers its chat partner to an email address to contact. Only then does a human service agent become involved.

Observing developments in the field of chatbots, it seems reasonable to think company websites will probably be visited more by bots than real people in the future. Amidst all the marketing noise, it is the bots that will lead (potential) customers to a relevant page. As a consequence, companies should make websites user-friendly not only for humans but increasingly for AI as well.

For companies, the advantages of artificial intelligence lie almost everywhere. Processes can be optimized and simplified, and repetitive tasks can be taken over by systems, saving resources and speeding up processes. Additionally, into customer behavior, market movements, and other areas can be gathered from data.

For users, the biggest advantage of artificial intelligence is availability. Customers can access chatbots and voice assistants 24/7 and need not adhere to working hours or business days. Minor problems, tasks, and questions can be solved immediately, which also saves customers time.

In CRM, artificial intelligence is a core topic for the coming years. All leading CRM vendors (Salesforce, Oracle, SAP, Adobe, and Microsoft) are currently investing in artificial intelligence and machine learning. In most modern CRM systems, the first apps using AI are even already available.

## 3 Action-Oriented Outlook on Expected Development

We can make the following conclusions in summary: The professional and technological CRM trends described above exhibit a very high degree of interdependence in terms of content; that is, there is a very close connection between them, and they can be directly linked to one another in terms of their application contexts, both functionally and in terms of content. Their true potential will come to fruition in consistent, orchestrated interplay; they will fully enable, complement, and reinforce each other, all in the spirit of creating an optimized customer experience.

The resulting functional interconnectivity and interchangeability will enable unprecedented flexibility in the selection of tools and in the architectural design of IT and business: Each party involved will select the Digital CRM components most suitable for them and combine them without substantial restrictions. This fundamental paradigm shift will come to bear on the businesses and on partners and customers.

What remains is the core idea of CRM, the elements of which continue to be designed according to requirements and purpose:

- Central customer databases.
- The historization of all transactions and interactions.
- The support of customer processes.
- The cross-departmental consolidation of the specialist functions of marketing, sales, and service.
- Integration of functions and data in ERP, logistics, and production environments.

At the same time, the optimization of the customer experience and the guarantee of secure and end-to-end business processes between customers, suppliers, and partners are becoming increasingly consistent and innovative.

What will change fundamentally, however, are the design options for customer management itself. What will the application contexts of the future look like for companies and customers? How will these expand? What possibilities, unthinkable today in terms of their feasibility, will they open up?

Due to ever-increasingly available communication channels, automation options, and intelligent mechanisms (relevant keywords here are virtual assistants, artificial intelligence, and machine learning), the core idea of CRM will be gradually expanded and optimized. This links individual functions better and more reliably, making them ultimately more user-friendly.

One thing is certain: Markets and competitors are transforming. This means that new opportunities must be seized and innovations driven forward to avoid lagging behind the competition. With the possibilities of digital transformation, organizations can use digital thinking and action to meet these challenges and unleash new innovative potential, especially in customer management.

## References


BrightLocal (2018) Local Consumer Survey 2018. https://www.brightlocal.com/learn/local-consumer-review-survey/ Zugegriffen: 7. January 2019

Chef Marketing Technologist Blog (2018) Marketing Technology Landscape Supergraphic (2018). https://chiefmartec.com/2018/04/marketing-technology-landscape-supergraphic-2018. Zugegriffen: 7. January 2019

Computer Security Resource Center (CSRC) (2011) The NIST definition of cloud computing. https://csrc.nist.gov/publications/detail/sp/800-145/final Zugegriffen: 20. February 2019

Gabler Wirtschaftslexikon (2018) Digitalisierung. https://wirtschaftslexikon.gabler.de/definition/digitalisierung-54195/version-277247 Zugegriffen: 7. January 2019

Greenberg P (2009) CRM at the speed of light. Mac Graw-Hill, New York

IDC (2018) Data Age 2025. The Digitization of the World From Edge to Core. https://www.seagate.com/files/www-content/our-story/trends/files/idc-seagate-dataage-whitepaper.pdf Zugegriffen: 7. January 2019

Maynard W (2010) Old spice guy brings 107% increase in sales. Kinesis Inc. https://www.kinesisinc.com/old-spice-guy-brings-107-increase-in-sales/ Zugegriffen: 7. January 2019

PR Newswire (2017) New research finds consumers use mobile devices for product information whether shopping in-store or at home. https://www.prnewswire.com/news-releases/new-research-finds-consumers-use-mobile-devices-for-product-information-whether-shopping-in-store-or-at-home-300434981.html Zugegriffen: 7. January 2019

Small Business Trends (2016) Paul Greenberg of The 56 Group: CRM, Customer Engagement and Customer Experience Aren't One in the Same. https://smallbiztrends.com/2016/09/customer-engagement-and-customer-experience.html Zugegriffen: 7. January 2019

TripAdvisor (2018) Über TripAdvisor. https://tripadvisor.mediaroom.com/de-about-us. Zugegriffen: 20. February 2019



**Dr. Martin Stadelmann** is an expert in advanced customer management and has been accompanying companies in all industries on their way to a holistic CRM for almost 20 years. This combines professional requirements and possibilities of technical implementation with each other—in every respect in the sense of realizing the most comprehensive customer experience possible and under consistent orchestration of the "customer functions" marketing, sales, and customer service.

Dr. Martin Stadelmann is a lecturer at the University of St. Gallen as well as co-founder (2002) of the executive study program "Master of Advanced Studies in CRM" at the Zurich University of Applied Sciences (ZHAW), where he is active as a lecturer in a number of core topics of the CRM courses offered. He is a sought-after speaker on topics of "Customer-Oriented Management" and author of numerous CRM publications. In 2004, he established the "Swiss CRM Expert Forum," where he has since served a number of leading Swiss companies as a coach and source of inspiration.

**Patrick Schäfer** is a managing director of ec4u expert consulting (schweiz) ag. He is responsible for all sales-related topics as well as partner management in the Salesforce area for Switzerland and also in an international context. With a degree in business administration, he has many years of experience as a proven expert in the telecommunications, banking, insurance, and financial services sectors. His work focuses on solution sales, business development, and professional services.

Since 2000, Patrick Schäfer has been dealing with CRM topics in various roles. He has a broad wealth of experience, which he brings to bear in mandates in the areas of CRM strategy and specialist consulting, CRM software evaluation as well as in classic CRM implementation projects. He also has several years of practical experience with large companies in the planning and implementation of CRM projects.

**Peter Tüscher** is a passionate designer and implementer of change projects driven by customer orientation and digitalization. As an executive with over 25 years of professional experience, including 10 years in management and technology consulting, he supports companies in the further development as well as the organizational anchoring of their customer- and data-centric business models. This ranges from strategic conception to implementation.

Peter Tüscher studied economics and sociology at the University of St. Gallen. He supplemented his business education with a postgraduate degree as Executive Master in Customer Relationship Management. The conviction that a differentiation strategy consistently oriented toward the customer is a central, goal-oriented success factor for companies drives his professional and private commitment to the topic of customer management.

**Juliane Waack** is marketing manager at Billwerk where she manages the company blog, develops marketing campaigns, and supports colleagues with any writing-related tasks. She has more than 10 years of experience as a writer with a focus on SEO, digitalization, and corporate communication. She is particularly interested in preparing complex technical topics in easy-to-understand formats and enjoys researching innovative tech topics and developing creative ways to present them.

# Sales Performance Management: Excellence in CRM with Digital Control Concepts

Mario Pufahl

**Abstract**

This chapter explains what successful sales performance management entails, why it is necessary for a holistic digital CRM strategy, and what it requires, particularly in terms of business and technology. From a technical point of view, the focus is a tried-and-tested sales methodology with the dimensions of strategy, organization, controlling, and personnel. An important success factor for digital CRM is change management that motivates digital transformation throughout the company. The concept of the "Digital Workplace for Sales" represents a professional and technological digital workplace for sales managers and employees through modern CRM cloud platforms, business intelligence, and artificial intelligence solutions. This digitizes the necessary professional requirements through CRM to unlock process efficiencies and intelligences.

## 1 Sales Performance Management As the Foundation of Digital Sales Management in CRM

CRM excellence in sales. This is a goal that every company and every sales manager should set for themselves. Outstanding performance is achievable, but CRM excellence requires sustainable and consistent development and optimization of sales.

Volatile markets, globalized business relationships, technological advancements, price transparency, and many other factors impact sales operations. In fact, they offer countless opportunities to develop sales, work new markets and customers, and find technological solutions. On the other hand, they aggravate the business

M. Pufahl (✉)
DIGITALL Nature Germany GmbH, Düsseldorf, Germany
e-mail: Mario.Pufahl@digitall.com





S. Kirchem et al. (eds.), *CRM Goes Digital*, Management for Professionals,
https://doi.org/10.1007/978-3-658-45798-3_6

climate and make the road to success more difficult. In this environment, it is essential to stand out from the crowd with CRM excellence in sales.

Sales managers from a wide variety of industries are intensively engaged in improving management options in sales and the associated efficiency increases in market cultivation, customer processes, the best possible support through (mobile) IT systems, and challenges for employees and their development. They use different approaches:

- "Sales performance management" describes the consistent and sustainable alignment of a company with customer needs along the customer lifecycle (customer journey) (Pufahl 2018).
- "Efficiency" describes the process of completing tasks in an economically effective manner. It measures the ratio of (current) output and input and represents, among other things, a guideline for short-term planning. It includes the effectiveness of activities and structures.

The board of directors or sales management can use the Sales Performance Management methodology to systematically monitor and control efficiency in sales on the basis of four dimensions (see Pufahl 2018):

- Strategy: Are all essential elements of a sales strategy sufficiently defined and documented, and are they sufficiently designed, regularly monitored and, if necessary, realigned? Are there early warning systems for market changes?
- Organization: Is the organizational structure sufficiently designed from the center and for local markets? Are they comparable with each other and equipped with sufficient resources? Are processes defined, documented, and adequately digitized by modern IT systems?
- Controlling: Is there a mature controlling concept for sales? Are the key performance indicators clearly defined and operationalized in a simple and understandable way through cockpits and reports? Is there consistent planning with sufficient detail? Is the achievement of the plan monitored?
- Personnel: Do sales staff have sufficient qualifications to achieve the targeted market goals? Are differences of employees' required and targeted competencies regularly identified and measures derived to eliminate them? Are top performers promoted and weaknesses among employees systematically eliminated?

The appropriately designed application of the methodology opens up the following advantages when defining and implementing a future-oriented CRM strategy:

- Strategy: Clear alignment of the sales organization on the basis of an overarching strategy, including recording of market and customer potential, definition of a pricing strategy, and alignment of the so-called customer experience (customer journey) in the relevant channels.

- Organization: Definition of tasks, competencies, and responsibilities in the sales organization (organizational structure) and the operational organization via processes and their digitalization via supporting IT systems in sales.
- Controlling: Quantitative and qualitative evaluation of sales efficiency via key performance indicators (KPI), dashboards, and reporting. Simple and fast determination of closing ratios for branches, area managers, and sales staff via a dedicated reporting system for the pipeline.
- Personnel: Comparability of sales performance via performance criteria and targeted strengthening of employee competencies via development plans.

## 2 Trends for Digital Sales Management in CRM

A volatile market environment, increasing competitive pressure, and ever higher demands for satisfying customer needs are particular challenges for sales and thus also for CRM.

Different market studies (McKinsey 2024, CIO Magazine 2024, CapsuleCRM 2024) show an advanced scope for CRM in 2024: 1. Generative AI: Generative AI is transforming CRM by automating content creation, such as marketing materials and customer call transcriptions. It also enhances business process automation and data analytics 2. Omnichannel Experience: Providing a seamless customer experience across multiple channels, including mobile apps, social media, and in-person interactions, is becoming crucial 3. Mobile CRM Apps: The use of mobile CRM apps is on the rise, allowing sales teams to access customer data and manage relationships on the go 4. Low-Code/No-Code Solutions: These solutions are gaining popularity as they allow businesses to customize their CRM systems without extensive coding knowledge These trends highlight the growing importance of AI, automation, and data-driven insights in CRM solutions, aiming to enhance sales efficiency and customer engagement.

### 2.1 Strategy

The survey results on the strategic orientation of sales indicate that every tenth sales department works independently of the strategic goals of the whole company. This represents an enormous waste of potential and synergy effects, as sales should be a core factor in a corporate strategy. In questions of customer orientation, it was found that three out of four sales departments already focus all or part of their sales activities on the prospects and profitable customers identified by target customer segmentation. This shows that customer orientation and the targeted handling of specific customer segments play an important role in today's sales. However, the expert barometer also found that customer orientation is not reflected in the amount of time spent on customer-related activities in sales. For example, 15% of the study participants said they spent more of their time on administrative tasks than on customer-oriented activities.

From the sales experts' point of view, the most important strategic fields of action for the immediate future are very customer-oriented. For example, they see leveraging customer relationships, focusing on selected target groups and products, and acquiring new customers as the most relevant fields of action for sales successful in the future.

## 2.2 Organization

The second dimension, "organization," was also evaluated by the participating sales experts. As many as 7 out of 10 study participants rate their sales organization and processes as supporting their strategy. Nevertheless, 10% of participants consider their sales organization ineffective and even 1 in 5 sales decision-makers cannot make a clear statement about the effectiveness of their organization. These are surprising and interesting results, which clarify a need for improvement from an organizational perspective. For example, half of the respondents state that not all achievable efficiency potentials in process design have yet been exhausted in their sales organizations. The distribution of roles and responsibilities is also unclear in 18% of the sales organizations.

On the subject of IT systems, survey results are telling. Here, one-fifth of sales experts still see a clear need for action and 17% describe the existing sales-supporting IT infrastructure as unhelpful. Since IT systems have the fundamental importance of simplifying complex work processes, sales-supporting IT systems in some companies do not appear to meet this requirement. This picture is also reflected in the use and acceptance of IT support. Once again, 17% of respondents state that there is no acceptance of IT support by employees. If IT systems are not a real support, they are not accepted by the employees.

The use of IT systems also reflects an uncertainty in dealing with IT solutions. For example, in one-quarter of the sales organizations surveyed, the level of utilization of IT support is not high. The results suggest:

a) Some sales-support IT systems are not helpful;
b) They are therefore not accepted by employees;
c) They are therefore not used.

One reason for this is the weak involvement of sales in system-related decisions. Thus, 27% of study participants state that their sales department is not sufficiently involved in the selection of IT systems for sales support. In other words, companies make decisions about IT support without precise coordination with the sales department. The fact that this behavior leads to misunderstandings and low acceptance is by no means surprising. In sales in particular, it is essential that the IT system is accepted, used, and maintained by all employees. This is the only way to work efficiently and consistently.

Results regarding the future fields of action are therefore also not surprising: 70% of the sales experts see the optimization of IT support as the most important field of action. They also rate cooperation with sales partners, the establishment of new sales channels, case-closing processing in sales, and the shift of administrative activities from customer service representatives to the back office as urgent areas for action.

## 2.3 Controlling

The expert barometer also addressed issues relating to sales controlling. Here, it became apparent that sales management is still immature in many companies. Although a large proportion of companies actively manage their sales, one-fifth do so only inadequately. Since this information was surprising and interesting, the participating sales experts were questioned further on the subject of sales management. The main interest was in the short-term improvement of sales management. Respondents rated improvement measures according to relevance. According to the survey, the most important means are improved control concepts, improved measure controlling, optimized control variables, and the use of mobile reporting.

Almost all proposed measures to improve sales management in the short term enjoy strong support. For example, the sales experts also see a need for action to intensify real-time analyses, shorten reporting processes, establish early warning systems, and change reporting content. In fact, there are numerous important levers that every sales department can and should use to improve sales management.

Since (key) performance indicators play the most important role in sales management today, the expert barometer also deals with key performance indicators. These need to be selected very specifically and adapted to the individual company. For this reason, the participating sales experts were asked to provide information on the key performance indicators they currently use. Performance indicators used by almost all companies are net sales and incoming orders. These two factors are the most important control variables in today's sales environment. Customer satisfaction, contribution margin, sales volumes, and gross sales also contribute strongly to most organizations' sales management. The key figure "customer satisfaction" has become increasingly relevant in recent years and plays a fundamental role in sales performance management. Customer satisfaction should be a central planning factor for strategic decisions in every sales department. However, customer value is currently one of the least used indicators. This, too, must be expanded through high-level customer orientation. In addition, indicators for compliance with price floors and ceilings, visit frequency, and costs of sales activities are hardly used.

## 2.4 Personnel

The fourth pillar for sales excellence is personnel. The expert barometer looked at sales staff, staff development, and compensation systems. The initial focus is the number of sales employees. Although 55% of the study participants say that the number of employees is sufficient, 30% of the sales experts surveyed feel their headcount is too low. Accordingly, companies need to ask whether their sales force really works efficiently, or whether the lack of employees is due to inefficient working practices. After all, three-quarters of the sales organizations operate a compensation system that supports their sales targets, and only 12% of the sales experts consider their compensation and incentive systems to be off-target. There is still a clear need for action in employee development. Almost one-quarter of the participants consider personnel development in sales to not be goal-oriented.

Three-quarters of respondents see an increase in employee qualifications as an important field of action in sales personnel management. However, the first priority here should be a strategic and targeted system. Only if employee development aligns with corporate strategy and sales targets can it make a sustainable and consistent contribution to sales success. The sales experts cite the improvement of consulting quality as the most important field of action in personnel management.

## 3 Digital Sales Management in CRM Practice: Business and IT Requirements in B2B Sales

The functional requirements for sales management have expanded considerably in recent years. Whereas in the past, the focus was on mapping sales processes and classic reporting or mapping dashboards, it has now shifted to the user experience and support of sales staff to enable operational sales management in everyday life. At the end of the day, what counts is the efficient support of the sales manager and salesperson in their daily work. Without data from daily work, no sales control is possible.

B2B sales faces the following professional requirements in this regard:

- Volatility and complexity in B2B sales are increasing as markets change faster and changes are harder to predict, customer ordering cycles are becoming more flexible, and the sales environment in many places is characterized by higher competition and pressure on suppliers.
- At the same time, customer expectations of companies and their sales staff are high, as high efficiency and response speed, GDPR compliance, and full transparency of customer history (ideally in real time) are required.
- This places greater demands on the daily efficiency and performance of sales staff, as available information must be evaluated as quickly as possible and decisions must be made more quickly than in the past.
- In addition, structures and processes on the customer side are more complex than in the past, especially in the case of major customers with different contacts in the buying center.

From a sales management perspective, the trend toward intelligence-supporting systems can be seen in sales management systems. In addition to marketing automation solutions for improving lead management, CRM systems for mapping classic sales processes, self-service customer portals, and classic reporting/DWH solutions, a new category of the so-called apps can therefore be identified, which have entered the business world in a manner analogous to apps on smartphones (e.g., Apple).

According to Gartner, Forrester, and IDC, the leading CRM providers such as SalesForce, Microsoft, SAP, SugarCRM, and Oracle offer a number of individual solutions as apps in addition to their standard solutions for sales. These are offered to the public and thus to business customers by their sales and implementation partners in dedicated app stores. This has the advantage that individual solutions—especially through the possibilities of cloud computing—can quickly achieve a high degree of efficiency in sales.

## 4 Solution Approach: Digital Workplace for Sales

An "Intelligent Workplace for Sales" is an intelligent, digital workplace for the sales employee and sales management that supports and continuously optimizes sales activities at any time, on any device, in real time. The Digital Workplace for Sales consists of a number of constituent elements. The interplay between these is presented below. For each of these elements, the added values that can be achieved for CRM as a result are described.

To address today's requirements in modern B2B sales, many companies are using the services and paradigms of an integrated platform. This approach creates an optimal user experience and efficiency gains for the sales rep by combining Modern Workplace, CRM, Business Intelligence, and Artificial Intelligence (AI).

Business Intelligence and Artificial Intelligence transform valuable data from sales and other customer interfaces into customer intelligence. Modern cloud platforms offer a comprehensive, fully integrated suite for reporting, including cognitive services.

Added value through a "Digital Workplace for Sales":

- Today's functionalities requested by sales staff can be fulfilled with an integrated approach based on Microsoft platform services;
- The solution is based on a modern, intuitive, mobile application platform that integrates well with the existing application landscape;
- The solution is highly integrated and synergizes with other Microsoft productivity solutions such as Office services (e.g., Outlook, Excel);
- The solution offers a wide range of automation capabilities and intelligent machine-learning capabilities to support sales goals;
- A modern cloud platform is an ideal starting point for improving sales performance and can scale in a modular way in line with growing customer requirements;
- BI offers comprehensive functionalities from information management to intelligence;

- The solution can address different data services and apps and can be comprehensively integrated into existing IT landscapes;
- A modern cloud platform offers a variety of predefined cognitive services and provides a bot framework, modern speech recognition (e.g., Cortana), and visualizations via BI.

## 4.1 Mobile Sales

Modern B2B sales are mobile and operate on a variety of devices. In the home office or while traveling, notebooks, iPads, or smartphones are used. All customer data must always be available in real time to ensure the shortest possible response times for customer requirements. Voice assistants such as Siri, Alexa, and Cortana facilitate visit documentation. Business card scans can easily be made mobile—e.g., snapAddy—and transferred to CRM as contacts. Solutions like Microsoft Copilot help the user based on AI to do be more efficient in CRM.

Added value through a "Digital Workplace for Sales":

- Relevant customer data can be viewed before a customer visit in order to find out in real time about possible changes, for example, if payment terms have been exceeded, reminders have been issued, or customer complaints have been received, and to conduct customer meetings with highly up-to-date information;
- All relevant customer information can be viewed on the move through the cloud, including integrated information from the peripheral systems, before or during customer meetings;
- Customer inquiries can be documented directly during or after the customer visit;
- Modern user interfaces can be used on all mobile devices with the same functionality, thanks to the cloud;
- Efficiency increases can be realized using mobile solutions, as travel times can be actively used.

## 4.2 Data Protection Compliance (GDPR) and Data Security

Since May 25, 2018, provisions from the "EU General Data Protection Regulation" (GDPR, also known as GDPR) have been implemented as part of the reorganization of data protection in the EU. B2B sales employees will be confronted with customer inquiries about the GDPR. These relate particularly to data subject rights and the GDPR, where the right to information, correction, deletion, and blocking of personal data is regulated.

Added value through a "Digital Workplace for Sales":

- A Digital Workplace for Sales supports employees from sales and other departments to be included in the data-protection–compliant processing of inquiries.

- By using proven components such as a GDPR solution (e.g., from ec4u based on Microsoft Dynamics 365), complexity can be safely managed and the risk of non-compliance with data subject rights can be significantly minimized.
- Information retrieval and rectification: All essential personal information about a customer from the CRM system is available at a glance, also as a PDF report. The report can be sent to the customer.
- Blocking and deletion: Personal attributes of data records are anonymized in order to withdraw them from individual users until "higher interests" such as contract fulfillment have been clarified.

## 4.3 Excel Integration and Excel2BI

Sales is individual. Information must be prepared quickly and easily and also sent out. That is why sales employees love Microsoft Excel. The disadvantage is that information is stored locally, creates media breaks, and in the end there is no traceability of calculations or lists. What is needed here is a simple, flexible, and yet Excel-based solution so as not to jeopardize productivity.

Added value through a "Digital Workplace for Sales":

- A Digital Workplace for Sales allows Excel to continue being used in sales.
- However, Excel is used in the cloud, fully integrated, and more standardized.
- A Digital Workplace for Sales allows existing Excel solutions that are used repeatedly in sales (e.g., calculations) to be integrated into CRM and accessible on SharePoint from anywhere.
- Standardized reports from Excel are easily and quickly transferred to BI (e.g., Power BI or Tableau) (Excel2BI). This enables possibilities for modern business intelligence solutions from the cloud to be used without losing the functions from Excel. This is ensured by a complete integration of Excel and BI.

## 4.4 Channel and Office 365 Integration

Customers want straightforward communication channels and quick responses from sales for their inquiries. One still widely used communication channel is email. Social platforms such as WhatsApp, chats, LinkedIn, and Xing are also on the rise in B2B sales. The sales employee must have all relevant information quickly available to answer inquiries and be able to document the communication quickly and efficiently in the CRM.

Added value through a "Digital Workplace for Sales":

- For the most part, customer communication still takes place via email and telephone. Within Outlook, sales employees can easily link email communication to customers, contacts, or sales opportunities with just a few clicks.

- Social platforms are becoming more and more widespread in customer communication. Customers want communication through their preferred channels. Companies need to document communication for a complete customer history. A Digital Workplace offers integration of different social platforms.
- Responding to customer inquiries and documentation is simple and straightforward for sales reps via SharePoint. The exchange between sales employees takes place via chats (Yammer) and relieves email inboxes.

## 4.5 Action Dashboard

Sales people are faced with more and more information and pressure is increasing every day. There is a need to condense information to quickly identify, prioritize, and complete important tasks. Detailed information is secondary to this, but can be viewed when needed.

Added value through a "Digital Workplace for Sales":

- A personalized, role-based action dashboard shows sales reps important information when they start their Digital Workplace:
  - Overdue activities;
  - Current complaints;
  - New leads;
  - New opportunities;
  - Resubmissions;
  - Overdue payments.
- The sales employee gets a clear view in the information jungle. All data entries now contribute the added value missed by existing CRM;
- Efficiency and reaction speed increase, which leads to increased process speed, higher customer satisfaction, and more deals.

## 4.6 Integrated Social Selling

In B2B sales, the relationships and access of a sales employee to the people (e.g., decision-makers, influencers) in the customer's purchasing area (the so-called buying center) are critical to success. Decision-makers—especially for new customers—are increasingly difficult to identify, and access is also limited by gatekeepers like assistants.

Powerful Digital Workplaces for Sales integrate the leading B2B social selling platform LinkedIn, with its 11 million members (as of 2018), in DACH.

Added value through a "Digital Workplace for Sales":

- In key account business, relevant people in the buying center can be saved as leads through special search functions and their activities and interests can be tracked. Leads can then be addressed directly and personally. Target customers are saved as leads. Relevant information about the company is displayed to the sales representative.

- The contact confirmation is legally compliant and confirms the so-called double opt-in as defined by the GDPR.
- Company and contact data from LinkedIn are integrated. The data is highly up-to-date, as it is maintained by the contact.
- Relationships between individual members in the buying center and beyond can be viewed and analyzed.

## 4.7 Campaigns and Lead Optimization

Every sales representative knows this situation: an exciting offer needs to be sent to selected customers at short notice. Unfortunately, however, the sales representative can only send this via email and has poor-to-no follow-up on responses. Alternatively, a central campaign is launched, which in turn means a lengthy marketing process and lots of work for sales with an open outcome.

Added value through a "Digital Workplace for Sales":

- Modern campaign management in the form of email and social selling campaigns are integrated in the Digital Workplace.
- Sales staff can set up and run their own sales campaigns quickly and efficiently and track the results.
- In turn, conclusions can be drawn from the results for new campaigns and follow-up activities to further improve efficiency.
- Marketing automation integrates the marketing lead funnel with the sales opportunity funnel. This enables an end-to-end process from first contact to close.
- Account-based-selling increases customer penetration with the right content for existing B2B customers.
- Artificial Intelligence (AI) provides support with intelligent suggestions for campaign participants and follow-up activities.

## 4.8 Customer Profiling: 360-Degree Customer View with AI Support

Many companies provide a 360-degree customer view to their sales staff. This is certainly a good first step, but unfortunately falls short, as sales representatives have to compile relevant information themselves. A sales employee only receives real assistance through intelligent recommendations for action that capture the customer and their wishes.

In the context of account management, sales employees repeatedly ask themselves which customer should receive an offer next, which specific components this offer should include, and which closing probabilities are associated with this. This usually involves manual desk research by the sales representative, based on empirical values and a good knowledge of the company's portfolio.

Added value through a "Digital Workplace for Sales":

- A Digital Workplace for Sales goes further than conventional CRM systems. It provides concrete assistance for the sales employee and creates transparency regarding customers and key contacts.
- Customer profiling supplements a sales employee's gut feeling with facts and sales impulses. It provides concrete recommendations for action generated using artificial intelligence (AI), providing a second, data-driven view of customers.
- The generated recommendations are based on cross-functional information from customer contacts and customer behavior. On this basis, possible customer actions can be evaluated through twin comparison and underpinned with success metrics.
- With its additional function of a "recommendation engine," a Digital Workplace for Sales goes further than traditional CRM and BI systems. It provides the sales employee with context-related and concrete recommendations for action.
- In the context of decision support and quotation support, a Digital Workplace for Sales distinguishes between two functions:
  - Decision support for more complex issues (e.g., offers, customer churn prevention): the sales employee receives information and suggestions based on artificial intelligence, but they choose the most suitable variant.
  - Automated decisions (simple issues such as forwarding emails to specialist departments for complaints): the modern workplace performs routine tasks automatically based on rules or artificial intelligence.

## 4.9 Personalized Analytics

Modern B2B sales are self-managing. However, they need the necessary information in real time. This can change over time as customer requirements or the sales environment change. B2B sales employees therefore demand personalized information at a glance that is tailored to their specific situation and provides them with optimal support for self-control and optimization.

Added value through a "Digital Workplace for Sales":

- Less is more. The Digital Workplace for Sales is not characterized by countless reports that no one uses.
- Instead, the sales employee compiles their personalized information so that the available information is visible in real time, in the most condensed form possible.
- Information can be presented and aggregated in the form they prefer:
  - Aggregated data in the form of KPIs;
  - Different graphs;
  - Maps.

- A Digital Workplace for Sales combines the possibilities of CRM, Business Intelligence, and Customer Analytics in one informative interface. Detailed information can be easily viewed by "drilling down."

## 4.10 AI-Based Forecasting

B2B sales in manufacturing companies are usually characterized by the fact that sales employees are supposed to provide resilient forecasts (often even multi-year) to optimize production. However, it is usually difficult for an employee to estimate the future and the forecast is often unreliable. AI-based forecasting remedies this by combining past-oriented data with future-oriented data to create a probability-based forecast.

Added value through a "Digital Workplace for Sales":

- A Digital Workplace for Sales relieves the forecasting burden on sales staff by providing concrete assistance in the forecasting process.
- A top-down forecast: based on sales data like customer data, opportunities, deals, prices, conditions, contracts, order rhythms, and production data from the past, as well as external market data for the future, forecast models generate a highly automated forecast via top-down machine learning and break it down for sales regions and employees.
- Bottom-up: the forecast data is fed to the employee for their sales region and the sales employee can make adjustments if necessary. The supervisor receives the aggregated forecast data and corrects it if necessary to commit the final forecast.

# 5 Conclusion and Outlook

In volatile times and against the background of the unconditional desire for sustainable growth, systematized and digital sales management should be an integral part of a CRM strategy and its implementation. With the appropriate concepts, control impulses, key performance indicators, and instruments, sales can be analyzed and controlled sustainably. However, this can only be achieved using increasingly sophisticated technical options based on modern CRM cloud platforms.

From a technical point of view, business requirements should be developed in an agile, collaborative manner, accounting for the extensive standards of the CRM solutions. This can minimize project lead times and costs. In addition, it minimizes the time-to-market until a solution like the Digital Workplace for Sales is available in the relevant application context.

A technical foundation includes systematic support for the digital transformation through CRM-specific change management. Concepts such as innovation centers and accompanying focus groups are highly suitable for this purpose and are recommended to ensure the desired technical, organizational, and process-related results.

In the technical foundation of sales performance management, in addition to the cloud capability of the solutions, mobility, integration in state-of-the-art reporting (BI), and the predictive capability of AI solutions are important prerequisites in order to be competitive in the long term and to ensure the necessary reaction speed in rapidly changing markets.

**Key Takeaways**

- Excellence in sales should be the goal of every company and every sales manager. Outstanding top performance can always be achieved in the short term, but achieving excellence requires sustained and consistent development and optimization of sales.
- Volatile markets, globalized business relationships, technological advances, price transparency, and several other factors influence sales activities. In fact, they offer countless opportunities to develop sales, work new markets and customers, and find technological solutions. On the other hand, they aggravate the business climate and make the path to success more difficult. In this environment, it is essential to stand out from the crowd with excellence.
- Employees in B2B sales should receive daily support in the best possible way through a modern sales platform such as a Digital Workplace for Sales, in order to increase efficiency, raise their closing ratio, and focus their valuable sales time specifically and consciously on key customers with high potential.
- The sales employee should be supported in their decisions by artificial intelligence (AI), in order to act quickly, purposefully, and as effectively as possible.
- The employee's personal "Digital Workplace for Sales" should be tailored and available on mobile devices with condensed information. Key KPIs are presented to the employee simply and comprehensibly.
- Cloud solutions are used to create the Digital Workplace for Sales that is highly integrated with surrounding systems, to display data in real time, to map processes end-to-end, and to consistently use artificial intelligence for decision-making.

## References

CRM trends for 2024, *CIO Magazine*, Accessed: 09 Oct 2024, 2 (2024).

McKinsey Technology Trends Outlook 2024, *McKinsey*, Accessed: 09 Oct 2024, 3 (2024).

Pufahl M (2018) Sales performance management, 2nd edn. Springer Gabler, Wiesbaden

The CRM trends that defined 2023 and will shape 2024, *Capsule CRM*, Accessed: 09 Oct 2024, 1 (2024).

**Mario Pufahl** is a board member and shareholder of DIGITALL Nature Germany GmbH and is responsible for the international sales of the entire portfolio including international business development and market expansion.

Mario Pufahl has over 20 years of practical experience with companies from DAX, M-DAX and medium-sized enterprises in the planning and implementation of digitization projects in marketing, sales, and service. Among other things, he was head of the "Sales" business segment at the international consulting firm Horváth and Partners, held a management position at Janssen-Cilag (subsidiary of Johnson & Johnson), and worked as a senior consultant at Capgemini. In his current role, Mr. Pufahl serves as a trusted advisor and board member for various major clients as well as various startups as an advisory board member in strategy development and implementation in marketing and sales.

Mario A. Pufahl is the author of the reference books "Vertriebscontrolling (6th edition)," "Sales Performance Management (2nd edition)," "Kosten senken mit CRM," "Vertriebsstrategien für den Mittelstand" as well as co-editor of the book "Innovatives Vertriebsmanagement." In addition, he is the author of numerous professional articles and studies as well as a lecturer at various universities. Mr. Pufahl is also a speaker and expert at trade congresses and company events.

# Building a Next-Generation Digital Marketing Strategy

Frédéric Demierre

**Abstract**

Digital has become a dominant component of customer experience. Previously, companies saw technology as a useful way to record information and transactions for analysis and post-processing. But we are now facing simultaneous, worldwide societal changes, precipitated by a pandemic that brought meetings and sales on traditional channels to a screeching halt, and accelerated digital commerce operations. The collective consciousness of consumers has also evolved, so companies must redouble their efforts to invent new business models, frequently in line with the circular economy and sustainability principles. Building a next-generation digital marketing strategy therefore requires a series of preliminary steps and investment before implementation.

## 1 Companies and Brands Are Under Pressure

Sales and marketing specialists face a competitive environment in which different players exploit technology to achieve revenue targets and improve return on investment (ROI). The customer is now more connected and more demanding than ever, which forces companies to accompany them throughout their journey.

Digital marketing has become unavoidable but remains intrusive by nature. It must therefore be targeted and personalized, which only automation through platforms can enable. Professionals must shift from a proactive to a reactive attitude, considering the multiple channels available and a fine segmentation that facilitates

F. Demierre (✉)
CX Platform Lead and Alliance Manager OWT Switzerland - a Swisscom Company, Lausanne, Switzerland
e-mail: fdemierre@owt.swiss





S. Kirchem et al. (eds.), *CRM Goes Digital*, Management for Professionals,
https://doi.org/10.1007/978-3-658-45798-3_7

the best targeting and distribution of the most relevant content. Other elements add complexity, such as reducing the cost of acquiring a connected customer, but particularly repeated requests from product and sales teams. Above all, companies are no longer on a level playing field when traditional marketing must compete against powerful systems based on artificial intelligence, robotization, or process automation.

Most modern companies already use CRM systems to manage customer relationships and interactions, but their limitations have become increasingly apparent. The emergence of the digital, well-informed customer now requires companies to go much further. The convergence of digital marketing, social media, e-commerce, connected objects, and after-sales service is leading companies to rethink their relationship with customers.

All these factors contribute to a digital transformation that is impacting organizations in all sectors. We no longer speak of Customer Relationship Management (CRM) but of Customer Experience Management (CXM).

## 2 A Customer-Centric CXM Strategy

Introduced in the 2000s, CRM systems have undoubtedly contributed to sales growth and profitability by improving customer relationships, helping to retain customers, and increasing customer loyalty. CRM systems primarily target sales and management. In contrast, CXM (customer experience management) is a more holistic business strategy. The goal is to provide customers with positive experiences that influence their behavior and drive loyalty, advocacy, and ultimately business growth. Although CRM and CXM do not oppose each other, the CXM strategy places customers at the center of marketing, sales, customer care, logistics, and all other touch points to drive brand loyalty and repeat business. Other company departments that directly or indirectly interact also need to be part of this "hybrid experience." Companies need to know customers' perception of their brands, products, and services, but also of their social responsibility.

A CXM strategy must also satisfy the new generation of more conscientious and "digital first" consumers, while accelerating the deployment of new business models like direct-to-consumer and the subscription economy, which aim to turn offers into services or align with the sustainable circular economy. The experience can be completely digital or hybrid, as many companies are yet to mobilize the relevant data and the orchestrating systems to visualize and aggregate it. Furthermore, cross-analysis of feedback from interactions with data allows companies to create new ideas from which to extract value.

Putting the customer at the heart of company operations is therefore the key question. Better analysis and understanding of customer behavior is sometimes a technological challenge, especially when IT systems are heterogeneous, or data is siloted or simply non-existent.

## 3 The Urgency to Mobilize Its Data

Specialists need a vast amount of data on their customers to manage their actions. Information is often fragmented, incomplete, and poor quality, which prevents the creation of personalized experiences for each individual because it is difficult, if not impossible to interpret. First and foremost, it is necessary to overcome this obstacle by providing modern, secure, and compliant solutions to gather this data and normalize it for future needs. Recent scandals such as Facebook-Cambridge Analytica have forced the internet giants to adopt new "cookie-less" systems that are more inclined to protect consumers but reduce simple targeting possibilities. The GDPR has also profoundly changed marketing practices based on personal data, forcing companies to introduce consent processes. Future targeting will therefore be contextual or semantic and will rely on clean, consolidated data. But the good news is that today, data is no longer an exclusive property. It can be bought, sold, and shared; in a way, it can be monetized. It is therefore imperative for brands and companies to mobilize and extend their data; it is a top priority for decision makers.

An excellent way to mobilize data is to retrace the customer journey by identifying precisely where the data comes from and how it is collected, based on the "where, who and when" principle. To do this, it is necessary to map all company information systems and processes, not forgetting those that could be delegated to third parties. The first priority is to introduce a real data policy that imposes discipline on employees in terms of entering and updating data. This is the responsibility of the data officer who, in addition to developing the data strategy, will ensure the information maintained follows regulations, as new laws (GDPR, for example) require a thorough review of customers' personal data. This thorough data audit will help identify gaps and inefficiencies in the data collection process.

The data identified at the audit stage should be categorized; transformed into digital format if necessary; consolidated into a centralized customer data platform ("CDP"); and interconnected with the company's CRM, ERP, commerce, and marketing systems. Most cloud-based "CDP" offer technical capabilities that previously took months or even years to implement at a high cost with low success rates. Today, these systems provide infinite high-performance data in no time.

This consolidated data is the foundation of your next-generation digital marketing strategy. It is linked to a unique identifier, that of your customer, which is more commonly known as the "golden record."

## 4 The "Golden Record" As the Single Source of Truth

The golden record combines meaningful, clean data from multiple systems into a single view that is ideally more precise, complete, and accurate than data from a single source. This unified customer profile is a reliable reference that provides the most up-to-date information. Marketing, commerce, and sales professionals will focus on this consolidated data to improve the customer experience through new and more personalized interactions.

The data that makes up the "golden record" comes from many different data sources and is usually mobilized in a customer data platform ("CDP"). The ingestion, cleansing, and transformation of structured and unstructured data are in principle delegated to orchestrating systems such as ETL/ESB or enterprise middleware. The frequency of data synchronization is reduced to a minimum and will ideally occur in real time if the architecture allows. The orchestrator takes care of the information distribution according to a logical and predictable sequence, directly linked to the data strategy.

Historical and transactional data like marketing preferences, buying experience, customer service, and social media interactions is relevant information that enables marketers to analyze and leverage customer behavior (through analytics or data science) and provide useful triggers for personalization and customer journey automation.

The closer specialists get to the golden record, the more likely they are to interact with customers and prospects through preferred channels and tailored offers. With this flexibility, creating and maintaining a golden record can transform customer engagement. This means that specialists, together with IT departments and data officers, must seek data management solutions that create an extended, 360-degree view of the customer.

## 5 Create a 360-Degree View of Your Customer Interactions Through Data

The 360-degree view is a complete and accurate representation of each customer, which collects structured and unstructured data from across all touchpoints of the organization in a hub. With this knowledge, specialists can personalize interactions, trigger next-best actions, and create new customer experiences. Typically, this view materializes in a CRM system, which then becomes the single source of truth.

A 360-degree view consists of declarative data and company-specific identifiers (also called "first party"). They are grouped in a logical and aggregated way, according to their end use (see Fig. 1). Modern CRMs also offer different views depending on the needs of departments or stakeholders.

The biggest challenge of the 360-degree view is to correctly identify all records belonging to a particular customer, due to inconsistencies between databases and poor-quality information. The idea is not to reproduce the entire dataset but to view it from the same angle by linking it to the golden record or source records in external databases.

Whether you operate in B2C or B2B, very similar data in this view is needed for marketing and sales. Automation and interaction personalization tools will also rely on this information to trigger the actions needed to cover the customer lifecycle and journey.

To illustrate the complexity of these new demands, let us look at a classic use case that sales and marketing professionals might face, which rests on a 360-degree view of the customer:

**Fig. 1** Client 360

> We want to orchestrate a direct marketing campaign for a new product aimed at parents in a specific location. The target customer is the homeowner. The customer who already owns an equivalent product to the brand will receive communication indicating an exclusive, time-limited offer. The members of the "club" will benefit from a 30% discount on the product and will be invited to a preliminary demonstration of the product in a showroom. The product is by nature obsolescent because its life span is entirely linked to the technology and its innovations; therefore the product warranty will have to be registered, allowing its return in the value chain and its subsequent replacement. Also, customer feedback on the product is desired as it will help to improve the product and stimulate innovation. Customers who are not satisfied with our products or who have a bad influence factor are to be excluded from this first campaign. The ROI and conversion rate of this initiative must be measured. With limited production of this new product, a daily sales and opportunity report must be established and shared with the supply chain.

To meet this demand, specialists need aggregate information to segment the audience (demographics, customer interests, purchasing preferences, questionnaire, and satisfaction level) but also indicators to trigger personalized interactions (personal invitation, product life cycle, promotional coupon, etc.). The ability to measure the success rate of campaigns is also essential, in order to adjust the strategy and the budget during execution.

So, here is what your 360-degree view could look like to meet this use case (Table 1):

In this use case, we understand that this 360-degree view of customers is a real game-changer for organizations that need to react under pressure from internal factors such as the embrace of new products or new business models, but also external

**Table 1** 360-degree view through data

| Data | Content | Usefulness |
|---|---|---|
| Identity | A unique identifier for your customer across all company and third-party information systems. Also known as the "golden record," it groups potential subsidiary accounts | Creation of the "golden record" allows you to create a 360-degree view of your customers across all online and offline organizational processes |
| Segments | Aggregate information such as demographics, buying and communication preferences, customer journey status, and satisfaction level | Key segments enable faster campaign management and automation throughout the customer journey |
| Finance | Credit score information to assess the customer's creditworthiness and purchasing power to make appropriate offers | Important information to qualify the sending of your offers and promotions |
| Sales operations | Sales made and opportunities in progress according to their cycle, but also aggregate information to trigger interactions that facilitate persuasion and conversion | Crucial data for triggering next-best sales actions. Enables the sales forecast; also useful for the supply chain to predic demand |
| Marketing operations | Targeted marketing operations carried out or in progress with lead tracking, scoring, and conversion ratio. Customer behavior analysis on digital channels (preferences, influence, etc.) | Knowledge of customer behavior, captivity, and conversion rate. This allows you to optimize campaign and advertising budgets |
| Customer service | Current and past customer service inquiries, feedback, and customer satisfaction with products or services. Warranty and end-of-life information. Social media reputation | Useful information for targeted campaigns based on customer satisfaction (or churn risk) and future upsell opportunities. Customer feedback is also useful for driving innovation |
| Loyalty | Level of customer engagement and retention, frequency of purchase, loyalty to the company, product, or brand. Customer categorization | Important indicators in the context of customer loyalty and incentive. Enables the creation of brand ambassador communities |
| Event | Events in which the customer has participated (online, offline) such as trade shows, exhibitions, or meetings at points of sale | Allows you to follow up on opportunities after the fact and to trigger commercial actions. Allows you to measure the ROI of events |

factors such as the expectations of a new generation of "digital first" consumers or the influence of the competition. Organizations are sometimes under-resourced and skills in the digital world are limited. It is therefore necessary to have this aggregated and segmented information to automate and fine-tune interactions with customers and prospects.

## 6 From Personalization to Automation of Marketing Interactions

Agility is key to overcoming new challenges and seizing new opportunities because, in today's dynamic digital world, the customer will not wait for you to catch up. They expect an exceptional experience, and you must satisfy them across all channels, even during peak demand. Every step of the customer journey must give customers what they need at the right time.

The pandemic has accelerated the use of existing and emerging channels, literally forcing companies to rethink how they address the market. New omnichannel customer journeys have been rapidly designed and deployed to keep customers on the brand's side and prevent the brand from being overtaken by the competition. This state of crisis has created additional pressure on sales and marketing specialists while propelling the digital world into another dimension. As a result, many investments originally planned for the long term have been granted overnight to facilitate implementation of these new strategies.

As already explained, the foundation of a CXM strategy is 360-degree visibility of customers and feedback on the experience created. This enables more consistent and personalized customer journeys when the experience is triggered by targeted pre-sales, sales, post-sales, and loyalty events. Personalized marketing is also associated with all advertising tools that allow for better-targeted ads, such as retargeting. The 360-degree view then facilitates visualization and analysis of all customer interactions. This is essential, since organizations often struggle due to withheld or poorly mapped information.

The customer experience must convey the company's values across all touch points, at every stage, and across all channels. When the customer leaves the traditional digital journey (e.g., during a customer interaction at the point of sale or when the next actions are delegated to a third-party supplier), the organization must ensure that the scope of the message is consistent with the level of service guaranteed and the company's social responsibilities. It is therefore essential to consider actions very broadly, especially when the strategy is hybrid or partially outsourced to a trusted supplier.

To create a quality custom experience, you need a diverse skill set. Bringing people from different disciplines together as a team and getting all the key participants involved is a key success factor. This means organizations need to ensure a good presence and content across existing and emerging channels.

However, you also need tools. Platforms today offer marketing automation solutions integrated with CRM and commerce solutions. When configured across the customer journey, they automate all interactions at different stages customers pass through: from visitor to prospect, prospect to customer, and customer to loyal customer. These tools are also valuable for companies with physical points of sale, whose salespeople are now equipped with smart POS systems (connected to the CRM) or mobile application type "clienteling" to advise the customer based on their historical data.

To sum up, personalization is a process that aims to adapt communication, product, or service as precisely as possible. But listening to and understanding your customers to match them to your business context is essential for this to work. This way, you can automatically and optimally trigger the next-best actions to reach your goals.

## 7 Understand the Needs of Each Customer and Recognize Your Prospects

To enable content personalization, you must first understand the wants and needs of each customer. Proper segmentation of individuals and accounts across their digital properties will enable the delivery of personalized campaigns or content, whether targeted marketing campaigns or interactions triggered along the customer journey (Fig. 2). Interactions with prospects (or anonymous users) can also benefit from personalized content by matching identities with named customers.

Generally, a fine segmentation is based on the following data:

- *Demographic data* (location, sex, gender, age, language, etc.), which is collected when the customer registers or when updating their profile.
- *Behavioral data* (purchase patterns and frequency, usage, navigation, etc.) that is recorded throughout the customer journey.
- *Interest groups* (purchase history, product preferences, etc.), which are determined by sales analysis.
- *Social data* (family status, level of education, interests, relationships, etc.) that are collected through social media.
- *Advertising data* (tracking, conversion rates, etc.) from tools and servers.
- *Audience data* (identity matching) that is sold by marketing agencies or made available by "Data Management Platforms" on a fee basis.
- *Scoring* (conversion potential), which is calculated according to the previous indicators and matched with conversion objectives to optimize interactions.

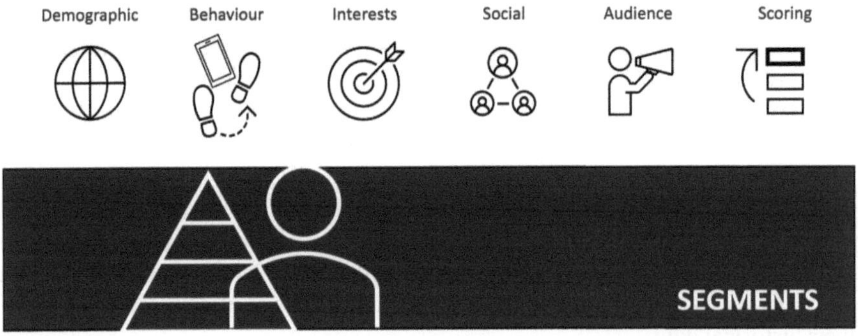


**Fig. 2** Segments

Effective, real-time segmentation can identify and deliver contextually relevant experiences that inspire customers to act. Segmentation can also be supported by artificial intelligence (AI) to recommend the most relevant products, content, and categories based on the unique characteristics and preferences of each customer.

## 8 Listen to the Customer Voice for Better Personalization

To satisfy your customers, you need to listen to them actively and regularly. It is about knowing what they think and feel about your brand, products, and services. Satisfaction surveys and customer service inquiries are your greatest asset because they address persistent challenges and create new sources of data to improve your customer experience. Feedback can directly impact your business results, especially when combined from all channels, like social media and online reviews.

Listening to the constant stream of comments can determine a customer's influence factor (ambassador versus detractor). Detractors will provide key information on lost sales opportunities, service quality issues, or analysis of unsubscribed accounts, whereas ambassadors contribute positive stories and future upsell opportunities.

The collected results are ingested and analyzed to create new segments that are used to automatically trigger personalized interactions along the customer journey, such as the creation of an after-sales service request, the generation of a promotional coupon, or the distribution of personalized content across all channels.

## 9 Connect the Customer to Your Business Context

Personalization must be part of a business strategy with well-defined objectives such as increasing turnover or sales, acquiring new customers, but also increasing the ratio of customer engagement on social media. Personalization can become a real, measurable lever of a CXM strategy.

To personalize interactions, segmented customer data must be relevant to the business context. Segmentation from the company's own data can be combined with other external parameters. Business context necessarily concerns the assortment of products, services, and content (and all the associated metadata) that needs to be catalogued to feed recommendations through machine learning. External parameters essentially concern reference source indicators (where the prospect comes from), geolocation (what can they buy here), societal context (why should they buy this now), and activities (how do they buy something).

The following example illustrates the need to correlate segmented customer data, business context, and external parameters:

> Our Garden Center department is programming a seasonal promotional campaign that will trigger recommendations on the e-commerce site and ad servers each day based on the weather looking like summer.

It will target customers and prospects who live with their families and have a garden or balcony. The personalized offer will prioritize outdoor furniture currently on backorder and delivery will be offered to new or existing customers who have made a purchase in the same category of items in the last three months. If interest has been shown in an item in the same category, it will have to be remarketed on social media for three days after the first interaction, whether it is a customer or a visitor. In addition, a promotional newsletter will be sent midway through the campaign to willing customers who meet the above criteria with personalized content.

To configure this campaign, marketers need to expose customer segments (demographic, interest, behavior) to the commercial context (product catalogue, promotion) by including external parameters (weather forecast, reference source). The journey is then built in the marketing automation tool, which listens to the user along the journey and triggers (when criteria are met) the different personalized interactions on all channels, at the right time, and for a defined duration and budget.

## 10 Know Your Customer's Next-Best Action

The next-best action is a customer-centric mechanism that considers several different interactions that can be taken in deciding which is best to provide. Typically, decisions are automated through self-learning and determined by a combination of customer interests and business objectives. Modern CRM systems are enriched with artificial intelligence (AI), including machine learning (ML) capabilities. They can monitor the customer's digital behavior, including times of activity and inactivity. Enabling these systems maximizes conversion at the point where the customer needs to make a purchase decision while continuing to learn on their own by improving over time.

When properly implemented, this mechanism provides an effective and continuous way to maintain the customer relationship online or offline, across all channels, and with the right message or offer. Also, the next-best action is a key indicator when talking about automated customer journeys, as its use can trigger all kinds of customer interactions (e.g., a promotion on a dormant cart and scheduling an appointment to renew a contract) in correlation with the sales cycle or the business context.

Even if CRM or data lake systems incorporate AI/ML, configuring the next-best action requires a lot of planning, good-quality data, and expert CRM skills.

## 11 Test, Analyze, and Optimize Your Personalized Campaigns

As mentioned earlier, the marketing world is changing. How marketers use data and how tools can be automated to trigger personalized interactions is fundamental. This shift is reflected in budgets, with a steady increase in data analytics spending expected now and in future. The bottom line is simple: when marketing decisions are data-driven and linked to business context, results follow.

By implementing CXM, companies gain a more complete picture of their customers' needs and preferences. Sales and marketing professionals can make decisions based on this data by eliminating assumptions and guesses. However, these decisions require a diverse set of channels (online and offline) and platform types (CRM, commerce, marketing, advertising, etc.) that generate masses of data. The analytical landscape has therefore become more complex than ever and only an integrated platform offers specialists a complete view of their marketing performance to provide valuable analysis with much more intelligence.

A data-driven approach to marketing remains at the heart of most marketers' concerns, and the implementation of marketing analytics platforms helps to improve the effectiveness of data and understand its impact to create new opportunities. Today, the role of analysts is no longer simply to report statistical data. Their mission has changed drastically because data is a strategic lever for company growth.

The main improvements sought by marketers and analysts are directly related to optimizing marketing and advertising spending, the ability to understand data to engage with the customer, and most importantly, revenue growth and campaign KPI performance. These improvements complement the ongoing need to understand sales performance, customer satisfaction (or NPS Score), and brand or company loyalty.

## 12 Conclusion

Building a next-generation digital strategy means rethinking the entire enterprise's processes by putting the customer at the center and reclaiming their data. Sales and marketing specialists benefit from systems that centralize, transform, and visualize a considerable mass of information that is too often under-exploited. This information is analyzed and enriched to create segments that are essential for setting up new experiences. The active or dormant customer journey can then trigger automated interactions, and the 360-degree knowledge of the customer enables the delivery of relevant and personalized content in line with the company's commercial strategy.

Specialists need platforms to perform cumbersome tasks to focus more on strategies, such as identifying performance indicators, building customer journeys, orchestrating campaigns, and other actions that improve customer experience and company results.

Although marketing is under pressure, technological developments bring new and exciting challenges as the value of the business to the organization is measurable and clearly established.

**Frédéric Demierre** Associate Partner and CX Platform Lead & Alliance Manager OWT Switzerland - a Swisscom Company, leads all aspects of customer experience and strategic alliances with the mission to accelerate OWT's business growth in Switzerland.

Before joining OWT, he was in various management positions at several companies as, for example, DIGITALL as CGO, where he was in charge of corporate strategy, business development, digital commerce, CRM, and marketing. He was also a Division Manager at Merkle EMEA, where he also served as a member of the executive committee Merkle DACH and a member of the partner advisory board Salesforce.org EMEA. Previously, Frédéric was a member of the management team at blue-infinity, where he built the largest Salesforce Competence Centre in Switzerland.

Recognized as a successful entrepreneur and leader, Frédéric is also a pioneer in e-commerce and CRM, having founded and developed several start-up companies in this field.

# Part II

# Implement

# How to Get a 360° Customer View

Steffen Deufel

**Abstract**

To keep an eye on all lead and customer activities, online and offline, and thus obtain a 360° customer view, companies must link applications from different software providers. Using Salesforce in cooperation with Google as an example, this chapter explains how data exchange and diverse, flexible functionalities help to keep lead management and the entire customer journey in view, across all customer phases and channels. Note: This chapter refers to an article in CRM goes digital 2019.

## 1 360°: Why the Holistic View of the Customer Is Necessary

The modern customer is active on many different channels. According to a 2016 study by Sopadjieva, Dholakia, and Benjamin, the average shopper uses neither the online store nor the in-store exclusively. Multiple channels, online and offline, are used by 73% of customers for their journey from initial consideration to purchase completion (Sopadejieva et al. 2017). During the Christmas season, for example, B2C customers still prefer to shop in brick-and-mortar stores because they can better evaluate goods, do not have shipping costs or delays, and they also enjoy the Christmas spirit and atmosphere (EY 2017). For research and product comparison, however, customers often use online stores and supplier websites. According to a survey by the German Retail Association, 11% of customers seek advice in brick-and-mortar stores and then make purchases online. Conversely, more than 30% inform themselves online and then buy in the store (Futurezone 2017).

S. Deufel (✉)
DIGITALL Nature Germany GmbH, Karlsruhe, Germany
e-mail: steffen.deufel@digitall.com



S. Kirchem et al. (eds.), *CRM Goes Digital*, Management for Professionals,
https://doi.org/10.1007/978-3-658-45798-3_8

For most companies, this is not new, and many offer various digital and analog channels to provide information and enable purchases. However, having numerous channels is not sufficient to guarantee customer satisfaction. The buying experience must also be seamless and satisfying from first to last contact. An increasingly significant challenge thus arises in combining many channels into a positive customer journey. For this to be guaranteed, all channels and customer movements must be documentable and measurable.

What companies need is the ability to refine desired 360° customer view by adding aspects of customer channels. These channels must be aligned with customer behavior in accordance with the 360° view, and processes must be adaptable. On the other hand, this view is necessary to successively adapt these very processes in real time—ideally—for individual customers.

## 1.1 The 360° View

The 360° customer view results from monitoring, measuring, and evaluating customer touchpoints on the customer journey, whether online or offline. Taking all touchpoints and channels together should provide a well-rounded picture of the customer or lead's behavior on their journey along all stages of the purchase.

Melissa Davis, Research Director at Gartner explains in the Gartner blog (Gartner 2017a): "The 360° view of the customer is important to ensure that the customer is recognized when they move among business units of an organization."

The 360° view specifically concerns recognizing customers to ensure a seamless customer experience in real time—not in the future—as the customer uses an organization's offerings and channels. Using all existing data generated by the customer is not essential, but rather asking "whether the data reveals anything new about the customer," Davis says.

What elements of the customer journey need to be considered for a 360° view?

Channels: All online and offline communication and information channels that a company offers to customers. These include, for example, the website, stationary sales (from store locations), emails, events, and call centers. In addition to the company's own channels, this can also include channels that are not directly controlled by the company, but which the company can nevertheless influence or monitor. These include, for example, marketplaces, social media, or comparison platforms.

Touchpoints: Touchpoints are all interaction opportunities on different channels that a customer or lead can have with a company. A channel can enable different touchpoints: for example, a customer can read posts on Twitter, like or share posts and comment on them, or contact the company directly via direct message. There are also touchpoints where no direct interaction is possible, such as viewing an advertising poster or receiving a no-reply email.

Purchase phases: Purchase phases are defined as different stages from consideration, to research, to purchase, and beyond (e.g., post-purchase support). Various models define the phases differently. In the context of the customer journey—that is the customer-centric journey—the "Need (need)–Buy (purchase)–Use (use/

service)" model has become established. What is relatively new is an understanding that the customer does not go through each phase chronologically, but can also skip individual phases or go through phases in parallel.

### 1.2 Companies Must Adopt the 360° View to Optimize Customer Experiences

Numerous possibilities make it easier online to link platforms and systems and to merge data and thus track customer movements, but the change from offline to online interactions has caused particular problems for companies. In B2C retail, there are numerous methods for documenting and digitally mapping in-store interactions, decisions, and behaviors. From loyalty programs that track members' purchasing behavior to ambitious systems that can document and evaluate in-store foot traffic, for example, there are countless ways to create digital links. The challenge is not just to implement these links, but to bring this data together for use by marketing, sales, and service—in real time if possible. This is not just about anonymized data on average customer behavior, but also about the possibility of making the customer a better offer online, for example, based on their offline activities, and vice versa. This is the only way for online retail to catch up with the dominant advantages of brick-and-mortar retail.

## 2 The Solution: Linking CRM and Analytics

Linking systems will become increasingly necessary to standardize processes and manage databases and business intelligence in future. As the customer database and core system of all customer-relevant processes, CRM is ideal for processing and supplementing the collected customer data with links. One example is the cooperation between CRM provider Salesforce and search engine giant Google. The Google Analytics 360 + Salesforce model developed shows how the 360° view can be implemented through the smart use of linked systems. In addition, the example illustrates how market leaders, as well as their respective customers, can benefit from cooperation with each other.

### 2.1 Google Analytics 360 + Salesforce

The concept is that sales data from Salesforce's Sales Cloud can be used in Google Analytics 360, for example, to apply it in audience creation, attribution, and bid optimization. Conversely, the information and data generated from Analytics 360 is mapped into Salesforce's Marketing Cloud for insights into campaign successes and failures. Customer segments created in Analytics 360 can also be used in Marketing Cloud for direct marketing efforts (including SMS or email), and customer interactions from Marketing Cloud are fed back to Analytics 360 to refine customer segments.

Especially in the context of the General Data Protection Regulation and other planned data protection laws, the collaboration is attractive for companies because the integration is consistent with the respective data protection regulations of Google and Salesforce and also allows individual settings for data use.

The platform can thus identify and track customer movements through the need, buy, and use phases. New information is generated from each customer interaction, which benefits both the individual customer and subsequent, similar customers.

In particular, linking offline conversions, for example by call center employees or salespeople conducting personal customer conversations, can be mapped with Google Analytics 360 and Salesforce. Comments from sales conversations flow directly into Analytics 360 analyses, and evaluations of campaign successes, preferred information channels, and other variables can thus be captured and used holistically, not just from digital customer journeys.

**Sales Cloud (Salesforce)** It provides information on offline events such as sales meetings and customer attributes, ML-powered metrics, and product data. This data is sent to Analytics 360.

**Marketing Cloud (Salesforce)** It delivers information about email marketing campaigns (e.g., click-through rates, open rates, conversions via email) to Analytics 360.

**Analytics 360 (Google)** The data sent by Sales Cloud is used to create customer segments for bid optimization or attribution. For example, data from existing customers can be used to target similar people via online campaigns and thus generate leads whose probability of conversion is correspondingly higher. In addition to its basic function, Analytics offers numerous additional functions that can be used to process and deploy the data. These include the following functions.

**Display & Video 360** Formerly DoubleClick Bid Manager, Campaign Manager, Studio, and Audience Center, this tool can be used to plan, measure, and optimize campaigns, control budgets, and determine and apply target group data.

**Google Ads** The tool to create, measure, and customize online ads via Google.

**Google Data Studio** A reporting tool to visually prepare data, create interactive reports, and share these reports.

**Surveys 360** Create and deploy Google Surveys, highly targeted user segmentation, and more accurate metrics through increased reach and therefore increased participants.

**Optimize 360** A/B testing and more to test online presences and present results meaningfully. Again, target groups can be segmented very individually.

**Big Query** Big Query is Google's Big Data database for performing analyses of huge amounts of data quickly and cheaply. Big Query is the basis for Google Analytics. It can and should be used for storing and linking any other data.

Analytics 360 then feeds back reporting and information about customer segments to the Marketing Cloud, where campaigns can continue to be optimized. In Marketing Cloud reporting, this data is integrated, resulting in more detailed reporting of the marketing funnel between online and offline.

Based on the reporting, actionable items can be identified and analyzed, for example, to create new segments or develop a campaign. For example, the system can recognize certain behaviors and merge customer segments accordingly. For example, customers and leads could be segmented by Analytics 360 after opening an email or filling out forms, and thus automatically receive further content through Salesforce Marketing Cloud. This can also be used when leads or customers have not behaved as desired to play out alternative campaigns. For example, if a customer clicks on an email containing a link but does not click on the link, they may automatically receive another email in an appropriate segment or be called or otherwise contacted depending on their contact preferences.

Whether these campaigns were successful can then be measured again via Marketing Cloud. The results can then be sent to Analytics 360 and Analytics can determine whether the campaign was successful and whether it needs improvements or should be completely replaced.

The linking of the two systems thus works in such a way that information is constantly exchanged and processed to create the basis for how current and future campaigns, strategies, and processes can be optimized. All results of optimized campaigns are fed back to the analysis and can thus be continuously optimized. At the same time, this creates a more comprehensive picture of the customer, their favorite channels and content, and even campaign formats and times can be evaluated and used to improve the customer experience.

## 2.2 An Example

Sonja has been considering buying a new bathroom for quite some time. On Google, she enters "buy bath" in the search box and then receives a number of results, including one from the provider "Baden & Entspannen." Sonja sees in the search engine suggestion that the provider offers a bathroom configurator with which she can virtually set up her dream bathroom. She clicks on the page and uses the configurator to specify the dimensions of her bathroom and her ideas. At the end, Sonja can receive the product list for her dream bathroom via email. She fills out a contact form within the configurator and can also enter her zip code to find out whether there is a branch of "Baden & Entspannen" in her vicinity, so she can look at the products on site. Immediately after submitting the form, Sonja receives the product list via email and a selection of local branches near her.

Three days later, Sonja receives an email from one of the suggested stores, informing her that "Baden & Entspannen" has a special offer week. She decides to visit the branch for personal advice. At the store, Sonja explains to the employee that she had made a product list but had forgotten it. The employee looks it up in his system and retrieves the list under Sonja's contact details. Sonja looks at all the selected products on the spot and decides at one point or another on another variant that she likes better. The employee works with Sonja to adjust the changes on a tablet. Sonja is so satisfied with the selection that she signs the purchase contract directly.

Even though this experience seems very simple from Sonja's point of view as the customer, processes were running in the background along the entire customer journey that were controlled by Salesforce & Analytics 360.

For example, Analytics 360 documented Sonja's search input, her click on the vendor's landing page, and sent the result to the Sales Cloud. Sonja's email behavior, meanwhile, as well as automated emails from the vendor, were driven by Marketing Cloud. The fact that Sonja would potentially respond positively to a particular store's offer after receiving the product list via email was determined by Sales Cloud's lead scoring and transmitted to Marketing Cloud to send the appropriate email.

Even in the store, the employee was able to enter Sonja's change requests to her product list directly into the system via tablet using Sales Cloud, to prevent confusion or shipping of the wrong products. Sonja's purchase completion was additionally recorded by the system through the employee, so that in the future she would not receive emails or Google ads asking her to buy an entire bathroom set, but rather send and display cross-selling offers for accessories or upgrades to her selected products. Additionally, Sonja's data can be used to generate likely behaviors of similar leads and customers to better respond to potential customers in the future.

Salesforce also introduced a new dimension for personalizing customer experiences at Dreamforce in September 2022 with the launch of the Genie platform, which offers security and privacy on Hyperforce, the new cloud infrastructure that promises to handle data ethically. The goal is to provide customers with personalized experiences in sales, service, marketing, and commerce that can be continuously customized in real time and over the long term to meet their needs and desires.

## 3 Technology Partnerships Are the Future

With the advancement of cloud technologies, a large number of start-ups developed for a long time, suggesting that the future in the software sector lay in many small providers offering very specific individual solutions. Even then, these solutions were not really an alternative for large companies, as they were often poorly compatible with existing infrastructures and could also only be linked to a limited extent to compliance requirements and other conditions of typical corporate IT.

Nevertheless, Silicon Valley companies appeared to be the future of CRM software precisely because they seemed to be able to respond to new needs more quickly than traditional vendors and were much more agile in developing and launching innovative solutions due to shorter decision chains and fewer requirements. In the meantime, however, it is becoming apparent that the traditional CRM providers are also catching up again, and are using a lack of expertise and even a lack of flexibility to their advantage by forming strong partnerships or making purchases. The Salesforce–Google integration is certainly one of the strongest examples of how valuable a meaningful partnership can be to close gaps and problem areas in the classic CRM system. Since hardly any marketer or salesperson can do without analytics touchpoints in their daily work, there is still the advantage that users do not have to get used to completely new software, but can use the combined advantages of familiar applications.

It is interesting to note that even competing companies—such as Adobe, Microsoft, and SAP, and (at least temporarily) Salesforce and Microsoft—are entering into partnerships with each other to mutually benefit from the respective technological and strategic advantages over short- or long-term periods and to develop joint projects.

In this way, CRM providers benefit from the exchange of knowledge, on the one hand, and become more attractive to customers on the other, as they can offer modern, diverse, and flexible solutions without having to fundamentally change or completely abandon their traditional offerings.

Incidentally, the cloud theme has already shown in recent years that this approach works. Salesforce has developed from a small SME solution into a leader in CRM software, not least because the company recognized early on how useful cloud-based CRM systems are for large companies, in saving hardware and maintenance costs and at the same time being flexible and mobile. Already, the share of cloud-based CRM applications is increasing, and the revenue generated by them is growing every year. For example, research firm Synergy Research Group reported a 20% increase in revenue from cloud-based (SaaS) CRM software among market leaders in the second quarter of 2017 (Synergy Research 2017).

It will be similar for analytics topics such as artificial intelligence, business intelligence, and customer analytics, Gartner predicts. According to the research company, virtually every new software product in the area of sales will be equipped with AI functions by 2020 (Gartner 2017b).

## 3.1 LinkedIn Linking for Social Selling

Other examples are linkages of popular social media platforms with common CRM systems. For example, the LinkedIn Sales Navigator, which is a valuable sales tool—especially in the B2B sector, for identifying relevant leads on the professional platform and managing direct communication—can be easily integrated with Salesforce or even Oracle. It should be noted here, by the way, that LinkedIn was acquired by Microsoft in 2016 and can of course also be linked to Microsoft Dynamics in the first place.

## 3.2 Microsoft, Adobe, and SAP for a Standardized Data Model

Elsewhere, Microsoft, Adobe, and SAP announced a partnership project called the Open Data Initiative at XY in September 2018, with the goal of creating a data model that could be more easily applied across platforms, making it easier to share data across platforms.

## 3.3 Adobe Acquires Marketo

Also in the fall of 2018, Adobe purchased the marketing automation/campaign management platform Marketo, which is particularly exciting because many Marketo users have been using Sales Cloud. Additionally, Adobe is working closely with Microsoft, particularly on the Microsoft Dynamics 365 linkage (Fletcher and Greenberg 2018).

## 3.4 Salesforce Datorama

As part of the Salesforce Marketing Cloud, the AI-based intelligence and analytics platform offers elaborate reporting and can provide a comprehensive and customizable view of target values, utilization, website numbers, and more from numerous data sources. Salesforce bought Datorama back in 2018 to strengthen its marketing intelligence.

## 3.5 Integration with MuleSoft

MuleSoft was also purchased by Salesforce in 2018, a then-high investment of $6.5 billion. The MuleSoft integration platform enables disparate systems and applications to connect to Salesforce clouds, providing clean interfaces and transparent, seamless data exchange.

## 3.6 Slack for Collaboration

In 2020, Salesforce acquired the collaboration platform Slack for $27 billion, bringing on board a strong competitor to Microsoft Teams for collaboration, planning, and data sharing. Meetings, chats, and groups help with organization and offer numerous functionalities and links to support digital teamwork beyond the office.

## References

EY (2017) Weihnachtsgeschenke 2017 – Deutschland Verbraucherumfrage. https://www.ey.com/Publication/vwLUAssets/ey-weihnachtsgeschenke-2017-deutschland/$FILE/ey-weihnachtsgeschenke-2017-deutschland.pdf. Accessed: 11.02.2019

Fletcher C, Greenberg P (2018) Adobe buys Marketo: who wins, who to watch. zdnet.com. https://www.zdnet.com/article/adobe-buys-marketo-who-wins-who-to-watch/. Accessed: 14.11.2018

Futurezone (2017) Umfrage: Kunden recherchieren online, kaufen im Geschäft. https://futurezone.at/digital-life/umfrage-kunden-recherchieren-online-kaufen-im-geschaeft/267.183.732. Accessed: 14.11.2018

Gartner (2017a) 3 Steps to get the most from Customer Data. https://www.gartner.com/smarterwithgartner/3-steps-to-get-the-most-from-customer-data/. Accessed: 14..11.2018

Gartner (2017b) Gartner says AI technologies will be in almost every new software product by 2020. https://www.gartner.com/en/newsroom/press-releases/2017-07-18-gartner-says-ai-technologies-will-be-in-almost-every-new-software-product-by-2020. Accessed: 14.11.2018

Sopadejieva E, Dholakia UM, Benjamin B (2017) A study of 46,000 shoppers shows that omnichannel retailing works. Harv Bus Rev https://hbr.org/2017/01/a-study-of-46000-shoppers-shows-that-omnichannel-retailing-works. Accessed: 14.11.2018

Synergy Research (2017) Microsoft Leads in SaaS Market; Salesforce, Adobe, Oracle and SAP follow. https://www.srgresearch.com/articles/microsoft-leads-saas-market-salesforce-adobe-oracle-and-sap-follow. Accessed: 14.11.2018

**Steffen Deufel** is Trusted Advisor at DIGITALL and was co-founder and board member of DIGITALL and ec4u expert consulting ag. As Chief Product Officer, he was responsible for the company's portfolio and its further development. Steffen Deufel holds degrees in computer science from the elite German University of Karlsruhe and an Executive MBA from the Swiss University of St. Gallen (HSG). With a team of CRM experts, Steffen Deufel advises DIGITALL's clients in all CRM needs of operational, analytical, and strategic CRM. He has years of experience and expertise in the financial services and telecommunications industries. His responsibilities are project management, business process management, and implementation of CRM systems. Before ec4u was founded, Steffen Deufel was an early adopter of CRM and his CRM experience dates back to 1997. The project team at that time decided to found ec4u in 2000.

# Implementing the Customer Interface of the Future: Requirements for Business and Technical Architecture

Peer Stehling

**Abstract**

This article highlights the changes in the customer interface over the last 20 years and explains which approaches companies can leverage today to adequately use the increasing number of customer interfaces for their own company or customer communication from both a company- and customer-perspective. In addition, it will be explained how technical solutions for customer interfaces can be evaluated and deployed from the requirements generated by customers and the company.

## 1 What Is the Customer Interface Anyway?

The CRM competence fields and the customer journey are, of course, central components of the customer interface, both professionally and technically.

But what is behind the customer interface? The customer interface concerns the many ways in which companies communicate with their customers, whether B2C or B2B. It is all about communication! This is not meant to be an chapter about communication, but it is a challenge for sender and receiver to always share the same understanding of an issue. This is what makes the customer interface exciting and challenging. There are several dimensions to consider:

- Customer expectations and expected benefits
- Channel
- Business process
- Technology

P. Stehling (✉)
Capgemini Deutschland GmbH, Berlin, Germany
e-mail: peer.stehling@capgemini.com





S. Kirchem et al. (eds.), *CRM Goes Digital*, Management for Professionals,
https://doi.org/10.1007/978-3-658-45798-3_9

The customer has certain expectations in communication and cooperation with the company. Now besides this, remember there is no such thing as *the* typical customer. Every customer is different, even if their expectations may be similar. Furthermore, from the customer's point of view, it is important they see a benefit. No benefit: no customer! An unexpected crisis, such as a global pandemic, also impacts the customer interface.

Before we delve more deeply into the digitalization of the customer interface from today's perspective, let us take a brief look back.

## 2 The Evolution of the Customer Interface Over the Last 20 Years

Today, the customer interface is always mentioned in connection with digital transformation. But of course it has been around for a very long time in both the analog and digital worlds. Here, we will just take a brief look back at the last 20 years. The focus here is on the digitalization and mechanization of the customer interface.

Twenty years ago, the Internet rose to prominence and companies now had to include it alongside telephone, in-store/in-person, and letter/fax communication channels. The origin of e-commerce was born. But let us first look at the classic channels of the time.

Telephony plays an essential role in digitalization. The large call centers of the 1990s are now optimized such that customers first clarify their needs through a computer before a conversation even takes place. A lot has been invested in inbound and outbound telephony to optimize and shorten communication with the customer. The sooner a case or call is closed, the less it costs.

If we look at the in-store channel, or face-to-face interaction on site, this has played a major role in some industries, both in the past and now (e.g., in telecommunications). In other industries, this channel is being increasingly cut back (e.g., in banking) to save costs. What about customer benefit in this context? Surely customers today should use other channels, such as the Internet. An improvement in customer benefit is not always clear. Here, customer perceptions certainly play a significant role. Generations Y and Z will not miss the store or local branch, but Generation X is simply used to this point of contact and remains reluctant to do without it. But today, the store contributes a lot to the digitalization of the customer interface. The customer experience plays an essential role here, and new technologies such as RFID (Radio-Frequency Identification) or NFC (Near-Field Communication) are worth mentioning. The customer's experience in the store, from the moment they enter to the moment they leave, must be the focus today.

Mail and fax are complex channels that have challenged companies in the past and the present. In the 1990s, mass mailing became popular. Then individualized communication arrived.

The customer was supposed to gain the impression they were receiving a letter that was tailored to them personally. In some industries, a lot of written communication with the customer is common (e.g., insurance companies). In this context, companies face the challenge of digitalizing incoming mail. To do this, scanned documents have to be examined for specific content using text recognition software. In the end, an employee still has to check the document and decide on an appropriate response. This process is costly to both implement and operate. Of course, the same applies to fax: here, only a few steps in the process, such as opening and scanning the letter, are omitted.

This brief look at the classic customer channels of the 1990s and the beginning of the new millennium shows us the challenges companies have to master at the customer interface, and shows that they predate the digital transformation. In the 1990s, the buzzword was "cross-channel," which involved marketing products on as many channels as possible. However, this did not yet mean that all business transactions were mapped across all channels and certainly not that customers could start a business transaction on one channel and continue it seamlessly via another channel. Who can forget having to begin the same inquiry all over again every time they called a company's call center? It was even worse if you wrote a letter first, then followed up with a phone call. This was more likely to cause confusion than resolve the inquiry, especially with large companies. At the time, the focus was not on the customer experience, but on the benefit to the company of being present across multiple channels.

With the Internet starting in the 2000s, e-commerce was on everyone's mind. Think of the dot.com euphoria, which saw many new e-commerce platforms spring up like mushrooms by 2001. When the bubble burst, the Internet was still important as a channel but the pressure to push it more than other channels withdrew for the time being. This didn't last long. From 2005, the Internet took off again. Social media was the new thing, and since its beginnings, social media has been more than just a channel for customers.

Facebook came out in 2004 for students at Harvard University. Today, I see it as a channel in its own right within the customer interface. Accordingly, many companies in the B2C environment take this channel seriously.

Twitter/X followed in 2006 and should also be considered a channel in its own right.

Another major pressure for change came to companies with the introduction of smartphones in 2007. Predecessor devices were already technically sophisticated, but hardly any customers used them to communicate with companies. They were primarily used for email communication in the B2B sector, or within companies (e.g., Blackberry, Nokia Communicator).

With smartphones came apps, and with each new idea and associated app (e.g., WhatsApp, Instagram, Telegram) new channels were added to the customer interface. Today, the younger generation (Generation Y and Z) aspires to exclusively use smartphones and tablets as an interface. Many therefore see the beginning of the digital transformation alongside the triumph of the smartphone.

The last ten years have increased the complexity of the customer interface. The classic channels still exist, even as companies attempt to make the new channels palatable to their customers. In addition, the volume of new channels means companies have to decide which ones they want to use for the customer interface. The terminology has changed from "cross-channel" to "omni-channel." Personally, I can well remember that this was already an important topic for the major CRM solution providers in 2008. Back then, they focused more on the customer experience than on marketing their own products. Since then, companies have faced increasing pressure to decide which channels to use and how, as new channels can be added all the time. In the 2010s, the term "customer journey" emerged. Originating in marketing, this term initially only described the customer cycle from the initiation of a purchase to its conclusion. However, the customer journey does not end there. The use of a product or service is also part of the customer journey. Today, it goes without saying that the customer journey covers marketing, sales, and service.

The customer interface of the future must therefore account for the touchpoints of the customer journey as well as its channels. The challenges have to be mastered both professionally and technically.

In retrospect, it can be said that the last 20 years have served to digitalize analog processes as much as possible. Technologically, there are significantly more opportunities to completely redesign customer benefits and experience today. But in doing so, it is necessary to step back a bit from the requirements and processes of the past. Otherwise, people will continue attempting to simply digitalize analog processes. However, this is not what's understood as the digital transformation of the customer connect.

## 3 The Business Architecture of the Customer Interface

Companies should first ask themselves the question: Do we need the digital transformation? How does the customer interface derive from this? Only if you can justifiably answer these questions with a clear "yes" should you start thinking about the customer interface of the future.

But where should you start? We describe a path that, while taking existing processes and requirements into account, should encourage new ideas and food for thought. Why? It could be that existing requirements do not influence or only partially influence customer value or experience. However, the customer interface can only be successful if these key issues are considered from the outset.

The following therefore shows how to move from customer journey management to the requirements for implementing the customer interface of the future.

Figure 1 shows the combination of two methods:

- Customer journey mapping
- Requirements engineering with an agile approach

Both methods together result in a 360-view of the requirements at the customer interface.

Let us first turn to customer journey mapping. For the development of the journeys, customer personas (fictitious persons representing typical customers) must be defined first. These are then brought into the CRM competency model, which focuses on the life cycle of the customer in customer journey management through

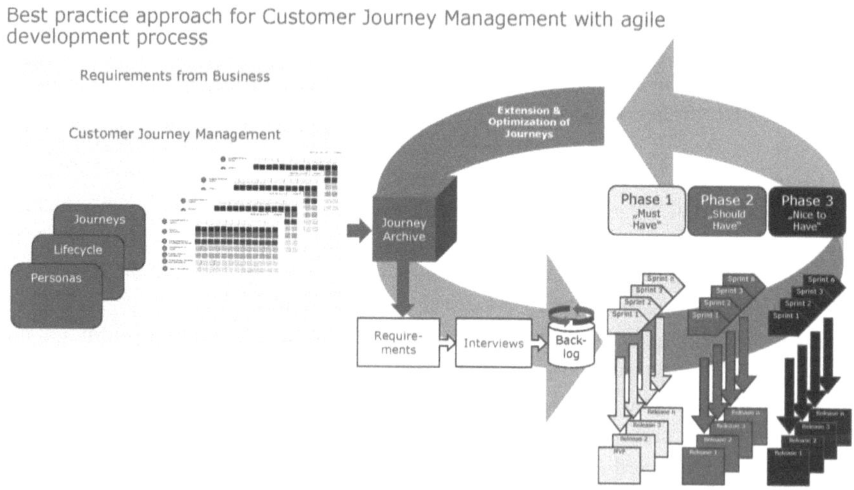


**Fig. 1** Best practice approach for customer journey management with agile development

marketing, sales, and service. The journeys derive from this. Journey development usually takes place in customer journey mapping workshops. The details of the method and its execution will not be further discussed here. The result of the journeys is appropriate communication. As stated at the chapter's outset, it is always about customer communication. The elements of successful communication result from customer journey mapping:

1. The right message
2. At the right moment
3. Via the right channel
4. To the right recipient

Once the right journeys have been defined, the process of translating them into requirements can begin. In addition to functional requirements, non-functional and technical requirements must also be considered. Since the introduction of the GDPR (General Data Protection Regulation), requirements for data protection and governance have increased.

The three pillars (functional, non-functional, and technical requirements) are then used to develop the specialist architecture of the customer interface. In any case, this should be part of the functional CRM target picture.

The domain-oriented target picture comprises various layers that should all map the requirements for the customer interface:

1. Interaction layer (omni-channel management, visualization)
2. CRM application layer
    a. Higher-level functions
    b. Functional components and focal points

3. CRM controlling and reporting
4. CRM profile data
5. CRM master data
6. Cross-functional components

Figure 2 shows an example of a functional CRM target picture.

The functional target picture encompasses more than the customer interface. From a business perspective, the focus should be on the interaction layer. Both the inside-out and outside-in perspectives must be considered, i.e. the company perspective and the customer perspective (see Sects. 3.1. and 3.2).

Both perspectives are equally important and must be taken into account accordingly in the requirements.

With the pandemic situation in mind, it is imperative that video be considered within the interaction layer. From my point of view, video does not represent a new channel but is resolved either via a web portal or an app (either responsive or tailored to the end-user devices). Interaction via video places new demands on companies and customers, both technically and professionally.

The business requirements include:

- Appearance of the company (e.g., background image) and the employee (clothing, etc.)
- Presentation of products and services via video (consulting)
- Appropriate communication based on the customer's visual and acoustic response (e.g., grimaces); employees must be properly trained in this area (e.g., recognizing cross-sell and up-sell potential)

The technical requirements include:

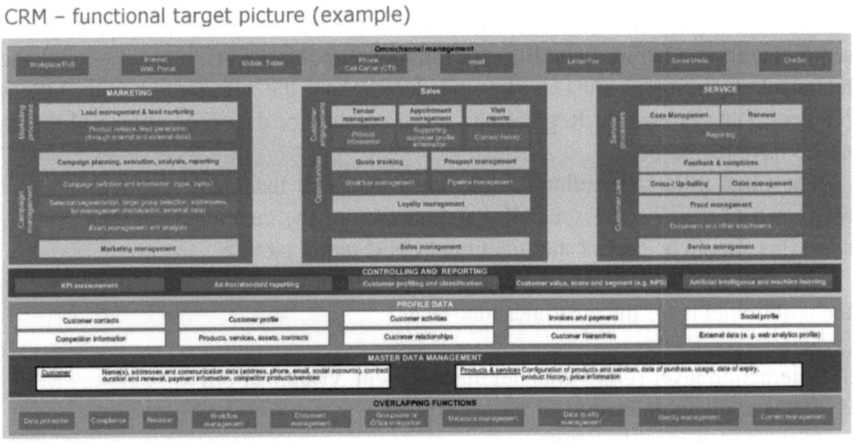


**Fig. 2** Example of a functional CRM target picture

- Sufficient bandwidth for video communication
- Proper lighting and sound conditions; can a headset be worn or does it not fit the company (e.g., wireless in-ear headsets are considered "trendy" or "cool")
- Resolution of the video image
- Avoidance of background noise
- Waiting time before video communication can start
- Privacy compliance of recorded video communication

This is of course only a selection of requirements, but it shows that bridging the spatial separation through video communication has its pitfalls. Even if a pandemic situation threatens high revenue losses, especially in the B2C environment, nothing should be rushed and video communication should first be tested and improved in a "friends and family" phase, i.e. a low-risk room with high feedback opportunities. After that, rollout can occur.

## 3.1 The Inside-Out View

From the company's point of view, the customer interface includes the following essential aspects:

- Complete information about the customer: master data, products, services, contact history, social media profile (increasingly in the B2C environment), web profile (for e-commerce platforms), GPS data (if allowed), etc.
- History and overview of all interactions
- High usability from the user's point of view
- Efficient process support without media breaks, preferably through automation

These points must be considered in all use cases. It does not matter whether interaction is automated, or occurs through a customer service representative, a sales employee, or a Chatbot.

Here, customer-facing communication is an important aspect. The customer always receives information through a chosen channel. This information should be customer-specific and precise. From the company's point of view, the interaction should quickly lead to the desired result (purchase, problem or complaint solution, mail campaign, etc.).

## 3.2 The Outside-In View

The customer sees the customer interface as a "monolith," communicating with one company. Customers want requests dealt with as quickly, efficiently, and cheaply as possible. In approaching the company, customers usually choose the channel that suits them best. If a request is not resolved appropriately, the customer could become an ex-customer. Particularly in the case of online shopping, customers can leave quickly if desired products and services are unavailable, only partially available, or are available at an unappealing price.

Service-related concerns are different. Here, the customers try to clarify their concerns conclusively and expect the company to find a solution through their chosen channel, if possible at the first point of contact. This is also desirable from the company's point of view, in order to keep service-request costs low. If a customer chooses a channel with asynchronous communication (e.g., email), they expect a timely solution. The company may well choose a different channel to the input channel, in order to have a better inside-out view.

Here is an example: A customer uses a web form to complain about a product or service. In this case, the customer usually receives an initial email confirmation that their concern has been received. Such emails are even better when the confirmation includes a case ID, so that a direct and automatic assignment can be made for each communication. Now, the customer waits for the company. Although the time taken to hear back often has nothing to do with digitalizing the customer interface, it can be important to the continuation of the customer relationship. In this example, the customer is called back by phone to resolve the issue. The outside-in view here can be subjective. If the concern has been satisfactorily resolved, the customer will respond positively. If not, their view will be more negative. However, from the customer's point of view, it is important that the concern is dealt with quickly and that communication is precise and accurate. A quick callback from a customer service representative about a concern makes sense if the customer does not have to explain the case again (the web form, for example, has already served this purpose) and the employee has the appropriate decision-making authority. Then, even if the request is rejected, the outside-in view can be positive.

In the example, the company has chosen telephone callback as the channel. Here comes the inside-out view again. This channel is a sensible choice because it can often help to clarify the concern conclusively, especially in the case of complaints. If the company responded by email, there would be more chance of further interactions with the customer about the concern. Thus, from the company's perspective, email would be inefficient because it would prolong the process. This example shows why the inside-out and outside-in views must always be considered when defining customer interface requirements.

The reverse case, when the company initiates communication with the customer, is of course just as interesting. The first thing here is that communication is prepared precisely and purposefully, preferably automatically and fully digitally. The idea is to generate a reaction from the customer. The customer will react in any case, but how, unfortunately, cannot be predicted. Of course, one could calculate probabilities for particular behavior based on existing data. Customers will react negatively if they see no benefit, consider the communication superfluous, do not feel personally addressed, or simply do not understand (e.g., in the case of a letter with lots of legal clauses). The customer must immediately feel like the communication is speaking to them personally. It needs to be a feeling of personalized communication. If this interest cannot be aroused, then there is no interaction with the customer.

The important aspects of outbound communication from the outside-in point of view are as follows:

- The choice of the right channel
- The personalization of communication
- Arousing interest within a few moments

This shows that standardized communications do not usually generate a high level of response. Let us go through these aspects one by one.

Every customer perceives a different channel as the "right" one. This can be directly evident from the customer profile, because the information is explicitly stored there. But it can also be implicitly stored in customer data, e.g., about the customer's age or previous interaction with the company.

Personalized communication is part of the digital customer interface. The right data and rules lead to good personalization.

The "interest" point is difficult. Of course, there are models today that calculate the next-best-action, etc., with a certain probability, but this still does not necessarily generate interest. Nonetheless, these models should be taken into account. Even if interest cannot yet be aroused, the enterprise can perhaps lead the customer to enter into interaction. Thus, at least a partial success has been achieved from the company's point of view.

When looking outside-in, companies should definitely look at how they can also address their customers with solutions they have not used before. Examples include virtual reality (VR) and augmented reality (AR). There are some industries where these can be useful.

Here are two examples.

In the real estate industry, residential and commercial buildings are offered for sale that do not even exist yet. Here, the use of VR and AR can be used to show customers what the future property will look like and how it will fit into the existing environment. The interior design of rooms can be brought to life using VR. There are already agencies today that offer such services.

The automotive industry provides a second example. Cars today are configured by customers using web-based product configurators. It would certainly be a better customer journey to sit down in an identical model and configure the vehicle virtually. In particular, colors, lighting, and the interior design of vehicles cannot be imagined very well in 2D.

These two examples could be expanded at will for other industries and use cases. The digital transformation offers many opportunities for companies to improve the outside-in view and generate positive results for the customer.

## 4 The Technical Architecture of the Customer Interface

From the customer interface requirements, this chapter moves on to a technical solution.

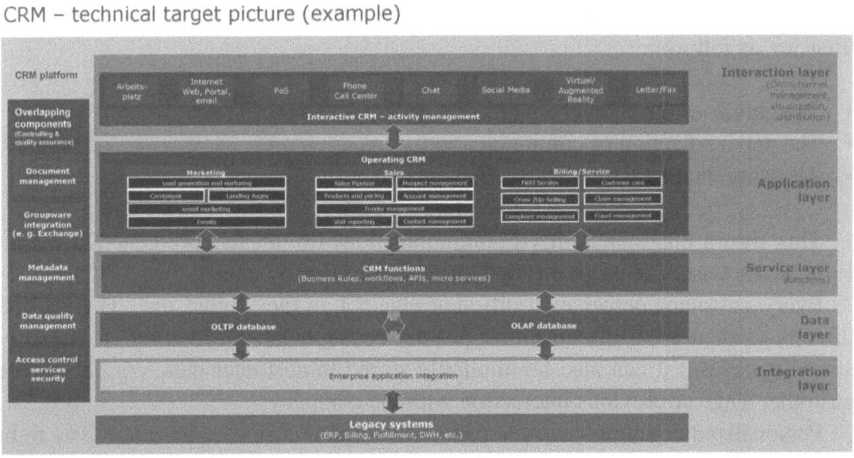


**Fig. 3** Example of a technical CRM target picture

The first step should be to develop a technical target picture in which all layers and components are considered. This also covers integration into the existing system landscape, technical and organizational framework conditions, legal requirements, and corporate guidelines (governance).

Taking these aspects into account, we then arrive at the technical target picture.

Figure 3 shows an example of a target picture for the CRM platform as the basis for the customer interface.

The next step should then be to define the complete integration into the enterprise application landscape. This usually involves complex integration scenarios with a whole range of important existing systems. This representation varies so much from company to company that it would not be helpful here to show an exemplary solution.

This is followed by the definition of the procedure for technical implementation. Most companies today already have a CRM platform and therefore the so-called greenfield approach, in which the CRM platform is newly added to the existing application landscape, is not possible. Based on experience and discussions with companies, four approaches have developed in recent years and are presented here:

1. Complete replacement of the CRM platform
2. Best-of-breed approach
3. Digital expansion
4. Overlay approach

## 4.1 Complete Replacement of the CRM Platform

Replacing an existing CRM platform with a new one is not an entirely new approach. This approach plays a role in relation to particular strategic decisions, which include the "one vendor" strategy and the cloud strategy. In both cases, the complete replacement of the existing platform is a favored solution.

The new platform must then offer the modules to appropriately map various functional blocks, including marketing, sales, service, and e-commerce. As with any approach, which business-critical processes are affected and how well these can be fully replaced directly with the new platform are important questions. The inherent risk must of course be evaluated by each company. Usually, these processes have been refined over several years and the new solution is unlikely to offer an adequate replacement immediately. The decision is often then to continue operating with the "old" platform until the risk can be minimized. Unfortunately, although this is intended as a transitional solution, this can lead to a situation in which an "old" and a "new" platform operate in parallel for years. The benefit for the company is then usually mediocre, since the parallel operation drives up costs.

This approach makes sense for companies if only one or two modules are used at the customer interface and the number of channels is low. For example, a B2B company mainly uses a CRM platform for sales activities handled by sales representatives. As a result, the number of processes and use cases is probably manageable and there is one major channel for the customer. Here, complete replacement makes sense if the solution is also expanded and future-proof for any further digital "journeys."

## 4.2 The "Best-of-Breed" Approach

The "best-of-breed" approach indicates what it is all about in its name. Here, the supposedly best solutions from different manufacturers are used to map the CRM platform. This approach is popular when there is already a high number of digital customer channels, complex processes are required in the background, and performance at the customer interface is of high importance: for example, when serving a high number of customers with services at the same time. In this approach, just as with complete replacement, the modernization of the IT landscape is pursued. However, different solutions are used. The "best-of-breed" approach can overlap with the overlay approach. The aim here is to continue operating certain existing systems. These are usually reduced to a few functions, or they are used as central data provision systems, but they probably no longer have a front-end function.

This approach is being taken in various industries today. It is possible to construct the customer interface in a modular way. Individual components and channels are added or newly built. Certain functions in existing systems are then switched off. In addition, there is little dependence on a single manufacturer. By using different solutions, it may even be possible to create a competitive situation between manufacturers, if there are functional overlaps in their solutions.

### 4.3 Digital Expansion

Digital expansion is essentially about adding a digital abstraction layer (digital layer) for the customer interface. This separates the entire interaction layer from the legacy systems (decoupling). Micro services can now be used for the different channels to provide new functionality to the customer. The advantage of this approach is it improves the "time-to-market." Once the digital layer is available, new products and services can be implemented quickly for different customer channels.

The challenge of this approach lies in the digital layer. Especially if there are already complex and extensive use cases at the customer interface, the development of the digital layer can quickly become a mammoth project. In this case, you should initially consider making only certain functions available via the digital layer. These will then be successively expanded. Other functions will continue to be offered via the existing CRM platform. Of course, this approach can lead to media discontinuities and impair the outside-in view, but it can control or reduce business risks.

### 4.4 The Overlay Approach

The overlay approach is a form of parallelization between the existing CRM platform and the addition of a new CRM platform. The overlay can be very small, e.g. only for particular new functions, services, products, or channels. But it can also affect complete CRM competency areas that are implemented in parallel. The overlay approach thus sounds unattractive at first, because parallelizations and complex integrations are required. Changes to existing systems are necessary and system maintenance incurs additional costs. However, this approach serves to minimize the risk that business-critical processes will no longer function properly as a result of changes and lead to disruptions in operations. The overlay approach must therefore have the clear goal of eliminating duplicate functions in the medium-to-long term. Otherwise, the so-called transitional solutions will quickly become the "target solution."

## 5 A Methodically Coordinated Approach as a Prerequisite for Successful Transformation

Every transformation needs a coordinated methodical approach. This is very important to achieving a successful result. For many years, the waterfall model was used as the approach. However, for some years now, various agile methods have been on the rise and have successfully established themselves in some companies.

In what follows, we will take a look at agile methods.

Most agile approaches are related to implementation, e.g., SCRUM, Extreme Programming, or Pair Programming, to name just a few. Many companies today rightly rely on agile approaches in order to see the results of implementation more quickly and still have the opportunity to introduce changes. In the classic waterfall model approach, changes were only possible at a late stage and were then usually time-consuming and correspondingly cost intensive. This is why agile methods have become so popular.

Transformation does not begin with agile implementation. Companies should take a holistic approach that uses agile approaches in business-requirements management in addition to implementation. Key to success is not only choosing the right transformation method, but the proper involvement of all stakeholders. Depending on the level of involvement, stakeholders must not only support the approach, but internalize and apply it. If there is resistance from some stakeholders here, it is essential to overcome it through appropriate change management. This point can be decisive for the success or failure of a project.

Because it concerns the customer interface, companies must embrace the outside-in view. The only way to do this is through new ideas, creative thought processes, and rapid prototype development. Design thinking is very suitable for this. It promotes new ideas from the user's point of view. Experience shows that even seemingly "weird" ideas can lead to great solutions for the customer in the end. When selecting the members of a design thinking workshop, the right mix is important. Employees from the relevant specialist department should be involved, but so should colleagues from outside the department who can contribute completely different views on particular topics.

Design thinking is a method of user-/customer-centered problem-solving that develops new ideas. It is often based on interdisciplinary teams as well as the phases "Scan," "Focus," and "Act," in order to identify and illuminate a problem or issue, creatively develop solutions, and then generate actionable steps.

One important aspect is the direct implementation of ideas in software. This allows business users to very quickly gain a picture and then introduce change requests and new ideas. If, after some iterations, the prototype stands, actual implementation of the project can begin. A product backlog is developed from the prototype and the results of the design thinking workshops, and the implementation project begins, for example, with SCRUM.

There are also other approaches if companies are not yet ready for design thinking. One starts with a classic analysis phase and then moves to an agile approach. This is the hybrid approach of waterfall and agile. Companies need to decide which approaches best suit their own culture and organization. In the end, it is always about the digital customer interface.

Agile approaches rely entirely or partially on face-to-face meetings. However, the pandemic has shown that many companies already working with agile have been able to switch to virtual meetings. This works very successfully for both small and large teams. Especially in large teams working according to Safe® (Scaled Agile Framework), there is project increment planning (PI planning) after each iteration. In the past, this was successfully conducted over three days in an in-person event with several hundred participants (even nearshore or offshore colleagues were flown in). In the context of the necessary virtualization of these face-to-face meetings, it has been shown that with the right technology, the discipline of the participants, and appropriate rules, it is also possible to work virtually in an agile and successful manner.

**Dr. Peer Stehling** (born 1968 in Berlin) is a German management consultant and author. He has been advising companies on all aspects of CRM for more than 26 years. Dr. Stehling studied chemistry with a focus on biochemistry at the Free University of Berlin. After completing his doctorate, he began his professional career as a management consultant at Accenture. He later moved to ec4u expert consulting ag as a consultant and later to Capgemini.

# Explore the Right Personas for Successful Marketing, Sales, and Service

Sabine Kirchem and Juliane Waack

**Abstract**

Personas are representative, fictitious, realistic profiles of customers, users, and other target groups. They support personal communication through careful examination of needs, challenges, and motivations. This chapter introduces the concept, offers guidance on developing your own personas, and provides numerous best practices and explanatory information for possible applications and complementary methods and processes.

## 1 Why Do You Need Personas?

Markus and Peter love coffee and frequent the same coffee shop nearby their workplaces. Peter worked as a barista during his studies and is well acquainted with the differences between different beans. He always orders a double espresso from his favorite café in downtown Cologne, trying a different variety every time. Besides his espresso, he usually tries the cake of the day. Markus, on the other hand, always orders a latte macchiato with caramel syrup during his lunch break. He likes caffeine more than coffee, so rather than trying something he might not enjoy, he always chooses the same thing. He does not buy pastries because the caramel syrup has enough calories.

If the coffee shop were to plan a customer campaign and target groups similar in age, gender, or profession, Peter and Markus would receive the same offer. They are both 30 years old, live nearby, and work in middle management. Although Peter and

S. Kirchem (✉)
DIGITALL Nature Germany GmbH, Karlsruhe, Germany
e-mail: sabine.kirchem@digitall.com

J. Waack
Billwerk+ Germany GmbH, Berlin, Germany
e-mail: juliane.waack@billwerk.com



S. Kirchem et al. (eds.), *CRM Goes Digital*, Management for Professionals,
https://doi.org/10.1007/978-3-658-45798-3_10

Markus share many similarities, they are completely different types of customers; one is an adventurous epicurean who likes to experiment, while the other is an habitual shopper, who doesn't take chances. For this reason, the coffee shop should not use "target groups" for its campaign; it should use "personas," to address Markus and Peter appropriately, not based on their demographics but rather based on their needs.

Personas (Kirchem and Waack 2021) refer to fictional characters that represent a particular customer group. They help an organization to market to the persona in a more targeted and personal manner. A persona should not only be based on classic demographics, such as gender, cultural background, age, and profession, but also on emotional needs, behavioral patterns, personality traits, and other factors. Buyer personas, or personas that represent customers, always include purchase motivations. What motivates this particular group of customers to purchase a product or service?

In this way, the persona enables targeted and personal communication. As the example illustrates, even two people of the same age and gender may not necessarily share the same characteristics simply because they love the same café in the same city. To communicate effectively with customers, personas highlight customer diversity. When applying personas, it is therefore important to not view certain characteristics and traits like dogmas; personas should only serve to make customers more "tangible" in their differences.

Even though personas may appear fictitious, they are ultimately based on real customer profiles, so they should not be treated as pure imagination. They are neither an unrealistic movie character nor an ideal customer; they are realistic representations of real customers. Embellishments should therefore closely reflect existing customers, to avoid the impression that the personas are not actually real.

## 2 What Is Typical of a Persona?

A persona combines several kinds of characteristics to provide a comprehensive view of a customer, while defining a realistic person. A persona's characteristics are broadly classified as "demographic" (age, gender, cultural background) or psychographic (behavior, attitude, motivation). Depending on a particular persona, other categories may be included. For example, coffee shops do not care about customer height, weight, or fitness. But for a fitness product, these characteristics are useful in targeting different personas.

A selection of the characteristics and information about the personas for a smart start could be:

- Work and profession
- Family status
- Education
- Gender
- Age
- Income
- Cultural background

- Location
- Living conditions
- Channels of preference
- Skills
- Hobbies
- Needs
- Plans and objectives
- Challenges and problems
- How can the persona act?
- What does the persona need in order to act?

Personas have the clear advantage of enabling a customized approach because needs, motivations, goals, concerns, problems, and challenges are well known to the business.

- By knowing what channels customers use (and why), the company can place targeted messages on the right channels
- Tone and address can be adjusted according to the audience (e.g., formal or casual)
- Typologizing the customer group is not only a matter of categorizing by demographic characteristics, but also by needs and motivations to buy, which can be derived from the characteristics listed further along this article;
- To effectively target your marketing, it is important to typologize customer needs and purchase motivations
- An effective communication system documents relevant customer information and problems clearly and centrally so that campaigns, processes, and strategies can be prioritized accordingly
- This process clarifies why a potential customer would not choose a product or service, and factors into the marketing strategy

## 2.1 How Are Personas Used?

The use of personas in communication can be varied. Personas are most often used for marketing: creating campaigns, email streams, content marketing, and advertisements. Using analytics can also benefit sales, customer service, and other customer-facing areas by better understanding customers' needs, communicating with them, and establishing a presence on appropriate channels. A persona provides you with an idea of what your communication partner might be like, so you can better address a group of customers with the right messaging and tone. Personas have almost limitless applications.

Here are some typical use cases:

- **Campaign management:** Formulating targeted campaigns, providing relevant keywords, images, and information.

- **Email marketing:** Finding the right form of address (especially in the subject line) and motivating recipients (sending links, registering).
- **Sales pitch:** Different personas ask different questions, want different information, and have different product, service, and offer priorities.
- **Application management:** Professionals have different requirements and needs compared to junior positions and early-career starters; students and pupils also have different needs.
- **Content development:** Any content (e.g., infographic, video, article, social media post, book, infographic) must consider specific audiences and purposes.
- **Event management:** An event must appeal to either one or multiple personas.
- **Marketing automation:** Using a persona concept in marketing automation systems can automate and measure customer processes.
- **Customer journey mapping:** In customer journey management, all business processes are designed to meet the customer's needs.

## 2.2 What Motivates Customers?

What makes personas effective is their focus on purchase motivation. Personas should clarify what motivates them to become buyers. How does someone decide whether to buy something? What is the best way to get them to buy? Which information do they need, how should processes be designed, and what is their expectation from the purchase experience and the follow-up?

Motivation is the differentiating characteristic that indicates how many personas should be approached. Analysis based on demographic characteristics or behavior can lead to endless personas, but analyzing motivation usually leads to only a few.

However, a good persona does not just include positive buying and behavior markers. Including reasons why a persona will not buy a product is helpful. The so-called pain points, such as specific challenges in customers' living environments, provide insights into which topics should be addressed, focused on, or even be avoided.

Personas are ideal for targeting people who are likely to develop into ideal customers. It is not necessary to setup every single customer type into a persona when evaluating customer information. Customer personas should only be used for people you really want to reach. Ideally, a persona summarizes the most attractive (potential) customers for a business.

# 3 One-Off: The B2B Buyer Persona and the Buying Center

In B2B, marketing activities and personas tend to be ignored because people assume they better suit B2C businesses. Typically, B2B communication occurs directly with customers, sales representatives know their clients, and do not assume they need personas. However, times have changed since B2B clients went right into sales.

Before their first face-to-face interaction with an enterprise, B2B customers increasingly research them online. Social media, review sites, and powerful search engines facilitate much of the research for potential business. Therefore, B2B companies should design their websites, social-media profiles, and content accordingly, so they cater to the needs of their customers. Companies can quickly lose track of clients, without the time to choose them correctly for their sales contacts. As a consequence, B2B marketing is increasingly relevant, alongside the need to engage with large audiences in a personalized manner.

This development is also being recognized by B2B companies. Allison+Partners (2020) found that British and German B2B leaders aim to present their brands in a more human and emotional way. With an eye towards people and an emotional approach to business, 58% of survey respondents believe they can increase revenue, 55% expect a higher level of engagement, and 55% expect greater customer loyalty. More than every second respondent believes that personal interactions that extend beyond product description can positively impact company success, brand awareness, and customer loyalty.

But according to the study, B2B communication is challenged by the emotional aspects:

- Lack of understanding of customer priorities and needs
- Tonality problems in content production
- Challenge in developing new customer partnerships

These hurdles prevent B2B marketing from establishing a strong connection with its customers; 57% of marketers do not use personas so they probably lack a clear insight into their customers' motivations, pain points, and preferences. This also indicates that there could be a communication gap between marketing and sales (e.g., when sales does not use personas provided by marketing). In the B2B sector particularly, finding the right contact and providing them with relevant information is important which is why a close relationship between marketing and sales and their customer insights is crucial for personalized, aligned, and relevant messaging.

In B2B, the term "buying center" determines which people (or personas) are involved in the decision-making process, when and how they can be reached, and what information they need to make an informed decision.

A buying center is an important asset because in almost all B2B sales cycles, sales does not just speak to one single senior decision-maker. According to a Google study, 81% of "non-C-suiters"—i.e. employees without decision-making power—are part of a buying center because they conduct research and ultimately influence decisions. Moreover, the contact person may not always make the final decision. This does not necessarily imply any less influence because, after all, they collect, structure, filter, and pass on the necessary information. As you can see, developing B2B personas can be quite a complicated process.

When creating a buying center, you need to ask yourself these questions:

- Who is involved and to whom should I reach out?

- Which contacts are involved at which point in the buying process?
- What information do each of these contacts need for each phase of the purchase?
- Where can I reach each contact on each communication channel?

Personas help communication with buying centers by identifying the people who are usually involved in a purchase. It is important not to base personas on decision-maker status alone. Instead, you need personas for the individuals you can actually reach through your communications strategy and campaigns, and whose decision-making processes differ heavily from one another. For example, creating a CEO persona may be useful because this person ultimately gives the "go ahead." But if they're only involved in listening to a marketing manager's pitch and saying yes or no, maybe creating a dedicated CEO persona is unnecessary opposed to addressing a marketing persona.

How can you gain information for your B2B personas?

- **Interviews with colleagues who have frequent customer contact:** Colleagues in direct contact with customers can provide helpful insight into customer behavior, motivation, and challenges, and should participate in the development process. You should use third-party data on customer behavior cautiously, and at most as a supplement to persona guides.
- **Customer interviews and surveys:** A persona should be developed based on real customer statements; these are best obtained through interviews and surveys, which should be conducted before the workshop.
- **Studies and benchmark analyses:** Many persona guides recommend to use third-party data to gain further insight into customer behavior. Various studies and benchmarks provide interesting insights into general behaviors and characteristics. Personas can contain an array of characteristics, traits, behaviors, and information.

It is important to consult different information sources when developing personas so they are as comprehensive and realistic as possible. In addition to customer information, marketing automation platforms and customer management systems accumulate lots of useful data for developing personas.

The value of information may vary, but the creator should determine which information is most important.

The main aspects of a persona are as follows:

The **name and image** of the persona can be chosen at the end of the process, after all the other information has been gathered. Hereafter, it becomes easier to choose a picture that fits the persona.

**Background and demographic characteristics should** include information like occupation, position (student, manager, CEO), educational path, family status, gender, age, residence, income, and preferences (city versus rural life). Characteristics relevant to customer objectives should be prominent during the process. Position and education may be much more important than cultural background. However, if a company, for example, sells baby nutrition products and wishes to attract marketing influencers, whether the persona has or works with children should be considered. Always fit attributes to your audience, product, and industry.

**Values and interests** tell us what motivates the persona, their hobbies, and special interest (also within their career). Moreover, values play a significant role in areas where political and social attitudes determine decisions. The values of an organization can significantly impact customer decisions on interaction and purchasing. When the persona, for example, is concerned with the environment, this could indicate that you should incorporate environmentally friendly and sustainable practices into their actions.

A persona's behavior with regard to the **Internet and information sources** is important besides classic characteristics. It is important to know where the persona can best reach a company and how they generally behave. Questions could include: where does the persona get information, are they tech-savvy, and how do they communicate with companies? How do they prefer to be addressed? Would they prefer to be addresses in a humorous, relaxed tone, or more formally?

**Personality and self-image:** What is the persona's self-perception and how does this affect their decisions? Are they impulsive, reserved, introverted, or extroverted? In marketing, how do personas envision themselves and what does this mean? In messages, how does the persona wish to be recognized and are they trying to create an ideal self-image?

**Goals and motivation** are among the most important factors in developing a persona. What goals and motivation does the persona wish to achieve when interacting with the company? Why is the persona buying a product, applying for a job, or donating to a charity? One single goal does not need to exclude others; primary and secondary goals often flow into each other. A persona should be based on real quotes regarding goals and motivations. It is possible to obtain these from interviews, surveys, or even from the extensive daily experience of colleagues who interact with the relevant personas.

It is important to distinguish between **primary and secondary challenges** when creating a persona. What problems, pain points, and challenges could the offering potentially solve? The primary issue for a marketing manager might be that they spend too much time setting up email campaigns. Additionally, they do not have an easy way to evaluate campaign results. Importantly, customer quotes should serve as a source of challenges and problems for your persona.

What **expectations** do customers have of the company and what does that mean for processes and communications? Are particular issues very important? Can their expectations be met or do processes need to be adjusted?

**Quotes**: When developing a persona, it is essential to speak directly with customers and users, and to collect quotations. This ensures a formulation of persona motivations from their point of view, as opposed to the company's. Face-to-face interviews are usually recommended to address talking points that may not have been considered when creating the questionnaire. Potential questions include:

- Are you interested in the product for yourself or for others?
- Where and how do you get information for recommendations?

- Do you get purchase advice from family, acquaintances, the Internet, comparison sites, or social media?
- Do you conduct online research?
- What is your most common method of informing yourself: providers, comparison sites, Google, social media?
- Which device are you most likely to use to access the Internet: computer, laptop, tablet, smartphone?
- What is most important to you when deciding on a product?
- Do you use your smartphone for research, payment, online shopping, event registrations, newsletter registrations, emails, and social media?
- Why would you decide against a purchase?
- What do you expect from your purchase?
- Through what channels do you prefer to receive product offers?
- Why would you decide against a purchase?
- On which channel do you want to handle problems?
- Are you interested in self-service or would you rather be assisted?
- How did you learn about us?

What **obstacles or concerns** might motivate the persona to reject a product or participation? Are there any known obstacles, such as price, effort, or other reasons why the persona might choose a different vendor? During interviews, it is imperative to identify these factors. As a result, the appropriate counterarguments—for example, that the price represents sustainable and fair manufacturing with a high level of quality—can be developed. Should the processes and channels attend to certain hurdles and specifically discuss how they hinder the persona on their journey? For complex issues, such as processes, and very sensitive areas (e.g., collecting data) that cannot be changed, the right communication strategy is important. This work can be sensitive and even hurtful, but companies will receive valuable information from concerns and obstacles, even if they are things that cannot be changed. If a current or previous campaign conflicts with these concerns, it should also be considered. A persona is designed to discuss why customers should find an offering attractive and precisely shows a different perspective from the company's view (i.e., not a company-centric or inside-out view). A realistic persona that reflects their goals, fears, and concerns is essential. Prejudices, rumors, and unvarnished criticism also play a role.

**How specifically does the offer** assist the persona in achieving their objectives? When communicating, it is very important to formulate the offer's benefits from the customer's perspective, and how the persona can overcome obstacles and solve problems.

The **message**: How can the persona best be persuaded? Core arguments should be summarized to correspond directly to the persona's goals and challenges. Although this may seem simple, it can be very challenging to phrase the general messages to appeal to a specific persona rather than simply repeating their needs. How can arguments be pitched or summarized concisely and succinctly? It is useful to prepare a short pitch consisting of a few sentences that summarize the offer, so it is relevant to your persona's life, within a maximum of one or two minutes. This pitch can be used verbally or in writing, and is a good template for colleagues who have a lot of contact with customers.

**Need-to-Know:** Every company is unique. A company may need information that is not covered in the classic persona template. If so, this should be added and filtered. Personas have the advantage of representing ideal customers and therefore should include characteristics that value specific customers or that are pertinent to addressing them as individuals.

It is helpful to include **concrete measures** directly in the "persona package," to ensure that personas do not collect dust in a drawer and are used beyond marketing as well. This can be done, for example, by adding a rough overview of the customer's lifecycle, highlighting key moments and interactions (touchpoints), and recommending actions.

## 4 How To Fill a Persona Template

Persona templates make it easy to document the most important elements, characteristics, and statements of a persona, along with recommendations for actions and messages. Our template is compatible with PowerPoint presentations, so it can be shared, incorporated into project descriptions, and used in campaigns. It is structured like a profile description and can be visualized when needed. A good template should be understandable and self-explanatory for all users. When creating it, make sure it follows these guidelines:

People who were not involved in developing the personas should be able to understand all information. When considering a short profile vs. a long profile, there can be different levels of detail in developing personas. Depending on purpose and resources, the persona does not necessarily need all characteristics, traits, and behaviors. Determine at the outset why personas are necessary and how they will be used. To better target communications, a small business may only need a rough picture of its personas, whereas a large retailer with multiple campaigns and customer groups should understand its personas more deeply for effective marketing campaigns, to ensure the sales process hits the right notes.

The persona short profile (Fig. 1 Persona Template Short) is no less valuable than the long profile that also can be find. The short profile summarizes certain topics more coarsely and omits details relevant for personas used for multiple topics, areas, and campaigns, but also for comprehensive customer journeys across all business areas.

However, neither short nor long profiles need to cover all topics. Before using them, you should agree, within your team, on what is really relevant for your personas, in order to clarify their scope and focus. The templates presented here serve as a kind of "serving suggestion."

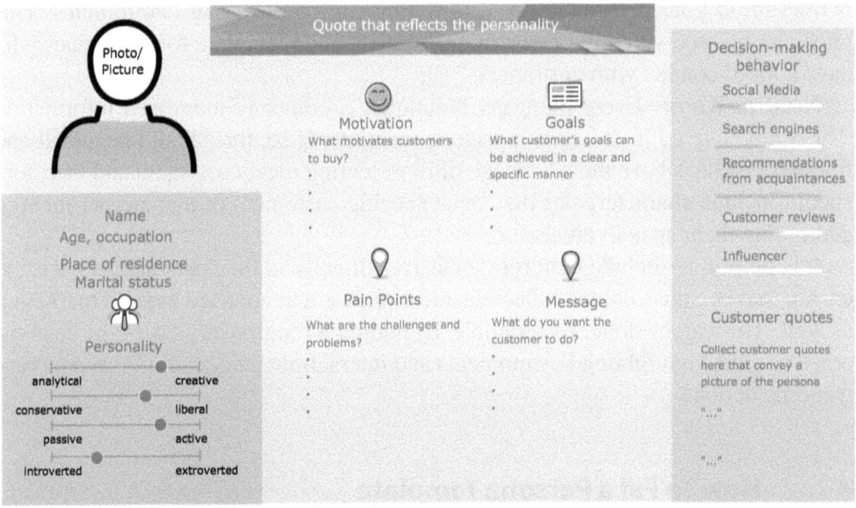


**Fig. 1** Example for persona short template

# 5 Personas: Frequently Asked Questions

There are always questions and challenges when developing and using personas. What to consider when creating them is often unclear, as is how to apply them. We explain the most common questions and challenges in what follows.

## 5.1 What Are Common Mistakes When Creating Personas?

Probably the most common mistake when developing personas is focusing too much on one's own wishes. Customer needs are assumed to be known, instead of asking them specifically.

- Creating personas without reference to the customer
- Including the company's own priorities in personas
- Prioritizing characteristics over motivation
- Not updating personas
- Not using personas

## 5.2 How Many Personas Do You Need?

Generally, companies tend to have more personas than they need. Personas should not be differentiated by demographic characteristics, but rather by purchase motivations and preferences (i.e., what do they buy, when, how often, and why?) or, in the B2B sector, according to professional requirements and areas of expertise. There is no "right" number. The size of a company's market also matters. On the one hand, personas should represent ideal and real customers and on the other hand, they should help to set up campaigns in a more targeted manner, addressing them more personally to reach as many different customers as possible.

## 5.3 Who Should Be Involved in Developing a Persona?

Marketing, sales, and service personnel often are a great mixture to gain a full understanding of customers' needs, behaviors, and challenges. Although in practice, development usually rests with marketing, people in direct contact with customers should participate. Depending on who will use the persona, this can also vary by company.

## 5.4 How Long Does a Persona "Last?"

Creating a persona is not a one-time thing, and regular reviews are important to ensure it is current. During times of disruptive change, such as abrupt events that result in quasi-immediate changes, personas should be considered in context. During the Covid-19 crisis, for example, almost everyone's behavior changed drastically. In any case, a review every one-to-two years is appropriate, as customer behavior is changing rapidly in parallel with digital transformation.

## 5.5 How Many "Fictitious" Details Does a Persona Need?

A persona does not need elaborate character studies or life stories, since the core of a persona lies in motivation, needs, challenges, and goals. In general, a persona should be given a name, a photo, and at least a few rough fictitious characteristics, so that it is "tangible." However, how extensive these characteristics are depends on the field of application.

## 5.6 How Many Interviews Do I Need to Conduct for a Persona?

There is a strong correlation between the number of interviews and the type of interview you use for your research. Online questionnaires, for instance, do not offer follow-up questions and are often anonymous, so numbers are higher. Additional more personal interviews, however, are important, especially when interview partners that represent the same persona provide strongly differing answers; these interviews can be more in-depth and help to avoid contradictions within the persona.

## 5.7 How Do You Measure the Success of Persona Deployment?

KPI are generally used to measure campaigns against your set goals. What these look like for personas depends on the area of application. In corporate marketing, personas can be measured against various KPI, such as conversion rates, engagement, purchases, and sales. Additionally, it is important to compare KPI across different personas to determine if any adjustments need to be made. Possible KPI include the following:

- **Sales:** Which personas make the most sales and could sales be increased by campaigns using personas?
- **Engagement**: Does engagement increase as a result of using personas, such as on social media channels?
- **Conversion**: Can growth in new members, subscribers, customers, and buyers be seen as a result of personas?
- **Customer retention:** Do customer groups that are addressed with the help of personas remain loyal to the company for longer or are they less likely to bounce?

## References

Allison+Partners (2020) Von Mensch zu Mensch, Download-Link: https://allisonpr.de/insights/von-mensch-zu-mensch.html (Accessed 13.11.2020)

Kirchem S, Waack J (2021) Personas entwickeln für Marketing, Vertrieb und Kommunikation. Springer, Wiesbaden

**Sabine Kirchem** is the Vice President of Marketing and Communications at DIGITALL. She began her career in the consulting industry and developed the areas of market research and corporate communications in different companies. Throughout her career, she has gained extensive knowledge in the CRM environment and is well-versed in current trends and technologies, such as cloud services, customer journey, and social media, thanks to her flair for innovation topics. Additionally, she is an author and has contributed to the creation of several books and written studies, and published numerous specialized articles on customer journey, CRM, and cloud computing.

**Juliane Waack** is Senior Content Marketing Manager and manages company blogs, develops marketing campaigns, and supports colleagues with any writing-related tasks.

She has more than 14 years of experience as a writer with a focus on content marketing, social media, SEO, digitalization, and corporate communication. She is particularly interested in preparing complex technical topics in easy-to-understand formats and enjoys researching innovative tech topics and develop creative ways to present them.

# Agile Design and Implementation of Digital Offerings: Holistically Realizing Customer Goals, Business Requirements, and Technical Implementation

Glenn Oberholzer and Sandro Ruberti

**Abstract**

Digital measures are only successful if they address customer needs and create benefits for organizations and employees at the same time. Keeping the needs of (internal) customers in focus throughout the entire development process is challenging and often unsuccessful. The key to success lies in involving all relevant roles throughout the entire development process and in clearly defining customer requirements. A case study helps to explain the recipes for successful customer-oriented development.

## 1 Are You Still Digitalizing or Already Supporting?

Everything will be digitized. The motivation behind many digitalization projects is to improve efficiency. Automated processes and activities outsourced directly to the customer are intended to better use existing resources. "Self-service" is the ambition and its key promise is that of a leaner service organization. Today, companies are trying to master this in-house challenge through portals, chatbots, virtual assistants, and deep-learning algorithms.

However, technology and digitalization themselves are rarely the solution: Many technology-focused initiatives fail to meet expectations, in terms of both customer acceptance and cost-benefit calculation. Digitalization is a means to an end. And the end must be to delight customers by making customer interaction easier, more enjoyable, and better at meeting their needs. Only then will customers use digital tools and channels as well, and result in a positive cost–benefit calculation for companies.

G. Oberholzer (✉) · S. Ruberti
Stimmt AG, Zürich, Switzerland
e-mail: glenn.oberholzer@stimmt.ch; sandro.ruberti@stimmt.ch



S. Kirchem et al. (eds.), *CRM Goes Digital*, Management for Professionals,
https://doi.org/10.1007/978-3-658-45798-3_11

The fact that many customers demand precisely this kind of simple and pleasant digital interaction was shown by the *Customer Experience Monitor 2018* from the customer focus experts at Stimmt AG (Oberholzer and Leuthold 2018): Qualitative responses from over 6000 people show that digitalization is now an increasingly central topic compared to respective data from two and five years ago. However, this is not so much a customer request as an expectation. If digital options are missing, this is often evaluated negatively. In the Kano model (Kano et al. 1984), digital options are therefore now no longer "enthusiasm factors," but performance factors or even basic factors. In other words, if you don't offer digital customer benefits, you disappoint customers.

The focus of any digitalization project that wants to optimize customer interaction must therefore be to implement only what customers actually need.

## 2 Potential "Savior" Customer-Centric Development

In order to adequately incorporate the customer's point of view into projects, approaches and procedures need to systematically enable innovation from the customer's point of view, while always ensuring feasibility and a business upside. The methods of customer-centered development of digital systems (user-centered design) have been known for decades (e.g., Norman and Draper 1986). Other approaches are now being added to this, the most prominent of which are Design Thinking, Human Centered Design, and Service Design. These approaches are all based on the following four principles:

1. Understanding customers is essential
2. Prototyping and testing in multiple loops quickly leads to certainty
3. Interdisciplinary, motivated teams are a prerequisite
4. Rigorous prioritization of individual action modules enables a short time-to-market

Advocates for these methods suggest that business and technical perspectives need to be included in addition to the customer perspective. In practice, however, the customer perspective often comes to bear more heavily these schools of thought. This leads to dissonance in implementation, if not earlier. Convincing concepts are developed with customers, which either cannot be implemented or do not make business sense.

Another weakness is that these approaches are often only applied in the early phases of a digitalization project. The result can then be an excellent concept based on customer needs, but which developers do not understand. Customer benefits are subsequently lost in the detailed elaboration toward implementation, which results in digital solutions that are far removed from the original concept. This is unsatisfactory for everyone involved and rightly calls into question the benefits of customer-centric methods.

## 3 Potential "Savior" Agile Development

The Agile Manifesto dates back to 2001 (*Agilemanifesto* 2001), the same time that customer-centric design methods (think of "design thinking") emerged. Indeed—possibly due to the zeitgeist—many similar principles exist: Agile development methods also focus on the validity of solutions; i.e. on "doing the right thing." Interdisciplinary and motivated teams are the basis of success, alongside quick response to new requirements and insights.

Another common feature of these approaches is that, besides the technical feasibility of the digital solution, the customer perspective and the business perspective—according to agile development advocates—should also be consistently prioritized. In practice, however, agile methods are still clearly software development methods. Technical feasibility often dominates the requirements.

Thus, product owners, who manage the interface between the developers and the concept's customer requirements, prioritize individual user stories. Often they prioritize feasibility in their decision-making, neglecting their role as "customer advocate and business representative." The result of this approach is a digital solution far removed from the original concept, but which arguably fits into the existing system and solution landscape.

## 4 Holistic Design and Implementation Without Compromises

The challenge is to properly including customer, business, and technological perspectives in the project, from initial strategic considerations to final implementation. In reality, the often linear process—first the relevant specialist department, then the concept creators, and then the software developers—must be changed for this purpose (Fig. 1).

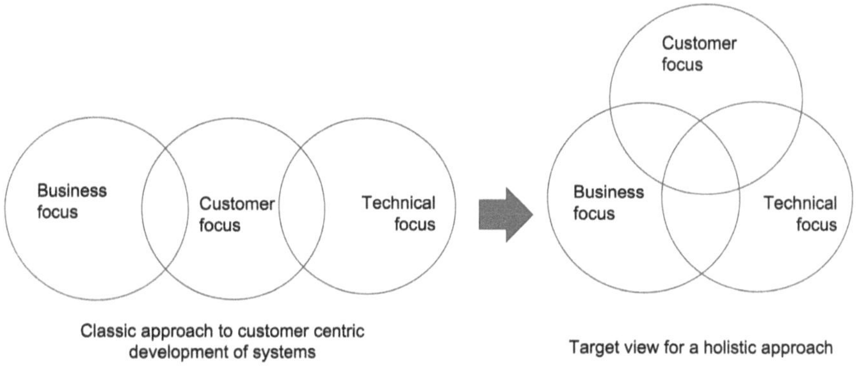


**Fig. 1** From the classic role of the customer's point of view as translator, to partner in a dialogue

There are various approaches to combining customer-centric design with agile development methods. Some experts suggest the close involvement of UX designers in the sprints, while others discuss conception and implementation sprints running in parallel. Still others place "Sprint 0" as a "concept sprint" before development.

Other approaches try to dovetail the strategic component with the customer view. Tools such as the Business Model Canvas (Osterwalder and Pigneur 2011) place a very strong focus on the customer's added value and the value proposition of a business idea.

However, the separation of competencies and phases in all these approaches is still very strong; strategic and operational components do not mesh well. There is arguably a role in all approaches for ensuring the customer view. For technical decisions, this role is often fulfilled by customer experience experts, who are supposed to validate solutions using tools like customer journeys and personas. User experience designers, information architects, and of course user interface designers come on board to effectively implement and design graphical interfaces. However, these people rarely work across the boundaries of technology and business and they are exposed to different interests and forces, depending on the phase of the project. At the beginning of the project, the focus is on added value for customers, while at the end, the focus is on feasibility. Neither is efficient.

In order to ensure that customer, business, and technical perspectives are recognized throughout the digital project, the perspectives and competencies must be integrated into the entire project in a much more overarching manner. It is not only translators between business and IT that are needed, but also mediators and moderators between all stakeholder interests. Active designers and implementers are required throughout the entire process. The role of a "customer advocate" or "customer experience agent" can fill this role very well.

The integrative approach is explained in this article based on a project at a leading health insurance company in the DACH-region (Germany, Switzerland, and Austria). The challenge was to design a customer portal that would be strategically sound for years and that could be implemented within seven months. A pure concept would have missed the target; and technological implementation alone would not have offered any strategic added value. Only a close dovetailing of the concept and the implementation made the goals set by the ambitious board of directors achievable.

## 5 How Agile and Customer-Centric Methods Can Be Successfully Interlinked

The basic idea behind the process is that the three disciplines of business, customer orientation, and development always work on the solution in parallel and in close coordination (Fig. 2). In each of the three phases—"conception," "prioritization and definition," and "implementation"—one discipline has the lead and the others are present for detailed content questions and with a veto right on fundamental decisions. The benefit is that the knowledge of each discipline is constantly available

| Concept | Definition | Development |
|---|---|---|
| Business in the lead | Business gives guidance | Business gives guidance |
| Customer Centricity gives guidance | Customer Centricity in the lead | Customer Centricity gives guidance |
| Development gives guidance | Development gives guidance | Development in the lead |

**Fig. 2** Different responsibilities in the various phases

throughout the project, the needs of different (internal) customers receive equal consideration from the beginning, the decision paths and thus the time-to-market are shorter, and the solutions are higher quality.

Furthermore, it is essential that solutions are repeatedly tested in every phase of the project, with all project stakeholders but especially with customers.

## 5.1 Conception

In this phase, the business unit has the lead responsibility. Customer orientation and development set the guard rails. At the outset of every digital project, a company needs to ask what it wants to achieve with a new digital application, and whether specific KPIs exist. How strongly the project is being shaped by considerations of internal efficiency or external customer benefit becomes clear at this stage. This is not a contradiction; on the contrary, it is only when both internal and external goals are achieved that a project is successful.

However, customer needs are often not known with the same clarity as internal requirements. Eliciting customer needs is therefore central to the project's progress. Existing market and customer data provide initial indications of what requirements exist from the customer's point of view. Qualitative survey methods, supplemented by quantitative methods, are a very productive way to more fully understand customer needs in specific contexts. Individual or group interviews about customer tasks and goals specific to the digital solution paint a very sharp picture of needs, goals, and behavior. Quantitative market research can quantify respective needs-based segments. The results are customer problems, customer journeys (descriptions of processes from the customer's point of view), and needs-based customer types (descriptions of goal- and motive-based target groups). This task is performed by customer experience experts.

In addition to customer needs, clarifying and building the foundations of technical requirements and framework conditions at an early stage is essential.

Development benefits from removing technical hurdles to possible functionalities at an early stage.

However, arguably more important than this basic work is to reflect on the findings from the business and customer requirements work and to begin considering solutions for how requirements can be implemented. This helps to consider technological possibilities and discard unrealistic ideas early on.

For the health insurance customer portal, once the business objectives were defined, dozens of customers were surveyed about their interaction with and administration of health insurance. This provided insights into what drives customers, which tasks were already well supported, and which less so. The deep understanding of the context then enabled new ideas and innovations to be generated. These insights allowed us to critically challenge ideas from within the organization.

It is often the very simple and self-evident functionalities, rather than the most technologically complex, that benefit customers most. The first approaches were already analyzed in collaboration with IT. In this way, it was already possible to roughly determine what was feasible and under what framework conditions. Functionalities that were needed anyway (basic functionalities) could be set up and partially implemented directly in this early phase. At the same time, the existing IT infrastructure was examined. Which technical components were available? How did these systems interact? Which interfaces existed, and which still needed to be built? This analysis developed a clear picture of the possibilities from a systems engineering perspective.

## 5.2 Prioritization and Definition

In this phase, customer experience management assumes the main responsibility, flanked by the business specialist department and development. The results of the first phase lead to prioritization and a roadmap that displays both the customer benefits and the feasibility of implementation. All roles are involved in the development process. The steering committee can already decide on which functionalities to implement in a first release: those that promise maximum benefit with acceptable complexity in implementation and that best support the business goals.

The prioritization is followed by the elaboration of the processes and the user interfaces. Here, too, giving the customer experience experts a lot of responsibility is a good idea. Defining epics and user stories in close coordination with business specialists and user experience designers leads to realistic requirements based on customer needs. The prototypes developed in this phase are sequences of screen designs (screen flows), as they should look in the final programmed system. These prototypes are then tested with users in an early phase. This leads to even more precise user stories and, most importantly, acceptance criteria (“Definition of Done” in agile frameworks), defined from the user’s point of view.

▶ **Definition** User stories and epics are used in agile development methods to define user requirements in a solution-neutral manner. Epics represent larger units of requirements that are then broken down into individual user stories. For example, "As an insurance customer, I want to be able to manage my insurance policies" is an epic that is detailed in several user stories: "As an insurance customer, I can see all my insurance policies at a glance", "As an insurance customer, I can change my address," etc.

Since the developers are already involved in the reviews, feasible alternatives can be identified. And the business department's involvement ensures that changes are also technically appropriate. The result is a very concrete target image, tested with real customers.

For the health insurance portal, multiple prototype runs resulted in viable and solid epics and user stories that required little further specification. Interactive collaboration saved time and money.

Defining the deliverable very concretely makes the complexity of implementation easier to estimate. In turn, this leads to better sprint planning. On the other hand, it is also easier for the business side, and management, to assess whether the deliverable meets expectations.

## 5.3 Implementation

From now on, the focus is on the technology, but customer orientation and business requirements serve as guardrails here as well. In this phase, collaboration between the parties is at its most intensive. A good understanding of each other's worlds and a willingness to work creatively and constructively on solutions are essential to achieving the joint goals. It is fundamental that the customer experience experts now work closely with the user experience designers, interaction designers, and developers. The functional managers must now provide quick answers. After all, what happens during the implementation when a query does not produce the expected results or a user interface element needs to be designed differently? In these cases, the fall back is the profound knowledge of needs from the previous phases. And this is possible because the customer experience experts are sitting at the same table. They know best what customers really need because they have screened the real behavior of customers in dozens of customer interviews and customer tests. If uncertainties remain, additional variants can be quickly tested with customers. It has been proven effective to either access customer panels online or test them in pre-planned test slots with detailed screens.

An important task for the customer experience experts is supporting the product owners by acting as sparring partners. In the heat of the moment, pragmatic and economic considerations often lead to decisions on content cuts that are central to the functioning of the overall concept.

In the portal project, customer experience experts worked closely with implementation partners and the client to develop, test, and implement the detailed screens. In the sprints, quick and efficient solutions were created that were convincing from technological, business, and customer perspectives. In close coordination with the product owner, new prioritizations were also made during sprints, always with the overall goal and the most important customer needs in mind.

Solutions often become more defined through the process: What happens if the portal cannot display PDF files directly from the data warehouse—an essential user requirement—due to system limitations? A "workaround" led to an email display, with attached files, that was very close to the central customer need, but technologically feasible with much less effort.

Another advantage of early prioritization based on customer benefits is that the communication for the commissioning of the system can be built on elements that show clear added value, both for the customers concerned and for the company itself. Together with the marketing department, campaigns can now be planned with a high probability of success. The clear roadmap across an initial release also enables storytelling across multiple releases.

## 6 Success Factors in a Nutshell

Agile and customer-centric approaches are not opposites. On the contrary, they are mutually dependent (*Agilemanifesto* 2001). Combined well, solutions can be convincing technologically, as well as from business and customer perspectives, and can be quickly launched on the market. In summary, the following factors are crucial for successful customer-centric and agile projects:

1. **Establish customer needs as a unifying element:** The goal of any business management trade must be to cover customer needs pleasantly and simply. When customer needs are solidly established as a kind of "north star," this forms a viable basis for decision-making across roles. Customer experience experts should also be directly involved throughout the project—from strategy to launch—to ensure a consistent customer focus.
2. **Design and implement in parallel, not one after the other:** Technical clarifications should not only play a role in the implementation phase. Rather, technical clarifications can be made at a very early stage of conception, when initial tendencies become apparent. This leads to a concept that considers technical hurdles at an early stage and is thus implemented faster and more closely in an agile manner through sprints.

   At the same time, the strategic and conceptual view should have a central role as a business and customer advocate, especially during implementation. Where tradeoffs, quick decisions with a holistic view, and further detailed concepts have to be worked out in the definition of user stories, the technical view must not dominate, since it is often the details that make the difference for customers and for business success.
3. **Enable cross-role collaboration and understanding in all phases:** Only when all people involved understand the "why" can they work toward a common goal. Having designers on the project team during the strategy phase and management representatives on the team when prioritizing implementation options prevents

misunderstandings and enables fast, focused work that fosters understanding for the whole initiative.

## References

*Agilemanifesto* (2001). http://agilemanifesto.org. Accessed 07.01.2019

Kano N, Seraku N, Takahashi F, Tsuji S-i (1984) Attractive quality and must-be quality. J Jpn Soc Qual Control 14(2):147–156

Norman DA, Draper SW (1986) User centered system design. New perspectives on human-computer interaction. Erlbaum Associates, Hillsdale, NJ

Oberholzer G, Leuthold S (2018) Customer experience monitor 2018. Stimmt AG, Zürich, Zürich

Osterwalder A, Pigneur Y (2011) Business model generation: Ein Handbuch für Visionäre, Spielveränderer und Herausforderer. Campus Verlag, Frankfurt am Main

**Glenn Oberholzer** is a founding partner of Stimmt AG and one of Europe's most established thought leaders in customer experience management. Based in Zurich with projects largely in Switzerland, Austria, Germany, and England, the consultancy has specialized for over 20 years in embedding customer focus in organizations and designing superior customer experiences for key moments in the customer's life cycle. As an electronics engineer ETH, he combines technological knowledge with profound experience to customer-centric development.

**Sandro Ruberti** is director at Stimmt AG and has won several prestigious awards for designing and supporting the implementation of digital solutions. Among them are several awards at the Best of Swiss Web. His background as a business economist at the University of St. Gallen and his years of experience in advising companies on value propositions, branding, and digital interactions enable him to be ever focused on customer needs, especially in IT-related projects, while never losing sight of the business priority.

# Voice and Speech Recognition for Banks and Insurance Companies

Jürg Schleier and Jakob Hauser

**Abstract**

The customer experience plays a crucial role in the foreground of intelligent customer relationship management. The latest technologies in the speech environment contribute greatly to optimize the customer experience. New approaches to speech recognition are already a reality today. In this article, this disruptive trend and the benefits that can be realized with it are highlighted.

## 1 Introduction

Customer experience plays a decisive role in intelligent customer relationship management. The latest technologies in the voice environment substantially contribute to a good customer experience. These new disruptive solutions are already a reality. In this chapter, we draw attention to the benefits of this area.

Voice and speech recognition is approaching us like a tidal wave. The first small waves are already visible, but on the horizon something very big is clearly heading our way.

We are already used to Siri, Alexa, and the new Sonos speaker or similar systems. Voice recognition is finding its way into the home and thus to people who previously had nothing to do with it. The list of well-known providers who want to

J. Schleier (✉)
Spitch AG, Zurich, Switzerland
e-mail: juerg@schleier.net

J. Hauser
TrustCom AG, Bern, Switzerland
e-mail: jakob.hauser@trustcom.ch



S. Kirchem et al. (eds.), *CRM Goes Digital*, Management for Professionals,
https://doi.org/10.1007/978-3-658-45798-3_12

play in the market with their own products is getting longer and longer: IBM Watson, Microsoft Cartana, Amazon Alexa, Apple Siri, Spitch AG, the list can almost be extended endlessly as it is growing constantly.

Speech recognition has similarly wide-ranging possible areas of application. These range from the simple recognition of a product or customer number spoken by a customer in a company's hotline queue (IVR) to the fully automated understanding, analysis, and evaluation of thousands of complete employee–customer conversations.

## 1.1 What Are the Different Disciplines of Speech Recognition?

Most of today's known applications of voice and speech recognition can be divided into the following areas:

- Automated Speech Recognition (ASR): The understanding and conversion of human speech. ASR is sometimes also referred to as STT (Speech-to-text).
- Voice Biometry (VB): The biometric testing and verification of a voice based on each person's unique voice characteristics.
- Text-to-Speech (TTS): The direct speech transmission of text, also sometimes referred to as synthetic voice.
- Emotion Detection: The recognition of human emotions and moods based on voice characteristics and/or spoken text. The latter is also referred to as sentiment analysis.
- Speech Analytics: The analysis and evaluation of (large amounts of) spoken or written speech. Who said what, when, how, and in what context.
- Statistical Semantics: The understanding and interpretation of sentences and word sequences; understanding the meaning of words.

Often, several of these disciplines are combined to produce meaningful results for the customer. For example, a bank wants to use speech recognition (ASR) to understand and serve customer requests without direct employee interaction. Moreover, by using voice biometrics (VB), the bank can additionally ensure that the person speaking on the phone is authorized to ask for the requested information.

Or a company may want to offer a voice-activated Interactive Voice Response (IVR) system that allows customers to independently and fully automatically request information about current orders. The "understanding" of the text spoken by the customer is thereby realized with ASR. The audio output of the requested information is provided by a synthetic computer voice (TTS).

## 1.2 What Is Automatic Speech Recognition (ASR) Suitable for and What Are Its Limitations?

Speech recognition can only understand what the system has been trained for in advance. Recognition values depend on the following three factors:

1. The acoustic quality of the audio signal. Just like human hearing, a Natural Language Processing (NLP) system (the AI-based science to understand language) can filter out certain background noise. However, if a fast train is running through in the background, understanding becomes difficult for the human as well as for the NLP system.
2. The vocabulary to be understood. The smaller the range vocabulary to be recognized is defined, the better the expected recognition rates will be. For example, if an NLP system has to recognize only four words, the recognition rate is always 100%. If 1000 words have to be recognized, there will be several that sound very similar and represent a possible source of error. The recognition rate drops marginally in this case. However, if 100,000 different words have to be recognized, the recognition rate drops further. Companies like Spitch try to take advantage of this circumstance by defining and training a "customer- and domain-specific vocabulary" in each case, whereas solutions like Siri and Google try to understand the entire vocabulary of a language, which is an approach that always reduces the recognition rate.
3. The available reference data. In speech recognition, the recognized audio signals are each compared with the available reference data and evaluated using AI, machine learning, and neural network technologies. In principle, the more reference data that can be used, the better the recognition rate. The aforementioned acoustic quality and vocabulary also play a role here.

If one or two of the previously mentioned points achieve only mediocre values, satisfactory speech recognition can still be achieved. However, if two or all three factors are of low quality, a good recognition result is no longer possible.

# 2 Biometric Voice Recognition Makes Closing the Deal with the Customer Easier

In addition to pure speech recognition, biometric voice recognition methods are continuously gaining acceptance. In this area, however, the wrong questions are often asked. In particular, prospective customers pursue the goal of using voice biometrics to make an already secure system much more secure. In most cases, however, this is a trade-off for customer and user friendliness. The customer basically wants only one thing: to access their data and services as easily, quickly, and intuitively as possible, with a guarantee that no unauthorized persons can access their data. In addition, it should be possible to adjust the security level to the risk. A bank does not want to prevent customers from doing business with it, nor does it want to make access to information difficult. This would lead to customer churn and make a mockery of voice recognition as a customer loyalty tool.

For the company, Voice Biometric (VB) Recognition offers the opportunity to significantly reduce call time for staff, as the customer has already been identified (the technology can recognize who is speaking) and verified (the technology can confirm identity) by the VB system (Fig. 1). For most banks, identifying and verifying the customer on the phone takes between 30 and 50 s. With typically 1000 or more calls per day for a mid-sized retail bank, the time savings can quickly amount to two-to-three fulltime employees, who could be used for more meaningful tasks like effective customer service.

By using a voice biometrics solution, the bank can set a very low yet sufficiently secure customer entry barrier for telephone service. For this purpose, the desired security levels (FAR) and (FRR) are defined on a case-specific basis, in close cooperation with the bank.

False Acceptance Rate (FAR): The percentage of identification instances in which unauthorized persons are incorrectly accepted.

False Rejection Rate (FRR): The percentage of identification instances in which authorized persons are incorrectly rejected.

It is important that biometric recognition is not considered in isolation. If the customer calls from a phone number known to the bank, states the correct customer name, asks for the correct account number, and the customer's biometric voice is confirmed as legitimate with a high FRR/FAR, then it is certainly appropriate to automatically give them their account information without any further security questions. However, if a transfer of several thousand US dollars is involved, then the FFR value should be considerably higher and the use of a further authentication factor is certainly recommended.

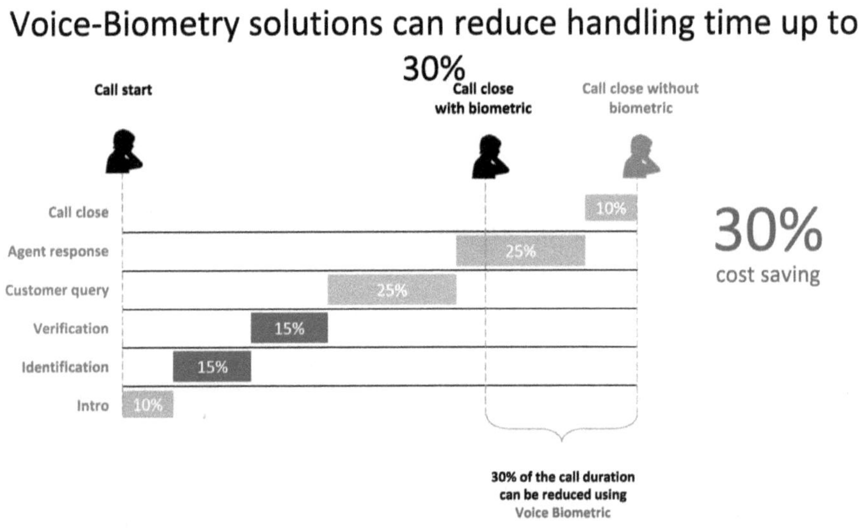


**Fig. 1** Voice-biometry solutions can reduce handling time

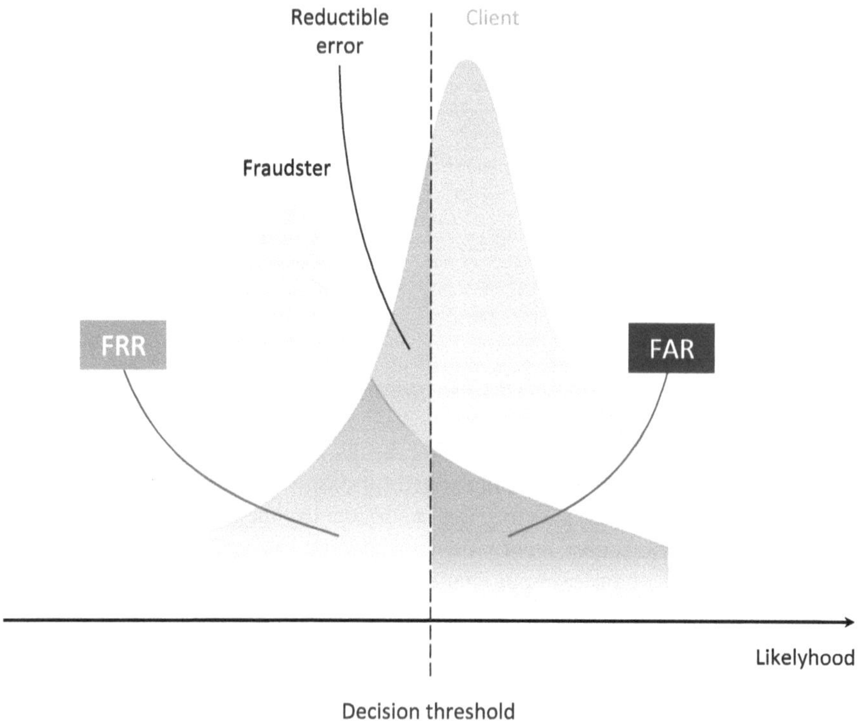


**Fig. 2** Case-driven decision

The trade-off between security and ease of use must always be decided on a case-by-case basis (Fig. 2). This applies to all security solutions.

## 2.1 Voice Biometrics Compared to Other Biometric Methods

Different biometric processes have different advantages and disadvantages. And not every method is suitable for every application. The factors to be weighed up are security requirements (how secure must it be), customer friendliness, technical feasibility, and costs (Fig. 3).

## 2.2 Voice Biometrics for Video Banking?

For around 40 years since the introduction of the first ATMs, banks have tried to make self-service palatable to customers. Video onboarding and video consulting have been further steps in reducing high branch costs and being able to serve customers "remotely," even for advice-intensive transactions. But even with video banking, customers need to be identified and verified. To avoid creating additional

| Characteristic | Fingerprints | Hand Geometry | Retina | Iris | Face | Signature | Voice |
|---|---|---|---|---|---|---|---|
| Easy of Use | High | High | Low | Medium | Medium | High | High |
| Error Incidence | Dryness, dirt, age | Hand injury, age | Glasses | Lighting | Lighting, age, glasses, hair | Changing signature | Noise, colds |
| Accuracy | High | High | Very high | Very high | High | High | High |
| User Acceptance | Medium | Medium | Medium | Medium | Medium | High | High |
| Long Term Stability | High | Medium | High | High | Medium | Medium | Medium |

**Fig. 3** Voice biometrics compared to other biometric methods

barriers to entry, security checks should be as customer-friendly as possible. Biometric voice recognition is ideally suited for this purpose.

During the initial login, the customer has to identify themself once, using an ID card. However, during subsequent video consultation sessions, the ID presentation can be omitted if the bank uses automatic biometric voice identification.

On the banking and solution-provider side, there are lots of ideas about how retail banking can operate more cheaply and efficiently, and about how to motivate customers toward more self-service. Banks occasionally make statements like, "We want our customers to increasingly inform themselves on our portal." However, customers will only accept these solutions on a broad scale if they see personal advantages. The device most frequently used by customers, the smartphone, is not suitable for inputs that go beyond a few letters or numbers. This is where an easy-to-use voice interface can lead to successful acceptance of new services.

Banks are trying to move customers away from the counter by making their counter services more expensive and complicated. Statistics show they are experiencing moderate success. Customers are apparently only partially switching to online offerings and are increasingly relying on the telephone. This behavior is adding to cost pressures.

A good combination of online offerings, voice recognition solutions, and a call center that focuses on special cases can be the answer here and help to reduce operating costs while increasing customer satisfaction. "Omni-channel" is the keyword here as banks seek a win–win for their customers and their business.

## 3 Why Today?

Voice and speech recognition has developed massively in recent years. Speech recognition rates today are very close to levels of human speech understanding. In some cases, these values are already exceeded. When customers call a company, they want (1) to be served quickly and efficiently; (2) to be understood correctly;

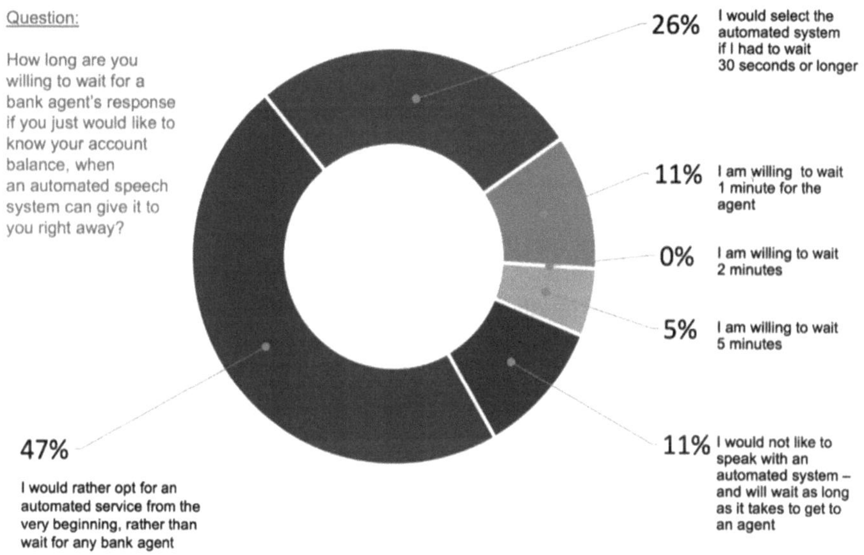


**Fig. 4** Result from survey at Swiss voice solutions provider Spitch

and (3) to receive the desired response or information. Most customers don't care whether the service is provided by a human or a computer.

Swiss voice solutions provider Spitch asked attendees at several customer events how long they would be willing to wait for service by a natural person, if the same response could be provided by a fully automated voice system (Fig. 4). Interestingly, 47% answered that they do not want to talk to a human at all for simple requests, and they would rather choose to use a voice recognition system. Twenty-five percent indicated that they would wait a maximum of 30 seconds for a face-to-face consultation.

An exciting study by CapGemini confirms these survey results and shows that today, 41% of consumers prefer a voice recognition system over a website and 49% even prefer a voice recognition system over contact with a call center employee (CapGemini 2018).

## 4 Data and Data Security

Data and data security play an essential role in the field of voice and speech recognition. All known NLP solutions are based on AI. The available reference data can significantly increase the speech recognition rates of the solution. One important question is therefore always, "Where does the reference data come from and was this data legally obtained?"

Companies using voice and speech recognition must comply with the legal regulations of the FDPIC (Swiss Federal Data Protection and Information Commissioner) in Switzerland and GDPR (General Date Protection Regulations) for the European Union area. The European Data Protection Regulation stipulates that the company that receives the customer's data (the so-called initiator) retains responsibility for compliance with the legal provisions, even if the company has a third party perform the data processing (the so-called processor). The company thus also remains liable for the external recognition and processing of customer voice data performed by a third party.

To make matters worse, at the end of 2020, both the European Union and Switzerland declared the "Privacy Shield" agreement with the US to be insufficient. This created an additional hurdle for the use of U.S.-based voice recognition solutions, because the companies that want to use these solutions must themselves ensure that their customer data is secure with the U.S. provider.

By means of the U.S. "Patriot Act" law, U.S. intelligence agencies can also demand access to the data of EU and Swiss companies managed at U.S. providers at any time.

There is of course a responsibility to customers as well, to ensure that their data is handled responsibly. This is where customers' greatest concerns about AI and NLP lie and is also evidenced by the CapGemini study mentioned earlier: "65% of respondents see risks in data protection." The Cambridge Analytica scandal is probably part of the background to this, and the careless handling of customer data by various U.S. companies has sensitized European data protectionists and customers to the data protection issue.

A company that wants to deploy solutions in the speech recognition sector should ask itself the following questions before moving ahead with a solution:

1. On the basis of what data does the solution being offered exist?
2. Can the provider demonstrate that it has legally obtained the reference data needed for the recognition solution?
3. Do I have the explicit consent of my customers to process the voice data (the active opt-in)?
4. Can the company trace, at any time, where the data is processed and evaluated, and in what form, and that all local legal requirements are complied with? This is especially important when working with foreign solution providers.
5. Can the company ensure, at any time, that the customer's voice data can be permanently deleted again at the customer's explicit request?

In many cases, the last two questions can only be reliably answered with "yes" if the speech recognition solution operates on the company's own systems (known as "on-premise").

## 5 Where Are the Possible Areas of Application?

NLP and AI are fundamentally based on statistical models. Simple and repetitive requirements are thus well suited for NLP. Replacing a complex customer consultation with an NLP system is a rather large and expensive undertaking. Inquiring about the account balance or similarly simple customer requests, on the other hand, are very well suited to a fully automated speech system.

Below are a number of application examples that lend themselves well to voice and speech recognition:

- Simple telephone queries, 24/7: What is my account balance? When is the next train from Zurich to Bern? What is the delivery time of XYZ?
- Simple phone orders, 24/7: Please block/unblock my credit card; Please load US$10 on my prepaid subscription; Ordering consumables.
- Identify biometrically via voice and/or reset password or order new password.
- Automatic call logs of calls that are often similar (e.g., bank advisor customer call logs).
- "Key word recognition" detection if predefined keywords occur in a conversation text. In the ongoing conversations or in the recordings, specific words or word sequences are searched for and an alarm signal is set in case of suspicion. For example, automatic detection of words and phrases that could indicate money laundering or tax evasion.

## 6 Two Concrete Use Cases in Switzerland and a Covid-19 Application in Russia

A large Swiss insurance company has decided to automate the "glass damage notification process" using voice recognition. The customer is taken step by step through the damage notification process by the voice recognition system. All information provided by the policyholder is received by means of natural speech, recognized, converted into text, and then the entire further processing procedure is started completely automatically. The first version of the system understands High German and Swiss dialects and is available 24 h a day, 7 days a week. The addition of further languages and the automation of further processes by means of speech recognition are planned in future.

A Swiss credit card company uses a "voice-to-text solution" that understands the Swiss dialect and processes it semantically. Instead of typing their way through a lengthy menu, customers can simply and naturally describe their concerns in the language of their choice. The customer concern is transcribed into High German in real time, semantically interpreted based on the company-specific AI logic, prioritized, and assigned to the right agent. This does not only improve the customer experience. Up to 30% shorter call times, higher first contact resolution, and shorter waiting times also pay dividends for the innovative solution. The transcripts serve both the agents, for an optimal entry into a professional conversation, and the Big Data analytics applications for which they can be further used.

In Spring 2020, a voice-based Covid-19 exit permit solution was developed for a Russian republic within 48 h.

In the first Covid-19 lockdown, a law was enacted that only people with a valid, time-limited, and justified "code" were allowed on the streets. Compliance was appropriately monitored by the police. Since not every household in the region had a computer, an automatic telephone system with voice recognition was set up. Each resident had to call the given phone number and verbally tell the system their personal details and the reason for the permit (e.g., grocery shopping, doctor's appointment, etc.). Afterwards, the caller received a code from the system automatically, which authorized their movement in public for a certain time. During the lockdown, the system automatically received an average of 25,000 calls per day and generated 15,000 codes per day.

## 7 When Does Voice and Speech Recognition Make Sense?

The voice and speech recognition wave is clearly rolling in. It makes natural sense to deal with the topic today and to gather initial experience.

The first question should be, "Are there possible business cases in our company that can be made more efficient using NLP?"

1. Does the selected business case make sense for the customer? Will the service be better, faster, or easier for the customer to use? Can customer satisfaction be increased?
2. Does the selected business case make sense for the company? How much capacity can it free up and to be used elsewhere? Can additional information and/or customers be gained? Will customer service be improved?
3. How much effort is required to create the NLP solution and how easy is it to integrate this solution into existing processes and infrastructure?
4. How easy is it to obtain and provide the required reference data?
5. Can the legal framework be complied with?

Speech and voice recognition is like Internet banking 15 years ago. It will increase efficiency, it can massively improve customer satisfaction, and it can reduce operations costs at the same time.

## Reference

CapGemini (2018) Conversational commerce. https://www.capgemini.com/wp-content/uploads/2018/01/conversational-commerce_brochure.pdf. Accessed March 4, 2021

**Juerg Schleier,** Country Manager DACH, Spitch AG, As a proven expert in voice and speech recognition solutions, Juerg Schleier has been responsible for the DACH region at NLP specialist Spitch AG for three years. Prior to that, he worked as a sales or country manager for various large IT and software companies such as BEA Systems, Oracle, Cisco, and CA for about 20 years.

**Jakob Hauser,** CEO TrustCom AG, Jakob Hauser has been active in the CRM, Contact Center, and Artificial Intelligence environment for more than 25 years. He is an expert in the digitalization of holistic customer interaction processes for large customers.

# Part III

# Use

# Customer Behavior in the New Normal: What Is Temporary and What Will Remain?

Sabine Kirchem and Juliane Waack

**Abstract**

COVID-19 has caused huge, irreversible changes all over the world. Lockdowns and social distancing have rapidly accelerated digitalization. But user behavior has also been forced to change. For companies, the question now is which behavioral changes are temporary and which are here to stay.

## 1 Purchasing Behavior in the Crisis

The pandemic has changed online retail purchasing behavior. According to a McKinsey report (Kohli S, Timelin B, Fabius V, Veranen SM, 2020):

- Customers shop at greater intervals; purchases are made less impulsively.
- Needs are prioritized differently, so that essentials (medicine, cleaning products, household goods) and product sustainability play a greater role.
- People seek cheaper variants and alternatives (depending on prioritization). For example, some kinds of products are more likely to be purchased and collected in bulk.
- The number of products in the (digital) shopping cart has also fallen.

Customers have therefore adapted their overall purchasing behavior to the conditions of the pandemic, but also to general crisis precautionary measures. In these

S. Kirchem (✉)
DIGITALL Nature Germany GmbH, Karlsruhe, Germany
e-mail: sabine.kirchem@digitall.com

J. Waack
Billwerk+ Germany GmbH, Berlin, Germany
e-mail: juliane.waack@billwerk.com


S. Kirchem et al. (eds.), *CRM Goes Digital*, Management for Professionals,
https://doi.org/10.1007/978-3-658-45798-3_13

particular areas, there is a strong presumption that post-pandemic behaviors will return somewhat to pre-pandemic norms, as current priorities are predominantly based on necessities or have been forced due to pandemic restrictions.

Ernst & Young have distinguished four customer groups in relation to the pandemic, which either react differently or are affected differently (EY, Rogers K, Cosgrove A, 2020):

Thirty-five percent of customers are saving while ensuring they have enough supplies. While they are less concerned that they personally will be severely affected by the pandemic, they do care about the future of their loved ones and therefore want to plan well.

Twenty-seven percent of customers—those most affected—are currently spending much less, whether due to financial worries, job insecurities, or health reasons.

Twenty-six percent have not changed their purchasing behavior and are not affected by the pandemic. Their biggest concern is rather the "hoarding" behavior of other customers.

Eleven percent are very concerned about the pandemic, but are financially secure and barely affected. This group—contrary to the behavior of the other groups—is currently spending more.

Ernst & Young expect many behaviors to shift or rebalance after the pandemic. Certain customer groups—especially those financially unaffected by the pandemic—will probably return to the market with more purchasing power, while customer groups that have suffered losses will remain frugal for longer.

But what specific characteristics could and can be observed among customers during the pandemic? And what changes will remain, keep developing, or regress after the pandemic? In what follows, we would like to highlight core trends in customer behavior identified in 2020.

## 2 Shift to Online Commerce

Lockdowns and social distancing have seen purchasing behavior naturally move toward digital offerings in many areas. While supermarkets are still preferred, particularly in the grocery sector, consumers in various industries were more likely to search for products and services in online stores in 2020 than before the pandemic.

A 2020 international study that asked customers about their purchasing behavior during the pandemic found that the following products were purchased more frequently online than in 2019 (UNCTAD 2020):

- Cosmetics
- Pharmaceuticals
- Electronics
- Furniture and household goods
- Tools
- Educational products

The big question will be for which industries customers still prefer the digital experience, even after the pandemic, and for which they will ultimately prefer the brick-and-mortar store. Particularly in cosmetics, but also furniture, the physical shopping experience is presumably necessary for a solid purchasing decision, since the smell, for example, but also the sense of comfort, cannot be fully reproduced through text and images.

At the same time, expectations of brick-and-mortar retail will be different. With the simplicity of digital order and delivery services, the demand for combined shopping experiences will probably increase. Customers will want more options, whether in-store research—which is often done online with a smartphone—or ordering options. Cross-channel options can expand the possibilities here, for example, through Click & Collect or Check & Reserve.

Click & Collect: Customers order products online, pay directly, then collect them from the nearest store. This supports local retailers, saves on delivery costs, and maintains the bond with the store. Meanwhile, customers can shop more flexibly.

Check & Reserve: Customers select products online and reserve them for checking and testing in the store. They do not have to purchase the product, and the product's presence is guaranteed. An advantage for stores is that products currently out of stock—such as certain sizes and colors—can be reordered.

Endless Aisle: Customers view all available product variations on in-store smart screens and order them if they are unavailable. This allows customers to access the entire product catalog, unlimited by the local inventory. The product is then delivered directly to the customer or to the store via Click & Collect.

## 3 Local Suppliers

Many studies of customer behavior during the pandemic have shown that customers are increasingly supporting local vendors and shop more regionally. Of the several reasons for this, not all concern vendor support:

- Contact restrictions and lockdowns reduce people's radius of travel, making nearby stores more useable. The pandemic's reduction of vacations and even day trips exacerbates this, as do the home offices of many telecommuters.
- Regional suppliers, especially local manufacturers, are less exposed to the supply chain constraints of restricted air travel, as well as the pandemic's workplace safety measures.
- Direct contact with local suppliers is more convenient, especially for questions about supply shortages. Goods returns and service problems can be discussed directly, and the entire process occurs without major detours.

According to the aforementioned Ernst & Young study, customers who expect an economic impact due to the pandemic are particularly keen to support locally produced goods: 42% would even pay more for them. A study of customers in the Southeast Asian region by United Overseas Bank found that more than 60% want to support local businesses (The Straits Times 2020). According to a survey by advertising provider Nextdoor, 72% of respondents also plan to shop more regionally in the long term.

## 4 Luxury Product Sales Are Dropping

Luxury products are currently experiencing a major crisis. First and foremost, this is certainly because many customers are shifting their purchasing priorities and buying more household products and necessities. Additionally, financially affected customers are currently more frugal. Customers are buying more groceries because they are working or studying at home and outings have been greatly reduced. Restaurant closures, some legally ordered, also reduce opportunities to dine out.

Meanwhile, spending on clothing and leisure has fallen sharply. In addition to frugality, the fact that people are spending much more time at home reduces spending. When outings, concerts, and other activities are no longer possible or permitted, spending naturally falls. Clothing is also often purchased in conjunction with events, which are currently largely cancelled. If you cannot go to the beach, you do not have to buy a new swimsuit.

The greatest cause of the decline in spending on luxury goods is the sharp drop in tourism numbers. In 2020, for example, small companies offering high-priced, handcrafted goods in tourist areas were particularly affected. Luxury fashion has also been affected, due to the loss of sales generated from fashion shows that were unable to take place or occurred with fewer visitors.

The absence of Chinese tourists has hit the luxury sector particularly hard. According to figures from consulting firm Bain, Chinese customers accounted for around one-third of total global luxury sales in 2018 (Bain 2018).

Furthermore, many suppliers are struggling due to a failure to expand online, in contrast to the fast-moving consumer goods market. The luxury customer also sees an exclusivity in the locality of stores, which is diluted by online stores.

It can be assumed that luxury goods customers will adjust their purchasing behavior again with new travel options after the pandemic. The problem here is not so much that customers will no longer need shopping trips, but that suppliers have abandoned their stores due to the lack of sales.

## 5 CSR Influence Is Growing

Corporate Social Responsibility—the measures, strategies, and philosophies a company implements to assume social responsibility—had already grown in importance before the pandemic, particularly in terms of customer loyalty. During the crisis, this influence increased significantly as various activities—employee treatment and what messages companies communicated—became more transparent than ever. In the aforementioned Ernst & Young study, customers that assumed the pandemic would have a strong economic impact placed a disproportionately high value on brands with a "purpose;" that is, brands pursuing a purpose customers shared. Accordingly, 62% were more likely to buy from companies making positive contributions to society.

Other studies reveal similar trends. When market analysts from YouGov asked German consumers how they rated the social attitudes of brands (Jahns 2020), 65% stated that they liked brands that openly communicate about and address social issues. However, this is only an advantage if companies treat these issues seriously. Customers pay attention to the difference between what is said and what is done.

Because CSR was already strongly positioned before the pandemic, companies presumably have to become more active after the pandemic, especially brands and industries that stand out due to lapses in the area. Poor working conditions at production sites in less developed countries, environmentally harmful products and manufacturing processes, and short half-lives in order to increase product cycles and sales have already been in critical focus during the pandemic, but customers will observe them much more carefully in future.

During the pandemic, customers have become much more attentive to the mechanics of consumption and manufacturing. Sudden supply shortages of essential products (e.g., toilet paper in spring 2020) have called outsourced production facilities into question. Supply chains, manufacturing conditions, and sustainability are increasingly important to purchasing decisions because they have sometimes been responsible for resource shortages and economic problems during the pandemic. Certainly, not all customers will retain this new perspective, but it will be more important than before the pandemic, especially due to climate change and other socio-economic issues.

## 6 Self Service Versus Personal Contact

The digitalization of the shopping journey increases the need for self-service solutions when customers are shopping online outside of service hours. For the many vendors who moved their business online due to the crisis, an initial challenge was accounting for the specifics in the digital space to create customer journeys that could match the analog experience. Self-service options in the analog space serve to reduce contact, particularly through self-service checkouts, but also information terminals and digital payment options. In some countries that previously offered hardly any self-service in stores, the pandemic alone has led to such options being introduced more frequently and more widely.

Customers are becoming more self-sufficient. On one hand, they have no choice; on the other hand, they have secure options to reduce human contact. This development will continue gradually after the pandemic.

However, increasing customer self-sufficiency results in a greater focus on moments that still happen in person, even in online commerce. For example, the charmingly personal email from a small bookstore that does not yet use marketing automation, a friendly service representative patiently assisting with a problem, or a helpful response to a tweet.

Customer service is particularly visible during a crisis because customers are already more sensitive beyond the actual customer journey; they feel more pressure due to restrictions in everyday life and worries about the future. A negative experience can be the proverbial straw that breaks the camel's back. Furthermore, if the crisis disrupts processes or reduces resources that delay packages or order processing, then customer service has to cushion the blow. Self-service offerings are important, but should not be the only option for customers. For example, in customer scenarios that often involve stress (e.g., bills, tech support, and health issues), phone is by far the preferred communication channel (CGS 2019).

According to another CGS study, the option to immediately contact a support representative is among the top three requirements for satisfactory customer service (CGS 2020). In addition, 44% of surveyed customers believe companies do not communicate how to contact customer service transparently enough.

## 6.1 An Example

A large telecommunications company offers customers a comprehensive self-service portal, help forums, and a contact form. Unfortunately, the portal suffers intermittent failures and the tone in the help forums is rather "rough." When seeking a contact person, one customer despaired because even the customer number provided only forwarded her to a chatbot, which was unable to help with her specific problem. Out of necessity, she turned to the company's Twitter profile and complained publicly.

She could in fact have reached a service contact via phone. But she needed to give the chatbot a very specific command, which was mentioned nowhere on the official service channels.

Obviously, the self-service options in this example were not sufficient to help the customer. What is more, the company—knowingly or not—"hid" the option to speak to a real service representative, so the situation escalated publicly on social media.

But of course, human contact must be positive. One in three customers lists friendly contact among the most important requirements of a positive service experience. Almost every second customer has had at least one negative service experience in recent months.

Especially in crisis situations, the need for empathy and positive interaction is higher. For Christmas 2020, one in two customers expected brands to design Christmas ads differently from previous years to better address the situation (Unruly, Waterhouse D, 2020). More customers wanted advertising messages that conveyed joy, warmth, and nostalgia. Informative or funny advertising, meanwhile, was secondary.

These needs do exist beyond advertising as well. In 2020, 64% of American B2C customers were depressed and/or anxious (McKinsey, Kohli S, Timelin B, Fabius V, Veranen SM, 2020). McKinsey therefore advises, among other things, that besides necessary process-related changes, the customer experience should be brought to the fore emotionally, remain responsive, and treat customers in a caring manner. This should not be a temporary pandemic priority; it can lead to stronger customer relationships and positive brand perception in the long term.

## 7 Loyalty

In recent years, with digitalization, customers have become increasingly "jumpy" when it comes to brand loyalty. This is certainly thanks to globalization, which offers many more options, product variety, and an almost infinite selection, even of unusual products and services, especially online. Whereas customer loyalty in brick-and-mortar retail was often shaped by customers' lack of other local options or due to their choice of favorites from a manageable number of suppliers, the Internet, with all its marketplaces, swap meets, and retailers, is a tempting source of alternatives.

Interestingly, however, the pandemic has prompted a return to the familiar, whether it is local vendors or brands that resonate with customers through their messaging and experiential journeys. As a result, customers are not only shopping more locally but also spending more money on brands that are trustworthy (EY 2020).

During a crisis, emotions are often important factors in decisions, but they are not always transparent. Customer psychologist Kit Yarrow explains in an interview with uschamber.com that people look for "allies" in stressful situations (Thau 2020). Companies on the side of their customers in word and deed, that support them, and take their problems seriously, are far more likely to be recognized as "allies." According to Yarrow, it is very important that this is not only communicated, but also actually implemented. Customers are once again paying more attention to real action, not least because the pandemic has provoked recognition of the need for people in system-relevant professions, for certain industries (for example, in the production of hygiene products), and for clear statements (companies that allow their employees to work from home).

This change in perspective will certainly have a post-pandemic impact. In 2019, the attractiveness of Direct-2-Consumer—i.e., companies that sell their products directly to customers without intermediaries—had risen already. The reason is the often direct communication and clear transparency of production conditions. Suppliers who communicate directly with their customers appear more authentic and can respond better to feedback. Even before the pandemic, customers felt the need to be closer to companies. The pandemic has only heightened this need.

## 8 Data Generosity

With the sometimes-forced shift to digital shopping, many customers need to evaluate how much data they want to share online. It is true that many online stores now offer so-called "guest accounts," which allow shoppers to make purchases without registering for a customer account. But presently, this far from the norm, and the customer account has more advantages than a temporary guest account, especially when it comes to tracking.

Concerns about data security are often closely linked to regional and cultural peculiarities. Particularly in the DACH region, the use of social media, and also cashless payment and smartphone shopping, is delayed and restrained. In China, for example, shopping via smartphone, conducting official business, and exchanging private messages, all through an app interface, is part of everyday life. In contrast, German users are often still seeking solutions that function as separately as possible, since it is generally considered unsafe to share too much data with one single app. One in three German consumers think personal data cannot be protected online (Statista, Brandt M, 2019). Yet, according to Deloitte, 46% of all consumers agreed to use personal data more often during the pandemic in order to be more comfortable in the digital space (Deloitte 2019). In the same study, more than 80% of respondents expected to be more critical of data use again after the pandemic.

However, it is precisely here that we should wait and see how behavior really develops. From a psychological perspective, it would be much more inconvenient for customers to change the "new" behavior again. The longer the pandemic lasts, the more customers get used to sharing their data sooner. Furthermore, many cases will result in positive experiences, such as existing customer discounts or easier access to support channels. The plan to return to data-saving and provider-critical behavior after the pandemic does not necessarily have to occur, especially if the new behavior adds value.

Incidentally, providers can also have a positive impact by clearly highlighting and enabling customers to experience the added value provided by customer accounts and personal data.

## 9 Conclusion: Back to the New Normal?

The new normal can be understood as a new status quo: customer behavior, markets, technologies, and society are changing continuously, making long-term planning for specific behaviors increasingly difficult. Companies need to become more flexible, more attentive to customer feedback, and more adept at interpreting customer behavior.

Not everything established in the new normal will remain after the pandemic. Despite speculation that people will shop, travel, and live more regionally, it is possible that travel opportunities after such extended restrictions will create an entirely new "travel boom."

At the same time, the shift toward social issues and how they are publicly embraced and acted upon by companies will potentially endure for the long term, as customers now have and want more direct contact with suppliers through social media. Customers can now engage in a public dialogue with companies, so companies need to be clearer about what "voice" they want to express in that dialogue.

In addition, some changes are currently not clearly foreseeable. Some studies cited in the chapter assume that some customers will be more frugal after the pandemic, while others will once again shop more extensively. How behavior actually develops depends on numerous variables, many of which retailers cannot directly influence. However, this is precisely why close customer contact is important, so retailers keep sight of their own clientele beyond the forecasts. Regardless of whether customers shop in person or digitally, frugally or generously, locally or globally, decisive fundamentals will be interaction, communication, and community.

## References


Bain & Company (2018) The personal luxury goods market delivers positive growth in 2018 to reach €260 billion—a trend that is expected to continue through 2025. https://www.bain.com/about/media-center/press-releases/2018/fall-luxury-goods-market-study/ Accessed: 05 Oct 2022

Brandt M (2019) Deutsche fürchten sich besonders vor Datenmissbrauch. https://de.statista.com/infografik/3220/angst-vor-datenmissbrauch-bei-internetnutzern/. Accessed: 05 Oct 2022

CGS (2019) CGS survey reveals consumers prefer a hybrid AI/human approach to customer service. Is there Chatbot Fatigue? https://www.cgsinc.com/en/resources/2019-CGS-Customer-Service-Chatbots-Channels-Survey. Accessed: 05 Oct 2022

CGS (2020) 2020 CGS Customer Services Preferences in Times of Distress Survey. https://www.cgsinc.com/en/resources/customer-service-in-crisis. Accessed: 05 Oct 2020

Deloitte (2019) How Covid-19 changes consumer behavior long-term. https://www2.deloitte.com/de/de/pages/consumer-business/articles/consumer-behavior-study-covid-19.html. Accessed: 05 Oct 2022

Jahns M (2020) Studie: Kunden belohnen Haltung bei Marken. https://www.ispo.com/maerkte/studie-kunden-belohnen-haltung-bei-marken. Accessed: 05 Oct 2022

Kohli S, Timelin B, Fabius V, Veranen SM (2020) How Covid-19 is changing consumer behavior - now and forever. https://www.mckinsey.com/~/media/mckinsey/industries/retail/our%20insights/how%20covid%2019%20is%20changing%20consumer%20behavior%20now%20and%20forever/how-covid-19-is-changing-consumer-behaviornow-and-forever.pdf. Accessed: 05 Oct 2022

Rogers K, Cosgrove A (2020) The EY Future Consumer Index on behavior and sentiment across five key markets shows how the pandemic is creating new consumer segments. https://www.ey.com/en_us/consumer-products-retail/how-covid-19-could-change-consumer-behavior. Accessed: 05 Oct 2022

Thau B (2020) A consumer psychologist details what businesses need to know during COVID-19. https://www.uschamber.com/co/good-company/launch-pad/consumer-psychologist-explains-effects-of-coronavirus. Accessed: 05 Oct 2022

The Straits Times (2020) Half of Singapore consumers prefer to shop local to help firms hit by Covid-19: Survey https://www.straitstimes.com/business/economy/half-of-singapore-consumers-prefer-to-shop-local-to-help-covid-hit-firms-survey. Accessed: 05 Oct 2022

United Nations Conference on Trade and Development (2020) Covid-10 and E-commerce findings from a survey of online consumers in 9 countries. https://unctad.org/system/files/official-document/dtlstictinf2020d1_en.pdf. Accessed: 05 Oct 2022

Waterhouse D (2020) UK consumers looking to advertisers to lift festive spirits this christmas. https://unruly.co/news/article/2020/10/21/uk-consumers-looking-to-advertisers-to-lift-festive-spirits-this-christmas/. Accessed: 05 Oct 2022

**Sabine Kirchem** is the Vice President of Marketing and Communications at DIGITALL. She began her career in the consulting industry and developed the areas of market research and corporate communications in different companies. Throughout her career, she has gained extensive knowledge in the CRM environment and is well-versed in current trends and technologies, such as cloud services, customer journey, and social media, thanks to her flair for innovation topics. Additionally, she is an author and has contributed to the creation of several books and written studies, and published numerous specialized articles on customer journey, CRM, and cloud computing.

**Juliane Waack** is a senior content marketing manager and manages company blogs, develops marketing campaigns and supports colleagues with any writing-related tasks.

She has more than 14 years of experience as a writer with a focus on content marketing, social media, SEO, digitalization, and corporate communication. She is particularly interested in preparing complex technical topics in easy-to-understand formats and enjoys researching innovative tech topics and developing creative ways to present them.

# Swiss Re Corporate Solutions: Transforming a Traditional CRM System into a Customer Engagement Management (CEM) Solution

Tobias Mäder

**Abstract**

B2B insurance is characterized by tailored offerings and higher premiums, with intermediaries pivotal in structuring insurance programs. Relationship management extends beyond sales to include functions like Underwriting, Claims Management, and Operations. Marketing in B2B insurance focuses on distributing tailored risk knowledge to known customer bases rather than generating leads. Strategic relationship management competencies include Sales Management, Customer Insights, and Digital Marketing, aiming to enhance customer and broker servicing quality.

## 1 Introduction: Swiss Re Corporate Solutions, the Commercial Insurer of the Swiss Re Group

Swiss Re Corporate Solutions (CorSo) is the commercial insurance arm of the Swiss Re Group. The business unit was established in 2010 and is headquartered in Zurich, Switzerland. It employs more than 2500 people globally.

CorSo operates on a Business-to-Business basis (B2B), providing corporate risk transfer solutions, risk services, and risk partnerships. Most insurance products are sold through specialized insurance brokers, that is, intermediaries acting on behalf of their customers. Insurance brokers play an important role in structuring insurance programs for corporate customers and representing them in their search for the best offering with different commercial insurers.

B2B insurance purchasing processes differ as they are multifaceted, as opposed to selling insurance directly to individual consumers. The corporate customer base

T. Mäder (✉)
Swiss Re Corporate Solutions, Zürich, Switzerland
e-mail: tobias_maeder@swissre.com


S. Kirchem et al. (eds.), *CRM Goes Digital*, Management for Professionals, https://doi.org/10.1007/978-3-658-45798-3_14

is usually more finite, requesting bespoke offerings, and the premium per policy is substantially higher. Corporate customers and their brokers have multiple touch-points with commercial insurers. A close or personal relationship may impact customer loyalty and hence represent a competitive advantage. Managing relationships and engagement with customers and brokers is not restricted to Sales. It also stretches across all insurance functions, such as Underwriting, Claims Management, and Operations. The harmonization of processes and technologies driven by a holistic customer strategy is the foundation of superior customer and broker management.

Whilst sales processes and customer insights across all customer-facing teams impact the customer and broker-servicing quality, these practices are closely interlinked with marketing. Digital marketing in commercial insurance is less about generating more leads (a lead is characterized as an individual linked to an organization with an interest in a company's offering), since the core customer base is largely known by established market players. It is all about identifying the actual needs of a target audience and distributing tailored risk knowledge more effectively. With B2B insurance, digital marketing is not designed to reach anonymous masses through social selling and identify the ultimate lead. Nomination of the relevant marketing audience (i.e., microtargeting) is rather driven by a sophisticated segmentation process of customers and brokers, based on intelligent customer profiles.

In essence, relationship management in B2B insurance is based on three strategic competencies (Fig. 1):

- Sales Management—articulating the sales value proposition and competitive market advantage.
- Customer Insights—generating insights across all customer-facing teams for high-quality servicing.
- Digital Marketing—utilizing engagement data to tailor relevant information to the target audience.

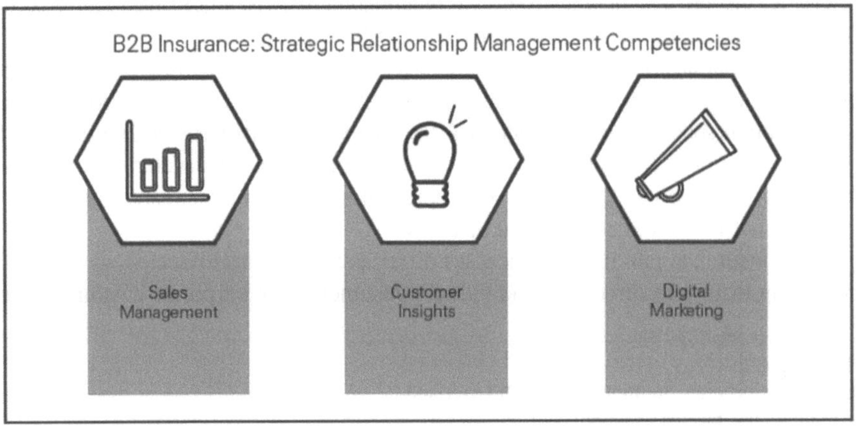


**Fig. 1** Strategic relationship management competencies in B2B insurance

## 2 Customer Strategy: Swiss Re Corporate Solutions Deepening Customer-First Culture

A customer-centric approach has been essential for CorSo since its inception to meet increasingly complex risk-management needs, which in turn create new business opportunities. Major trends and challenges are reshaping the corporate risk landscape and business models. These forces are redefining corporate demands and expectations of commercial insurers, which CorSo meets by growing complex international programs operations, including supply chains, tech-driven transformation, as well as expanding the relevance of sustainability and cross-industrial partnerships.

Through a customer-centric approach, insurers must respond to these challenges by enhancing the customer experience and the services offered. These can be achieved by providing risk knowledge combined with data- and tech-driven solutions and by supporting the co-creation of new ecosystems across industries.

CorSo is well positioned in the evolving corporate risk landscape. Indeed, in recent years it has invested significant effort and resources into building a deeper understanding of its customers, while working on differentiating offerings such as Primary Lead and Innovative Risk Solutions. For future success, CorSo will leverage data and technology to stay at the forefront of the industry. The emphasis will continue to systematically gather insights on CorSo's customer needs, their industries, and expand existing relationship intelligence.

To deliver value, it is paramount for CorSo to facilitate needs-based customer value propositions. The critical starting point is the generation of relevant customer insights. The key element in delivering these insights to the business lies in engagement-enabling technology. This entails a digital transformation of the way CorSo engages within and across its business and with customers themselves. It involves applying advanced analytics to create a 360-degree view of CorSo's customers.

Leveraging new technologies and data enables a fundamental shift in ways of working. It means that customer managers will gain more time to focus on customer engagement and generating value for those customers.

## 3 Insurance Industry Trend: Legacy CRM Applications Causing Operational Inefficiencies

Aligning strategy and technology permits businesses to approach both problem-solving and innovation with greater agility and consistency. However, it is essential to realize that this endeavor is not a one-off action. In the early 2000s, commercial insurers made substantial investments into new generation Customer Relationship Management (CRM) solutions. At that time, single-vendor CRM systems were praised as the gold standard of business applications. In recent years, most companies maintained "one-size-fits-all" CRM solutions in isolated environments, rather than incorporating these into everyday business practices.

CorSo has experienced a similar effect. For years, it has invested heavily in its proprietary IT infrastructure, turning into a competitive advantage. While CorSo's core business applications were modernized over the years, the company continued to operate its external CRM platform with limited integrations. In the past, CorSo's CRM practices were restricted to sales functions supported by the following system capabilities:

| | |
|---|---|
| Account management | Accounts represent the foundational element of any CRM application, covering basic entity information such as company name, address, and management of its lifecycle stages (target, prospect, customer). In its initial configuration, accounts act as the central hub of all contextual sales management activities |
| Contact management | Contacts are associated with accounts and enable consistent recording and tracking of human interactions, that is, they mainly relate to the manual creation of discussion notes. Central contact management further serves as the master data management platform for company-wide nomination of contacts in the context of the Net Promoter Score (NPS) process |
| Pipeline management | Pipeline management refers to the tracking of leads (accounts across all lifecycle stages) and opportunities throughout all sales phases. In simple terms, a pipeline provides an overview of the expected revenue, including conversion ratios |
| Account planning | Enabling systematic and consistent bottom-up planning of growth targets, facilitating the allocation of resources, and prioritization of actions. An annual strategic process supports the achievement of strategic business objectives |

These core CRM capabilities were supplemented with base CRM application features such as sales campaign management, tasks management, document management, reporting, and dashboard visualization.

A, industry-wide trend characterized by the lack of upgrades, integrations, and process alignments leads to the following operational inefficiencies:

- Extensive manual effort to obtain holistic and accurate information about customer relationships.
- Data integrity and quality deficiencies result from compiling from multiple disconnected sources.
- A growing information gap impacts customer-facing teams due to the lack of relevant insights.

In consequence, CorSo concluded that its sales-centric legacy CRM solution was not suited to expand its customer-first strategy across all customer-facing teams to enable best-in-class customer and broker experience. This realization resulted in a fresh approach, entailing delivery of a digital strategy that has transformed CorSo's sales-focused CRM system into a more holistic Customer Engagement Management (CEM) platform, which has the following priority functions:

- Elimination of redundant system capabilities by utilizing CorSo's IT infrastructure investments.
- Provision of an insights tool, changing a data-entry culture into data-consumption culture.
- Delivering insights into the native business applications by introducing a service-based architecture.

Transforming legacy CRM technology into a data-driven CEM solution and leveraging proprietary technology and data is not simply a matter of "in-housing" core sales management capabilities. CorSo's objective was to introduce a more holistic CEM solution and expand across all customer-facing teams, generating a new layer of customer insights. The goal was to position the new CEM platform as the central intelligence hub, to expand the sales management capabilities with enhanced customer insights, and to act as an integration point into digital marketing. Essentially CorSo had formulated its ambition to put all customer-relevant data to work to empower its employees to drive decision-making.

## 4 Digital Vision: Transforming Swiss Re Corporate Solutions' Legacy CRM into an Insights Platform

Successful digital transformation requires a bold vision and thinking outside boundaries. CorSo's goal was not to fix a market-standard CRM tool but to do things differently and deliver an intelligent platform with significant business impact. The main business driver was to strengthen CorSo's customer-first culture by targeting a higher engagement level with its customers and brokers.

Throughout the process of developing the digital strategy, two things were crucial:

1) Practicality of the digital transformation strategy.
2) Gaining management support to pursue a bold strategy.

The following themes set the direction of CorSo's digital transformation strategy:

| | |
|---|---|
| Leverage Swiss Re Technology | Dealing with data, enhanced analytics, and technology is part of Swiss Re's DNA. CorSo's ambition was to leverage its native IT environment and eliminate redundant system capabilities, including data capture. The analysis phase revealed that most CRM capabilities provided by CorSo's external vendor solution were already embedded in CorSo's proprietary business applications. This led to a "paying more than you need" effect. The focus, then, was to utilize the native IT infrastructure and make the new CEM solution an integral part of CorSo's core business applications. This is driving re-usability, lowering costs, and raising efficiency, reliability, and consistency |

| | |
|---|---|
| Introduce data-driven culture | In the age of digitalization, insurers have access to an unprecedented volume of information. In contrast to the initial phases of CRM where there were integration limitations, today's technologies provide flexible data integration and analytics capabilities. CorSo's strategy in this context is a company-wide effort to make better use of information, supporting its ambition to become a data-driven commercial insurer. Supported by a robust governance framework, this effort empowers the entire organization to democratize all relevant data sources. The design and implementation of CorSo's CEM platform reflects legal, regulatory, and contractual requirements and adopts good practice in relation to areas such as data protection, privacy, and fair competition, as well as ensuring that we meet customer expectations. Moreover, it enables the organization to construct contextual customer insights based on advanced analytics, which delivers more personalized services. This process has triggered the transformation from a data-entry to a data-consumption culture |
| Make the target system invisible | Sales-centric CRM systems are important to every organization. That said, users often perceive such systems as administrative tools by nature. Having to manually register calls, track relationship activities and sales progress mainly results from poor system architecture. On the other hand, demand to increase the usage beyond sales functions is low. Key to overcoming these challenges is to expand the value of insights across all business functions and to provide a holistic CEM relationship overview on one platform. The system architecture design is key to avoid a system overload—In other words, the need to access too many applications<br>CorSo's desire was to move away from one single vendor solution and to deliver a "bouquet" of CEM services across the core business applications of all customer-facing teams. Eventually, a service-based system architecture will enable the delivery of contextual customer insights to the users in their native environment, without switching from one system to another |
| Foster technological innovation | Growing out of a "one-size-fits-all" external CRM solution does not rule out the option of searching for complementary innovative niche technology and aiming for its re-usability across the organization. An important topic here was CorSo's ambition to introduce business relationship intelligence with customers and brokers. Whilst standard CRM solutions offer integrations into established social media network platforms, CorSo took an alternative approach. In the B2B space, traditional social media network tools do not help in understanding an insurer's relationship strength with its customers and brokers. CorSo has addressed this challenge by analyzing, visualizing, and contextualizing various internal and external information sources and converting metadata into relationship insights |

## 4.1 Architecture View: Leverage Swiss Re Technology and Utilize Data

CorSo's implementation was divided into multiple phases. Focusing on service-based design principles has allowed it to deploy capabilities as components and services in a consumer-agnostic architecture, providing higher flexibility in combining many internal and external services. Consistent application of agile principles helps strengthen cross-functional co-development of outcome-driven reusable services. In turn, this enables organizations such as CorSo to integrate existing application components in a single harmonized web front-end. This has resulted in the replacement of CorSo's vendor-based CRM solution. Here are the benefits of this internal delivery decision:

- Introducing a consistent user front-end that automates everyday business processes.
- Removing redundant capabilities by integrating (reusing) application components.
- Changing from a data-entry approach toward a holistic data-consumption culture.
- Building the foundation to distribute customer insights across business applications.
- Eliminating third-party licensing costs for an external market standard CRM solution.

> "The key to winning in this new digital age is to put your data to work, empowering your employees so that they can make winning decisions" says Prasad Naik, Technical Area Lead Customer Engagement at Swiss Re Corporate Solutions.

A strong focus on a public cloud and a flexible architecture approach enabled CorSo to connect proprietary application components and various data sources into one front-end, supported by an analytics backbone that generates actionable insights. Introducing a single engagement layer harmonizes business, logic, process functions, system services, and data sources. Figure 2 represents the vision architecture of CorSo's holistic CEM platform:

The emphasis of CorSo's CEM platform (internally branded "Customer 360") is enhancing its sales management capabilities. A new analytics layer of customer insights was generated. This was created from various systems of records and engagement tools centered around accounts and contacts, including integrating external tools such as digital marketing and customer feedback management. CorSo's CEM platform is built on an enhanced data analytics framework that produces contextual insights for the relevant business function.

> "Customer 360 – CorSo's new CEM platform – is transformational in addressing the inverse relationship we had with 'data in' vs 'value out' for our users, ultimately leading to better relationship and customer engagement" says Paul Fitzgerald, Global Distribution Management Leader at Swiss Re Corporate Solutions

Following the themes of CorSo's digital strategy ("leverage Swiss Re technology" and "introduce data-driven culture"), the delivery of the CEM platform represented a key step in the agile digital transformation journey. CorSo's CEM approach

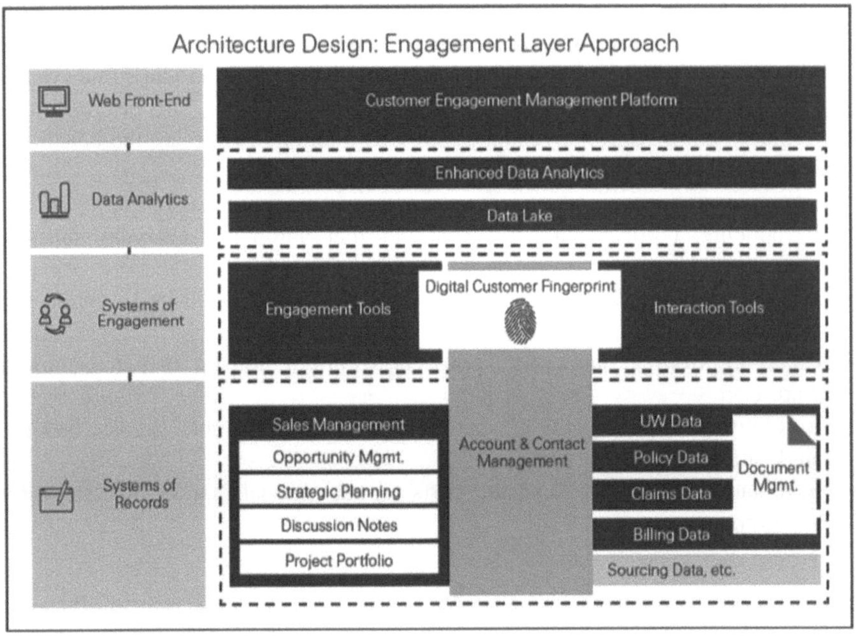


**Fig. 2** Four-layer CEM application architecture representing CorSo's digital vision

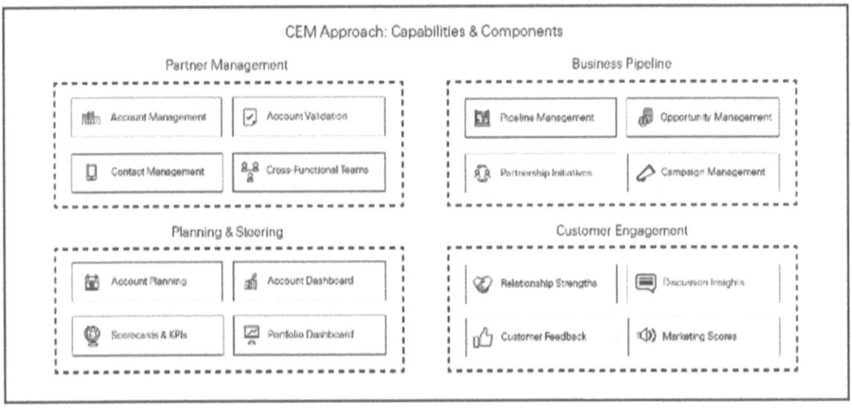


**Fig. 3** Core customer engagement management capabilities and components

(Fig. 3) was not restricted to sales-centric CRM capabilities but offered a new set of capabilities and components:

| | |
|---|---|
| Partner management | CorSo's account management capabilities no longer cover entity and address data solely used to associate sales activities. The new components include a high degree of automation and sophistication, covering:<br>- Single entity validation (KYC) against external sources, increasing data quality.<br>- Grouping a company's universe[a] of entities, enabling reporting consistency.<br>- Contact record creation, derived email signatures, including entity resolution.<br>- Classifying customer-servicing employees across all customer-facing teams.<br>The partner management practice has evolved into the CorSo-wide company and contact repository. This leverages external legal entity and regulatory compliance databases and automates the KYC processes, including auto-association of related contacts. Partner management acts as the data backbone of CorSo's customer data management with embedded data quality standards and enhanced information integrated into the central customer profile |
| Business Pipeline | The Business Pipeline capability was extended to cover CorSo's full sales activities for traditional risk transfer solutions and more complex partnership projects, including sales campaigns. Any expected revenue generation (premium or fees) will be managed centrally, supported by visual pipeline representation |
| Planning and Steering | The Planning & Steering capability enables "true" 360-degree views of customer and broker business activities, turning the new CEM tool into a data-driven engagement platform. Planning covers the forward-looking elements of strategic positioning and forecasting. Steering is represented by portfolio- and account-level dashboards with a holistic account overview based on the data sourced from the core business applications. Planning and steering values converge into scorecard views that indicate the business development against the plan |
| Customer engagement | The customer engagement capability acts as the central customer intelligence hub, converting transactional engagement, interaction, and business information into a globally consistent customer insights view introduced as a digital customer fingerprint. The purpose of the digital customer fingerprint is to standardize relevant information and turn it into actions. The digital customer fingerprint is agnostic to platforms and can be distributed into any CorSo business application. The main components of the customer engagement capability are:<br>- Relationship network generation of "who knows who"<br>- Customer interaction capture, including topic modelling<br>- Central feedback management, including user actioning<br>- Digital marketing integration (nomination and analytics) |

[a]Concept combining all validated and non-validated company entities that belong to the same global group of companies into one cluster; account clusters facilitate the retrieval of the corresponding business data and are the baseline for generating consistent account and portfolio views in CorSo's CEM platform

## 4.2 Service-Based Architecture: Making the Swiss Re Corporate Solutions' Insights Platform "Invisible"

In a second phase, CorSo expanded its service-based architecture with an inclusive service catalogue to bring contextual insights and CEM system components directly into the native business applications of its customer-facing teams. The CEM platform was no longer restricted to a single application front-end but instead provided a flexible service offering. Uniquely, there is not one web front-end in existence combining sales management, customer insights, and digital marketing capabilities. The new service-based architecture represents a paradigm change as core business teams are now presented as real-time contextual customer and broker insights, delivered directly into their business applications.

Reusable services make the establishment of an infrastructure enabling more intuitive customer and intermediary journeys possible. Such an infrastructure can serve multiple consumers and use-cases delivered as:

- Consumable Business Application Programming Interfaces (API).
- A micro front-end to integrate where visualization is an asset.

Figure 4 visualizes the interplay of insights and services:

The Digital Customer Fingerprint represents the Composition Layer (business logic) that processes all account and contact-related real-time data, turning these into insights. Transactional data is taken from the following systems and transformed into a consistent insights view:

- Systems of engagement that process and aggregate customer response and behavioral data.
- Systems of interaction that transform different data points into a business relationship network.
- Systems of records that provide account performance history and strategic (forward-looking) views.

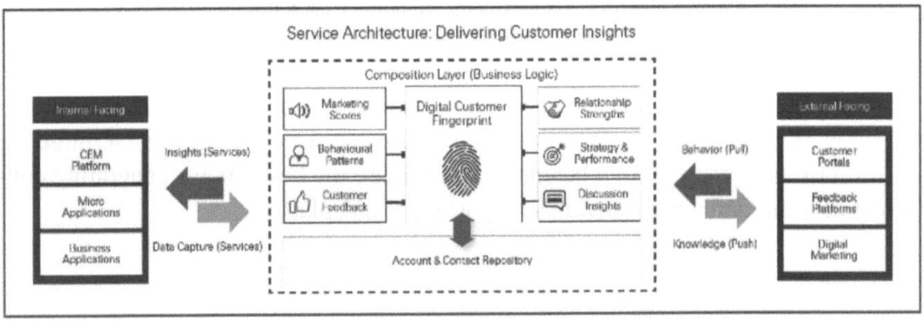


**Fig. 4** Digital Customer Fingerprint representing the customer insights composition layer

For example, the Digital Customer Fingerprint transforms data into a holistic view such as the strategic positioning of an account (derived from account plans), relationship views of "who knows who," and it aggregates behavioral insights extracted from external engagement platforms. The concept of the Digital Customer Fingerprint is flexible and spans all customer-facing teams. New account or contact-level insights will be integrated into the Digital Customer Fingerprint and contribute to the 360-degree view of customer or broker accounts.

The Composition Layer is the key enabling element to steer relevant customer insights into any internal-facing application, such as:

- CorSo's CEM platform, also known as Customer 360.
- Email clients via plugin, delivering contextual insights.
- Business applications, for example, for Underwriting and Claims.

In reverse, new customer data captured via the internal-facing business tools (data capture service) will be processed centrally and embodied by the Digital Customer Fingerprint. CorSo has eliminated its data-capturing redundancy, introduced a company-wide data-consumption culture, and transformed its sales-centric CRM into a CEM insights solution utilized by all customer-facing teams. Following the flexible IT architecture, the Digital Customer Fingerprint can be consumed as a global service via API or integrated through a micro front-end by any business application.

> "Our vision was to transform our legacy CRM system into a data-driven insights solution and make it invisible (headless) by transferring relevant insights into the native business applications of the market-facing teams" says Tobias Mäder, Digital Transformation Leader at Swiss Re Corporate Solutions

Beyond the distribution of customer insights, the Digital Customer Fingerprint is also used to nominate contacts for digital marketing campaigns, feedback requests, and other engagement activities. The Digital Customer Fingerprint provides consistent functional and relationship content at the contact level. This has significantly changed how CorSo nominates contacts for marketing and feedback requests. In return, CorSo can systematically and centrally capture the customer's behavior; this leads to better content push and product recommendations, as well as internal actioning.

## 4.3 Technology Innovation: Unlock CorSo Network Relationships Based on Interaction Data

One of the biggest challenges in B2B insurance is to understand an insurer's business relationships with its customers, brokers, partners, and suppliers. Business relationships are connections among single contacts associated to a business account. The stronger the network, the greater the potential for success. A close or even personal relationship has a decisive influence on loyalty and can be a competitive advantage.

Traditional CRM systems and conventional social media network platforms do not solve the problem of providing transparency into a company's relationships with its stakeholders. CRM applications are limited to manually capturing contact data, tracking business relationships, or narrowly integrating with social media platforms as social media accounts are proprietary to their subscribers, that is, the employee and their connections. On the other hand, their social media connections rather represent loose relationships; how many social media connections can be deemed strong enough to be used in a corporate environment?

Considering these challenges, CorSo has established a dynamic business relationship network intelligence solution by introducing innovative technology. CorSo's focus was to identify different sources of interactions and transform these data points into a dynamic relationship network. This form of "who communicates with whom" represents a technological innovation, since it leads to calculating relationship strengths in real time. These calculations are based on the intensity of interactions and provide a multi-dimensional network view of individual contacts.

The underlying data sources are key for network intelligence. While interaction data addresses the problem of the existing customer network, the evaluability and reliability of external data sources represent an ongoing challenge. Expanding relationship intelligence supports data-driven decision-making and has a lasting effect on the generation of new business and the reduction of transaction costs for customer care.

CorSo's business relationship graphs are tightly embedded in the Digital Customer Fingerprint, supporting data-driven decision-making. At the same time, information flows are no longer manually controlled, but determined by interaction points provided by the relationship graphs. The network acts as a control center and enhances customer profile information, tightly integrating with digital marketing (e.g., identification of strong contacts) and the nomination process for customer feedback.

## 5 Benefits Cases

### 5.1 Benefits Case 1: Efficient Meeting Preparation with a Coherent Customer and Broker View

Customer-facing teams in commercial insurance often lack a coherent, comprehensive, and accurate overview of a single customer or broker relationship. This leads to:

- Extensive manual effort to obtain a holistic and consistent interrelation view.
- Data integrity and quality deficiencies when compiled from disconnected sources.
- An information gap affecting market-facing teams that lack relevant insights.

The challenge in addressing such issues is mainly that businesses have multiple applications, relevant to different functions. This causes conflicts with disconnected CRM systems, resulting in redundant and incoherent information capture.

CorSo has tackled this issue by introducing its company-wide data-driven insights approach. One of the main components of CorSo's CEM system is the so-called "Meeting Preparation Form," which is automatically distributed to customer-facing teams in preparation for upcoming customer and broker meetings. The purpose of such a feature is to outline key discussion points and a coherent insights view. Every user can define the geographical level (global, regional, country, or city) to connect the following relationship history and metrics:

- Business overview (in-force numbers and timeframe comparison)
- Claims overview (progressing, closed claims, and large movements)
- Company description (extracting data from external data sources)
- News and social media (company- and contact-related information)
- Customer interactions (relationships, topics discussed, and meetings)
- Engagement notifications (updates based on, e.g., NPS or marketing)

The Meeting Preparation Form has particularly addressed the "left hand doesn't know what the right hand is doing" organizational issue and is composed through the Digital Customer Fingerprint.

## 5.2 Benefits Case 2: Deeper Understanding of Customers and Brokers Driving Loyalty

CorSo's CEM platform follows a "data first" approach, seamlessly integrating insights and analytics into its customer and broker views. It leverages operational and behavioral data that is both actionable and contextual. In addition to having all data in one place, the application also processes customer-related information from external sources such as social media and industry news. The motto is to provide every employee with cross-functional information.

This level of connectivity and context helps CorSo achieve greater effectiveness through a deeper understanding of trading relationships and transparency around the customer's engagement level. It will make it vastly faster and easier to prepare, reconcile, and understand multiple sources of customer and broker data for use in engagements. This ultimately leads to higher conversion and retention through a greater understanding of our holistic trading relationships. It also impacts CorSo's annual Net Promotor Survey scores where customers reflect on their experience in dealing with CorSo across all business functions. The NPS in insurance is the key metric to demonstrate loyalty and the likelihood of recommending the insurer.

## 5.3 Benefits Case 3: Data Analytics Unlocking Business Relationship Intelligence

In B2B, social network platforms are not suited to understanding the strengths of a company's relationship with external stakeholders. Linked connections between individuals do not represent the company but rather individual relationships and are proprietary to their subscribers. As relationships are key to a successful customer management strategy, CorSo has introduced an innovative technology to establish a "Who Knows Whom" network insight based on email interactions and calendar entries of their employees with external Customers, Brokers, Partners, and Vendors. This insight is changing the entire Partner Management (central company and contact repository) discipline (also referred to as "Customer Data Platform"). Going forward, a single contact is no longer static. CorSo understands the following:

- Activeness of the contact based on the frequency of interaction.
- Strength of the relationship ("known" or "known of" contact).
- Ownership of the contact ("exclusive" or "broadly connected").
- Functional affiliation, for example, a contact serviced by Sales and Claims.
- Management access of a contact: whether they are connected with C-Suite.

Network intelligence in the B2B space is not about operational metrics. The focus is not measuring email response times or monitoring employee interaction statistics. Filling the network transparency gap changes how companies operate. Interaction data points (not limited to email exchanges) act as the central insights-distribution mechanism of the Digital Customer Fingerprint. This transforms conventional and administrative Customer Data Platforms into highly dynamic data-driven intelligence hubs.

CorSo has introduced technology innovation by transforming interaction data points into a real-time business relationship insights view, augmented with content. The network insights are delivered in a contextual form (based on emails), fully integrated into the email client of all customer-facing teams. This will immediately tell a user the strongest relationship of that contact into the organization, their past and future meetings, plus connecting topics discussed, as extracted from meeting notes.

Network intelligence is multi-dimensional and advances gradually. There is next-level potential in integrating commercial register data that serves as an additional source of new or alternative contact generation ("Next-Best Contact – NBC"). Any data source with relationships to companies and individuals (e.g., alumni and associations) can be integrated into CorSo's business network technology, which extracts:

- Connections with employees of the company (direct path).
- Connections into external contacts with existing relationships (NBC).
- Contacts without any connections that are potential leads for marketing.

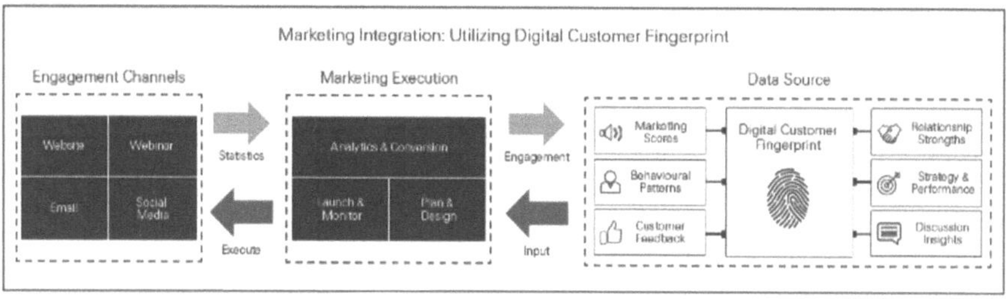


**Fig. 5** Utilizing the digital customer fingerprint in the context of digital marketing

## 5.4 Benefits Case 4: Advancing Digital Marketing Contact Nomination by Provision of Better Insights

The Digital Customer Fingerprint transforms transactional data related to customers and brokers into one consistent intelligence layer for internal consumption, such as for nomination of contacts for digital marketing campaigns and feedback initiatives including NPS. It provides extended context to the registered external contacts on the account (overall performance ratios and strategic positioning) and engagement levels (relationship, topics, feedback, behavior, etc.). This leads to a more sophisticated contact segmentation and nomination process for marketing purposes.

As the following image shows, the Digital Customer Fingerprint will act as a central source for the external digital marketing platform (system agnostic). The rich context of the Digital Customer Fingerprint enables more targeted contact-sourcing. Other than in traditional marketing, contact nomination and segmentation will not be limited to core contact attributes like functional titles and preferences. The fingerprint-based contact-targeting will consider various additional engagement insights of the contact like activeness, relationship strengths, and functional affiliation.

Once a marketing campaign is successfully executed, the behavioral and engagement results will be processed and transformed into information or actionable insights and distributed to the relevant customer manager's native business application (Fig. 5).

CorSo has introduced an advanced approach to B2B marketing through the Digital Customer Fingerprint and integrated marketing results into the overall CEM approach across all customer-facing teams within CorSo.

**Tobias Mäder** As the Digital Transformation Lead at Swiss Re Corporate Solutions, Tobias Mäder oversees the design and delivery of digital solutions and innovation by utilizing advanced analytics and modern technologies. He has introduced an internally developed customer engagement management platform, replacing a market-standard CRM system, to enhance client engagement and customer loyalty.

# Trigger-Based Marketing: Tiki-Taka for Digital Customer Relationship Management

Frank M. Hannich and Marcel Hüttermann

**Abstract**

The following chapter postulates that the Tiki-Taka style of play with high agility and low error interaction is also the right style of play for digital CRM and trigger-based marketing is the means of choice to get close to this style of play. The following questions will be addressed from a business perspective: What is trigger-based marketing and how can companies proceed? A three-step process is presented for this purpose. How do you systematically find the triggers of your own customers? Five main sources of triggers are identified. What is the connection between trigger-based marketing and digitalization, especially marketing automation and personalization? Overall, the chapter shows that the digitization of CRM is an enabler of trigger-based marketing, but that trigger-based marketing also helps to demonstrate clear and timely successes of digitization and automation.

## 1 Why Tiki-Taka Is the Right Tactic for the Digital CRM

His unique interplay enabled the Spanish national team and the FC Barcelona team under its coach Pep Guardiola to be the unrivaled role model in world soccer for years. The style of play that has come to be known as "Tiki-Taka" is characterized by activity, agility, short and reliable passes and, as a result, overall superior control of the game (Fig. 1). Does this sound familiar as a vision from your own working world? A comparison with the trends from the current "Swiss Marketing Leadership"

The original version of the chapter has been revised. A correction to this chapter can be found at https://doi.org/10.1007/978-3-658-45798-3_23

F. M. Hannich (✉) · M. Hüttermann
ZHAW School of Management and Law, Winterthur, Switzerland
e-mail: hanf@zhaw.ch; huet@zhaw.ch



S. Kirchem et al. (eds.), *CRM Goes Digital*, Management for Professionals,
https://doi.org/10.1007/978-3-658-45798-3_15

**Fig. 1** Tiki-Taka as a style of play for CRM (*Source*: Own illustration/Marcotti 2008)

study (Hannich et al. 2018) shows that, in the course of the digitization of marketing and CRM, companies are faced with the challenge of reconciling fast and reliable—preferably automated—processes with customers' demands for individualization. Salesforce also noted the increased demands on the (digital) customer experience as one of the main findings in its "State of the Connected Customer" study (Salesforce Research 2019).

On the one hand, you should be agile in responding to customer demands, and on the other hand, you should not just be driven by the latest digital hypes. The Marketing Science Institute in Cambridge, MA. also put "Understanding Customers and the Customer Experience" at the forefront of marketing research for 2014–2016 to develop the marketing of the future (www.msi.org). Digitization is an important enabler here in two ways. First, digitization improves data availability, especially in digital channels. In addition, immediate automation is possible in digital channels without changing channels. The "Service Benchmark" study by PIDAS (a European provider of customer service and service automation) in collaboration with ZHAW also showed that customer acceptance of automation is significantly higher if contact has already been established via a digital channel.

An important question for marketing managers in companies is therefore currently: When does speed matter and when does consistency matter? Customer segmentation is a good illustration of the difficulty of the question of speed vs.

consistency. In order to develop segment-specific strategies and, for example, to develop services for specific personas during implementation, consistency is required. Automated ad-hoc campaigns and rapid micro-campaigning responses to triggers, on the other hand, require speed. The example of customer data also highlights the difficulty of prioritizing between consistency and speed. On the one hand, customer data is essential that is collected over a long period of time (e.g., address and preferred products); on the other hand, customer data is also very relevant to respond "live" (e.g., wedding, birth, and change of address). In contrast, maintaining data quality is a never-ending task in companies. The topic of customer value management should also be mentioned here. On the one hand, customer values are calculated on average (e.g., average annual sales), but they are also quite relevant on an ad hoc basis if something serious changes in the customer's life that could have an impact on the customer relationship, e.g., a house purchase and the associated potential additional or reduced revenue for the company.

If we apply the Tiki-Taka style of play to digital CRM, the following requirements come to light:

- Always be on the ball, i.e., close to customers and their needs.
- Link company functions and channels with reliable and direct processes along the customer journey.
- Implement one-to-one marketing and still automate where customers want or accept it.

Trigger-based marketing can be a means to get close to Tiki-Taka in digital CRM as a company. Therefore, this chapter explains:

- What is trigger-based marketing and how can companies proceed?
- How do you systematically find the triggers of your own customers?
- What links trigger-based marketing with digital CRM, especially marketing automation and personalization?

## 2 What Is Trigger-Based Marketing and How Do You Proceed?

In order to generate attention among customers and ensure an efficient customer approach, organizations must constantly think of new methods. Because while customers increasingly tune out and ignore irrelevant advertising measures, their tolerance for undesirable marketing measures, which are perceived as a nuisance, is also declining. Due to this, it is existential for a modern company that not only the right person is addressed with the right message, but that this process also takes place at the right time. To achieve this, the current life events of the clientele must be optimally identified and responded to: An approach followed in trigger-based marketing. These life events influence both the behavior and the needs of the clientele. In doing so, trigger-based marketing enables an agile and personalized one-to-one concept that is able to combine automation and individuality and thus helps to address customers more successfully (Dyché 2002, pp. 40–41; Gustafsson et al. 2005, pp. 210–212; Hannich 2018, p. 64).

Trigger-based marketing is also referred to as event-based or event-driven marketing. The image of pulling the trigger of a gun to "shoot" customers certainly no longer fits into modern dialog and relationship marketing and is therefore rather unfortunate. Hitting the target with pinpoint accuracy and being as fast as a bullet, however, does. Above all, trigger-based marketing aims to increase relevance for customers and reduce annoying, because irrelevant, communication. For technical reasons, however, the term trigger-based marketing is chosen here because otherwise there is too great a risk of confusion with event marketing, i.e., the experience-oriented addressing of customers with the help of live communication (cf., e.g., Drengner 2006). Trigger-based marketing forms a new approach that identifies relevant events in the lives of the clientele that change their behavior and needs. As a CRM principle, it pursues the claim of being present with customers on four dimensions with pinpoint accuracy:

1. With the right customer
2. ...at the right time
3. ...on the right channel
4. ...with the right message or the right content

The goal is to be present with the right customers at the right time with a personalized communication in order to enable a more successful customer approach. Automation made possible by digitization is often used for this purpose, as is the goal of an omni-channel (Belz 2016, pp. 19–20; Cebulsky and Günther 2015, pp. 145–147; Dyché 2002, p. 40).

Trigger-based marketing thus forms an important component of digital CRM, as it enables agile one-to-one marketing that combines automation with individuality. Marketing automation is understood to mean the use of marketing systems that perform processes independently and regularly that would otherwise have to be performed manually.

This means that triggers can be used more efficiently and additional trigger moments can be integrated into a corporate strategy without causing additional work for employees after implementation. However, in order to operate effective and efficient trigger-based marketing, the relevant events, questions, and problems of the customers must first be determined, which trigger the (partially) automated process.

In practice, however, this does not result in individual customers, but rather in micro-segments for which a predefined trigger applies at the current time. A simple example might be car insurance. As soon as a person reaches the age of acquiring a driver's license, he or she has a need for car insurance for the first time, especially since the first car of one's own is a popular gift for graduation or coming of age. So a regular micro-campaign with a congratulatory message and special offer to anyone who turns old enough to get a driver's license that week would be obvious. What would still need to be determined is the right channel and the right content.

This can be determined classically through market research or experience and optimized through test-and-learn cycles.

If customers can be addressed precisely on the four dimensions, far-reaching benefits for the CRM of companies can be expected. Typical motivations of companies pursuing trigger-based marketing are:

- To better exploit large, untapped potential among existing customers in a data-based manner.
- Triggering wow effects in the customer in order to increase customer enthusiasm and engagement.
- To increase effectiveness and efficiency in digital CRM compared to mass marketing—especially efficient channel selection and use in omni-channel strategies.
- Harness potential of marketing automation in the enterprise.
- Achieve individualization through personalization.

Figure 2 shows three basic steps are necessary. First, the necessary customer understanding must be established, i.e., an understanding of which situations and events lead to a relevant change in customer needs (typically these are referred to as "critical events"). In addition to entering a new phase of life, as in the example above, this could be, for example, a move or the recognition of a pregnancy. A planned move is a highly relevant trigger for an insurance company (and numerous other industries), as it requires, for example, taking out or canceling a homeowner's insurance policy, depending on whether, for example, a child is moving out of the parents' home or a couple is moving into an apartment together. Triggers, then, can fundamentally represent an opportunity or a threat to the company. The goals can be acquisition, customer development, or customer retention in the sense of actively preventing customer churn. As a rule, pregnancy entails both diverse and far-reaching changes in the purchasing behavior of a woman or a couple. This has been demonstrated by the well-known example of the US retailer Target, which is able to identify the pregnancies of its female customers (insofar as they are part of the customer loyalty program) at an early stage on the basis of purchasing behavior data. It is not absolutely necessary to first comprehensively understand all the triggers of one's own customers before starting to implement them.

Experience at the Institute for Marketing Management in cooperation with numerous companies in research, training, and consulting has shown that individual

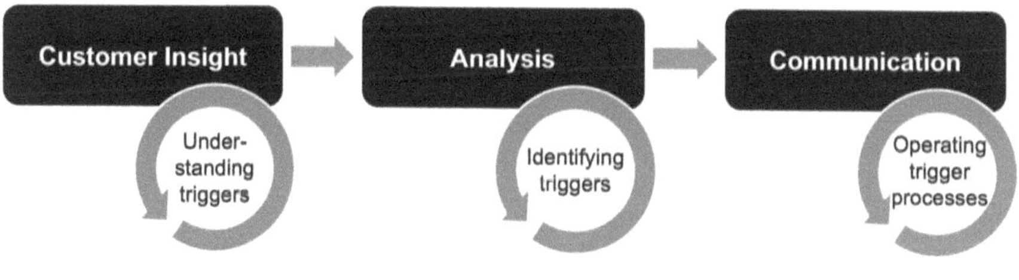


**Fig. 2** Trigger-based marketing process (*Source*: Own illustration)

pilot triggers can also be implemented initially in order to gain experience and assess the potential in one's own company. Once you have sharpened your eye for trigger-based marketing, the ideas often really start to bubble up. In addition, proving the benefits in a pilot case is often useful to drive the necessary changes in the company. Axa Insurance is one of the most prominent current use cases presented in a whole series of conference papers. Axa reported on a preparatory project that lasted several years and included adjustments to the company's strategy, organization, IT, and culture. Currently, more and more trigger-based marketing processes are gradually being implemented and the implementation optimized in individual cases. At the same time, the project is bearing fruit beyond trigger-based marketing in terms of agility and data availability in the company as a whole.

Knowing which triggers exist among one's own customers is highly relevant but not sufficient on its own. In an analysis phase, three things must be checked.

1. Is there a clear indicator for the occurrence of the trigger and does the company has the possibility to reliably and promptly determine the occurrence of the trigger? An example here would be the relocation notification to the postal service.
2. Is it economically worthwhile to track the trigger (e.g., to examine it in a business case)?
3. Can the company ensure continuous and timely identification of the occurrence?

Data sources (Fig. 3) can be the company's own existing customer data, data from third parties, as well as ongoing behavioral observation of customers, e.g., through web monitoring. An example of behavioral monitoring could be the detection of negative opinions about the company via web monitoring, which then

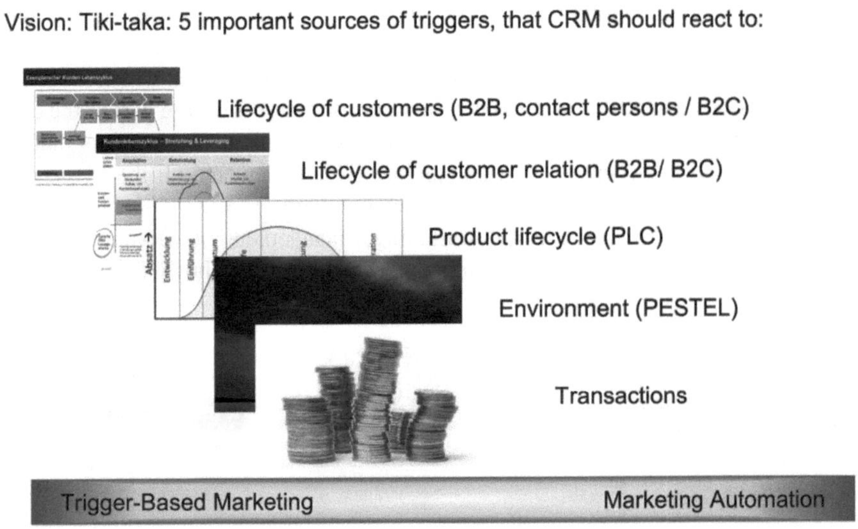


**Fig. 3** Emotional opportunities and threats to the customer relationship from customer events (*source*: Own illustration)

triggers a customer loyalty process on the one hand and a process for preserving the company's reputation on the other. This is also one of the most widespread applications of web monitoring for companies and is used by Emirates and Dell, for example.

A now quite established example of the use of predictive analytics to identify triggers is the prediction of help requests on websites. In the telecommunications industry, it is already very common to offer a live help chat based on this trigger in each case, reducing customer dissatisfaction and disgruntled as well as more expensive calls to the hotline.

For years, PostFinance (the bank of Swiss Post) has been a positive example of how trigger-based marketing can be done using sophisticated analytics. This involves searching for predefined so-called business events in the customer data, e.g., unusually high cash receipts. In the financial industry, this is already standard practice in connection with compliance issues such as money laundering, terrorism, or suspected fraud, but it is not necessarily also used for trigger-based marketing. If such a business event is found at a customer, a trigger process is triggered—especially in B2B business usually in the form of an automated notice to the sales department—i.e., the third step in the trigger-based marketing process.

Implementing the three steps of the trigger-based marketing process smoothly often proves considerably more difficult in practice than in theory. The three process steps require different competencies and are therefore often located in different areas of the company. Customer understanding requires input from customer experience management, market research, but also front-end units with direct customer contact, while the second step calls for analytical units in the company and the third step for marketing communications or units providing personal customer support. Here, responsibility for the process not only changes several times, but different cultures and interests in the company often have to be bridged. If this does not succeed in every single step, the success of trigger-based marketing is acutely endangered. The fact that appropriate communication must take place at the end is often forgotten.

Here is a small (anonymous) anecdote: A B2B industrial goods company uses the web monitoring function of the CRM system to monitor its key accounts or their main contacts on the Internet and to identify suitable triggers for a positive reason for contacting them, such as success stories and important events. The implementation is going perfectly and appropriate communication must take place at the end. The implementation is running smoothly and it is indeed possible to provide the key account managers with very relevant occasions for contacting them. Numerous customers respond by asking "How do you know that?" The answer may then be "We're watching you on the Internet." or "You're one of our key accounts - of course we're very interested in what's going on with you." Both are formally correct answers, but only one alternative will make trigger-based marketing successful for this company. Often, trigger based marketing processes rely on statistical analysis with some probability of confidence, typically high, but not 100%. Similarly, other databases for identifying triggers are typically not error free. It therefore makes sense to design the communication in such a way that it is possible to make a mistake without causing strong irritation among customers. Especially since the creation of positive emotions in CRM—especially on digital channels—is becoming increasingly important (Hannich and Hüttermann 2018).

## 3 How to Systematically Find the Triggers of Your Own Customers?

While much research is devoted to analyzing and predicting customer behavior using customer data, there is relatively little literature on how to determine what to look for in the data. In addition, external or internal data science specialists are often available to identify triggers in the data on a one-time or ongoing basis, while a good knowledge of one's own customers is not so easily replaced. Therefore, the focus of this section is to provide guidance on how to systematically identify your customers' triggers as a company. Figure 3 shows five sources of triggers (Fig. 3).

Firstly, the current life situation of customers should be mentioned here, whereby this applies to B2C as well as B2B customers. Less sensitive than the previously mentioned pregnancies are birthdays, anniversaries, promotions, retirements, etc., which can be identified from customer data or via web monitoring. Such triggers exist not only in the lives of B2C customers, but also B2B contacts and in the life cycle of companies. Companies are founded, contacts change jobs, companies launch new products, establish new locations, get into trouble, and end after a sale, for example.

Similarly, the lifecycle of the company's services can be a third source of triggers, such as new product launches, digital add-ons, disruptions that should be responded to quickly and automated, or systematic notification when the purchased service or associated contract becomes obsolete. An example of the latter is notices of upcoming subscription renewals, which require reliable automation and timing, as is often used by rail companies or cell phone providers.

A further distinction related to triggers takes place between Situational and Reactional triggers (Gustafsson et al. 2005, p. 211). Situational triggers involve a change in performance evaluation by the clientele. This is caused by changes in the clientele's life situations—e.g., demographic/financial changes in the family, changes in the job, environmental changes, and many more. Due to the change in life situation, the company's performance no longer meets the needs of the clientele. In the systematization presented here, this type of Situational Trigger is most closely associated with the triggers in the customer life cycle.

Reactional triggers are extraordinary situations in which a service restriction may occur—in the pre-purchase, purchase or usage phase. An example of this would be the failure of a service at a telecommunications company, which is also not communicated. This may even have a negative impact on customer retention.

Suitable sources for identifying triggers include the customer lifecycle, the customer relationship lifecycle, and the product lifecycle, as well as the consideration of environmental changes (PESTEL) and transactions (Hannich 2018, pp. 58–66), resulting in a fourth and fifth source of critical events as a basis for triggers. The PESTEL model of corporate situation lists five basic areas of environmental change: political, economic, social, technical, ecological, and legal. For example, a bank should use environmental triggers for information campaigns of affected customers and at the same time can identify the right moments for advisory meetings. Triggers based on transactions are heavily used in e-commerce—mostly as direct, automated reactions to customer behavior, e.g., the request for a rating on Trip Advisor after completion of a trip, retargeting when a shopping cart has not been redeemed (English: abandoned cart) or so-called threshold triggers when a limit has been reached or the next step in the bonus program.

If a company knows in principle what the decisive events are for its B2B and B2C customers, it must identify these as triggers and then trigger-based processes. Digitization, advanced data analysis, and automation are making it possible to bring the Tiki-Taka principle from soccer ever more effectively into digital CRM: Always being on the ball and on the attack, agility and an optimal passing of the balls within the company and between the company and its customers.

Data availability is important here. The new regulation of data protection in the European Union came into force on May 25, 2018, and has caused a lot of uncertainty among companies worldwide. The increasing difficulty of obtaining customer data and permission to use it is raising awareness of the value of data. So, it is logical that the willingness to invest in data quality and CRM remains very high overall. This is confirmed by the "Digital Data Insights 2018" study, according to which 84% of the companies surveyed see the areas of customer intelligence and analytics as suitable means of being able to act better in the interests of customers—which in turn should have a positive impact on sales. It should therefore be more possible to conduct trigger-based marketing in the future.

## 4 Digital CRM: What Trigger-Based Marketing Has in Common with Marketing Automation and Personalization

Advances in data analytics and digitization are creating a high potential to identify triggers in an automated way and then trigger automated processes when a trigger has occurred. Examples include automated monitoring of the Internet for trademark infringements and purchase requests or automated live chat pop-ups based on behavior on a website. So, there is a close connection to marketing automation.

But you can also see the connection the other way around: the possibilities for automation that are technically quite available are not worth much if you do not know what and when something should be automated. Understanding the triggers of your customers is an essential basis for marketing automation. This is the only way to answer the question of what should be automated. The results from the analysis step can trigger the automated processes in each case and thus answer the question of when. Automated processes, in particular, have the potential to greatly annoy customers because they lack the flexibility to react if they start from incorrect planning, identification, or a misunderstanding of the customer's situation or need. Trigger-based marketing can help reduce these errors. Since trigger-based marketing can also be introduced gradually, it also serves as a kind of catalyst for digital transformation, especially marketing automation, for pioneering companies. The benefits of automation can be clearly demonstrated here in a relatively timely manner, but it also becomes obvious what needs to change in processes, organization, and culture for these benefits to be achievable.

Personalization as automated individualization ideally bridges the gap between cost efficiency through automation and the need for customers to be treated in a tailored way. Trigger-based marketing can also be very useful here by providing design cues and stimuli. Not only is timing improved, but also the content and channel of personalized communication can be driven by trigger-based marketing. Conversely, it can be said that every communication based on trigger-based marketing is personalized at least on the levels of customer and timing.

Companies that are thinking about personalization or more generally about marketing automation in direct customer contact should therefore make use of trigger-based marketing. Nevertheless, it is not a pure automation topic. Particularly when scarce and expensive resources for personal contact are involved, it is worthwhile to use them in a more targeted manner through trigger-based marketing.

## References


Belz C (2016) Marketing Heatmap II—Marketing-Effizienz, Marketing-Organisation und -Prozesse, Cross Channel und Kunden zum Kauf führen. Swiss Market Rev 2(1):14–21

Cebulsky M, Günther J (2015) Der digitale Versicherungskunde: anspruchsvoll, vernetzt und mobil. In: Linnhoff-Popien C, Zaddach M, Grahl A (eds) Marktplätze im Umbruch: Digitale Strategien für Services im Mobilen Internet. Springer, Berlin, pp 141–148

Drengner J (2006) Imagewirkungen von Eventmarketing: Entwicklung eines ganzheitlichen Messansatzes. Springer-Verlag, Berlin

Dyché J (2002) The CRM handbook. A business guide to customer relationship management. Addison-Wesly, Boston

Gustafsson A, Johnson MD, Roos I (2005) The effects of customer satisfaction, relationship commitment dimensions, and triggers on customer retention. J Mark 65(5):210–218

Hannich F (2018) Analytisches CRM, zentrale Kundenmanagementaktivitäten: Entwicklung (inkl. Trigger-based Marketing)—Vorlesungsskript. Frühlingssemester 2018. Zürcher Hochschule für Angewandte Wissenschaften (ZHAW), Institut für Marketing Management, Winterthur

Hannich F, Hüttermann M (2018) Kundenbeziehungen emotionalisieren. Emotionalisierung im digitalen Marketing: erfolgreiche Methoden für die Marketingpraxis, 47–63

Hannich F, Hüttermann M, Fuchs R, Suvada A, Kübler D, Barth L, Heierli R, Rozumowski A, Kiarostami T (2018) Swiss Marketing Leadership Studie 2018 - Geschwindigkeit vs. Beständigkeit im Marketing. Winterthur

Marcotti G (2008) New coaching breed gives heart to Spain in the times. https://www.thetimes.co.uk/. https://www.thetimes.co.uk/article/new-coaching-breed-gives-heart-to-spain-3jc08jh58jq. Zugegriffen am 22. März 2021

Salesforce Research (2019) State of the connected customer. Salesforce, San Francisco

**Marcel Hüttermann** is faculty member and Head of the MarTech Lab at ZHAW School of Management and Law. His research interests focus on marketing technology and customer engagement. He holds a doctorate in business administration from the Technical University of Munich (TUM).

**Frank M. Hannich** holds a doctorate in the field of CRM and is a professor and senior lecturer at the Institute of Marketing Management at the ZHAW Zurich University of Applied Sciences and deputy director of the institute. He is responsible for research and consulting projects related to customer relationship management. His current work focuses on automation and AI in customer management as well as the emotionalization of customer relationships.

# Artificial Intelligence Meets Homo Sapiens: Possible Applications and Limits of Artificial Intelligence

Jochen Werne

**Abstract**

A special encounter: Algorithms developed by humans meet everything humans and nature embody—from industrial processes to our very own behavior. A race has begun between countries and companies to decide for themselves the enormous potential of AI and its impact on our consumer behavior and society. But it is important to go beyond the euphoria by understanding the topic, its potential applications, and also its limitations to mitigate the risk of getting lost in techno-believing magic.

## 1 Introduction

Two letters electrifying the economy: AI or artificial intelligence. After decades of disinterest, artificial intelligence is suddenly being seen as the decisive guarantor of companies' future viability. The immediate integration of AI into company business models seems indispensable, even necessary for survival. Without "smart" software, especially for the customer journey, companies feel they are doomed to irrelevance and ruin.

In the world of Amazon, Google, and Facebook, it's hard to disagree. Cognitively, computer programs are already superior to humans in many ways. Artificial intelligence can beat humans in games like chess, "Go," and poker. The Libratus poker AI even can bluff; according to the research team, this is one of its specialties.

It is interesting that soccer-playing robots cannot hold a candle to humans. Wolfgang Wahlster, a professor at the Artificial Intelligence Research Center in Karlsruhe explains that they lack social intelligence during a lecture at the Munich

J. Werne (✉)
Experian, Duesseldorf, Germany
e-mail: JW@JochenWerne.com



S. Kirchem et al. (eds.), *CRM Goes Digital*, Management for Professionals,
https://doi.org/10.1007/978-3-658-45798-3_16

Media Days (Meyer 2015): "They always want to score the goals themselves and can't pass." In his view, the first wave of digitization is complete. After numbers had predominantly only been collected, stored, and processed, the next step would be to interpret, refine, and actively monetize digital data with the help of algorithms.

Data is considered the most valuable raw material of the twenty-first century, and artificial intelligence makes it clear why. Yet only a few years ago that experience and gut instinct were still considered acceptable means of decision-making. Many a customer relationship management expert even saw these as their most valuable assets. One allocated one's budget by coupling yesterday's experience with feelings for tomorrow and, for the professional touch, with some studies and statistics. Nowadays, with a clear definition of goals and a sufficient amount of well-prepared data, an algorithm can visualize statistically clean connections and compensate for the enormous, scattering losses of many a gut feeling. This in turn has a direct influence on company results.

Human decisions are basically intuitive, but those of a program are based on data. An autopilot would certainly not have let the Costa Concordia collide with a rock years ago—the reason for the disaster was emotion-driven human behavior. But an autopilot would also not have been able to intuitively land an Airbus 320 on the Hudson River. That requires human experience and spontaneous creativity. Only our brains can do that; artificial intelligence reaches its limits here.

## 2 How Witty Can Software Be?

Generally, the words "artificial" and "intelligence" contradict each other. Can a computer actually be intelligent? Can it possess what we call a "mind?" Can it be creative, abstracting, intuitive, and ultimately emotional; all that constitutes intelligence? Indeed, the term artificial intelligence is misleading. John McCarthy first coined the term "artificial intelligence" in 1955 while soliciting funding for a research workshop that resulted in the Dartmouth Summer Research Project on Artificial Intelligence on July 13, 1956 (McCarthy et al. 1955). McCarthy, who had a pretty good gut instinct, thus coined a generic term for how to teach software to learn: the ability to abstract and possibly extend existing data. The term "learning systems" was born. In this context, machine learning plays a crucial role. This involves a self-adaptive algorithm that interacts with itself and its environment. Deep learning goes one step further: It includes the ability of a system to evaluate and make autonomous and reasoned changes to an implemented structure (Wedekind 2018). However, it only does so within its world, which it sees as a hierarchy of concepts.

Since the invention of AI, some have seen it as the salvation of humanity, others as its demise. While the creation of strong AI, i.e., intelligence, that is supposed to mechanize human thought has failed due to philosophical issues, significant progress has been made in recent years on the side of weak AI, whereby concrete application problems of human thought are solved. But for all the supposedly clever machines that play unbeatable chess, for example, one must not forget that this program does not even know it is playing chess. It only executes its programming and is able to perfect it on its own. In fact, learning systems are nothing more than a tool for humans. They can support creativity, but they cannot replace it. Also, most experts are convinced that AI programs will not be capable of a primal human trait like emotion for a long time. Some believe this will never be the case.

A simple example from the field of visual pattern recognition illustrates machine learning: If you show a computer what a glass is and then demonstrate a million versions of it, it can recognize another glass as such with a precisely defined percentage probability and distinguish it from a set of objects. Of course, scanning a million glasses would be a highly time-consuming affair, and the result unsatisfactory by comparison. Today, however, thanks to the Internet and effective data storage, computers with modern computing power are learning by leaps and bounds, and it takes only a limited time to compare a million glasses. However, the old principle of the quality of the data—i.e., the input—always applies. Then the system finds correlations and can make a prediction as to whether an object it does not know is a glass. Meanwhile, AI can also abstract. If it is a glass of red wine, for example, AI is able to recognize the origin of the grape based on the coloration. This has nothing to do with intelligence, but rather with machine learning. However, its speed exceeds that of human learning many times over in special applications. Hawkins and Blakeslee (2005), who coined the term "hierarchical temporal memory" as a model of machine learning has said, "Prediction is not just one of the things your brain does. It is the main function of the neocortex and the foundation of intelligence."

Five years ago, this was not possible. The computing power required for abstraction was simply not available. However, it now seems to be increasing exponentially. Gordon Moore, one of the co-founders of Intel, formulated a law as early as 1965, a few years after the invention of the integrated circuit, which was later named after him: "Moore's Law." According to this law, the complexity of integrated circuits doubles within 12 months while costs remain the same. Later, Moore relativized the period to 24 months. What does this mean? Transistor performance doubles every 2 years without increasing the price. And after 2 years, it doubles again. This phenomenon has been going on for several decades. The computing power of two Cray supercomputers today costs as much as a McSundae from McDonald's.

## 3 The Limits of Human Thinking

The problem with understanding consequences is that humans are barely able to think exponentially. Another example may illustrate what the rapid development of computing power means. If you fold an A4 sheet in half, its thickness doubles. This works exactly six times, after which the sheet cannot be folded any further. However, if it were possible to fold it 42 times, the thickness would correspond to the distance from the earth to the moon—an incredible 380,000 kilometers. Converted to computing power according to Moore's Law, this means we are already some distance away from our starting point. And the moon by no means has to be the final destination.

We are in an era of epochal upheaval, but above all of a widely unnoticed revolution. Strangely enough, the two letters AI still electrify society disproportionately less than the economy. Artificial intelligence is commonly associated with Hollywood figures such as the Terminator or the Amazon series *Westworld*, and thus tends to be associated with humanoid robots and strong AI, which has led some discussions astray ever since C3PO from the Star Wars film series. Existing AI programs such as Alexa or Siri, on the other hand, are not considered overly intelligent, and online advertising offers based on personalized customer data still have large wastage.

## 4 The Predictive Power of AI Will Revolutionize CRM

But that is set to change. A key area of application for artificial intelligence is forecasting. This will essentially change the customer journey. Classic CRM today looks for ways to best reach and address people, how to awaken and satisfy consumer desires and needs. In the future, this will be a matter of using the data collected to identify the customer's needs in a targeted manner before they are expressed, indeed before they are thought of, in order to make an appropriate offer. The more powerful artificial intelligence becomes, the more refined and accurate its predictive ability will become. Professor Ajay Agrawal of the Rotman School of Management has presented a thought experiment for this purpose (McKinsey and Company 2018).

Prof. Agrawal's thought experiment aims to show that AI tools not only increase efficiency, but are potentially transformative, and to show how quickly this can happen. Imagine that Amazon's current recommendation engine (i.e., the AI tool that presents product recommendations to customers) can be calibrated like a volume control toward accuracy.

Currently, we can imagine Amazon's product recommendations rated, on a scale of ten, as two. This means that out of approximately 20 products presented, the customer buys one product, which is 5% accuracy for the recommendation engine. At first glance, this does not sound like much, but it is technologically amazing when you consider how many products Amazon offers in order to suggest just 20 to a single customer.

Let us now imagine that the "volume control" is upgraded, i.e. the recommendations become more precise. The customer suddenly buys 5, 8, or 10 products out of the 20 suggested. This not only increases sales; it also opens up the possibility for Amazon to decide not to suggest the products at all, but to ship them directly to the customer. Even if customers then return some products, they have firstly not been able to buy the products they keep from the competition and secondly they have not had time to think about a purchase decision for too long; the decision has effectively been taken away from them by the algorithm of the recommendation engine.

Of course, this is just a thought experiment, but it shows how disruptive even small changes in the area of AI application can be, from the optimization of processes to the transformation of entire business models.

Consequently, we are already in the midst of a disruption. And such a disruption always has the greatest success when it is not noticeable, at best in a surprisingly pleasant way. We always judge upheavals on the basis of our current knowledge and our current ability to assess. In order to really judge and give directions, however, we must abstract and at least attempt to foresee the positive, as well as negative, consequences of a development. It is a bit like the invention of the automobile. At the time, New York was in danger of suffocating in horse droppings, which were all over the streets and—as we would say today—represented a massive environmental problem. The automobile, of all things, solved this environmental problem. That it would 1 day become one itself was unforeseen. Would such foresight have been possible back then?

Despite all the uncertainty, we have to make judgments today about the technologies of tomorrow. This also applies morally, especially in times of exponential AI growth. Is there a danger of a loss of morality due to an increasingly greater power of man or the machine over all areas of life? Reacting with fear does not prevent progress; but it rather prevents the access to and handling of technology. It is therefore more appropriate to approach new technologies with confidence, foresight and, above all, to focus on the possibilities of constructive rather than destructive use. Politicians are of course responsible for creating the optimal framework conditions for the use of artificial intelligence.

Used constructively, technologies such as the Internet of Things can make our world a better place. IBM, for example, has fitted the vines at one of the world's largest wineries, Gallo in California, with sensors. They measure the supply of water and minerals, soil conditions, and more. They also networked this data with weather data from The Weather Company, satellite data, and many of their own sources to gain not only the most accurate weather report possible, but also insights into the composition of the rain. The result was that 25% less water was needed than before, when the—certainly highly experienced—Gallo managers still decided on watering quantity according to gut feeling. In addition, the quality of the grapes improved (IBM 2017). This results not only in business models, but above all in opportunities to feed the world's population in a more resource-conserving way. Gallo's optimization of water use certainly provides fundamental insights for other initiatives, such as the United Nations World Food Programme. Technical systems usually excel at increasing our prosperity. With the technological revolution of the Internet and the interconnectedness of society, we have even seen a fall in the global poverty index.

## 5 Should We Do Just Because We Can?

Nevertheless, the use of new technologies always leads to questions of ethics. Of course, AI programs cannot be used exclusively for constructive purposes; like all technical instruments, they also harbor risks of misuse. For example, a truck can be used today to bring relief supplies that are essential for survival to a disaster area, and it can be misused by assassins to carry out a terrorist attack on innocent bystanders. Gottlieb Daimler certainly did not have the latter in mind when he made the first truck, which at the time had 4 horsepower, delivered to the British Motor Syndicate in London on October 1, 1896.

When Mark Zuckerberg founded Facebook's predecessor in 2003 while a student at Harvard, he probably didn't think that just a decade later, targeted social media campaigns from abroad would be influencing the voting behavior of American or British citizens. Facebook's increasing importance as a news outlet was evidenced in 2015 by the Reuters Institute at Oxford University (2015). According to the report, 23% of 1969 respondents across Germany in all age groups obtained their news from Facebook. Of course, the dangers posed by new technical possibilities must be identified, assessed, and prevented.

Mark Zuckerberg repeatedly pointed out at his hearing in the U.S. Senate in the spring of 2018 that "AI tools" are absolutely needed to filter the vast amounts of data in order to effectively weed out the so-called fake content with an illegal background. However, the discussions also led to the observance of an increasing public vigilance. In this context, how the public has built up pressure on American corporations is noteworthy (Werner 2018).

Microsoft, for example, is cooperating with Homeland Security on data storage issues. Its Azure cloud service uses artificial intelligence to determine people's identities in real time. The introduction of a decree to separate children of illegal immigrants from their parents shocked large portions of the American population, and criticism was also directed at Microsoft. As a result, company CEO Satya Nadella, himself the son of Indian immigrants, finally spoke out and announced, "We at Microsoft are shocked by the forcible separation of children from their families at the border crossing," and demanded that Congress pass appropriate laws against the practice.

At Google, public pressure led to concrete consequences. The corporation pulled out of "Project Maven" with the Defense Department following pressure from employees. The program helps the Pentagon to better recognize people, vehicles, buildings, or weapons caches in drone videos with the help of AI. Some employees had indignantly left the company, and thousands had signed a petition saying that Google had no place in the "business of war."

It is understandable that a single corporation has this option. However, states, specifically in their national security and defense policies, can ill afford to be at a strategic disadvantage by not using AI. According to reports in *The New York Times* on August 26, 2018, Secretary of Defense James Mattis was working on dialogue with Silicon Valley experts (Metz 2018). For this purpose, the Joint Artificial Intelligence Center, JAIC, was launched in June 2018, which is to receive US$75 billion from the defense budget over the next 5 years and where, among other things, the aforementioned "Project Maven" will be further developed.

The American startup Botnik is even working on teaching computers a profoundly human characteristic: humor. The goal is simply to make interaction more interesting for humans in a human–machine interaction. For example, Amazon is funding the company founded by comic book artist Bob Mankoff and neuroscientist Jamie Brew to further develop the digital assistant Alexa. A humor update would also be conceivable—and possibly appropriate—for care robots, such as those already in use in tech-savvy Japan. The founders are well aware of the limitations: Mankoff compares artificial intelligence to a child learning English by sitting in front of the T.V. It has never met people who speak the language, yet it is fluent in it.

## 6 The End of Work?

Whether a computer can crack jokes or play chess is not crucial to the major social upheavals AI will bring about. We should be clear that artificial intelligence will change the world of work as we know it. And it will do so in the near future. Experience shows that machines will take over tasks that were previously performed by humans, and by no means only in the low-wage sectors, at the supermarket checkout or on the assembly line in the factory. Today, for example, lawyers are already being assisted by intelligent AI programs such as ROSS Intelligence, in combination with IBM's Watson. This does not mean that there will be no more lawyers in the future. But the job description will change, and the requirements for specialization will increase. Lawyers will still be needed for more complex cases. Likewise, new job descriptions will be created. For example, lawyers who help programmers translate contexts into codes.

From a country-specific cultural perspective, it is interesting to observe how differently people see the impact of AI on their current jobs. In a global survey commissioned by the Boston Consulting Group (2018), 58% of respondents assumed that AI would not threaten their own job. Germany and France delivered the highest scores in this regard: 67% and 69%, respectively. In China, on the other hand, less than one-third of respondents were of this opinion. There, however, AI has been elevated to a topic of national interest, such that many Chinese people have come into contact with it in practice, not only in the media. An interesting thesis for future studies could certainly ask whether the more people come into contact with artificial intelligence, the greater they rate its potential. On the other hand, social or cultural resentment could lead to a different assessment.

On the other hand, as history shows, new technologies always create new jobs, and often even more meaningful work than before. But will this also be the case with digitalization and artificial intelligence? No one is in a position today to make reliable predictions. The only thing that is certain is that there will be major changes in all branches of industry and an international race, also driven by states, in all areas around all technological innovations. Many other statements that we will have to deal with in the future require everyone to have a solid technical knowledge base in this area. All the more so if one even has to make political or social decisions in this context. We will have to deal with predictions of mass unemployment, massive economic crises, high dissatisfaction among the population, and empty social coffers.

The supposed speed of development and the social upheavals attributed to the further development of artificial intelligence make the issue one of the most important tasks for policymakers.

Germany, which counts itself a pioneering country in learning systems and artificial intelligence, has already launched an artificial intelligence platform initiated by the Federal Ministry of Education and Research (BMBF): "Learning Systems." With its 200 members, the platform brings together leading experts from science, industry, and society to address technological, economic, and social issues relating to the development and introduction of learning systems in an interdisciplinary and cross-sectoral manner. The composition of topics shows the interwoven, culture-specific discussions that will later lead to scenarios, recommendations, guidelines, and roadmaps.

The banking industry, for example, is a sector in which the supply of jobs will shrink. Here, disruption by new technologies has long since begun, and here, too, artificial intelligence is the new buzzword for future viability. FinTechs are causing traditional financial service providers to think in new ways. Things like self-learning algorithms for highly complex investment strategies or chatbots in digital customer centers are being discussed. "Artificial intelligence and Big Data are currently the strongest and most vibrant forms of innovation in the financial sector," was one of the guiding principles of Prof. Joachim Wuermeling, member of the Executive Board of the Deutsche Bundesbank, in his speech on artificial intelligence at the second annual FinTech and Digital Innovation Conference in Brussels in February 2018 (Wuermeling 2018).

However, a representative study published in June 2018 by GfK (2018) on behalf of the Association of German Banks shows that perceptions still seem to be in the initial stages of development. Most Germans associate "artificial intelligence" with self-driving cars (83%), speech recognition using a voice assistant (70%), and facial recognition (54%). Banking services such as voice banking (24%) and financial advice through robo-advice (16%) are mentioned less frequently. Germans generally have low levels of trust in digitally controlled processes: When it comes to completing important tasks, they have considerably less confidence in robots (3%) than in humans (77%).

This undoubtedly gives AI a competitive edge for financial market actors who master the subject's complexity and the correct use of the available data. However, the investment manager's dream of being able to predict tomorrow's market will remain unreachable in the era of algorithms.

In contrast to stand-alone solutions for specific application areas, some companies rely on dedicated development departments that scrutinize existing solution processes in a kind of technology transformation and aim to investigate where AI technologies can make a meaningful contribution. For example, Prosegur, one of the global market leaders in the security and value industry, created the so-called

GENZAI platform in its AI Tech Studio in 2020, based on which the company tackles all AI-related issues centrally. Through a diverse network of surveillance cameras, detectors of all kinds, and a growing number of IoT devices, the security industry already has the necessary volumes of data to create new and highly effective security systems using video and audio pattern algorithms. These systems will be able to detect threats more accurately and significantly reduce high false alarm costs. During the Covid-19 crisis, the infrastructure created has already been leveraged to develop an application at short notice that assures employees of a work environment free of Covid-19. This is provided through a combination of data and its analysis, such as mask wear and temperature detection or social distancing and contact tracing. Simple feedback in the form of a traffic light system to the employee creates practicality and feedback to the access control systems in the company creates the necessary security.

## 7 A Question of Trust

At present, it is too early to say exactly which operational areas will be supported—partially or even completely—by using AI systems. In the financial sector, which was the focus of the previous analysis, the use of intelligent features in the areas of risk management and money laundering can, as things stand, reduce operational costs and labor-intensive processes. Business models are becoming leaner, data is used more efficiently, and customer journeys are optimized. Technological progress stands and falls with concretely defined, successful deployment scenarios. The technical revolution in the form of AI systems will only be lucrative for companies if customers accept the innovations and if the new technologies are socially accepted. For example, the practice of dealing with customers in the private banking environment will become an interesting testing ground for the limits of human–machine interaction. Likely, a purely virtual contact person will not be sufficient for all target groups to offer fully sustainable advice and special support.

Why does the human factor remain relevant here? The origin lies in the findings of behavioral finance, a subfield of behavioral economics, which show that emotional—i.e., human—behavior must lead to mistakes when it comes to investing. These mistakes can only be avoided or corrected by artificial intelligence to a limited extent. In the event of an unforeseeable stock market crash, a digital investment advisor with a high level of trust from the customer will find it difficult to offer worried investors the support they need via chatbot at this moment of great imbalance between "ratio" and "emotion." In the final instance, the advantage lies in human and personal exchange, not only to articulate and share fears and concerns, but in the emotion of the moment to minimize the risk of wrong decisions and even to take advantage of possible opportunities. The notion of a true "confidant" could thus experience a renaissance in banking.

Previous financial crises have repeatedly shown that trust is crucial when it comes to money—trust in the markets, in the banking world, and not least in human contact as the intermediary with a complex issue. The banking industry knows very well from its own experience how easily the customer's trust can be squandered. Mark Zuckerberg and Facebook learned this through experience in connection with the Cambridge Analytica scandal.

Similarly to Facebook, the financial industry is sitting on a valuable mountain of data, the extent of which is currently difficult to estimate. Maturing AI systems will not only make it easier to prepare and process this data, but do so much more quickly, cheaply, and in a more targeted manner.

Nevertheless, the data is private and sensitive. To harness this resource in conjunction with external data, the industry must simultaneously place its security at the top of the priority list. Data must only be used in the interests of the customer, i.e., the human being—an objective that certainly applies to all AI-based approaches. Artificial intelligence offers an enormous range of opportunities for companies to serve and operate more closely with their customers. But it also has its limitations. These are not only technical, but rather based on the limits of human characteristics such as emotions, irrationalities, and trust.

How well new technologies are accepted by the end customer is ultimately always a task for the top levels of management. Technological progress and the acceleration of product cycles are forcing executives to constantly reposition their companies. The question is no longer whether and why companies should transform themselves and introduce a more flexible form of organization, but only how quickly and sustainably they can do so. The need for successful change management is not new, nor are the opportunities presented by digitalization unpredictable events.

What is new, however, is the sum of the technical innovations, the possibilities offered by the leaps in technology, and the resulting need for an extremely high speed of implementation. This circumstance has far-reaching spillover effects on the entire corporate management, as it often leads to the fact that various change processes overlap and have to be interrupted, modified, or restarted at the same time. Organizations are thus in a state of continuous change at best. In this context, management must take the boldest steps to future-proof their own companies and thus also contribute to digital social development.

"AI is by no means about perfectly replicating human behavior with all its strengths, but also its many weaknesses; rather, we want to assist humans with AI where it makes sense to do so," is how Wolfgang Wahlster (Meyer 2015), head of the German Research Center for Artificial Intelligence in Saarbrücken, sums it up. And he reassures skeptics, "A current AI system will still need many years before it could take the Abitur [the final exams at German high schools]. Even elementary school graduation would not be possible today." Humans remain indispensable after all, the masters of all things.

## References

Boston Consulting Group (2018) Towards a reskilling revolution a future of jobs for all. http://www3.weforum.org/docs/WEF_FOW_Reskilling_Revolution.pdf. Accessed: 20 June 2019

GfK (2018) Customer journey banking. https://www.thinkwithgoogle.com/intl/de-de/insights/markteinblicke/neue-studie-uber-banking-im-digitalen-zeitalter-radikaler-wandel-im-konsumentenverhalten/. Accessed: 26 Aug 2022

Hawkins J, Blakeslee S (2005) On intelligence: how a new understanding of the brain will Lead to the creation of truly intelligent machines. Times Books, New York

IBM (2017) E. & J. Gallo Windery is working with Watson to develop an intelligent irrigation system that increases the quality of its grapes. https://www.ibm.com/watson/stories/ejgallo/. Accessed: 07 Jan 2019

McCarthy J, Minsky ML, Rochester N, Shannon CE (1955) A proposal for the Dartmouth summer research project on artificial intelligence. http://jmc.stanford.edu/articles/dartmouth/dartmouth.pdf. Accessed: 26 Aug 2022

McKinsey & Company (2018) The economics of artificial intelligence. https://www.mckinsey.com/business-functions/mckinsey-analytics/our-insights/the-economics-of-artificial-intelligence. Accessed: 07 Jan 2019

Metz C (2018, August 26) Artificial intelligence is now a pentagon priority. Will Silicon Valley help? *The New York Times*. https://www.nytimes.com/2018/08/26/technology/pentagon-artificial-intelligence.html. Accessed: 18 Feb 2021

Meyer JB (2015) Künstliche Intelligenz ist besser als natürliche Dummheit. Interview mit Wolfgang Wahlster. *Computerwoche*. https://www.computerwoche.de/a/kuenstliche-intelligenz-ist-besser-als-natuerliche-dummheit,3210426. Accessed: 20 June 2019

Reuters Institute (2015) Social media and the 2015 general election. https://reutersinstitute.politics.ox.ac.uk/risj-review/social-media-and-2015-general-election. Accessed: 18 Feb 2021

Wedekind K (2018) Was heißt hier eigentlich Künstliche Intelligenz? *NTV*. https://www.n-tv.de/technik/Was-ist-Kuenstliche-Intelligenz-KI-maschinelles-Lernen-und-Deep-Learning-article20226460.html. Accessed: 07 Jan 2019

Werner K (2018, June 20) Im Dienste der Nation? *Sueddeutsche Zeitung*. https://www.sueddeutsche.de/digital/microsoft-und-amazon-im-dienst-der-nation-1.4022591. Accessed: 07 Jan 2019

Wuermeling J (2018) Rede "Aktueller und künftiger Status der KI im Finanzbereich" auf der zweiten jährlichen FinTech- und Digital-Innovationskonferenz im Februar 2018 in Brüssel. *IT Finanzmagazin*. https://www.it-finanzmagazin.de/chancen-ki-finanzbereich-prof-wuermeling-bundesbank-66848/. Accessed: 07 Jan 2019

**Jochen Werne** is an international manager, public speaker, and NGO founder with a track record in business transformation. In December 2020, he was listed in the TytoPR Top 500 ranking as one of the 50 most influential Germans in the tech scene. He is also an expert in public diplomacy and is committed to developing international diplomatic and intercultural relations. He is a relationship builder and influencer with a large network in politics, technology, and business who can drive change within the leadership team of organizations. In his current role as Chief Executive Officer of Experian DACH, he is responsible for the growth of the technology and data giant in the heart of Europe.

# The Digitalization of Customer Contact in Healthcare

Kolja A. Rafferty

**Abstract**

Digital transformation is changing the landscape of many industry sectors. Healthcare, and health insurers face particularly significant challenges. On the one hand, technical innovations create opportunities; on the other hand, they have disruptive potential. Insurance carriers have to solve key tasks besides the societal problem of rising healthcare costs. They need to digitize their limited customer contact points. Modern technologies offer new solutions to promote healthier lifestyles for insured people and to monitor ongoing treatments. Prevention and monitoring of therapies are thus moving into insurance companies' sphere of influence. In this way, the health of policyholders can improve sustainably in the long term. The cost burden caused by medical absences and illness is relieved. Effective methods include intelligently using loyalty technologies and customer dialogue through digital and mobile platforms.

## 1 Status Quo in Healthcare: When Will Real Progress Come?

Healthcare is being digitalized at all levels. Initially, this was limited to the modernization of existing IT infrastructures within insurance, an enormously data-hungry and data-heavy industry. The primary focus was parameters like processing speed, storage optimization, and automation. Initially, this renewal of IT capacities did not improve the customer experience. The focus was improving operational efficiency. New technologies supported more efficient internal processes, insofar as they were used. But they were not a basis to improve external processes or for new business

K. A. Rafferty (✉)
Leverage Experts, Zurich, Frankfurt, Germany
e-mail: kolja.rafferty@leverage-experts.com





S. Kirchem et al. (eds.), *CRM Goes Digital*, Management for Professionals,
https://doi.org/10.1007/978-3-658-45798-3_17

models. This primary focus on efficiency improvement is a classic example of digitization within an industry.

Today, electronic data exchange between healthcare service providers and stakeholders remains in its infancy, although approaches for efficient solutions and processes exist. The focus is not exclusively to increase efficiency, but mainly to avoid errors at the interfaces between care providers. Of course, intelligent networking of hospitals, physicians in private practice, cost bearers, and nursing staff will cause lasting change in patients' customer experience during treatment. But initially, this "only" concerns the digitization of preexisting communication processes.

In the meantime, many insurance companies have begun to digitize established customer processes. This includes the following examples:

- Electronic customer support via a website
- Increased email communication
- Digital customer accounts to view products, services, and statements
- Options to send medical bills to the insurance company through a smartphone app

For the customer, even such small advances represent a significant facilitation of functional communication with the insurance company. However, the insurance company's services have not yet changed. With the purely functional digitization of existing processes, the potential of digital transformation and new technologies—such as Internet of Things (IoT), Artificial Intelligence (AI), and Big/Smart Data—is not being exploited.

## 2 Where Does That Leave the Customer?

A McKinsey study shows that life insurance companies average 15 customer contacts per year (Berger-De-Leon et al. 2016), equating to 12 monthly bills and 3 doctor's visits. Although insurance companies play a central role and approval of a patient's costs influences decisions on possible treatment, these contacts are negatively charged, even in ideal cases. Neither a premium bill nor a doctor's visit is likely to induce emotionally positive patient/customer experiences.

From the customer's point of view, the insurance company is only a commodity provider. The insurance carrier cannot accept this role. Besides its basic service mandate, it has competition: the insurer is not a sole player on the market, which is a competitive environment. Various sales and marketing measures play a role in positioning, as do customer loyalty and customer satisfaction. Insurers have a business responsibility to shape customer relationships positively. However, traditional measures are often one-way streets, as with conventional customer magazines, mailings, and even a static website, for example. The ubiquitous over-abundance of information quickly turns such one-way streets into dead ends.

This contrasts with the phenomenon of our time: social media. Depending on the industry, channel, and topic, hundreds-to-tens of thousands of customer contacts can be quickly generated every year. These are often banal ("here's a picture of my lunch"), yet they still trigger intense reactions in the target audiences' network (e.g., comments, re-postings, likes, dislikes). Social media activities often have only a short-lived social background, but arbitrarily-linked thematic activities exist as well. Commercially, social media platforms are now far superior to traditional advertising and communication channels as places for targeted information, communication, and advertising.

You would think "1 + 1 = 2" easily adds up. Using social media to address the insurance industry's needs and challenges and to interface with healthcare customers is obvious. But the equation is actually more complicated.

## 3 Looking Out for the Black Swan: Digital Trends in Healthcare

A "black swan" is a highly unlikely and unpredictable event. A popular example is the discovery of America in the search for a new sea route to India. Economically, it often refers to disruption from competitors outside the market, like the Internet's effect on the music industry. What black swans have in common is an unexpected appearance that can be explained logically and comprehensibly in retrospect. Black swans are the blind spots in the perception of our industries.

Healthcare decision-makers have recognized opportunities and threats in digital transformation. While opportunities are predominantly seen in the digitization of functional processes within insurance companies, and sometimes in customer service, digital transformation also poses risks for insurance carriers. These can be summarized in two areas: customer contact and health literacy.

### 3.1 Customer Contact

Insurance companies risk losing their already relatively limited contact and access to their customers. This can happen through new intermediaries or new market players. Ultimately, market share and pricing strategy are at stake. The potential role of supplier to a powerful intermediary is tantamount to commoditizing, and thus marginalizing, one's own service offering. The Swiss insurance industry experienced a wake-up call in 2014 with the company Knip. As the first "digital insurance broker," Knip gained significant market share in just a short time through an innovative app that allowed customers to bundle and manage their insurance relationships. While Knip ultimately failed to gain traction, its adoption of customer dialogue challenged the role of insurance companies.

### 3.2 Health Literacy

Due to unstructured and unregulated access to pseudo-medical information in the internet, people can easily make a supposed self-diagnosis, establishing the "right" treatment as well, from their personal computer. "Dr. Internet" is feared by medical professionals and can significantly, but inconspicuously, change the relationship between customers and insurance companies in contact over matters of health. Negative notices and bans are of no use at this point. Innovation always seeks an outlet. Answering medical questions with information from questionable sources, however, is dangerous and misleading for individuals and for the wider insured population. When processes cannot be regulated by restrictive measures, it is only mutual trust that enables recognition of an advisor or partner in difficult situations. Trust is built through shared experience. However, intensive customer experience based on partnership cannot be established through 15 customer contacts a year. To sustainably build trust takes numerous positively charged customer interactions.

Whereas the customer-facing influences of digitization are often mentioned first, healthcare as a whole is in a kind of "sandwich position." The disjointed influences of digitization on the end-customer relationship contrast with highly structured processes on the industry side. Watson, IBM's AI application, focuses heavily on the healthcare sector. "Dr. Watson" is expected to support doctors in future diagnostic processes. For cost bearers, this can have cost-reducing or cost-increasing effects; cost-reducing through greater efficiency in diagnostic processes and cost-increasing because another service is offered and obtainable for compensation.

Numerous individuals use Google to research their own symptoms and self-diagnose. Both iOS and Android-powered cell phones can collect, track, and share health, fitness, and medical data across multiple applications and devices. The collection of this data works through built-in sensors in the cell phone or through externally connected devices, such as pedometers. The data, with user consent, is sent to the respective app developers. Apart from the data protection concerns of transferring sensitive health-related data to the U.S., it is difficult to estimate which business cases benefit from this high density of personal data on a global scale.

Compared to traditional insurance companies, with only historical (disease) data, the providers of operating systems and healthcare applications have a clear advantage. While Apple has yet to communicate a healthcare strategy, initiatives to collect and archive personal health data cannot be overlooked. Google's holding company Alphabet has invested $375 million in U.S. health insurance company OSCAR Health. Currently, OSCAR Health is focusing on expansion within the U.S.; if and when it will enter the European market is unknown.

Amazon is also involved in the insurance environment and is busy establishing an insurance arm in Europe, with London as its headquarters. Although generating and collecting big data is an obvious starting point for the healthcare initiatives of companies like Google and Apple, this does not apply to Amazon. A publicly traded company is under constant pressure to grow and must continually identify and explore areas for growth. Being able to use extensive preexisting customer relationships for future insurance services was probably the driver for Amazon. To what extent a digital bookstore should be a trustworthy source for insurance services remains to be seen. Initially, Amazon will focus on property insurance.

It is impossible to predict whether and when an effective disruption will occur in the healthcare sector and how various market players' roles will change as a result.

However, it is clear that opportunities are being sought from various directions to shape and distribute healthcare processes and budgets differently using new digital applications. The vulnerability of the healthcare sector is systemic. On the one hand, the aging of Western industrial societies makes it easy to calculate rises in different disease patterns. There is always a business case for this too. On the other hand, the financing basis of today's healthcare system cannot be scaled. A contribution-based pay-as-you-go system inevitably comes under pressure as the number of care cases rises. Meanwhile, healthcare is the last major sector for which the digital transformation has not yet advanced, due to its considerable regulations. Regulations lead to inefficiencies and ultimately slow adaptation to new realities.

The Uber example demonstrates how a disruptive digital competitor "invaded" a highly regulated market. Where Uber was able to leap over existing artificial hurdles in the cab industry, the established market players had little or nothing to offer the new provider. The disruptive power of digital business models can be demonstrated in various industries: Facebook, AirBnB, Opodo, Amazon, and YouTube are just a few examples. In the current situation, healthcare decision-makers must assume they are the targeted prey of digital sharks. Black swans cannot be predicted, but it is clear that numerous non-industry initiatives are already being driven by much effort and large investment. The emergence of a truly disruptive offering will be no surprise in this context.

## 4 Technologies and Trends

A brief inventory of Western societies considers us "overfed and under-mobilized." This is already leading to an increase in hypertension, cardiovascular disease, and Type II diabetes. This trend will continue in coming years, driven by demographic change. At the same time, around 90% of the Swiss population already has a smartphone (Statista 2018) and for several years, the quality of the sensors built into cell phones has accurately determined users' movement patterns. We are still in the early stages of measurement technology, and this is the first time suitable measurement devices have been available to the wider population. The consequences of unhealthy lifestyles are already costing our healthcare systems, a trend bound to intensify in coming years, yet we already possess the technical means to closely monitor the entire population's health and exercise.

### 4.1 Stakeholders and Their Views

Stakeholders in the healthcare system assume different roles. Whereas society (here a synonym for citizens and government agencies) focuses on ensuring optimal provision of healthcare services, healthcare providers (physicians, hospitals, etc.) primarily confront treatment of increasing numbers of (often chronic) cases. Consistent quality can only be ensured with increasing utilization, by either a significant increase in efficiency or an expansion of resources. Healthcare spending already accounted for 12.2% of Swiss GDP in 2016. On average, this accounted for 803 CHF per month per person for Swiss residents. This value has doubled in just 24 years (Swiss Federal Statistical Office 2016).

For insurance providers, this creates a double challenge in shaping customer relationships. On the one hand, the focus is on building trusting and stable customer relationships for the sake of commercial and market strategy, and sustainably influencing lifestyles of the insured can influence long-term healthcare costs. If enough insured people adopt a healthier lifestyle, this permanently reduces the impact of behavior-induced disease patterns. A "healthier lifestyle" is an abbreviated term for active prevention programs. Healthy nutrition and regular exercise belong to the active design area. On the other hand, moderate consumption of stimulants, avoiding harmful substances, and mindfully dealing with personal health all require rethinking or sustainably changing behavior.

These challenges mean insurance companies are moving far beyond normal CRM frameworks, which are mostly geared to comparatively one-dimensional behavioral patterns. Common metrics such as ARPU (Average Revenue per User), NPS (Net Promoter Score), or RFM (Recency, Frequency, Monetary Value) are useless in this context. Complexity arises from heterogeneous insured portfolios. Depending on socio- and psychographic characteristics, individual interest and needs show great differences. Health and time are only perceived as important when they are no longer available. Getting attention for prevention-relevant topics is a special challenge. SWICA Health Insurance divides situations of need within the insured portfolio into the following groups:

- Being healthy
- Getting healthy
- Living with limitations

This shows how different objective needs are and the possibilities to address customers accordingly.

## 4.2 Digital Customer Relationships in Healthcare

The Federal Electronic Patient Dossier Act (EPDG) has been the legal basis for the introduction of the Electronic Patient Dossier (EPD) since 2017. The EPD describes a platform through which health-critical data can be exchanged by service providers. The patient–customer is involved in the process as the data owner, and thus gives permission for the release or transfer of their personal health data. The EPD is an infrastructure-oriented application that digitizes processes between service providers. Customer relationship design does not occur (BAG 2018).

Since 2016, insurance companies have introduced proprietary online platforms or mobile apps to address prevention-related topics. These range from general health tips to nutrition and advice on stress management. Some programs include measuring physical activities. In most cases, this involves counting steps. Overall, however, the platforms fall far short of the offerings of dedicated fitness platforms (such as Garmin, Suunto, and Fitbit). Incentives are mostly offered through discounts on products from the company's own portfolio. In some cases, cash payments of premium amounts are also offered.

### 4.3 Customer Reluctance

Customers are generally willing to share what they see as positive information, even outside of contractual relationships with insurance companies. However, there is no willingness to share disadvantageous data. People are happy to tell the insurance company, for example, about their participation in a triathlon, but reluctant to tell it about their all-nighter. In connection with exercise programs—for example, incentivizing step performance—this behavior leads to self-selection, in which only athletic persons participate in a program. A broad effect in the customer portfolio thus remains absent. For people who do not feel addressed by the offer, however, this can have a negative effect. The feeling of not meeting the (unspoken) demands of the insurance company can trigger frustration and the impression of rejection in the customer relationship. Many platforms experience a significant drop in participant engagement after only a few weeks. When competing with diverse media and entertainment content, customer loyalty offers have to hold their own and prevail in the long term. The requirements for the design and content of successful customer loyalty programs are high.

## 5 A digital Customer Loyalty Program in the Swiss Health Market

A Swiss insurance has operated a digital customer platform since 2015. As technological basis a customer engagement platform, offered as a white label solution, specifically for the needs of insurance companies, has been chosen. The platform is focused on the performance of customer engagement programs in the healthcare industry.

Another implementation partner is a local pharmacy association. Combining different stakeholders of the healthcare system unlocks economies of scale: the technical effort is shared, and on the other hand, the benefits for consumers increase significantly.

The health platform is designed to motivate participants to adopt health-oriented lifestyles, for which they receive personal health tips, take on fun challenges, and win attractive prizes. This gives them the chance to influence their premiums for individual insurance policies through active and healthy behavior.

## 5.1 Customer Experience 1.0

On the platform, participants find information on various health-related topics. An important component is an interest-driven content management system. Through participant self-declaration and actual content consumption, content distribution is controlled in a user-specific way. The user interface differs in appearance accordingly, and, in this respect, the user experience is unique.

Within the platform, steps can be counted and participants take part in step challenges. Within the step challenges, they compete in game-like competitions. An important part of the design is that implementation of the step challenges is non-discriminatory. The most athletic person does not automatically win. Especially for participants with a low body image and negative experiences of their own athletic performance, it is very important to experience success within the customer loyalty program. This approach makes it possible to successfully address traditional risk groups (Fig. 1). Participants are rewarded with virtual points on the platform for various actions. This applies to marketing and sales processes as well as prevention and health-related behavior. If a participant reaches a predefined number of points, rewards can be redeemed.

The platform is integrated into the CRM processes of the pharmacy association: personal health tests for cardiovascular and pulmonary functions are performed and archived through the platform at the point of service within the decentralized network. Advantage offers can also be accessed via the platform.

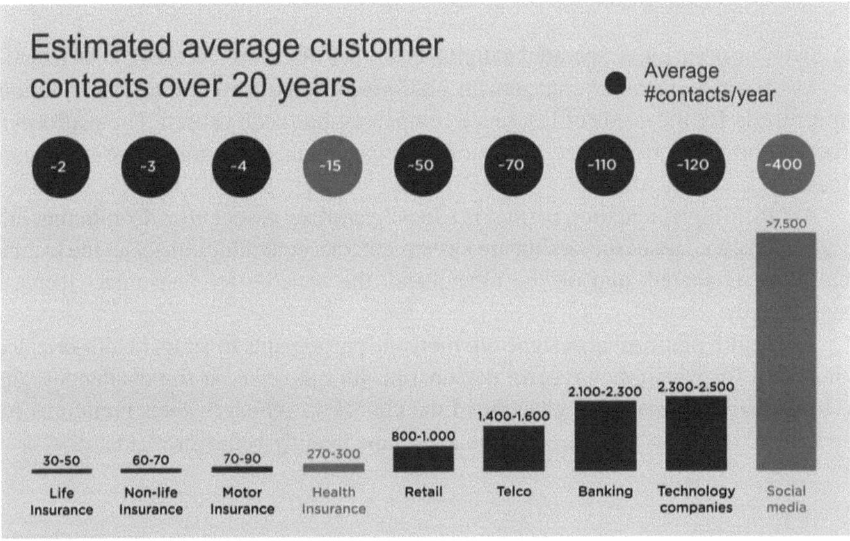


**Fig. 1** Addressing traditional risk groups and motivating them in the long term (author's creation)

### 5.2 Stumbling Blocks and Success Factors

Due to the external operation of the customer loyalty platform, the health insurance itself does not have access to customer data. This is both contractually fixed and an important element of customer communication. The "danger" that the insurance company uses participants' personal data and that participants suffer disadvantages is thus safely excluded. This is also reflected in the participant profiles. Self-selection, as observed in other (proprietary) customer loyalty platforms in the healthcare sector, cannot be detected. The inclusion of groups of people with a low level of motivation and significant risk factors is a central building block for implementing a comprehensive customer loyalty program. Applications for persons with acute illnesses to support therapy (patient adherence) are also conceivable in future.

Stable usage behavior (engagement) requires different channels to reach participants. In addition to the integration of classic media channels, incentivization (through rewards and discounts) and interaction through various offers and channels are important. This includes general information on insurance-specific topics, integration of events, and even editorial contributions on health-related topics. Here, professional quality and the acceptance of the editorial contributions and content by participants are decisive. Professional quality represents the insurance company's competence, and high-level interest of participants in the content is important for contact frequency with users on the platform.

## 6 Customer Experience 2.0: Health in the Eco-System of Different Stakeholders

Health has many dimensions and fundamental importance. Accordingly, a health platform cannot develop effectively on just one isolated channel. Success criteria will include integrating different communication media and channels to reach the customer and the creation of multidimensional touchpoints. This means communicating the health platform's content online and offline, for example at events, through sponsorship, and through personal customer contacts. Partnerships with other stakeholders in healthcare and compatible industries are also important; for example, connecting the insurance customer platform with corporate healthcare partners. Employers, like insurance carriers, are cost-sensitive to employee absenteeism, which poses significant challenges for employers. At the same time, organizations have numerous touchpoints through their employees. These can be used for communication to raise awareness and as an incentive channel to reward health-conscious behavior.

Another dimension is numerous touchpoints in retail stores. Here, strong customer experiences, especially for redeeming rewards, can be created. This is how a multi-partner loyalty program is established in healthcare. It is conceivable that participants will one day redeem their points balance with a morning coffee or local transport ticket. An eco-system with the most diverse and comprehensive partners possible from the retail and service sectors is an important building block.

## 7 Looking Ahead: New Trends, New Technologies

The digitization of customer relationships is now effectively beginning in healthcare. Combined challenges are accelerating this development. In particular, demographic change is forcing market players to go beyond pure CRM approaches. Confirming this trend is the September 2018 announcement by U.S. insurance company John Hancock that insured customers will receive exclusive discounts and benefits if they wear a tracker and provide the insurance company with their health data.

While insurance companies are still dabbling in proprietary customer loyalty programs, multi-partner programs are well proven in other industries. Especially because a health program's impact requirements go beyond classic CRM requirements, high customer value is considerably important. However, effective reward models benefit from multiple sponsors, and from comprehensive redemption opportunities. The future of loyalty programs in healthcare will therefore lie with multi-partner networks. New technologies will help solve problems around loyalty programs in healthcare. For example, blockchain applications can facilitate transactions between different partners in a multi-partner program and securely transmit healthcare data.

**Key Takeaways**

Health and time are not perceived as important until they are not available. Groups who are not intrinsically motivated for a healthy lifestyle place little importance on health-related behaviors. Sustained behavior change requires significant motivational support.

The goals of a CRM program in healthcare go beyond common CRM goals. Successfully influencing customer lifestyle habits requires a comprehensive approach and attractive incentives.

Achieving interest and relevance for health-conscious behaviors, as well as an active dialogue with insurance companies, requires a carefully coordinated dialogue and engagement strategy. This cannot be achieved through a proprietary in-house program. Key factors are the competencies of the program operator, a wide variety of reward options—for health-seeking behavior—and a ubiquitous and comprehensive partner network.

## References

BAG (2018) Projekt Bundesgesetz über das elektronische Patientendossier. https://www.bag.admin.ch/bag/de/home/strategie-und-politik/nationale-gesundheitsstrategien/strategie-ehealth-schweiz/bundesgesetz-elektronische-patientendossier.html. Accessed: 11.10.2022

Berger-De-Leon M, Kühn J, Ring I, Straub M (2016) Transforming life insurance with design thinking. McKinsey. https://www.mckinsey.com/industries/financial-services/our-insights/transforming-life-insurance-with-design-thinking. Accessed: 11.10.2022

Bundesamt für Statistik (2016) Ausgaben für das Gesundheitswesen. https://www.bfs.admin.ch/bfs/de/home/statistiken/querschnittsthemen/wohlfahrtsmessung/indikatoren/gesundheitsausgaben.html. Accessed: 11.10.2022

Statista (2018) Statistiken zur Smartphone-Nutzung in der Schweiz. https://de.statista.com/themen/3581/smartphone-nutzung-in-der-schweiz/. Accessed: 11.10.2022

**Kolja A. Rafferty** is an international executive and expert for critical and complex transformation and a founding partner of the global boutique consultancy Leverage Experts AG. One of his competencies is the development of disruptive business models.

# Part IV

# Optimize

# Digital CRM: From Disruption to Business Model

David Laux

**Abstract**

This article explains how customer behavior and digitalization act as disruptors for markets and businesses and how they change the way communication, services, and customer relationships function in this day and age. In examples, Laux explains how these changes can be used to innovate business models and get closer to customers.

## 1 The Influence of the Customer in Change

In an age when the change from the salesman market to the buyer market is advanced in nearly all industries and competitive pressure is rising constantly due to the globalization of markets, enterprises have recognized for over 20 years that only customer connection and customer orientation will create a long-term competition advantage. A new business strategy is therefore increasingly establishing itself in companies. This is leading away from the product orientation that has prevailed towards a holistic customer orientation.

In addition, customers of our time are undergoing a social change that is making them more demanding and selective, as well as more sovereign and individualistic. The modern customer wants to be involved throughout the entire life cycle. Against this background, mass marketing and product differentiation alone are no longer sufficient to motivate customers to buy and to then retain them. Instead, customers want individual overall solutions that are tailored to their personal wishes. Particularly in times of crisis, such as the global Covid-19 pandemic, these wishes

D. Laux (✉)
DIGITALL Nature Switzerland AG, Pfäffikon, Switzerland
e-mail: david.laux@digitall.com



S. Kirchem et al. (eds.), *CRM Goes Digital*, Management for Professionals,
https://doi.org/10.1007/978-3-658-45798-3_18

intensify, as the desire for a reliable basis of trust between customers and companies grows on both sides.

Achieving this requires extensive knowledge of customer needs, business processes, and the working environment. Customer needs must be recognized and understood; only then can products and services be optimized and customer satisfaction generated. For customers, meeting these needs has become a standard, and failure is punished with abandonment.

According to an Accenture study (2018), every second customer leaves an online store or homepage if the offer is not relevant enough to their own needs. Of the customers surveyed, 91% prefer companies that offer a personal experience by recognizing the customer and generating offers based on subjective purchasing behavior.

A significant contribution is made by the global information network, which makes it much easier for customers to research alternatives and find products and services beyond local offerings. In addition, social media platforms and rating portals provide unprecedented transparency when it comes to customer feedback.

According to *Our World in Data* (Roser et al. 2015), there are approximately 7.7 billion people in the world, of which 3.5 billion are online. Of these, no less than 2.4 billion are on Facebook and one billion each on YouTube and WhatsApp. According to Statista (2021), smartphone use grew from 1.06 billion to 3.5 billion from 2012 to 2020. So more and more people are using the Internet, communicating via social media, and always reachable (and connected), even when on the move.

The relationship between people and machines in particular is changing significantly, as interaction with end devices is becoming increasingly individualized, especially due to the increasing and popular use of smartphones and advancing developments in artificial intelligence, such as search engines, virtual assistants (Siri, Alexa, etc.), and recommendation algorithms. The smartphone has thus become the extended arm of the user, who can obtain information anytime and anywhere and also communicate directly with companies. For this very reason, however, these interactions are also becoming more immediate and individualized, since the user determines when and how contact is made with the company.

With these developments, the classic "inside-out" company view can no longer deliver what the customer or user demands. Whereas companies used to guide the customer's purchasing cycle (keyword: sales funnel) and the customer was led along a firmly planned marketing, sales, and service route, modern customers want to act, interact, and inform themselves in a self-determined manner. The view from the inside to the outside must therefore be reversed.

"Outside-in" therefore describes the customer viewpoint that companies must adopt in order to learn about the demands, behaviors, and needs of customers in the digital and analog space and implement them throughout their communications strategies and all internal and external processes. The classic funnel, in which the lead enters at the top and exits at the bottom as a customer, thus becomes a self-determined customer journey. Customer journey management is the planning and implementation of customer-centric processes throughout the company and along the entire customer journey.

If companies execute digital strategies in the classic inside-out mode, the worst-case scenario threatens costly development projects that ultimately fail to gain acceptance in the market and among customers. Meanwhile, an outside-in perspective, that is, taking customer needs into account as part of business planning, can ensure that digital trends are adapted at an early stage, enabling companies to become market leaders. In short, digitalization will only succeed in the context of customer centricity.

**Inside-Out: Google Glass on the B2C Market**

The virtual smart glasses Google planned to introduce to the B2C market in 2012 were praised in advance by evangelists, the trade press, and tech experts, and hailed as the next big technological and disruptive development after the smartphone. But the market decided otherwise: With a purchase price of US$1500, the glasses were not only too expensive, but also offered little added value to the already established smartphone. In addition, data protection concerns and the threat of bans in countries with stricter data protection laws caused the glasses to fail.

The mistake: Instead of developing glasses with normal B2C users in mind, only experts and digital trendsetters were involved in the development and marketing. Since interest in the possibilities of new technologies outweighed pragmatic value at this stage, the glasses were unable to demonstrate any recognizable added value on the "real" market when compared with other, less expensive devices, particularly due to their high price. ◀

**Outside-In: Skype Replaces SMS and Phone Calls**

The development of Skype and Facebook's Messenger service was quite different. After years of SMS and phone calls being restricted to mobile phone contracts, users were suddenly able to send messages to friends, relatives, colleagues, and acquaintances, and even make calls abroad at no extra cost. Within 10 years, Skype's worldwide user base grew to 300 billion. For the telecoms industry, this was an unexpected development that became a significant disruption to the pre-existing telco offerings and continues to have a major impact on the way we communicate. Skype met an existing customer need and adapted to customer behavior by disrupting at a gap in the customer experience (i.e., cheap communication). ◀

While many companies recognize the need, they unable to apply customer centricity–that is, the strategic implementation of the outside-in perspective—and design successful customer experiences in a truly holistic way.

A Gartner study (via marketingcharts.com 2020) argues that process-related and strategic hurdles primarily prevent companies from meeting changing customer needs. For example, 47% of respondents lack a concrete CX strategy; 39% find it difficult to establish a uniform definition of terms within the company. If customer experience is interpreted differently in different departments and by different people, implementing a uniform strategy is impossible. If the right processes to centrally collect, manage, and store customer data are absent, then the necessary levers are missing to develop a CX strategy for all company areas and processes and to measure these processes sufficiently.

Data on customer interaction and customer behavior are fundamental for measuring success and failure. Although general studies and benchmarks help to a certain extent, companies must discover for themselves what their own customers prefer, which channels they use to communicate, and which technologies they want to use and how.

Gartner's Hype Cycle also demonstrates how the customer is becoming increasingly important in the development and use of digital technologies, especially when technologies are developing at an ever-faster pace. Compared to 2010 (Gartner 2010), the number of trends that actually end up in market-wide implementation beyond initial developments has been minimized dramatically. While 28 trends were identified in 2018 (Gartner 2018) that have currently reached their "hype peak," there is only one trend that is on its way to productive use after the initial disillusionment phase (the "Valley of Disillusionment"). Not a single trend is actually being used productively across the board. By comparison, there were still eight trends in production in 2010.

Now, in principle, one can assume a peak phase of technological developments, characterized by many different developments, from which individual market leaders emerge. At the same time, however, the hype cycle can also indicate that user feedback on modern trends is now more immediate. And there are many more technologies which, as a result, are either discontinued early due to lack of acceptance or require a longer phase of further development to gain acceptance. In short, the user has shown with the popularity of the smartphone, but also through failures—for example, of Google Glass—that the user now determines the market.

## 2 The Need for Change in Existing Business Models

There are numerous reasons why the existing business model must change for long-term competitive survival on the market. In addition to digitalization, which is currently on everyone's lips, many parallel and linked areas are currently changing and forcing companies to change. The global pandemic has also caused an acceleration of digital transformations which, according to McKinsey, have skipped several years of development (McKinsey 2020). Although various changes in everyday work and customer life will return to some "normalcy" after the pandemic, numerous irreversible changes are forcing companies to strengthen their digital presence or establish it for the first time. Additionally, experts warn that Covid-19 is not a one-time phenomenon, but signals a future of more unpredictable events due to technological development, climate change, and other globally influential issues. Companies therefore need to become much more flexible, and digitalization will help them.

## 2.1 Disruption

Innovation, but also world events that turn entire markets upside down, is increasingly likely. The Internet, digitalization, globalization, and lower barriers to development and networking are constantly creating new opportunities to rethink services and products. Numerous topics (artificial intelligence, self-service, blockchain) have the potential to disruptively penetrate markets. Meanwhile, political, social, and cultural (world) events ensure that long-term plans can rarely be adhered to with certainty. Accordingly, companies balance fundamentals that ensure stability, even in volatile markets, with the flexibility to reformulate entire business models.

With an eye on their own customer base, companies are much more likely to embrace innovative disruptive elements if they understand early why these innovations are so positively received and how to adopt them. If the music industry had recognized the potential of streaming services earlier, YouTube, Spotify and co. would not have influenced the market so strongly. Likewise for TV broadcasters and the influence that Netflix, Amazon Prime, and Apple TV on TV viewing behavior and revenue distribution.

▶ **Definition** "Disruptive" is a term that describes a technology or development that changes an entire process or market by creating new added value or even a new market in a positive sense, thereby endangering or displacing established business models. Fundamental to the disruptive element is the immediate transformation of the market. An innovation that is initially only adapted by a small target group due to high acquisition costs or a limited area of application, for example, and only gains long-term market influence, cannot be described as disruptive.

The automobile, for example, was not disruptive at all in the beginning because it was a luxury good available to only a few individuals and thus only replaced the transportation of goods and people by horses and other beasts of burden in the long term.

In a negative sense, a disruption can be an event that threatens markets through external influences and developments. A current example would be the weakening of numerous industries by Covid-19. However, even negatively disruptive events also provide positive changes, for example in the acceleration of vaccine development cycles.

## 2.2 New Competition

The above examples show that disruption also gives rise to new competitors, some of which can act more flexibly and quickly due to their start-up status. In the financial sector in particular, the so-called fintechs are seen as strong competition by many banks, as they have to meet lower regulatory requirements by focusing on individual areas of financial services.

In addition, digitalization is causing local competitive boundaries to disappear, which is strongly impacting the retail sector. Besides Amazon as the market giant of online retail, numerous global offerings are cheaper or more convenient and thus outcompete local providers.

## 2.3 New Business Models

The fintech business models are fundamentally different from traditional banks, as they focus on a pain point in the life cycle of a financial customer and optimize it such that the customer outsources the service to the fintech, bypassing their own financial institution. PayPal, for example, is replacing credit card payments on online platforms worldwide, enabling easy payment without cumbersome wire transfers.

Traditional companies have to keep an eye on these new business models, but they cannot always easily adopt them because of sometimes different foundations, specifications, and infrastructures that complicate the idea of simply copying the model and adding it to their own offering.

## 2.4 New Channels

While hardly any new channels for reaching customers have emerged for decades, this has changed dramatically with the arrival of the Internet in private households and, latterly, with the spread of the smartphone. The shift to the home office has additionally established technologies that were previously only used selectively or predominantly privately (video meetings, virtual event platforms, live streams on social media).

In addition to the classic homepage and search engine, there are now numerous, constantly new social networks, platforms, apps, and opportunities to interact with customers, whether directly via chat, telephone, social media, and live chat or indirectly via blog, rating portal, and marketplace.

For companies, each new channel raises the question of whether it is worth including in their mixed offering. Even if the company's own existing customers do not use the channel, new customer groups can potentially be tapped. However, the half-life of social media channels and apps in particular is often impossible to predict, while implementation is resource-intensive.

## 2.5 Changing Customer Behavior

Due to disruption, channels, digitalization, business models, and globalization, customer behavior is also changing at an ever-faster pace. This is because modern innovations are far less likely to consist of expensive hardware, such as the television in the 1950s and 1960s or the computer in the 1980s and 1990s. Instead, many innovations are software-based at the user level and can thus be used immediately without a large investment. Virtual assistance, for example, comes with Apple's smartphone operating system, and even Amazon's Alexa and Echo services can be used with devices priced well under €100. In short, customers can react much more quickly to innovations and use them for their own purposes. However, this makes them increasingly independent and also more unpredictable in terms of how and when to reach them.

For companies, these fears or leverage effects of the digital transformation should not be deterrents, but rather lead to a rethinking of how customer relationship management should be defined and work in the future. Classic CRM can thus become dCRM, digital Customer Relationship Management.

From now on, every corporate brand will be defined by the customer through the experience. The product or offer is no longer solely representative of the image, but also the customer experience. Silo thinking and the strong demarcations between corporate divisions must be abandoned in favor of a central, holistically planned corporate strategy. Processes, workflows, and IT must be thought through and set up across divisional boundaries.

Key figures, cost–benefit analyses, and reports must provide the necessary information, from the CEO to the team leader, to point out potential for action in every case and to feed into individual and overarching goals. IT must be aligned with corporate strategy and processes first, not the other way around. This requires close cooperation between IT and management, ideally with a mediator at management level.

The "new" must always be aligned with customer behavior and needs. Innovation for innovation's sake cannot lead to success either in the company or with the customer, if it fails to offer clear and distinct added value (see inside-out example: Google Glass). Accordingly, modern digital CRM must be thought of as a toolbox that can be individually adapted to the business model and customers.

## 3 The Role of CRM in the Digital Age

If companies must increasingly align themselves with customer needs, rather than prescribing them, then CRM systems must also evolve accordingly. The question, meanwhile, is whether they have kept up for the past 10 years and whether CRM systems are prepared for potentially disruptive developments in customer behavior and the marketplace.

Paul Greenberg, one of the leading thinkers in CRM, defined the understanding of CRM in the early 2000s as technological "enabling" to help companies generate positive customer experiences. He consistently excluded from his definitions the philosophical considerations of what customer relationship management can mean beyond technology. This questions, as elsewhere in this book, what the right step is for successful long-term use of CRM.

For a long time, the CRM system served more to collect data in databases. It was, so to speak, a company's "memory" of all past and present customer relationships.

Today, software solutions help companies to collect and evaluate customer data in a targeted manner to ultimately identify, analyze, deepen or, if necessary, terminate profitable customer relationships. However, CRM requirements now far exceed solid data management. In particular, they cover collaboration and links with other systems (e.g., marketing automation), proprietary automation functions, analytics, and a wide range of applications to inspire customers individually. CRM systems must therefore also serve their users more individually to cover different industries, customer groups and needs, and areas of application.

CRM must maintain an interesting balance by improving the user experience, for example in the UX area, compatibility with other systems, and mobility, to correspond with the lifeworld of users and to provide information "on the go."

At the same time, CRM systems should reflect the customer's lifeworld to optimize and generate customer experiences. Software users can only benefit from the functions if they also support customer management on the channels that modern customers demand.

The integration of the right channels and means of communication is particularly important so companies can reach customers where they are present in the digital space. According to a 2017 study by InsideSales.com, salespeople use only 18% of their time with their CRM system, while they spend nearly 62% with other sales technologies, primarily email.

This result shows that in most cases, the CRM system cannot cover the sales fields that are desired and needed to accomplish tasks. One inevitable question is whether this is because these options are not provided by CRM vendors or because companies do use them.

One leading topic, for example, is "social marketing," that is, communication and interaction with customers on and via social networks. Especially in times of crisis—when supply chains collapse due to the pandemic, shipping is delayed, or companies have limited resources due to home office or social distancing regulations—communication to the customer must take place in dialogue and be transparent. On social media channels, all concerns and issues become public and can significantly influence how customers and their networks perceive a company.

In the summer of 2020, U.S. companies invested an average of 10% more in social media than in the preceding months. This figure has since fallen, but is still higher than proportions of recent years (Moorman 2021).

## 4 Today's Megatrends and Their Impact on CRM

Megatrends like digitalization have a major impact on customer behavior through manifestations like mobile, cloud, and the Internet of Things, which are changing dramatically as a result. Customers sit in the "driving seat" and control their own information behavior. They no longer have to be familiarized with a topic by the company, but often enter the purchasing cycle pre-informed. In B2B business particularly, an added factor is many customers' high expectations of digital, personalized experiences from their B2C experiences, especially when it comes to eCommerce, social media use, product recommendations, and self-service options.

As a result, companies adopt a reactive mindset and lose out if they cannot identify the "next-best offer" ("the next-best deal") for the customer. There are currently numerous trends, innovations, and areas in the CRM market that can support, measure, and enable precisely this connection.

These trends include:

### 4.1 Using Artificial Intelligence to Automate CRM Workflows

Data analytics can help use artificial intelligence used to successively optimize workflows. Frequencies, times, and content can be successively adapted to customer behavior and, based on this, enable communication that generates the best customer reactions (conversion, interaction, contract conclusion, etc.).

### 4.2 CRM Data Flow Optimization through IoT Integration

The Internet of Things (IoT) is fundamentally changing services through smart machines and individual apps. Through a data flow from, for example, household appliances, the appliance performance can be optimized "remotely." However, information on usage (lifestyle, health, maintenance) can also be communicated to the customer through the app, or the customer can check and activate the devices on the move. For CRM, this opens up completely new possibilities for contacting customers and offering services, depending on the cooperation partner and device use.

### 4.3 Seamless Customer Experience Through Realization of Omni- or Multi-channel Options

Omni-channel approaches enable a seamless customer experience across different analog and digital channels. CRM systems can support this by making it easier for marketing, sales, and service to collect and merge information across different channels. Links with point-of-sale systems, social platforms, and online stores can provide a 360-view of the customer and thus document and process customer queries and interactions regardless of the communication channel.

### 4.4 CRM Self-Enablement Through Self-Service Processes

Self-service provides customers with options for dealing with a problem independently on the company website (or via an app) and finding a solution. With the help of portals, but also chatbots that can answer simple queries using artificial intelligence, customers can receive services 24/7 without having to queue.

## 4.5 Targeted Market Presence Through Social CRM

The aforementioned link with social networks will be necessary in the future, especially due to the complex use of channels by customers. While social marketing is already practiced across the board in companies, customer behavior shows that sales and especially service also benefit from a presence on social networks. A link with the CRM system ensures clean, fast processes (e.g., combined with a ticket system for service requests) and can positively support lead management in sales (keyword: social selling) with analytical functions.

## 4.6 Enhanced Information Access and Capture Through Enhanced Mobility

Mobility has been one of the most important requirements for CRM systems for years. Not only information access while on the move, but above all information entry (e.g., during or after a customer meeting or event) can support sales work. Information can be documented immediately and thus completely synchronized with the data system. This means automated workflows can be activated immediately, for example by assigning leads directly to responsible owners. Follow-up can occur directly and newly acquired leads and opportunities are not lost.

## 4.7 Increased Targeting of Customers Through CRM Analytics and Predictive Analytics

The use of data analytics, especially predictive analytics, is one of the most exciting areas of CRM development. Process data, but also customer data, is analyzed for specific goals and can calculate probabilities to make statements about close rates or next steps. Offers and content can thus be determined in a more targeted manner based on customer behavior. Likewise, opportunities can be automatically flagged based on potential success rates using various variables, some of which are dynamic.

## 4.8 Power Apps for Individual Automation

CRM vendors have increasingly recognized that the balance between standardized solutions and individual customization can be achieved through apps. Usage is varied, but often consists of "shadow IT"—that is, software and tech used outside of a company's IT knowledge. This creates data silos and, in some cases, data protection problems. With the option of "Power Apps," however, CRM systems can set up simple automations individually. This is not done via complex programming languages, but in intuitive drag and drop mode. CRM users can thus automate individual reporting, notifications, and simple tasks. Everything is done via the CRM, which means all data can be used and stored centrally at the same time.

Users can, for example, keep a closer eye on individual customer activities and thus identify customers at risk of dropping out at an early stage, react immediately to special activities, and manage appointments more easily.

## 5 Digitalization as a Lever for Customer Management

The customer journey and digitalization together contribute to a good approach to transforming customer communication. From push to pull or—as we like to put it—from customer relationship management to customer journey management. However, it is important that opportunities emanating from digitalization are also covered in the CRM system. Additionally, companies must accept and try out available functionality to find the right mix for their customers.

In this process, marketing controls communication and sales is used where it achieves the greatest efficiency, in the closing phase and in cross-selling and upselling. Services can be optimized through digital offerings and customer satisfaction can improve as a result. Customers have emancipated themselves because they are the masters of their own research and expect the company to accommodate them as they wish and need. This is precisely why companies must adopt a customer-centric view. This includes not only the use of new technologies, but rethinking the approach to processes, communication strategies, and content. Change management plays a major role and can, if necessary, lead to old structures being questioned and rebuilt. CRM must no longer be understood solely as a sales topic, but must be applied to the entire company; only in this way can seamless customer experiences succeed. Companies must move away from a product- or company-centric approach to a customer-centric approach. The CRM system, as a database and enabler, will play a key and growing role in this process in the future.

The modern, now-feasible dCRM has two different, central tasks:

### 5.1 CRM as the Central Digitalization Platform of the Customer Interface

Particularly in the context of digitalization, it is necessary to link different processes and company divisions. CRM can be a central digitalization platform from which other linked systems can be controlled and monitored. In this way, processes can be planned and implemented throughout the company.

To achieve this, all necessary customer interfaces must be digitized above all. Where does the customer make contact with the company, for what purpose, and with what expectations? Digitalizing these interfaces ensures greater transparency customer interactions and thus identifies weak points more quickly (e.g., long waiting times).

## 5.2 Consistent Implementation of Customer Requirements for the Company

With the growing number of digital and analog channels, the CRM system is ideally suited to bundling customer requirements centrally and forwarding them to the appropriate company departments or owners. Customers will not pay attention to the internally defined areas of responsibility and channels; they will also make service requests via social media, if possible.

For this reason, individual company divisions should not use channels solely for their own purposes and ignore all requests that do not fall within their area. Internal processes need to enable queries to be forwarded internally to externally reflect uniform corporate structure and communication. Since the CRM can be the central customer database of any company, it is ideal for accessing customer history, enabling automated workflows, and identifying responsible parties to handle requests.

## References

Accenture (2018) Making it Personal –Why brands must move from communication to conversation for greater personalization. Pulse Check 2018. www.accenture.com/t20161011T222718__w__/us-en/_acnmedia/PDF-34/Accenture-Pulse-Check-Dive-Key-Findings-Personalized-Experiences.pdf Zugegriffen: 7 January 2019

Gartner (2010) Hype cycle for emerging technologies, 2010 https://www.gartner.com/en/documents/1414917. Accessed: 5.10.2022

Gartner (2018) Gartner identifies five emerging technology trends that will blur the lines between human and machine https://www.gartner.com/en/newsroom/press-releases/2018-08-20-gartner-identifies-five-emerging-technology-trends-that-will-blur-the-lines-between-human-and-machine Accessed: 5.10.2022

marketingcharts (2020) Here's where marketers are struggling most with the customer experience and personalization. https://www.marketingcharts.com/customer-centric/customer-experience-115587 Accessed: 5.10.2022

McKinsey (2020) How COVID-19 has pushed companies over the technology tipping point—and transformed business forever. https://www.mckinsey.com/capabilities/strategy-and-corporate-finance/our-insights/how-covid-19-has-pushed-companies-over-the-technology-tipping-point-and-transformed-business-forever Accessed: 5.10.2022

Moorman C (2021) The transformation of marketing: emerging digital, social, and political trends. https://cmosurvey.org/wp-content/uploads/2021/02/The_CMO_Survey-Highlights_and_Insights_Report-February-2021.pdf Accessed: 5.10.2022

Roser M, Ritchie H, Ortiz-Ospina E (2015) "Internet" https://ourworldindata.org/internet Accessed: 5.10.2022

Statista (2021) Number of smartphone subscriptions worldwide from 2016 to 2021, with forecasts from 2022 to 2027. https://www.statista.com/statistics/330695/number-of-smartphone-users-worldwide/ Accessed: 5.10.2022

**David Laux**, CEO of DIGITALL, drives the company's global strategy, growth, and execution. With a proven track record of implementing successful practices and keeping up to date on emerging trends and technologies, he has established the value framework and relevant network for a sustainable business. David is a respected visionary leader known for combining a focus on growth with innovative thinking and a clear commitment to business objectives with a uniquely human touch. Before DIGITALL, he co-founded and led ec4u expert consulting ag as CEO, the leading customer management consultancy in the DACH market. David also held various management positions, including District Manager with Siebel Systems Inc., Key Account Manager, and CRM Manager at Nova Data AG/entory AG. With a business administration and industrial engineering background, David has consulted and supported international companies in the telecommunications, banking, and insurances industries for over 25 years. Beyond his work at DIGITALL, he is an active business angel and investor in innovative startups and serves on the advisory boards of several European companies. He has also taught CRM at the University of Cooperative Education in Karlsruhe and is an author of several books and publications.

# Using Customer Data and Feedback to Optimize Products and Services

Laura Braun and Sven Reinecke

**Abstract**

The market's increasing diversity of providers, products, and services confronts today's companies with expanding customer demands and desires for immediate, individual treatment. Systematically managing customer data and concretely collecting and using feedback makes an effective and efficient customer approach possible, and also facilitates the individualization and optimization of services and products. This chapter deals with the preconditions, options for action, and effects of individualized service design. First, we discuss the necessity of data collection and enrichment as a basis for the use of customer data. Subsequently, we demonstrate possibilities and design measures in interaction and performance optimization through concrete examples. At the end of the chapter, we summarize relevant findings for decision-makers with guiding questions for a management-oriented approach in customer-data-centric product and service design.

L. Braun (✉)
Dr. Braun Innovation GmbH, Zurich, Switzerland

University of St. Gallen, Institute for Marketing & Customer Insight, St. Gallen, Switzerland
e-mail: hello@drlaurabraun.com

S. Reinecke
University of St. Gallen, Institute for Marketing & Customer Insight, St. Gallen, Switzerland
e-mail: sven.reinecke@unisg.ch



S. Kirchem et al. (eds.), *CRM Goes Digital*, Management for Professionals,
https://doi.org/10.1007/978-3-658-45798-3_19

## 1 Increasing Effectiveness and Efficiency Through Data-Centric Service and Product Design

The growing choice of providers, products, and services on the market means companies are faced with increasing customer demands as well as the desire for immediate and individualized treatment (see Bughin et al. 2010; Kunz et al. 2017; Lehrer et al. 2018). Today, new technologies and the comprehensive digitalization of customer interaction open up the mapping of online and offline customer behavior and the exploiting of corresponding potential on the basis of holistic customer profiles. Systematic management of existing customer data and the targeted collection and use of customer feedback not only increase performance, but also facilitate the individualizing and optimizing of a company's own services and products. Companies such as Zalando, Amazon, Nike, Harrods, Modomoto, Ovomaltine, and Swiss Airlines provide examples of successful implementation.

A data-based outside-in perspective in service design and optimization offers various advantages for a more effective and efficient customer approach: customers can be served more adequately by designing relevant interaction content, processes, and measures as well as by adapting the company's own range of offers. Various cases show positive effects on the effectiveness of personalization and customization measures and prove that customers not only respond more frequently to personalized offers, but are also more likely to make a purchase than with standard offers.

Furthermore, knowledge of customer behavior and preferences makes it possible to avoid ineffective marketing activity, leading to resource savings and increased efficiency. The corresponding effects of increased effectiveness and efficiency can be summarized in essence as follows in Fig. 1:

**Increasing effectiveness**

1. Increasing the relevance of offers, higher turnover rates
2. Strengthening customer loyalty
3. Derivation of schemes to optimize future interactions
4. In general: increasing the achievement of set goals in terms of costs, time, quality, flexibility & security

**Increasing efficiency**

1. Less resources required per converted customer (output/input ratio)
2. Fewer resources required per converted customer compared to standard measures
3. Possibility of automating processes and thus reducing costs at the same time

**Fig. 1** Effectiveness and efficiency of individualized services (Source: Author's illustration)

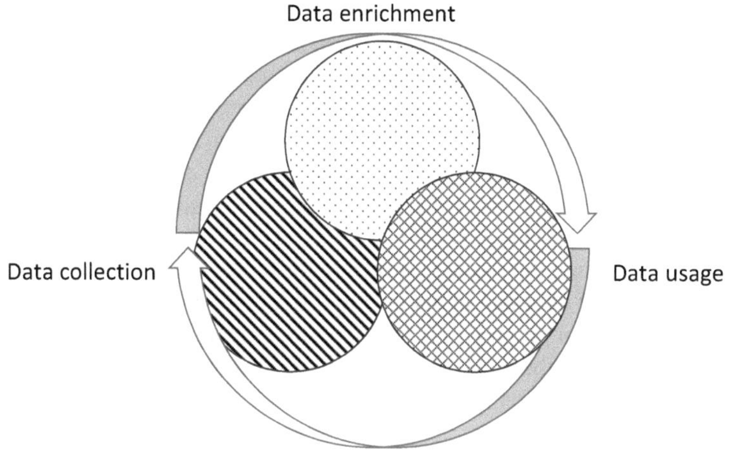


**Fig. 2** Schematic representation of the interrelationship of data collection, data enrichment, and data use (Source: Author's representation)

In what follows, we offer recommendations for systematically using customer data and feedback for service and product optimization to exploit potential for effectiveness and efficiency. We will not only demonstrate the advantages of such a data-centric and thus customer-centric approach, but we will also explain the relevant prerequisites for appropriate management.

## 1.1 Data Collection and Enrichment as the Basis for Data Utilization

The successful integration and use of customer data and feedback poses key challenges for companies. To meaningfully transfer information about customer interests, needs, and behavior into product and service design, an objective, reliable, and valid database is required, characterized not only by quantity, but especially by quality. Companies that strive towards customer-centric or data-centric service design must therefore closely examine possibilities for data collection and enrichment to identify the potential and the limits of their use. Data collection, enrichment, and use should therefore not be seen as separate processes, but as three integrated tasks of the company (see Fig. 2).

Beginning with explanations of data collection, the following sections detail the opportunities and challenges of these activities and how they interact.

### 1.1.1 Data Collection

The goal of customer-based product and service optimization is to design services that not only serve the needs and behaviors of today's customers, but also, if possible, address future interaction behavior between customers and companies. For this reason, not only the quantity but also the quality of collected data is of particular importance. General quality criteria from social research can orient assessments of data quality (e.g., Wolf and Best 2010). These are objectivity, reliability, and validity, and we outline them briefly now against the background of the current topic.

### Objectivity

Objectivity in this context describes the extent to which data generated about customers and their behavior was collected, evaluated, and interpreted independently of any influences. First, this applies to the type of survey or the person responsible for the survey; second, the evaluation method or process; and third, the interpretation of the generated data should not lead to different findings (see also Rammstedt 2010; Rost 1996), for example all information generated about a customer in a consultation should be the same, regardless of whether salesperson A or salesperson B conducts the conversation or collects the data.

### Reliability

Reliability describes the accuracy with which a certain characteristic is recorded by the survey method or, conversely, how susceptible to error the data in the survey are due to situational factors (e.g., Rost 1996). For example, the measurement of basic product interest can be very susceptible to bias and thus very inaccurate, depending on the situation and the survey method.

### Validity

The validity of information concerns how well data actually measure what is to be observed. Since measuring customer opinions directly is often impossible, indirect survey methods are used, for example, which aim to discover underlying characteristics (e.g., Rammstedt 2010). For example, it is not possible to directly ask customers about their intentions to make an online purchase, but it is possible to record this indirectly through measures like the number of visits to the product website, the length of time spent on the site, and interaction with customer ratings. Prerequisites for the validity of collected data are the other two quality criteria of objectivity and reliability.

If we now turn to the concrete collection of data, the range of data reference sources is clearly growing rapidly, especially in the course of technological progress (e.g., Bughin et al. 2010). In addition to offline-generated data (e.g., from employee logs of direct in-store customer interactions), online- or sensor-generated information is now available, enabling endless potential for companies to shape performance (e.g., Kunz et al. 2017). Online- and sensor-generated information offer companies the particular advantage of generating large volumes of data directly and in real time with comparatively little effort (see also Braun et al. 2017).

Online and offline sources together result in a wide range of information about current customer preferences and behaviors and can thus form a basis for service design. Two mechanisms must be distinguished here:

1. Data collected by companies or generated in interaction with customers
2. Data provided by customers themselves on their own initiative

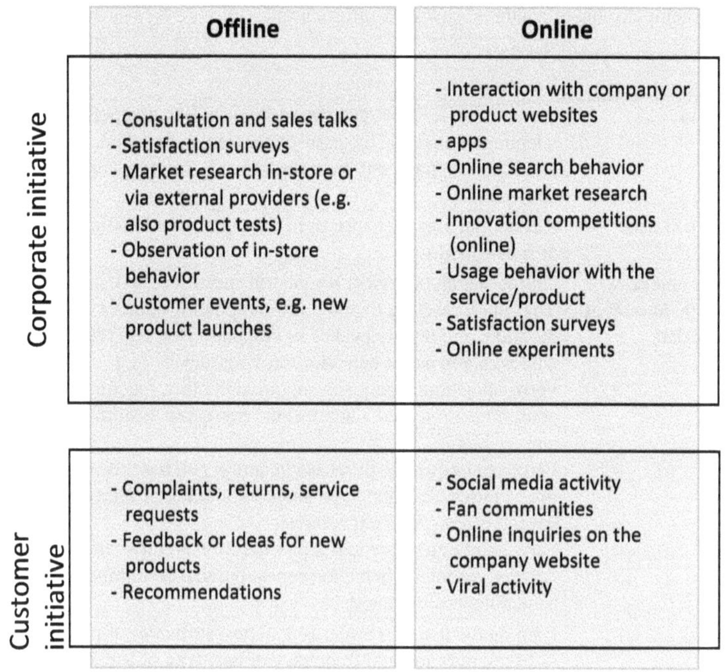


**Fig. 3** Illustration of exemplary sources of customer information in the online and offline environment (Source: Author's illustration)

Figure 3 shows examples of these two processes:

To exploit the full potential of data collection, providing customers with various dialogue options to interact with the company is beneficial. Particularly online, companies can use numerous measures, such as contact forms, online surveys, direct help functions, chat options, and feedback forms that efficiently collect, document, and evaluate information (Bliemel et al. 2000).

Even though offline customer interaction is significantly more resource-intensive in comparison, it offers the advantages of responding more specifically to customers and thus the chance to seek more in-depth and direct information (see also Braun et al. 2017).

In addition to classic qualitative and quantitative market research, targeted customer conversations in the context of sales can generate insights that can assist with the interpretation of other data, such as online interactions (see also Reinecke and Wortmann 2018).

Furthermore, tools such as company-owned or cross-company loyalty programs offer a direct way to integrate information from individual customers from online and offline channels. By using a program to identify customers at diverse touchpoints, concrete information about a customer's socio-demographic characteristics can be collected and correlated with individual search and purchase behavior (see also Braun et al. 2017).

**Table 1** Exemplary list of available customer information

| Excerpt of possible customer data | |
|---|---|
| Category | Examples |
| Master data | Surname, first name, gender, address (billing and delivery addresses), telephone numbers, age, household size, occupation, educational qualification, payment methods and data, relationships with other customers |
| Geographical data | Residential area; distance to nearest company location, store, service or repair facility |
| Marketing and sales history data, as well as after-sales data | Online search behavior; activity on social media (e.g., Facebook or YouTube); reaction to company campaigns; number of visits, duration, and thus relevance of company websites (especially via IP address); app usage behavior; browser, device (e.g., Ipad, laptop)<br>Form of customer acquisition, initial contact, reactions to different communication media and means, expressed customer preferences and wishes<br>Purchase frequency, purchase quantity, purchase location, purchase times, purchase value, type and combination of services, use of special offers, payment behavior<br>Service, maintenance and repair inquiries, returns and reasons for returns, complaint behavior, repeat purchases, number of friends and acquaintances recruited |
| User data | Data on the use of services (e.g., apps, software) or products; number of users; duration and frequency of use; type of use, e.g., differentiated consideration of the use of individual functions, error occurrence |

Source: Author's representation

Diverse reference sources result in numerous pieces of information on individual customers, as well as customer groups, which can be used for service design. Table 1 summarizes some examples of the available data points.

Although diverse and plentiful customer data show a more concrete profile and are thus better suited for service design, customer interests and data protection mean it is not always possible to collect and enrich this data (Rygielski et al. 2002). In addition to legal conditions such as the GDPR, it is important to ensure customers never feel observed by the company or deprived of their privacy, as this can have enormous negative consequences for the development of a trusting customer relationship.

### 1.1.2 Data Enrichment

To create holistic customer profiles and sharpen them with regard to relevant interaction offers, integrating different data sources and types is particularly important. Many companies thus rely not only on their own integrated online and offline data (e.g., social media data, information from loyalty programs and customer surveys), but also on procured information from third-party providers. By purchasing external customer data (e.g., via the so-called customer data marketplaces) and using the company's own profiles, holistic perspectives on individual customers or segments can be formed (cf. Braun 2017; Forbes 2018). A distinction must be made in this

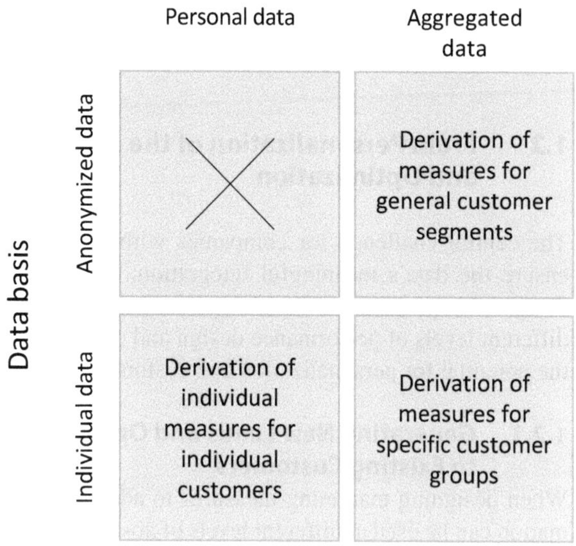


**Fig. 4** Illustration of exemplary sources of customer information in the online and offline environment (Source: Author's illustration)

area between central procedures of data enrichment and subsequent data use processes.

1. Enrichment/use of personal data: Concrete information from individual customers through various channels—for example, in-store purchases and social media or Google data—is linked together to develop individual measures like personalized advertising on recent Amazon purchases that is shown on various websites.
2. Enrichment/use of aggregated customer data: Customer data is enriched by anonymized information from other customers of a similar profile and thus bundled into stereotypes. Examples here are further product recommendations based on the customer's own purchases and the purchasing behavior of comparable customers (e.g., Apple iTunes, Amazon, nu3, Zalando, booking.com).

Figure 4 shows an example of the resulting four possibilities for data enrichment and use. It should be noted that in the case of anonymized data, a match with personal information is only possible if the so-called link variables are available for a concrete assignment. The four approaches differ significantly in their potential for individualized customer processing.

### 1.1.3 Data Utilization

There are many possible uses of generated data or comprehensive customer profiles for interaction and service design (see Lehrer et al. 2018). These range from adapting existing advertising measures or addressing new contacts to generate new leads, to optimizing existing services and products. As explained previously, data collection, enrichment, and use should be viewed as integrative processes. Even after implementing developed measures or services, data is again generated by customer interaction using the corresponding marketing measures, services, and products (e.g., Kunz et al. 2017). These can consequently be re-used as information sources for future service developments and optimizations.

## 1.2 From Personalization of the Address to Service Design and Optimization

The central challenge for companies with regard to diverse customer data is to ensure the data's meaningful integration, in order to make it usable for service design and optimization. We now present various possibilities for data utilization at different levels of performance design and optimization, paying special attention to the potential for personalization and customization.

### 1.2.1 Generating New Leads and Optimizing the Approach to Existing Customers

When designing marketing measures to address new or existing customers, information can be used at different levels of abstraction. The more concrete information one has about relevant target groups, the more one can design specific actions. One example of successful implementation of a target-group-appropriate address is from the company nu3, a provider of nutritional products in the areas of sports, health, and beauty. nu3 systematically collects customer information about interests, food preferences, and purchasing behavior. Data generated online (e.g., website interaction) and offline (e.g., nutritional advice for athletes by phone) is correlated and subsequently used for the design of personalized newsletters, product recommendations, and adjustments of website content.

### 1.2.2 Interaction Design and Optimization

The inclusion of customer data offers many possibilities for the design of interaction at concrete touchpoints between the customer and the company. Information on current customer needs, interests, and behaviors can be used to recommend specific products, adjust the assortment and product portfolio, change consulting options, and train sales staff. Harrods, for example, optimizes its own in-store advertising by considering socio-demographic customer data, which is collected in real time by video and evaluated to aid product recommendations that are shown on screens in the stores.

Another exciting case from the business-to-business environment is of the company CLAAS. The agricultural machinery manufacturer uses not only customer data, but also sensor-based product data to target consulting and sales activities at customers with past experience of maintenance, repairs, or increased error messages and thus with more limited product experience.

A similar example for the use of customer data to optimize service can be found at SWISS International Airlines. Customers who belong to the HON Circle or have previously flown First Class receive individualized service based on information about personal preferences (e.g., food) and routines.

For digital services, there are many opportunities for data-driven personalization of services. For example, as part of BMW Connected Services, BMW identifies previous driving patterns (times, recurring trips) and routes to home and work, which produce additional options. Customers thus experience, for example, that the fastest route to work is determined and displayed via Google or Apple Maps as a direct push message when they get into the car. In addition, the app offers functionalities in predictive maintenance that account for individual driving behavior. Also from the business-to-consumer area, Apple iTunes systematically uses data on customer behavior to improve user experience through personalized recommendations.

### 1.2.3 Performance Development and Optimization

A basic distinction can be made between data- or customer-based development and optimization of services, two approaches that frequently combine. Companies can rely on existing customer information for personalization and carry out product development and adaptation independently. Addition, customers can be included in the process by customizing customer integration in the development of new services. For many enterprises therefore, considering customer information and directly integrating customers into different stages of the value-creation process is part of the daily routine (Kleinaltenkamp et al. 1997).

In corporate practice, customers are involved in all phases of performance development, from the generation of ideas and the development of initial prototypes to final product testing and optimization (e.g., Hofbauer 2013). This approach has many advantages: With the help of concrete customer ideas and consumer feedback, new products and services can be developed, expanded, and optimized in line with the target group, so that discrepancies between customer and company perspectives are already revealed during the innovation process. Consequently, early customer integration can shorten innovation cycles and thus save resources (e.g., Kleinaltenkamp et al. 1997). The intensity of customer integration can vary. Three levels can be distinguished (e.g., Hofbauer 2013; Reichhart 2002):

1. Passive involvement: Customers can provide feedback, but have no influence on the integration of the feedback into the development of company services.
2. Active participation: Customers can, in part, develop new services and actively contribute alongside the producer.
3. Active participation: Customers take over entire subtasks in performance development (e.g., idea generation or prototype development) and thus make a significant contribution to the result.

Nike, Whirlpool, and SAP all provide corporate practice examples of using customer data and feedback for performance development and optimization. As part of Nike iD, for example, customers can personalize their own sports shoes in terms of shape, pattern, and color, which are then manufactured exclusively. On the one hand, customers are involved in the manufacturing process, but on the other hand, by disclosing their preferences, they are used as a source of information for future additions to the standard range.

Whirlpool, as a manufacturer of home appliances, integrates sensor-generated product interaction information with user-generated content from social media and other CRM data to generate insights into customer preferences and usage behavior.

This dataset subsequently forms the basis for optimization of existing products and performance development (see Woerner and Wixom 2015). Successfully collecting customer feedback and considering it in new product development is also common practice in the business-to-business sector. For example, SAP offers various opportunities for customers to not only provide feedback on existing software, but to also directly innovate new software solutions together with the company in the so-called co-innovation projects.

## 1.3 Management Implications for Implementing Data-Based Performance Development and Optimization

To be devoted to the concrete concept development and implementation of customer-data-based performance design, decision-makers need a comprehensive and targeted analysis of the status quo. They must account for their own activities and the competition. On this basis, assessing existing competencies and possible market opportunities is possible. To exploit the latter, the prerequisites for implementation in the company must be clarified. In addition to the existing infrastructure (in this context, primarily the IT infrastructure and the data basis), existing human resources and competencies should also be analyzed.

To ultimately measure the effectiveness and efficiency of existing and future measures, defining systematic monitoring and optimization is essential. Comprehensively assessing the cost–benefit ratio and effectiveness is only possible when alternatives are accounted for alongside individual performance measures.

Structured into four successive phases, the following checklist in Table 2 provided assistance in identifying possible approaches to strategy development.

## 1.4 Conclusion and Outlook

Systematic management of customer data and the targeted collection and use of customer feedback offer companies the opportunity to not only increase the effectiveness and efficiency of their customer approach, but also of their service design. The prerequisite for exploiting this potential is to ensure a high-quality quantitative and qualitative database that adequately and holistically maps customer needs and behavior. This chapter provides an overview of the initial conditions, opportunities, and recommended actions for using data to develop and optimize performance.

Technological possibilities, especially through the Internet of Things, artificial intelligence, and increasing process automation, offer companies varied potential for data enrichment and sharpening future customer profiles, using fewer resources. To avoid jeopardizing this potential, decision-makers must reflect on the possible consequences for the customer–company relationship when collecting and using data, in addition to legal issues.

**Table 2** Management checklist for implementing data-based performance development and optimization in the company

| |
|---|
| (A) Analysis of the status quo—data-based performance design and optimization. |
| To what extent do you currently use customer data for performance development and optimization (services and/or products)?<br>What response do you receive to these measures compared to the standard offering?<br>What statements can you make about customer feedback or usage? How are the corresponding KPIs of standard measures or data-based actions (e.g., conversion rate) currently shaping up? |
| Look at your competition: What measures are your market competitors currently pursuing in terms of customer-centric service design and optimization?<br>Where do you currently differentiate yourself in corresponding actions?<br>Where do you see market potential and opportunities to differentiate yourself from your competitors through a data-driven or customer-centric approach?<br>Are there opportunities for cooperation (e.g., in the area of data exchange) in your environment to increase your own data base or to enrich your offering? |
| (B) Analysis of future, possible, and relevant activities (short- as well as long-term). |
| Which of the existing activities offer potential for expansion against the background of market resonance and competition? |
| In which area of the customer journey do you see new starting points?<br>Which opportunities could be relevant for your company's current commercially interesting customer groups (e.g., to increase rates of repurchase, cross/up-selling, recommendations)?<br>What additional opportunities in this area would existing customers of your company like to take advantage of?<br>Are there target groups not yet served that you could attract by designing appropriate measures? |
| (C) Analysis of the company's own infrastructure and competencies for the implementation of corresponding measures. |
| How could additional activities in the area of data-based interaction and service-design be realized in the short or long term, i.e. within one-to-two years? |
| What customer data is currently available to enhance existing measures?<br>What data would need to be collected or processed from customers in the future to implement existing actions?<br>How can the technical means in the areas of data collection, storage, processing, and evaluation of the information be evaluated?<br>In general, how can the quality of the IT infrastructure be assessed against the background of the analysis of complex data volumes in real time?<br>What in-house competencies in the area of data-based service design are already available in the company today (especially action-planning, implementation, coordination, and maintenance)?<br>To what extent can existing personnel resources drive additional actions or is it necessary to acquire additional personnel? |
| (D) Definition of the monitoring and optimization process. |
| What are the specific objectives to be pursued by the activity under consideration?<br>What KPIs can be used to determine whether the activity is achieving its objectives?<br>What do possible comparison groups look like? Which standard processes or services can be used to compare the effectiveness and efficiency of a data-based approach?<br>How must the process be designed so that the results of the success estimation can be used to optimize the measures under consideration?<br>Which department/function is responsible for monitoring the success and optimizing the measures or is authorized to give cause for future measures? |

Source: Author's representation

## References

Bliemel F, Fassot G, Theobald A (2000) Electronic commerce: Herausforderungen - Anwendungen – Perspektiven. Gabler, Wiesbaden

Braun L (2017) Marketing trends 2017. Personalization. Aus: http://marketing2017.ch/beispiel-seite/personalization/. Accessed: 18.10.2018

Braun L, Reinecke S, Tomczak T (2017) Kundenbindung durch Loyalitätsprogramme. In: Bruhn M, Homburg C (eds) Handbuch Kundenbindungsmanagement. Springer, Heidelberg

Bughin J, Chui M, Manyika J (2010) Clouds, big data, and smart assets: ten tech-enabled business trends to watch. McKinsey Quarterly 56(1):75–86

Forbes (2018). The rise of the customer data platform and what it means to businesses. Aus: https://www.forbes.com/sites/insights-treasuredata/2018/06/20/the-rise-of-the-customer-data-platform-and-what-it-means-to-businesses/#60aea8c053a1. Accessed: 18.10.2018

Hofbauer G (2013) Customer Integration Prinzipien der Kundenintegration zur Entwicklung neuer Produkte. Working Paper. Ingolstadt

Kleinaltenkamp M, Ehret M, Fließ S (1997) Customer integration in business-to-business-marketing. In: Advances in services marketing. Deutscher Universitätsverlag, Wiesbaden, pp 27–48

Kunz W, Aksoy L, Bart Y, Heinonen K, Kabadayi S, Ordenes FV, Theodoulidis B (2017) Customer engagement in a big data world. J Serv Mark 31(2):161–171

Lehrer C, Wieneke A, vom Brocke J, Jung R, Seidel S (2018) How big data analytics enables service innovation: materiality, affordance, and the individualization of service. J Manag Inf Syst 35(2):424–460

Rammstedt B (2010) Reliabilität, Validität, Objektivität. In: Wolf C, Best H (eds) Handbuch der sozialwissenschaftlichen Datenanalyse. VS Verlag für Sozialwissenschaften, Wiesbaden, pp 239–258

Reichhart S (2002) Kundenorientierung im Innovationsprozess. Deutscher Universitätsverlag, Wiesbaden

Reinecke VS, Wortmann C (2018) Google Knows it Better? In: Praxis der Sinus-Milieus®. Springer VS, Wiesbaden, pp 193–207

Rost J (1996) Lehrbuch Testtheorie – Testkonstruktion. Huber, Bern

Rygielski C, Wang JC, Yen DC (2002) Data mining techniques for customer relationship management. Technol Soc 24(4):483–502

Woerner SL, Wixom BH (2015) Big data: extending the business strategy toolbox. J Inf Technol 30(1):60–62

Wolf C, Best H (2010) Handbuch der sozialwissenschaftlichen Datenanalyse. VS Verlag für Sozialwissenschaften, Wiesbaden

**Dr. Laura Braun** combines academic expertise with practical business acumen. As a former research associate at the Institute of Marketing at the University of St. Gallen (HSG), she has built a successful career in business strategy, innovation, marketing, and CRM. With extensive experience in consulting, innovation management, and customer strategy across diverse industries, she now serves as Director for Data-Driven Transformation at SWISS International Air Lines. Additionally, as the founder of her own advisory company, she empowers organizations to achieve growth in both business and workforce development.

**Prof. Dr. Sven Reinecke** is managing director of the Institute for Marketing at the University of St. Gallen (HSG). His main research and application areas are strategic marketing and CRM, marketing controlling, and management decision behavior. In particular, he has worked on developments in (digital) customer relationship management. Furthermore, he leads the "Best Practice in Marketing" excellence program in cooperation with leading marketing companies such as Bühler, Continental Reifen, Covesto, Hansgrohe, Geberit, Miele, Swiss Life, and UBS Switzerland.

# How "Smart Technologies" Will Change Customer Relationship Management

Evangelos Avramakis

**Abstract**

This chapter shows how key business dimensions have changed over time and how they can be simply characterized today. The use of smart technologies is more central today, supporting relationship processes efficiently and effectively. Smart technologies allow companies to better understand customer journeys and design personalized interactions. The chapter will also describe which digital, technological developments are of particular relevance for relationship design. Furthermore, it will show which four relationship dimensions characterize customer relationships in general, to what extent smart technologies impact customer relationships and design, and how these influence customer touchpoints, supply chains, and relationship dimensions, and impact existing and established customer relationships and touchpoints.

## 1 Context and Introduction to the Relevant Issues

In a world inevitably subordinating itself to enormous dependence on digitized processes, data and technology play a crucial role (Dhawan et al. 2018; Manyika et al. 2017). Technology merely provides the substructure and foundation upon which data can be generated, transported, stored, and processed. Data, in turn, through its use and refinement, and by skillfully applying analytical tools and methods, reflects a modern foundation of newly minted customer interactions and relationships. In other words, those can use data-based insights for their own benefit, and remain transparent and preserve consumer privacy, gain a decisive and immediate competitive advantage: consumer trust. Trust is the greatest asset a provider can build and

E. Avramakis (✉)
Swiss Reinsurance Company Ltd, Zurich, Switzerland
e-mail: Evangelos_Avramakis@swissre.com



S. Kirchem et al. (eds.), *CRM Goes Digital*, Management for Professionals,
https://doi.org/10.1007/978-3-658-45798-3_20

earn in the market, because any sustainable relationship is based on trust (Papadopoulou et al. 2001).

This chapter aims to show how the highest possible level of customer retention and loyalty can be achieved in the digital age. In this context, the so-called smart technologies that provide essential support for managing relationships play an increasingly central role (Boudet et al. 2017). This chapter does not aim to highlight a specific industry, but to explain the topic in general. It will describe simplifications, ideals, and stylistic escalations in order to describe the outlined relationships in a more striking and pointed way.

## 2 How Have Business Environments Changed from the Past to the Present?

The business environment is in a constant state of change; indeed, this is nothing new. What seems to be changing faster, however, are technological developments and their transformative business nature. For example, technology adoption rates and cycles have accelerated markedly within the last century. Among other things, this has been characterized by end consumers adopting and using established technologies much more quickly (Desjardins 2018).

The so-called exponential companies with data-based business models operating purely through "data-driven engines" have become indispensable to everyday life. They pose a major challenge to the management of existing business models of competitors (cf. Ismail 2014; Brinker 2016).

Furthermore, the so-called disruptive innovations enable new business models that are oriented toward "non-consuming" masses and make products and services affordable. On the one hand, this accelerates sales; on the other, it creates fertile ground for new products, services, and channels (Christensen et al. 2015). This change is reflected in different business dimensions, which are roughly summarized in Table 1.

As already noted, these are rather generic developments, which are not intended to focus on a single market. However, they are intended to indicate which dimensions are changing and how, particularly in the shaping of relationships. Furthermore, the first foundations have been laid, which are closely associated with the technological developments presented in Sect. 3.

Technological change is a driver with different facets. On the one hand, the Western world is particularly confronted with old system landscapes that are increasingly perceived to inhibit innovation, and on the other hand, embedding cutting-edge, highly data-driven technologies is indispensable for highly competitive market players (Mims 2018).

With technological advances come simultaneous efficiencies and effectiveness. Things are far simpler, but definitely require adjustment from a Western perspective. In the Asian region, technology-enabled and data-rich business models have become indispensable and have already reached a stage that could be a competitive disadvantage for Western economies in the medium-to-long term. This will have a

**Table 1** Changing realities of selected business dimensions

| Business dimension | Today | Tomorrow |
|---|---|---|
| Customer | Customers are not really at the center, despite the good intentions of many companies. Processes, products, and services are developed without involving the most important customers and/or stakeholders. | The customer forms the core of any product and service development, be it the optimization or new development of products, services, or processes. The company consistently bases its actions on insights gained by observing its customers. |
| Customer experience | Insufficient attention is paid to the overall customer experience. Products and services alone define the customer experience. Upstream and downstream processes play a subordinate role. Technologies and data are usually only functionally relevant in the product core or in the core service. | The customer interface and the entire product/service experience are understood as an "end-to-end" product. Upstream and downstream processes are essential to provide the customer with a unique customer experience from A to Z. This is enabled through supporting processes, technologies, data, supply chains, and partner networks. |
| Social environment | The social environment remains a very important foundation for communication; interaction ultimately creates trust. Opinions are aggregated, so individuals are mostly ignored due to the challenge of sufficiently mobilizing and influencing the mass population. | Technological developments enable new communication channels and the transporting or "sharing" of lived experiences. As a result, new opinion leaders are developed, which must be reworked and cultivated by brands. As a result, established channels of interaction, advertising, and communication are shifting in some cases. |
| Market | Markets and market sizes are clearly defined and can be well delineated. The customer perspective does not play an overriding role, as the focus is on the product or service in the market and industry served. | Overlapping, blurred industries prevail. Diverse, new market participants operate in cross-industry fields and link products and services along "natural" customer interactions and experience chains. |

(continued)

**Table 1** (continued)

| Business dimension | Today | Tomorrow |
|---|---|---|
| Market participants | Due to high-level market, product, and service complexity, intermediaries establish themselves and create new dependencies, but also new market-dominating relationships. | Value and supply chains become more efficient and effective; market participants are partially or even completely eliminated, especially as the balance of power in the markets mostly shifts to strongly data-driven participants due to the newly gained insights from data exchange. |
| Regulation | Regulation takes effect where regulatory intervention has become necessary. However, the necessary adjustments take a long time due to complex processes. Where necessary, accelerated processes are applied (e.g., in the financial crisis of 2007). | Regulation cannot keep up with the speed of predominantly technologically supported developments, especially since new market participants are opening up market segments that are predominantly still unregulated (e.g., Uber, Airbnb). |
| Marketing and sales | Many parallel players have enormous influence on stationary distribution. There is hardly any differentiation in the omni-channel environment. Marketing focuses predominantly on communication and is still understood as a support function. | Customer experience dimensions—independent of channel interaction—are becoming more and more important. Digital, and sometimes also fully automated customer experience chains, are increasingly enabled by technological progress. Marketing is understood as an integrative and data-driven, central function and is thus far more comprehensive. |
| Products and services | Products and services are sometimes very complex and require a high degree of willingness on the part of the customer to deal with them, which causes high opportunity costs for many market players. Limited personalization is possible because the majority of technological prerequisites are lacking. | Products and services are increasingly equipped with sensors and thus linked digitally and with a variety of supplementary data. This not only creates personalized opportunities, but also new relationship fields and opportunities. At the same time, data volumes enable better understanding of behavioral dimensions, thereby providing essential clues to further improve the customer experience. |
| Vendors | Traditional product and service suppliers are hardly ever directly involved in the customer interface and predominantly supply functional and decoupled value-creation elements. | Suppliers are closely involved in the value-creation process, and data and insights gained are shared among them. Technological interfaces enable new collaboration models. |

(continued)

**Table 1** (continued)

| Business dimension | Today | Tomorrow |
|---|---|---|
| Technologies | Technologies are highly proprietary and predominantly closed in the high-relevance backend, leading to high opportunity and transformation costs. Integrations and frontend are perceived by the majority as a major challenge and are understood as digital transformation inhibitors. | Technologies are seen as drivers and enablers of digital transformation and business models. Partner-oriented, decentralized, network-like, and open architectures are gaining importance. Technologies are becoming commoditized and thus enormously inexpensive and non-differentiating. As a result, tapping proprietary data is gaining importance (e.g., sensor data from vehicles). |

Author's representation

significant impact on the West, particularly in the context of artificial intelligence (Linn 2018; Gerbert et al. 2018; CB Insights 2018).

Section 3 profiles selected technological developments that will play a significant role, predominantly in customer relations.

## 3 Which Digital Technological Developments are of Particular Relevance for Relationship Design?

This section identifies enabling technologies that will have a significant and growing impact on relationship design. It should be noted that strategies, not technologies, drive digital transformation, and technologies act only as enablers (Kane et al. 2015; Ernst and Young 2015).

Contemporary business models are increasingly data-driven and increasingly include digitally critical aspects. In this context, sensors play an important role, especially since they generate data and thus represent the most important suppliers of data streams. On the one hand, smartphones and smartwatches, for example, are equipped with more sensors. On the other hand, this challenges network transport capacities. The majority of built-in sensors, as well as the partially decentralized computing capacities in various chips, enable continuously improved data processing, which indirectly generates a better customer experience.

Decentralization is also seen as the next step in the connected world, in that many decisions can be made and executed in a technology-assisted yet securely decentralized manner. The rapid speed is evident, for example, when logging into portals, smartphones, and apps. While the finger sensor was celebrated as a revolution just a few years ago, facial recognition and tactical biometrically controlled 3D technologies are spreading today. Much of this happens on-site, round the clock, by means of the so-called edge computing, without the need for a network connection or mandatory reliance on central authorization mechanisms. Cloud computing reflects centrally managed data flows in both capacity and processing. Large volumes of data are outsourced to data centers, where computing capacities and services can be adjusted almost arbitrarily according to demand. Increasingly, business-critical applications are also being transferred to the cloud, in the hope of reducing costs and maintenance. Furthermore, data points can now be linked and processed with each other more easily. Where possible, collaborative data robots are being used to fully or partially automate process chains.

This has a significant and further cost advantage, since processes can be designed more productively, on the one hand, and process quality massively improves on the other hand. Where manual or semi-manual tasks used to have the upper hand, specialized data robots now perform monotonous mass work cost-effectively. These data robots are equipped using algorithms and specialized data analysis methods such as artificial intelligence (AI) (see Davenport and Ronanki 2018).

Where robots process large amounts of data, for example, structure-recognition methods help to cope with these immense volumes. In the context of customer relationships, they seek to identify data points and patterns. Where cluster analysis used to generate customer segments, modern AI-powered analysis methods (e.g., behavioral dimensions of different data points, sensors, and devices) can recognize and structure them much more easily, making them interpretable for marketers. In some cases, human-like neural networks are also used (e.g., deep learning approaches).

The application possibilities are still in their infancy, but today they already include descriptive, prescriptive, or even predictive—i.e., anticipatory—models that are very efficient and allow new application possibilities in relationship design. For example, data points obtained through sensors can be easily linked to external data sources like social networks, socio-demographic data, and internal company customer value models over a longer period of time. Insights into customer behavior patterns are now yielding new opportunities by allowing more specific and personalized customer interactions to be designed. Finally, interaction devices such as smartphones and smart assistance-driven devices (e.g., Apple's HomePod) continue to evolve, so we will be able to use smart-integrated interactions to design customer relationships and develop them much more effectively and efficiently (see Solis 2018) in the near future. These are described as "smart interfaces" in Fig. 1.

For relationship design, this therefore results in a chain of closely related, technologically driven elements that must indispensably act quasi-synchronously with each other and in real time. This requires mastery and application of individual, interdisciplinary, technological elements and knowledge of industry-specific business disciplines. The fusion of technological and business-relevant domains is necessary. The maturity of these interactions is defined by the maturity of the disciplines. This can be described as follows (see also Evans and Forth 2015).

Based on collected data, behavioral insights are gained, which usually lead to an improved customer experience. This in turn provides important indications and insights for relevant customer added value, which is used to design or optimize products or services. This in turn provides important indications for improving relationship design.

This ultimately leads to sustainable customer relationships, which create customer trust, on the one hand, and organic growth on the other (Fig. 2). The potential

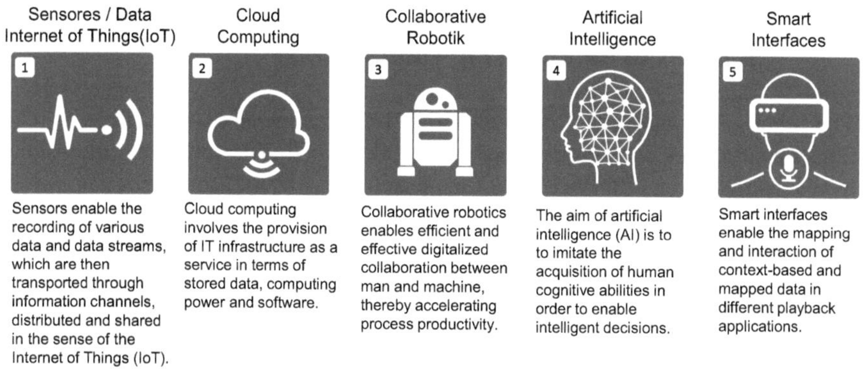


**Fig. 1** Basic technologies used in relationship design (Author's creation)

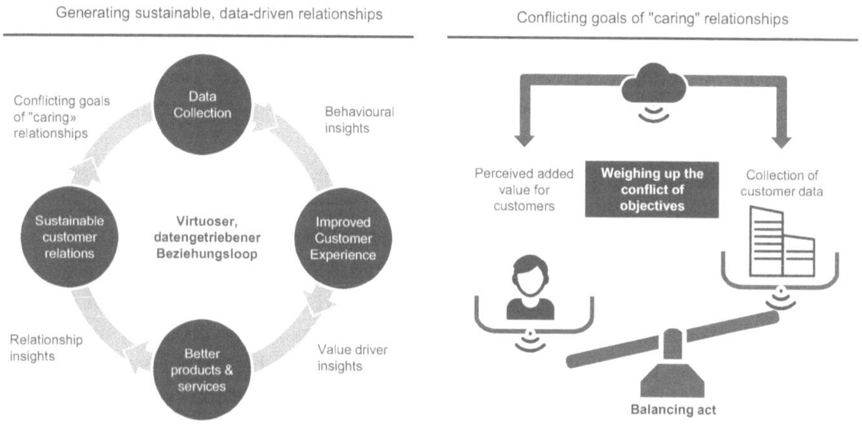


**Fig. 2** Balancing act of data-driven relationship design (Author's creation)

conflict between the goals of data collection, privacy, and data use to optimize one's own business model is a critical balancing act. If true customer value cannot be delivered, or if data and insights are misused, relationships and trust can be massively disrupted. Customer trust is a critical asset that must be nurtured over the long term. The use of data is a fundamental building block for trust towards any customer interaction, and it must be protected and preserved.

In this section, the focus was essential basic technologies and to list necessary processes, from data collection to sustainable relationship design. Section 4 focuses primarily on four different relationship dimensions that arise in customer interaction and relationship design.

## 4 Which Four Types Characterize Customer Relationships in Terms of Relationship Dimensions?

The canon offers numerous theoretical approaches, how value dimensions of relationship structures can be characterized and described. The following approaches by Parasuraman et al. (1991) and Liang and Wang (2007) are particularly well suited to describe service industries.

These dimensions are described as "bonds," which set the bar as high as possible for a change of provider or relationship breakdown. In other words, the stronger the impact of these relationship dimensions, the less customers tend to dissolve the relationship or switch providers. These relationship dimensions can be financial, social, functional, or structural in nature and can also act simultaneously or singularly, depending on the application.

1. Financial dimension: The financial value driver refers to the financial incentives of lower transaction prices or incentives. Service providers hope to provide customer loyalty benefits through economic benefits like price, discounts, and other financial incentives. However, this relationship dimension is weak, hardly sustainable, and very easily copied.
2. Social dimension: The social value driver affects personal attitude through values, expertise, communication skills, and customer similarity. This direct, personal, emotional, and somewhat empathic interaction between customer and service provider consists of familiarity, friendship, and social support.
3. Functional dimension: The functional value driver refers perceptions of the process of service delivery and customer interactions. Thus, products or services can be endowed with features representing perceptible added value and that complement the core product or service. This occurs in the process design of customer interaction.
4. Structural dimension: Structural value drivers are characterized by the fact that customers remain virtually logged in and locked into a system or product (e.g., through long contract retention periods or dependence on products or systems). This dimension is perceived as enormously unpleasant by many customers, especially since the lock-in is near-indirectly enforced. Examples include e-banking applications, customer portals or apps, and social networks, which make it enormously difficult to "get out" because data cannot be easily exported or can be lost, which can result in high opportunity costs.

The decisive factor now is which relationship dimensions should be applied from the company's point of view, since the customer experience usually results from a combination of different dimensions. Obviously for purely transaction-related customer relationships, the focus is predominantly the functional and structural dimensions.

Providers in the e-commerce environment such as Amazon, Alibaba, Tencent, Hotels.com, and iTunes constantly have to optimize the effectiveness and efficiency of customer processes to maintain the structural bond for as long as possible.

Customer loyalty programs are not the chief solution because they do not represent sustainable loyalty values, as described above. In contrast, current digital platforms like Airbnb, Uber, Pinterest, and LinkedIn use functional and structural dimensions and generate loyalty by integrating social media and human networks. In this way, social attachment dimensions are indirectly and very cleverly integrated.

However, social interaction rarely takes place at the corporate level. Modern technologies like AI-supported robots allow companies to offer automated social interactions. This means human interactions can be used, for example, when product or service complexity is medium to high or when customers can no longer progress in the process and depend on "human" help. Empathic bonds are still best gained through human interaction. They exhibit positive social attributes through personalization and they strengthen competitiveness (Shetty and Basri 2018).

In this respect, personal interactions should not be underestimated as they create trust and connectedness. However, in the near future, AI-powered machine interactions will become an everyday norm. In some cases it will be difficult to tell them apart from true human interactions. It will become clear how customers adapt this and where concessions have to be made and thus other solutions favored.

Section 5 will focus on the influence of enabling technologies on relationship dimensions and design. So far, we have not addressed the question of how relationship dimensions might be affected in an increasingly digital business world.

## 5 What Impact Do Digital Technologies Have on Relationship Dimensions and Design?

The introduction of new mobile and flexible technologies has had a massive impact on our everyday lives. Where once phones and fax machines were a prominent part of impersonal communication, mobile technologies are now integral (Solis 2018). Here, the huge shifts have made information available anywhere, anytime. Business models predominantly based on information are heavily impacted; the value of information itself is more important when it is inaccessible to other market participants. On the other hand, publicly available information is degraded to a mass commodity and gains importance where it can be skillfully linked with other information sources, thus creating new knowledge.

In a world where information can be shared and accessed digitally through diverse information channels, touchpoints gain importance when knowledge and insights can be transported and harnessed over long supply chains. These touchpoints are at risk of becoming enormously powerful, which could increase dependence on these services if valid alternatives are not available. In the following, an attempt is made to describe this development and to derive implications for customer interaction and interfaces. This is discussed by means of three different time dimensions: (1) yesterday, (2) today, and (3) tomorrow (cf. Fig. 3).

(1) Yesterday: Historically, many products and services were delivered through face-to-face channels; that is, human interaction with the retail or enterprise customer was predominant. While products were predominantly produced in factories,

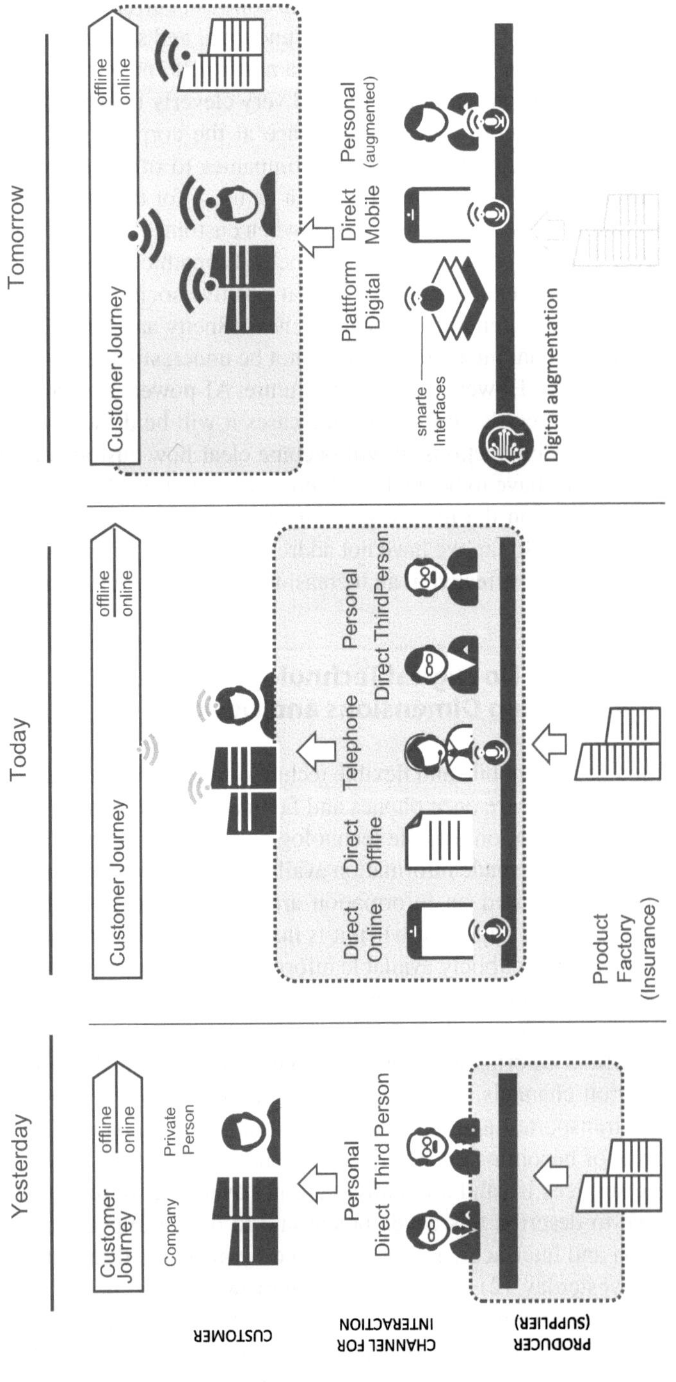


**Fig. 3** Development of changing channel interaction (Source: own representation)

direct interaction channels had the task of communicating the good or service so that it could be sold, which sometimes involved high consulting services and opportunity costs.

Therefore, the more complex the good to be communicated, the more personal the necessary relationship, and dependence and information asymmetries were created in favor of intermediaries. Knowledge and knowledge mediation were therefore understood in very close dependence with personal interaction channels, and associated with high mediation costs for the producing companies. Maintaining and expanding producer relationships and their interaction channels for distribution was thus key, but the latter held control of the end consumer due to information asymmetry. Social and structural connection dimensions were not uncommon.

With the advent of newer information and interaction channels such as the telephone or the Internet, the balance of power shifted toward the end consumer. Information became more transparent and accessible. Those who took advantage of the balanced information asymmetry gained a new, competitive edge and in some cases displaced existing market players.

(2) Today: Personal interaction channels still dominate the customer relationship, especially for complex issues. Nevertheless, digital interaction channels are increasingly popular and are established very differently, depending on the industry (Bjørnland et al. 2016). This is unlikely to change fundamentally, even in the short term. However, with the advent of new information technologies, knowledge will be made available digitally anytime and anywhere, and in some cases it will also be accessible to laypersons.

This will further even out the information asymmetry and increase the knowledge of the end consumer. Consumers are therefore empowered to take control of interaction and action themselves, which means that direct and digital channels are increasingly preferred. However, the newly gained transparency also gives rise to new service providers who make the needs of the end consumer easily, directly, and transparently accessible in the sense of transparent producer information by aggregating the information. Aggregators, new predominantly direct marketplaces, or digital platforms that cleverly link supply and demand are emerging (Van Alstyne et al. 2016).

Whereas "yesterday," personal interaction channels dominated, today one encounters a broad number of diverse and directly competitive channels, which can lead to massive channel conflicts in complex product or service categories. This increases financial relationship dimensions and incentives, which are played out by direct channels—at least in the short term—but not sustainably.

As a result, functional dimensions gain importance and product or service elements become transparent and easily accessible. Social dimensions, meanwhile, are becoming less important and are only relevant when complexity remains high or empathetic human interactions are indispensable. It is the aggregators and digital marketplaces in particular that are trying to hold on to structural dimensions whilst attracting their clientele with financial incentives and customer loyalty programs, apparently a dominant strategy for the short-to-medium term, but which risks an inability to sufficiently differentiate their services in the market.

(3) Tomorrow: The information, which is mostly available in digital form, is enriched with additional, digital data sources. These are mainly sensors and their information, which can be further refined and cleverly combined. Personalization is becoming increasingly important due to the density of information and behavioral insights. It is equally valued, provided it is transparent and privacy is preserved. The knowledge and insight can thus be made available when relevant for the customer.

The product or service is produced almost "on the spot" and is personalized in real time. The relevant and contextualized information required for this is obtained en masse during the customer journey. Given the digital fooprint and data points provided on various touch points, the consumer needs can be therefore identified much earlier before the consumers are becoming even aware of their needs. All digital channels are digitally enriched and augmented. It is therefore the functional dimensions that are particularly predominant.

Although mobile interaction channels continue to predominate, new digital platforms are being added that are equipped with smart interfaces. In addition to audio-visual control features, these include learning interaction functions and are massively superior to today's smartphones. This creates new dependencies and power relationships, which can lead to further customer convenience by projecting a data-driven parallel reality (see Tao et al. 2018). Financial and structural dimensions could be eroded due to information and digital service technologization and thus become massively less important. Where smart, automated interactions can be used, empathetic values become increasingly relevant. Social dimensions may thus experience a renaissance in the medium-to-long term (cf. Pistrui 2018; Schrage 2017).

Having described and estimated the implications of enabling technologies for the four engagement dimensions and interaction channels above, we will now discuss the impact on the supply chain. This is important because supply chains now have direct end-to-end interaction with consumers, and proximity and flexibility are becoming significantly more important. Again, only indications can be given. In the following, three states of supply and interaction chains are described, which increase with the number of linked and networked sensors and data across all supply chains. The first state (1) reflects (digitally) decoupled chains; the second state (2) describes digitally coupled chains; and the third state (3) discusses digitally networked interaction and supply chains (Fig. 4).

(1) Digitally decoupled interaction and supply chains are characterized by insignificant, if any, digitally connected data. It is not unusual to find individual chain components or isolated, functionally optimized, digital interaction channels. Accordingly, not all value chain elements benefit from digital data streams. The whole supply chain is thus ineffective and inefficient, resulting in relevant information for the end consumer being missing and, with higher competitive intensity, the need for the customer relationship to therefore be compensated for with other relationship dimensions. There is a lack of transparency and control in addition to closely interlinked information.

(2) Digitally coupled interaction and supply chains that enable or even promote the digital exchange of information as a foundation are already proving more promising. This means that products and services can be enriched and made available in

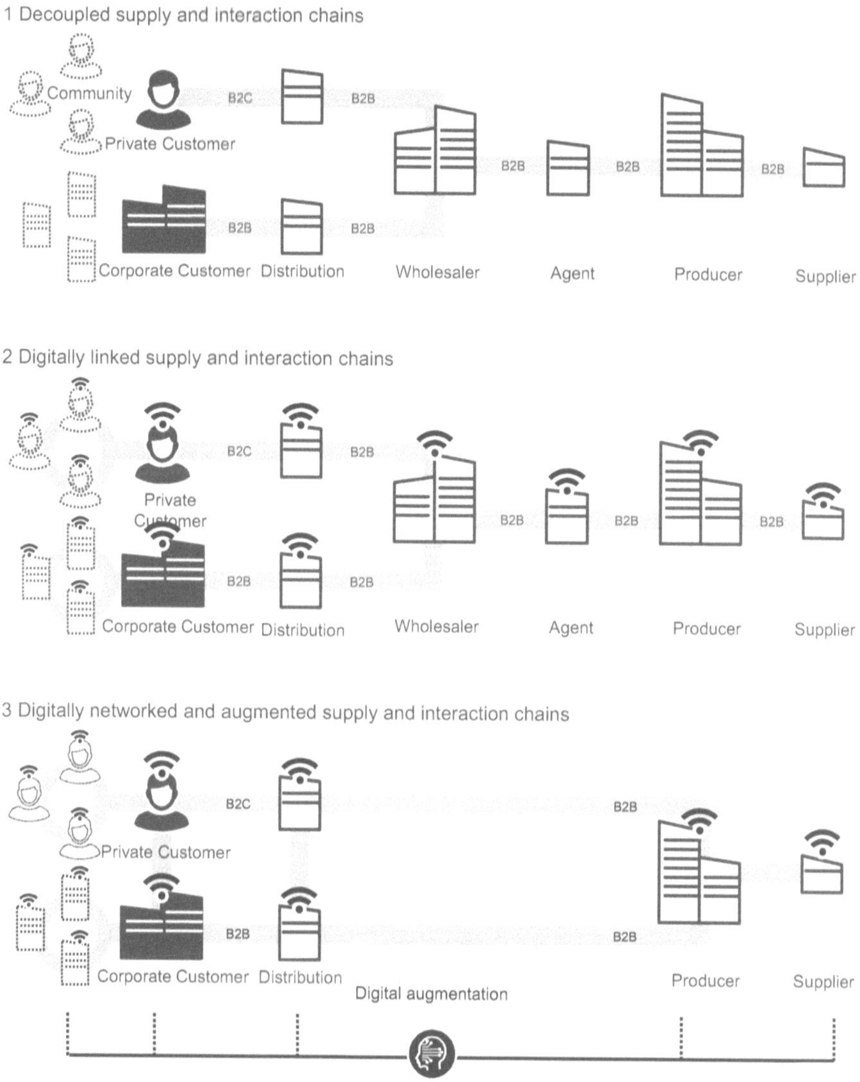


**Fig. 4** Impact of digitally networked states of supply and interaction chains (Source: Own representation)

digital form, usually with supplementary information that has significant advantages for all parties and favors digitally supported customer relationships.

In addition to better control and transparency, this also results in new opportunities to further solidify the customer relationship and enrich it with additional, supplementary data sources and analytical tools. This strengthens the functional relationship dimension. In part, this can lead to newly emerging structural relationship dimensions and thus significantly raise the hurdles to using other competing supply chains. On the other hand, these supply chains must constantly evolve or optimize in order to sustainably maintain competitive advantages.

(3) Digitally networked and enriched interaction and supply chains, due to purely digital information available, are enriched with further data (e.g., from third parties), creating massive data streams. Newer methods in artificial intelligence (e.g., machine learning or deep learning) can process this data to lead to new insights and even new services.

These are of high value when unique data sources can be tapped and processed (for example, sensor data that is unavailable to participants in other supply chains). This in turn shifts the information asymmetry within the supply chains to such an extent that unequal power relationships arise and, due to the effectiveness and efficiency of the entire system, individual market participants or interaction parties can disappear altogether, or become highly dependent.

If such new services can now be offered to all participants in the supply chain, the entire supply chain becomes near-unique, differentiating, and "powerful" in that it can control everything, optimally manage it, and provide it with relevant information and insights. All interaction parties are therefore constantly enriched with more knowledge. The interactions themselves are further improved and the supply chains as a whole are digitally enriched.

This creates new functional value in the customer relationship, which predominantly benefits digital customer interactions by enabling new and high-value interactions to be offered to customers in a quasi-robotic manner. This digitizes the entire supply chain. Suppliers receive relevant information and insights from many interaction points and can develop products and services in a very targeted manner, especially since they benefit from the dynamics of all relationship interactions and insights.

In extreme cases, these supply chains leverage intermediaries and create new distribution channels through their power, but this requires knowledge of the distribution domain. The personal interaction channel is predominantly used for complex, emotional, and empathetic interactions. Depending on the openness of the supply chain and the system, structural ties are created that have very different effects. Privacy and data transparency particularly need to be carefully weighed as insights are available to all parties.

In this section, the impact of digital enabling technologies and their information density and insights on relationship design within changing channel interactions and supply and interaction chains was discussed in more detail and possible implications were derived. Section 6 will consider how customer relationships might further develop, particularly if individual touchpoints, interactions, and market participants within existing supply chains partially exit the market due to the emerging information asymmetry described above.

## 6 How Will Digitally-Enabled Relationship-Building Evolve? A Bold Outlook

Digital, fully automated, and robotic interactions may provoke the triggering of (too) many customer interactions. This hardly represents significant added value from the customer's point of view. On the one hand, there are positive indications that they can contribute greatly to customer loyalty (Bain and Company 2014), increased sales, satisfaction, and referrals (Rawson et al. 2013). At the same time, however, new points of contact arise due to the enrichment of context-based and relevant customer information, further supported by the use of artificial intelligence (Kihlstrom 2018). These are then particularly valuable from a customer perspective if they consider relevant customer characteristics in the context of the customer journey, as well as behavioral dimensions. However, these customer interactions do not always occur on dedicated interaction channels. For example, it is quite common for the customer journey to pass through a very large number of contact points that are independent of one another. In technical jargon, this is referred to as "owned," "paid," and "earned" touchpoints.

- Owned: Under the control of the company, as with its own website.
- Paid: Purchased interactions, like web banners or Facebook ads.
- Earned: Attributed or earned touchpoints, from personal recommendations or good ratings from independent service providers.

Finally, the so-called social touchpoints occur when social platforms predominate or are integrated at touchpoints (cf. i-Scoop 2018). Some touchpoints even occur outside the direct, perceptible framework, for example, when a customer visits a competitor's website.

In the following, only two dimensions are to be assumed in order to simplify the whole thing, namely the company's own contact level and external contact levels. Basically, the two are independent of each other, so an understanding of the entire customer journey cannot be present. The gaps in interaction and knowledge make a personalized customer experience much more difficult. Due to this, new technical aids and tools (e.g., fingerprinting methods) are emerging to fill these information gaps (Szymielewicz and Budington 2018).

At the same time, however, the customer—and the customer journey—naturally make use of other interaction points and third-party service providers. It must be assumed that customer touchpoints can change over time and service providers will lose control of individual, previously strategic, points, so to speak, and therefore have to seek new forms of cooperation and partnership. This is usually accompanied by the adaptation or transformation of the business model (Weill and Woerner 2015; Naujoks et al. 2017). Therefore, it is even more important to tap relevant partners with natural customer touchpoint interaction at an early stage, especially as customer topics shift to the so-called ecosystems.

Atluri et al. (2017) predict that by 2025, around 30% of global economic revenue will be generated in these digital ecosystems, which is likely to pose a major challenge for individual service providers and market players. These ecosystems will be closely linked to the consumer lifestyle and will involve an aggregation of products and services from different industries.

Examples would be health, education and work, housing, leisure, and mobility (Fig. 5). As a result, the view of the customer journey takes on even greater significance, especially as the points of contact become more concentrated at platforms or in ecosystems. On the other hand, very large interdependencies are created, which means that relationship dimensions probably assume new roles as they become dependent on the interests and objectives of ecoplatform operators (cf. Candelon et al. 2018). Again, this probably strengthens the functional and structural relationship dimensions. At the same time, these relationships will be strengthened on the platforms to such an extent that niches will emerge, which must exhibit a compulsory differentiating character to hold their own against the new, digital ecosystems. This is where the provider's handling of the customer's privacy and integrity may play a key role.

Interactions become value-adding where information is exchanged and knowledge is shared with all interaction points involved. On the customer side, on the other hand, there may well be skepticism with regard to privacy if data is exchanged uncontrollably or quasi-automatically with various links in the interaction chain. It is therefore important to weigh up the extent to which data is exchanged and how customers should be informed about this. This ultimately goes hand in hand with the company's objectives, incentives, culture, and image (cf. Gerbert et al. 2018; Geneva Association 2018).

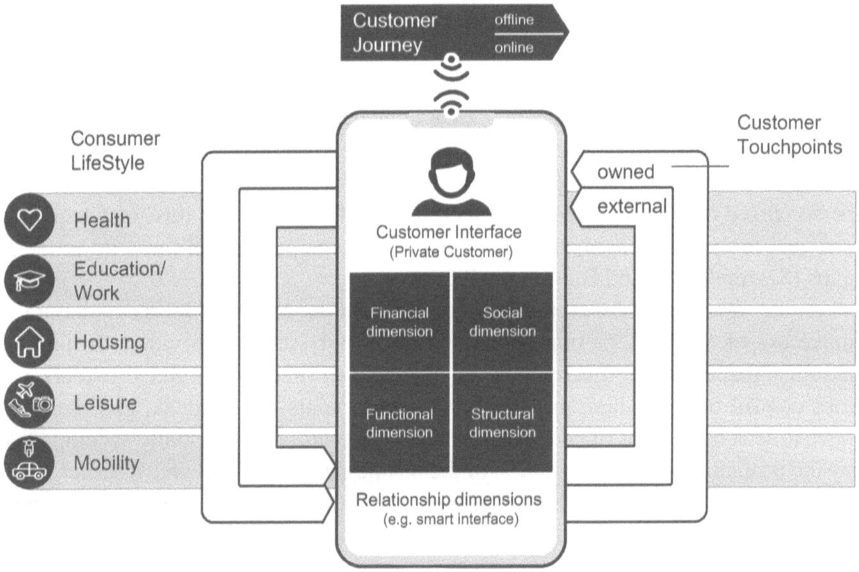


**Fig. 5** Consumer-oriented external and internal customer contact and interaction points using smart interfaces (Author's illustration)

In healthcare, for example, patients express little difficulty with historical health data, movement and activity data, and genetic data being shared with doctors. In contrast, real skepticism and reluctance can be observed among insurance companies and research institutions, as patients rarely want to share data with pharmaceutical companies, the government, or tech companies (Zweig et al. 2018).

Accordingly, context plays a significant role with insurance companies. Depending on the focus of the insurance context, such as vehicle, home, or health, openness to sharing data varies massively (Maas et al. 2008). It is therefore very conceivable that depending on the industry and context, consumer sensitivity to sharing data may vary.

In this chapter, we have shown how the business environment can change from one day to the next, which characteristics of previous business dimensions could be affected, and how. The rapid development of digital technologies will have a huge impact on the design of customer relationships and will make a significant contribution to effectiveness and efficiency, thus significantly supporting or even fully automating many customer relationship processes. Four basic relationship dimensions have been described, namely the financial, functional, social, and structural dimensions, which are influenced by existing relationship design through data-driven technologies. As a result, it is increasingly possible to digitally personalize products and services, as well as customer interactions along the entire customer journey, with contact points and supply chains equally affected (Dias et al. 2016). If data points and insights can be shared along entire supply chains, then new, powerful providers will emerge who, depending on their motivation, can dictate new rules of the game to supply chains.

It is likely that individual intermediaries or market participants will adapt their business models if they are forced out of the market due to newly emerging information asymmetry. Some customer touchpoints could change as a result to become partially dominated by previously outside market players, which could lead to new dependencies as the previously owned, controlled customer relationship is redefined (Evans and Forth 2015). Associated adjustments to the existing business model cannot be ruled out if new contact points and providers have to be served. In the end, however, it is always a matter of building, maintaining, and further expanding customer trust–regardless how this is realized, through the company's own or external contact points. This creates sustainable competitive advantages in the medium-to-long term, which result from the targeted balancing of the use of relationship dimensions. All this can be managed with smart technologies. The future of customer engagement is smart but also "smart vulnerable."

## References

Atluri V, Dietz M, Henke N (2017) Competing in a world of sectors without borders, McKinsey, July 2017. https://www.mckinsey.com/business-functions/mckinsey-analytics/our-insights/competing-in-a-world-of-sectors-without-borders. Accessed: 11.10.2022

Bain & Company (2014) Customer loyalty in retail banking: global edition 2014. Bain & Company Study, 18 December 2014
Bjørnland D, Harlé N, Luisada F (2016) Digital technologies raise the stakes in customer service. Boston Consulting Group. 18 May 2016
Boudet J, Gregg B, Heller J, Tufft C (2017) The heartbeat of modern marketing: data activation and personalization. McKinsey Study. March 2017
Brinker S (2016) Martec's Law: the greatest management challenge of the 21st century. 06 November 2016. https://chiefmartec.com/2016/11/martecs-law-great-management-challenge-21st-century/. Accessed: 11.10.2022
Candelon F, Reeves F, Wu D (2018) 18 of the Top 20 tech companies are in the Western U.S. and Eastern China. Can Anywhere Else Catch Up? May 03, 2018, Harvard Business Review
CB Insights (26.04.2018) Rise of China's big tech in AI: What Baidu, Alibaba, and Tencent are working on. https://www.cbinsights.com/research/china-baidu-alibaba-tencent-artificial-intelligence-dominance/. Accessed: 11.10.2022
Christensen CM, Raynor ME, McDonald R (2015) What is disruptive innovation. Harv Bus Rev 93(12):44–53
Davenport TH, Ronanki R (2018) Artificial intelligence for the real world. Harvard Business Review, Ausgabe February 2018
Desjardins J (2018) The rising speed of technological adoption. Visual Capitalist. 14 February 2018. www.visualcapitalist.com/rising-speed-technological-adoption/. Accessed: 11.10.2022
Dhawan R, Heid B, Küderli P, Laczkowski K (2018) How industrial companies can respond to disruptive forces. McKinsey Study. April 2018
Dias J, Ionuţiu O, Lhuer X, van Ouwerkerk J (2016) The four pillars of distinctive customer journeys. Digital McKinsey. August 2016
Ernst & Young (2015) Megatrends 2015 – Making sense of a world in motion. Ernst & Young Study. https://www.ey.com/Publication/vwLUAssets/ey-megatrends-report-2015/$FILE/ey-megatrends-report-2015.pdf. Accessed: 23.03.2018
Evans P, Forth P (2015) Borges' Map: Navigating a world of digital disruption. Boston Consulting Group. 22 April 2015
Geneva Association (2018) Big data and insurance: Implications for innovation, competition and privacy. 14. The Geneva Association. March 2018
Gerbert P, Reeves M, Ransbotham S, Kiron D, Spira M (24.07.2018) Global competition with AI in business: How China differs. MIT Sloan. https://sloanreview.mit.edu/article/global-competition-of-ai-in-business-how-china-differs/. Accessed: 11.10.2022
i-Scoop (2018) Content marketing: on owned, earned, paid, shared and converged media. i-scoop.eu https://www.i-scoop.eu/content-marketing/content-marketing-owned-earned-paid-shared-converged-media/. Accessed: 11.10.2022
Ismail S (2014) Exponential organizations: why new organizations are ten times better, faster, and cheaper than yours (and what to do about it). Diversion Books
Kane GC, Palmer D, Phillips AN, Kiron D, Buckley N (2015) Strategy, not technology, drives digital transformation – becoming a digitally mature enterprise. MITSloan Management Review. 14 July 2015
Kihlstrom G (19.06.2018) How to use artificial intelligence, personalization and automation in the customer journey. Forbes. https://www.forbes.com/sites/forbesagencycouncil/2018/06/19/how-to-use-artificial-intelligence-personalization-and-automation-in-the-customer-journey. Accessed: 11.10.2022
Liang CJ, Wang WH (2007) Customer relationship management of the information education services industry in Taiwan: Attributes, benefits and relationship. The Service Industries Journal, 27(1), pp.29–46
Linn TC (2018) Race to develop artificial intelligence is one between Chinese authoritarianism and U.S. democracy. San Francisco Chronicle. 20 August 2018. https://www.sfchronicle.com/opinion/openforum/article/Race-to-develop-artificial-intelligence-is-one-13189380.php. Accessed: 11.10.2022

Maas P, Graf A, Beck C (2008). Trust, transparency and technology. European Customers' Perspectives on Insurance and Innovation. IBM und I. VW-HSG, St. Gallen
Manyika J, Chui M, Lund S, Ramaswamy S (2017) What's now and next in analytics, AI, and automation. McKinsey Study. May 2017
Mims C (26.07.2018) Why do the biggest companies keep getting bigger? It's how they spend on tech. The Wall Street J. https://www.wsj.com/articles/why-do-the-biggest-companies-keep-getting-bigger-its-how-they-spend-on-tech-1532610001. Accessed: 11.10.2022
Naujoks H, Mueller F, Darnell D, Singh H (2017) Ecosystems: How insurers can reinvent customer relationships. Bain & Company Studie. 14 September 2017
Papadopoulou P, Andreou A, Kanellis P, Martakos D (2001) Trust and relationship building in electronic commerce. Internet Res 11(4):322–332
Parasuraman A, Berry LL, Zeithaml VA (1991). Refinement and reassessment of the SERVQUAL scale. Journal of retailing 67(4), p.420
Pistrui J (2018) The future of human work is imagination, creativity, and strategy. Harvard Business Review, 18 January 2018
Rawson A, Jones C, Duncan E (2013) Managing the complete customer journey. Harv Bus Rev, 17 September 2013
Schrage M (2017) Bots won't just help us buy stuff. They'll help us become better versions of ourselves. Harvard Business Review, 01 June 2017
Shetty A, Basri S (2018) Relationship orientation in banking and insurance services – a review of the evidence. J Indian Bus Res. https://doi.org/10.1108/JIBR-10-2017-0176
Solis B (2018) Smartphones are reshaping customer journeys; marketing must now align With CX to improve experiences. Forbes. 16 May 2018. https://www.forbes.com/sites/briansolis/2018/05/16/smartphones-are-reshaping-customer-journeys-marketing-must-now-align-with-cx-to-improve-experiences. Accessed: 11.10.2022
Szymielewicz K, Budington B (2018) The GDPR and browser fingerprinting: how it changes the game for the sneakiest web trackers. Electronic Frontier Foundation (EFF). 19 June 2018 https://www.eff.org/deeplinks/2018/06/gdpr-and-browser-fingerprinting-how-it-changes-game-sneakiest-web-trackers. Accessed: 11.10.2022
Tao F, Cheng J, Qi Q, Zhang M, Zhang H, Sui F (2018) Digital twin-driven product design, manufacturing and service with big data. Int J Adv Manuf Technol 94(9–12):3563–3576
Van Alstyne MW, Parker GG, Pipelines SPC (2016) Platforms, and the new rules of strategy. Harvard Business Review. April 2016 Ausgabe
Weill P, Woerner SL (2015) Thriving in an increasingly digital ecosystem. MIT Sloan Manag Rev 56(4):27. http://ilp.mit.edu/media/news_articles/smr/2015/56417.pdf
Zweig M, Shen J, Jug L (2018) Healthcare consumers in a digital transition. Rock Health. https://rockhealth.com/reports/healthcare-consumers-in-a-digital-transition/. Accessed: 11.10.2022

**Evangelos Avramakis** is a thought leader in insurance and innovation management, who works for the Swiss Re Institute. He is a design thinker and a holistic, interdisciplinary, and implementation-oriented strategist and doer. After working as a strategy consultant, he worked in the primary insurance industry in life and health insurance in various senior management and tax positions such as marketing and sales, business development, and market strategy (B2C, B2B, and B2B2C). In his current role, he is closely connected to academia, insurtech, medtech, and the start-up ecosystem. His main focus is digital ecosystems, omni-channel management, and business model innovation. Evangelos studied Sports Science (minor in Mathematics and Fine Arts), Information Systems, and Business Administration. He holds a PhD in Business Administration.

# Customer Experience of Today and Tomorrow

Frank Müller

**Abstract**

Today, customer experience increasingly differentiates good from not-so-good brands. Customers want to be understood and do not expect abstract addresses or experiences. They expect a seamless journey across various touchpoints with a brand. Customers do not mind whether they interact online or offline. The necessary emotions must be present to bind customers to the brand in the long term and thus increase their customer value.

## 1 Customer Experience Is Crucial for Modern Business

Customer experience (CX) is one of the most important differentiating factors for companies in today's world. According to a study by Salesforce (Salesforce Connected Customer 2018), 80% of customers say a company's customer experience is as important as its products and services. Customer experience is described as a consumer's experience with a company. Each point of contact, or touchpoint, is relevant and must be perceived as unique for the customer.

According to 67% of customers, their standard for a good customer experience is higher than ever. This holds irrespective of B2B or B2C context, because ultimately people lie behind all ideal-typical customer profiles. For 51% of customers, most companies do not meet their expectations for great experiences, which is why they migrate to competitors.

Many customers switch to a competitor after just one bad experience. The more bad experiences that follow, the faster customers turn from the brand. The market in many industries is saturated and competition is fierce. Many companies are now

F. Müller (✉)
Müller Beteiligungs GmbH, Böchingen, Germany
e-mail: frank.mueller@mktgadvisors.com


S. Kirchem et al. (eds.), *CRM Goes Digital*, Management for Professionals,
https://doi.org/10.1007/978-3-658-45798-3_21

realizing that the only way to stand out is through an outstanding customer experience. To put it another way, when product quality and competitive pricing can no longer ensure customer loyalty, personalized and customer-centric experiences must be the unique selling proposition that strengthens long-run customer relationships.

After all, whether it is a call to the service center, receiving an invoice, or browsing the website, every exchange between customer and company cultivates a relationship, good or bad. This perception has increased significantly during the pandemic, as the frequency with which people spend time online has also increased (Statista, Digital Media Usage, 2022). The pandemic was thus an accelerator for companies to think increasingly about a very good customer experience. After all, the customer experience often has a direct impact on a company's bottom line. Only when customers are loyal to a brand does this promote customer loyalty and retention. In turn, this directly impacts customer lifetime value, the value that a company generates with a customer over the customer's life cycle.

Of course, winning over customers in a competitive environment and retaining them over the long term is a real challenge. But only companies which offer customers a seamless customer experience across various contact points will win their loyalty and retain them over the long term. For this reason, it is essential that companies first think about the brand's ideal-typical profiles. Only those who have defined and communicated this so-called customer persona can consistently take an outside-in view and look at the brand from the customer's perspective.

First, you should ask yourself the following question: What challenges characterize the objectives of the persona and how can the company respond? It is also important to find out the customer's lifecycle phase. A potential new customer wants to be addressed differently and has different goals and challenges than an existing customer who has been known for many years and who buys from the same company again and again. As a company, I have to say goodbye to the inside-out view or product-centric view that I have become so fond of and consistently adopt the customer-centric view.

## 2 How Can You Create a Good Customer Experience?

What matters is how the customer perceives these collected experiences when interacting with the corresponding company. A good customer experience is when a customer can do business with a brand effortlessly and without abandonment. It is also important that marketing, sales, service, and commerce work closely together. This is the only way to create a seamless experience for the customer.

In many companies, however, departments deal with customer relationships in silos and consider them as individual interactions. The corresponding key figures then also reflect false facts. Appearances of respective department may seem quite positive, but in fact are deceptive. You have to look at the big picture and understand that the customer's relationship with a company is an ongoing, hopefully very long-lasting, interactive relationship.

Customers do not mind who they interact with from the company. They want to be understood at every point of the customer journey, and have their needs addressed. We all know stories of long-standing customers calling the company and undergoing lengthy identification processes. A good customer experience in this case would be the customer's phone number being recognized by the company and the employee in the service center addressing them personally. It is also helpful if sales staff know which marketing materials a corresponding customer has reacted to, for example, in the form of clicks or downloads. In other words, a great customer experience is only possible if the company knows exactly who the customer is, what they need, and then focuses on these needs throughout the customer journey.

For all the reasons above, it is therefore advisable and essential to introduce a customer experience management approach throughout the company. Or as Gartner puts it, "Customer experience management (CXM) is the discipline of understanding customers and implementing strategic plans that enable cross-functional efforts and a customer-centric culture to improve satisfaction, loyalty and advocacy" (Gartner, CX Strategy Research).

The most important department in the company for such an approach is marketing. Marketing provides the customer with their first business card. Marketing must also frequently respond to changing customer requirements, at short notice, and must therefore be very flexibly positioned. The brand presence, the adverts, and the social media marketing all create the customer's first impression, which determines whether customers will continue interacting with the brand or turn away disappointed.

Sales departments need to take their experience of customers in marketing and address them accordingly. This should be timely to maintain momentum. The longer the process, the more likely it is that a customer will infer a lack of interest and turn away. A good degree of customer processing from the sales department is required, alongside a personalized approach with appropriate offers. Only if all this is taken to heart and the customer feels well looked after can repeat purchases or cross-sell and upsell potential be increased and the churn rate reduced.

A company's product range defines the goods and services it offers. These go hand in hand with the customer experience. Many customers would pay more for the experience itself than for the product received. In addition to the direct experience, details such as reliability, affordability, overall ease of use, and product lifecycle play a role and contribute to the corresponding customer experience. The experience that the product provides affects the reputation of the company, which in turn affects other areas of the customer experience.

The customer service department, or service area, of a company, often estimates whether a customer will commit to a company in the long term. Just think of a claim reported to an insurance company. How does the service employee deal with the customer, how do they react, and what is offered to the customer? These details all make a huge difference to the overall customer experience. Service employees themselves are able to collect timely feedback on the customer's perception of their experience: they hear and experience how customers interact with the product or service on a daily basis. They learn first-hand how and whether customer

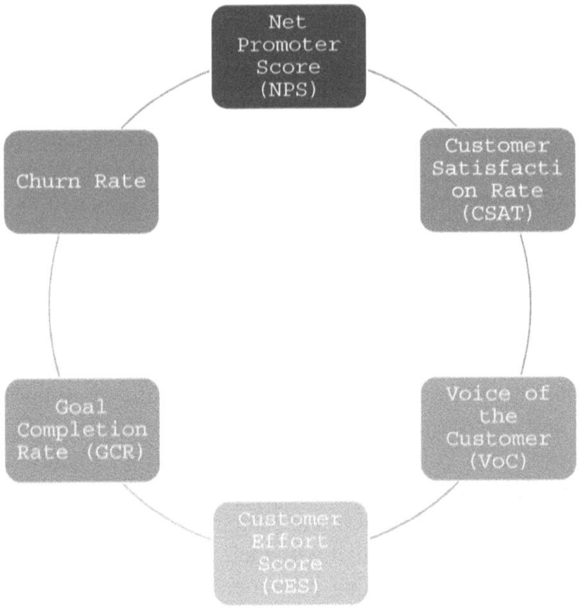


**Fig. 1** Frank Müller (own illustration), Key figures for measuring the customer experience

expectations are met and how the customer base is changing. Feedback is the most important part of the customer experience. Without feedback, a company stops. Or as Steve Jobs said, "You've got to start with the customer experience and work back towards technology—not the other way around" (Steve Jobs Interview, 1997). Customer experience can be obtained through appropriate customer feedback.

So how can you make customer experience measurable, and what metrics can help?

Some insights are accessible using the following key metrics (Fig. 1):

## 2.1 Net Promoter Score

The Net Promoter Score, or NPS, is a method of measuring customer satisfaction. It is based on a two-minute survey and provides an insight into customer loyalty: the NPS determines the willingness of a customer to recommend a company to friends or acquaintances.

The NPS differs from other benchmarks, such as the customer satisfaction rate, because it captures a person's general attitude toward a brand rather than their opinion about specific interactions or purchases. It is therefore particularly relevant to the customer experience.

In addition, the Net Promoter Score is a standard reference used by companies worldwide. This allows companies to compare meaningful performance assessments with their competitors.

## 2.2 Contact Satisfaction Score (CSAT)

It is well known that customer satisfaction is a key indicator of long-term business success. It naturally follows that it is enormously important to measure this indicator on a regular basis. One of the most popular methods for this is the Customer Satisfaction Score (CSAT). The Customer Satisfaction Score is a simple method for quantifying customer satisfaction. In surveys, customers rate concrete experiences with a company's services on the basis of a predefined scale. The result is a concise key figure that expresses the degree of customer satisfaction as a percentage. In practice, supporters generally assign a value between 9 and 10: they were satisfied with the experience and are very likely to recommend it. Neutrals assign a value of 7 or 8.

The Customer Satisfaction Score can be used to track customer satisfaction throughout the customer lifecycle. It highlights how customers feel at different touchpoints with a company and whether or not the respective experience has contributed to their satisfaction. This makes it easier to uncover weaknesses, for which appropriate action can then be taken.

## 2.3 Voice of Customer (VoC)

The voice of the customer is made up of customers' experiences and expectations relating to a company. To enhance processes and align new products with customer needs, the Voice of Customer primarily focuses on product development. However, nearly all departments can benefit from the often detailed feedback it provides. The collected customer feedback on a company, the Voice of Customer, covers many different aspects, including marketing measures, products, and the quality of customer service—basically all areas of the company that can subject to customer evaluation. It therefore makes sense to use Voice of Customer findings in the departments described above, among others.

## 2.4 Customer Effort Score (CES)

Customer Effort Score (CES) is a service metric that measures how much effort customers spend interacting with your organization. These interactions might include how much effort it takes to use your product or service, or how easily their problems were solved by your service representatives. A customer spends a lot of effort if they have to dig through pages and pages of knowledge-based articles to find the item they want, and very little effort if they call a service representative and their refund is processed immediately. There is ample evidence that the simplicity of a particular experience is sometimes a better indicator for customer loyalty than simply measuring customer satisfaction. Moreover, in an increasingly competitive environment, loyalty is a real pillar for successful businesses. The Customer Effort Score gained prominence in 2010 with the publication of an HBR article titled

"Stop Trying to Delight Your Customers" (*HRB*, July–Aug 2010). The article is insightful, not so much for the quality and depth of the research, but for the unexpected insight that the easiest way to increase customer loyalty is not to delight customers, but to make their jobs easier. This quote is an excellent summary of the article: "When it comes to service, companies create loyal customers primarily by helping them solve their problems quickly and easily." We illustrated this previously with the example of insurance.

## 2.5 Goal Completion Rate (GCR)

Goal Completion Rate measures the number of website users who complete a given goal or set of goals. Analytics services calculate this metric, but you can also calculate it yourself by setting goals you want your users to achieve, then tracking actual achievements of those goals. The specific goals one sets depend on the type of business. For example, if you run a blog, you might want users to subscribe to your newsletter, which costs a certain amount per month. To calculate the full rate for this goal, one would track the number of people who reach the goal and measure it against the total number of visitors to the site.

## 2.6 Churn Rate

The term churn rate (German: *Abwanderungsquote, Kundenverlustrate*) describes the ratio between customers who no longer use a service and the total number of customers of a company. As a rule, the churn rate relates to a specific period of time—for example, one month. The result is a value that provides information about any decline in the customer base and average customer retention. The churn rate is used for subscription models and newsletter registrations in order to react promptly to a decline in the customer base. Churn is a portmanteau of change and turn. Business models based on registrations and contracts can use churn rate to optimize their portfolio and customer service. It provides an initial indicator of dissatisfied customers and customers willing to switch. Ideally, the churn rate should be zero.

However, the value of the churn rate depends on factors like business model, industry, product, and service on the entrepreneurial side; and satisfaction, loyalty, and retention on the customer side. If the churn rate is particularly high, it is advisable to analyze it precisely and initiate measures. A solid customer base is crucial for profitability. Measures such as customer recovery, customer acquisition, and targeted marketing can be used to maintain profitability in the face of high churn rates. However, the causes of high customer losses should first be identified before the customer base is increased. These causes can lie along the entire value chain and include not only customer service, but also the entire customer journey and all associated processes and technical solutions, such as CRM, marketing automation, commerce, or service solutions.

### 2.7 Retention Rate

Winning customers is one thing; keeping them is quite another. But existing customers who bring in revenue without costing much are worth their weight in gold. You should therefore keep a close eye on how many of your customers are repeat buyers. For this, you need the "retention rate."

The retention rate is a way of calculating the percentage of customers that a company retains in its customer base over a certain period of time. As an indicator of customer loyalty, the retention rate can be improved in various ways. If a company focuses too much on acquiring new customers, existing customer relationships may be disregarded, resulting in customers leaving. If customers feel neglected or that their complaints are not taken seriously, they will eventually say goodbye. Acquiring new customers is more difficult and costly than retaining existing ones, so companies should focus on maintaining and intensifying existing customer relationships. In this way, buyers and business partners become more loyal to the brand and its associated products.

## 3 Where Is Customer Experience Heading?

What are the customer experience trends of tomorrow? Improving customer experience encompasses everything from service levels to how well products fit into customers' lives. This is a critical focus for businesses. In the coming years, brands will need to build on their successes (and learn from failures) by leveraging technology-enabled solutions for the challenges of building long-term customer engagement and relationships. Artificial intelligence (AI) and the Internet of Things (IoT) are being enthusiastically embraced in marketing, product design, and service, primarily because they enable companies to improve the experiences customers have when interacting with brands or using their respective products or services. Thankfully, sporadic focus group testing and customer satisfaction surveys are no longer the only way to obtain feedback on how well companies are meeting our needs as consumers. Technology and our data-driven, ever-online world mean deeper connections, sometimes in real time, with customers. But before that happens, brands need to earn our trust and show they can provide value. This will be the strongest trend driving customer experience in the coming years. Here are five ways we can see this happening in the future.

### 3.1 Experiential, Hybrid Experiences

This can mean marketing-focused experiences that help companies communicate their message and engage new audiences in new ways. This will be increasingly visible in sales, service, and products. The term "metaverse" has emerged as a key trend, promoted by companies such as Meta, Nvidia, and Microsoft. It describes persistent online environments where we can connect, communicate, and collaborate in increasingly intense ways. The ability of brands to deliver new and engaging customer experiences through virtual platforms is likely a key reason why the concept will be attractive to businesses, especially as the integration of virtual and augmented reality (VR/AR) will be a key feature of the metaverse. In 2022, companies will have their first experiences to create new ways for us to interact and engage from home, such as Ikea's Everyday Experiments. A growing number of services, such as Snapchat's AR Lab, will make it easier for companies of all sizes to join this trend.

## 3.2 Competition Over Customer Experience

Forget trying to undercut competitors' prices; delivering a superior customer experience is quickly becoming a priority for brands trying to differentiate themselves from the competition. Brands are now focusing on the customer experience, in part because they know people will pay more for great experiences. A look at Douglas' flagship stores is beneficial: they offer excellent shopping experiences to users inside as they know that part of the experience is building trust, and when we trust companies, we are much more willing to share our data with them. Technology offers countless opportunities to create and deliver such experiences. This comes through good service experiences, targeted experiential marketing, or simply discovering that your products and services fit well into customers' lives. As society transitions to a service-based economy in which customer lifetime value is paramount, from 2022 onward, there will be increasing investment in technology designed to enhance our experiences and earn our trust.

## 3.3 Smarter Products and Services

Thanks to the IoT and wearables revolution, the devices we carry and interact with are increasingly able to collect data about us and our world. Gartner estimates that the global wearables market will be worth $93.8 billion by the end of 2022 (see Table 1).

**Table 1** Global wearables market 2019–2022

| Device type | 2019 | 2020 | 2021 | 2022 |
|---|---|---|---|---|
| Smartwatch | 18,501 | 21,758 | 25,827 | 31,337 |
| Wristband | 5101 | 4987 | 4906 | 4477 |
| Ear-worn | 14,583 | 32,724 | 39,220 | 44,160 |
| Head-mounted display | 2777 | 3414 | 4054 | 4573 |
| Smart clothing | 1333 | 1411 | 1529 | 2160 |
| Smart patches | 3900 | 4690 | 5963 | 7150 |
| Total | 46,194 | 68,985 | 81,499 | 93,858 |

Source: Gartner (January 2021)

The extra free time many of us enjoy thanks to the shift to remote and home working is one reason for the IoT and wearables revolution, as is the growing interest in personal health. Companies focused on experience are becoming more adept at using this data to enhance the variety and utility of our interactions with them. New smart materials will enable the creation of smart clothing that is self-powered, can be washed in a regular machine, and can relay many different types of data to apps on ours phones and watches to provide insights into our health. We're also expected to see the first fruits of Google's acquisition of Fitbit, which may lead to more innovation in the smartwatch space. In 2022, many companies focused on improving user experience will develop better integrated products through their use of data to provide us with more valuable insights and richer user experiences.

## 3.4 Service Automation (Customer Service)

The level and quality of service customers receive from companies is a key feature of their experience. We have heard this many times. If customers know they will be on hold for a long time, shuffled between multiple departments, or will have to talk to poorly trained advisors who cannot help them solve their problems, they are unlikely to view their experience with the company positively. Automated call handling systems were originally introduced to solve some of these problems, but unfortunately have not always had the desired effect, as callers have become increasingly frustrated while navigating menus and interacting with voice recognition systems. Companies are banking on the ability to augment these systems with AI—for example, customer service chatbots that use natural language processing (NLP). This means chatbots will become increasingly capable of understanding our input and predicting the response we want. One application that could become a reality in 2022 is voice assistants in offline retail. In a supermarket, for example, we could ask Alexa to tell us where to find the products we want. McDonald's will likely begin rolling out voice recognition at its drive-through terminals this year. And sentiment analysis will increasingly be used to understand the content of written and spoken communication, to route customers more efficiently to the people or machines that provide the best solution. Perhaps Hey-Charles will enable us in the area of conversational commerce to select and order goods via WhatsApp, on the one hand, and to register returns and receive return labels, on the other hand.

## 3.5 Personalization

Increasing personalization will be a very strong trend this year as brands embrace the idea of using technology to develop closer and more personal relationships with their customers. Customer Data Platform (CDP), in conjunction with Marketing Automation, is a case in point. Personalized email headers and subject lines, for example, have been known to increase click-through rates, but that is just the beginning. A hot topic in personalization over the next year will be the opportunities to identify and take advantage of micro "moments:" sales opportunities that are only open for a few seconds, but can be extremely profitable for brands that understand how to identify and leverage them at scale. These micro-moments can occur when a customer goes online to make a purchase or simply to learn about a topic, such as what tool they need to do their job. Increasingly, brands will invest heavily in ways to identify and leverage these moments to find the right time to make a personalized offer that helps solve the problem the potential customer is facing at that time. This is about reaching the right customer at the right time and it represents a cutting-edge marketing challenge, which is increasingly solvable thanks to the technological solutions available to us today.

A great customer experience has a lasting positive impact on customer satisfaction. Long-term customer loyalty, the likelihood that customers will recommend products and services—indeed entire companies—to their friends is then very high. Last but not least, this ultimately increases the probability customers will *remain*. A very good customer experience thus helps turn customers into loyal fans and cements an exceptional market position.

**Frank Müller** has extensive experience in digital marketing, customer journey management, B2C and B2B commerce, and strategic marketing and commercial consulting. After graduating with a degree in industrial engineering from the Karlsruhe Institute of Technology, he completed an MBA at the renowned management school WHU (Wissenschaftliche Hochschule für Unternehmensführung) together with the Kellogg School of Management. He has more than two decades of professional experience as a consultant and manager in various companies and consulting firms in the digital economy and start-ups and teaches as a guest lecturer at various universities.

# Behavioral Economics and CRM: Improved Prediction of Customer Behavior

Herbert Bucheli

**Abstract**

Behavioral economics is a research field that studies decision-making behavior in real decision-making situations. Our decisions are not always as rational as we believe; very often they are irrational, i.e., they contradict the predictions of the standard model of homo economicus. However, there are also generally valid patterns behind irrational behavior, meaning that irrational decision-making behavior can also be predicted.

This chapter provides a brief overview of *behavioral economics* and links its approaches with *predictive modeling* methods. This enables the modeling and forecasting of customer behavior in new decision-making situations, such as the acceptance of new products or services, and thus helps to derive optimal courses of action.

## 1 Introduction

This short practice-oriented chapter aims to show how findings and methods from behavioral economics and predictive modeling (machine learning) can be combined and incorporated into the CRM framework as a methodological approach to prescriptive modeling for an in-depth study of customer behavior.

*Behavioral economics* observes decision-making behavior in the real world, studies its effects, and develops possible explanatory models. Consumers, and individuals generally, do not always make rational decisions, contrary to predictions by classical economic models.

H. Bucheli (✉)
Viseca Payment Services SA, Zurich, Switzerland
e-mail: Herbert.Bucheli@viseca.ch



S. Kirchem et al. (eds.), *CRM Goes Digital*, Management for Professionals,
https://doi.org/10.1007/978-3-658-45798-3_22

The primary model, and something of a cornerstone of classical economics, is *homo economicus*, which describes humans as rational utility-maximizers. In real decision-making situations, however, we frequently exhibit irrational decision-making behavior. The good news is that this irrationality is also subject to generally valid patterns: Our irrational behavior can be predicted. Incorporating these insights and anomalies into the CRM framework enables us to understand customer behavior in greater depth and to better predict customer behavior in new decision-making situations.

*Predictive modeling* concerns the application of machine learning algorithms—a subfield of artificial intelligence—and classical statistical methods toward the prediction of specific events. Usually, the events to be predicted are in the future. For example, predictive modeling tries to answer questions like "Which customers will cancel their bank accounts or credit cards in the coming months?" Using historical customer data, appropriate predictive models can be developed for this purpose. Historical data is systematically examined for patterns (i.e., similar customer behavior) that effectively announce the event to be modeled.

*Prescriptive modeling*, in contrast to predictive modeling, goes one step further and supports the extraction and development of optimal courses of action. That is, prescriptive modeling attempts to answer questions like "How can the termination rate be reduced?" Typically, optimization and simulation methods are used for this purpose.

After introducing the most important ideas and concepts from behavioral economics and predictive modeling, the chapter will look at a possible synthesis of the two research areas. The chapter does not provide a complete overview but aims to further a basic understanding of fundamental principles.

## 2 Behavioral Economics: A Short Introduction

Behavioral economics has been the talk of the town, even before Richard Thaler of the University of Chicago was awarded the Alfred Nobel Memorial Prize in Economics in 2017 for his work on market anomalies and decision-making processes (see, for example, the seminal article on the theory of consumer choice by Richard Thaler 1980). We experience behavioral economics, or its effects, every day without even realizing it. When going to a restaurant with friends, we are influenced by the first person to order when there is uncertainty in the menu selection; when tasting and evaluating a new and unfamiliar wine, we are influenced by available expert opinions; when estimating (or overestimating) the risk of an accident on an upcoming flight when boarding the plane, we are influenced by an article about an air accident we have recently read in the news. Given the choice between a safer or a higher but riskier gain, we tend to choose the safer side. However, when faced with a certain loss versus a chance to avoid loss at the cost of a greater expected value, we are more likely to choose the risk.

Behavioral economics is a research field that systematically studies such biases and apparently irrational decision-making behavior. The standard model of classical economics, homo economicus, actually states that we make rational decisions in the name of utility-maximization at all times: that we have all the information needed for a rational decision in each situation and are able to process it thoroughly. Behavioral economic experiments, however, show the opposite. Our ability to process information is limited. We are subject to bounded rationality. People acting in the real world not only make frequently irrational decisions, but they even do so to their own disadvantage. The founding fathers of behavioral economics, Daniel Kahneman and Amos Tversky, demonstrated various irrational anomalies in experiments investigating decision-making behavior.

Table 1 describes a selection of anomalies that play a role in the CRM context. The table is not exhaustive but provides initial insight into these anomalies. For a comprehensive overview, see Kahneman and Tversky (2000).

Can these anomalies be described as a model? What is the theory underlying these anomalies? The Prospect Theory explains at least some of these anomalies. What follows focuses less on the technical details than the central concepts, including a graphical representation, thought as a valuable and helpful guide for daily work.

Motivated by the observations and findings from their experiments on the decision-making behavior of individuals in uncertainty or risky situations, Daniel Kahnemann and Amos Tversky extended the classic standard theory, the Expected Utility Theory (EUT), to include psychological aspects. EUT goes back to the work of John von Neumann and Oskar Morgenstern in the 1940s and describes the decision-making behavior of rational decision-makers in uncertain situations (for a profound introduction, see Von Neumann and Morgenstern 1953). Kahnemann and Tversky's Prospect Theory introduced the two central concepts of *reference point* and *loss aversion*.

The reference point concept states that in decision-making processes, we do not understand and incorporate utility as an absolute quantity, but rather align ourselves with a reference value and evaluate utility as a relative gain or loss. In other words, there is no generally applicable scale for utility; rather, we weigh gain versus loss with respect to a reference value. The reference value reflects somewhat simplified previous experience and also our expectation according to our *beliefs* and *impressions*. Reference values, therefore, differ individually and are varying over time. In concrete terms, this means profit-loss considerations and perceptions of product decisions change over time. This means a product feature that was once evaluated as surprising and different comes to be expected by customers as a matter of course.

The concept of loss aversion describes the observation that a loss hurts us more than a corresponding gain helps us: a loss of $10 hurts us significantly more than a corresponding gain of $10. The rule of thumb is that we value a loss versus a gain more highly by a factor of 2. Figure 1 shows a graphical representation of the two concepts.

The different gradients of the profit and loss curves illustrate and reflect different perceived values. The concavity of the profit curve reflects disappearing marginal utility, such that, for example, the fourth roll for breakfast no longer tastes as intense as the first. The central point is that this curve shifts with respect to a reference point, depending on the concrete situation.

**Table 1** Selection of anomalies from the research field of behavioral economics that play a role in the context of CRM

| | |
|---|---|
| Reference dependence | Reference dependence is a central concept in behavioral economics. It states that customers, or people in general, do not evaluate offers on an absolute scale, but in terms of gain or loss relative to what they already have (or expect). People do not think in terms of absolute values but in terms of gain or loss relative to a reference value. Reference values are not constant over time, i.e., people get used to a status quo. Over time, customers come to expect what were once new and exciting product features as a matter of course.<br>Translated into the CRM context, this means innovations in products, services, and terms and conditions must always be evaluated in comparison with the *current* state of affairs, or even to the current competitor product (for an in-depth discussion of reference dependence, see Kahneman and Tversky 1979). |
| Anchoring | Anchoring refers to the observed anomaly that individuals use reference values to guide them in the estimation of tasks of unknown quantities. Even though the reference values may be completely independent of the problem being estimated, estimates may be substantially influenced by these reference values. A well-known example from Tversky and Kahnemann (1974) links the task of estimating the percentage of African countries that are members of the United Nations to the prior spinning of a wheel of fortune. The experiment showed that subject estimates were significantly influenced by the randomly obtained number. |
| Framing | Framing refers to the fact that how information is presented can influence how it is received and evaluated.<br>A well-known example of framing is the so-called Asian disease problem, in which inconsistent aggregate decision-making behavior can be provoked due to a reformulation of the same question. Subjects are asked to choose between two alternative programs to combat a fictitious epidemic. The two questions differ only in the formulation of the potential for success, once as rather safe potential and once as rather risky potential for success, but with identical expected values. Tversky and Kahnemann's experiments showed significant differences in aggregate decision-making behavior between the two formulations of the problem (Tversky and Kahnemann 1981).<br>In the CRM context, this means the choice of communication strategy is central to influencing customer decisions and behavior. For example, a particular formulation of a loss is not simply the neutral opposite to the formulation of a gain. |

(continued)

**Table 1** (continued)

| | |
|---|---|
| Loss Aversion | Loss aversion is another central concept in behavioral economics. People tend to perceive the extent of a loss as more painful than a corresponding gain. $10 is not equal to $10: On average, losing $10 makes people unhappier than winning $10 makes them happy. Emotionally, the loss is perceived more intensely than the gain.<br>In the CRM context, when communicating performance adjustments for example, whether this could be perceived as a loss or a gain by the customer must be well thought through. For further reading, please refer to the original article by Daniel Kahnemann and Amos Tversky (1979). |
| The Endowment Effect/Status Quo | The endowment effect describes the phenomenon that people assess the value of an object more highly if they own the object. In other words, people are not willing to sell the item at the price they paid for it themselves. The mere fact of owning a cup makes it more valuable. Exchange processes are more complex than traditional economics assumes and every trade is influenced by the initial situation.<br>For CRM, this means that if customers have to pay a perceivably higher service cost to own an item, product, or status, they will value it more highly. The IKEA concept shows that customers experience and perceive their possession more intensively by assembling their own furniture.<br>For further reading, please refer to the article by Kahnemann et al. (1991). |
| Trust | Trust is the central glue that holds a society together or makes an economy work. Trust is the foundation of social relationships and is based on dimensions such as:<br>– Open, honest, and regular communication to foster collaboration;<br>– Identification with the partner's values, goals, and needs;<br>– The development of an emotional bond, for example, through mutual sympathy.<br>In the CRM context, this means customers must feel their needs, values, and preferences are taken seriously and do not want unemotional or standardized communication.<br>For further reading, please refer to the article "The commitment-trust theory of relationship marketing" by Morgan and Hunt (1994). |
| Fairness | Fairness is another central concept in behavioral economics. Although people take advantage of social situations, they repeatedly reject behavior perceived as unfair and are also willing to pay a price for such rejection. For this reason, people punish those whose behavior they perceive as unfair. The majority of people are apparently not pure profit maximizers, but have social preferences. At the very least, fairness is important to them.<br>For CRM, this means that when a company's behavior is perceived as unfair, it is punished even if customers are not directly affected by it. This can be seen, for example, in the spread of negative customer experiences via social networks via word-of-mouth (see Fehr and Schmidt 1999, for further reading). |

## 3 Predictive Modeling (Machine Learning): Forecasting Customer Behavior

This section briefly introduces the field of predictive modeling. The aim is not to present a complete and detailed overview of possible procedures and methods for predicting customer behavior, but rather to highlight and describe the underlying

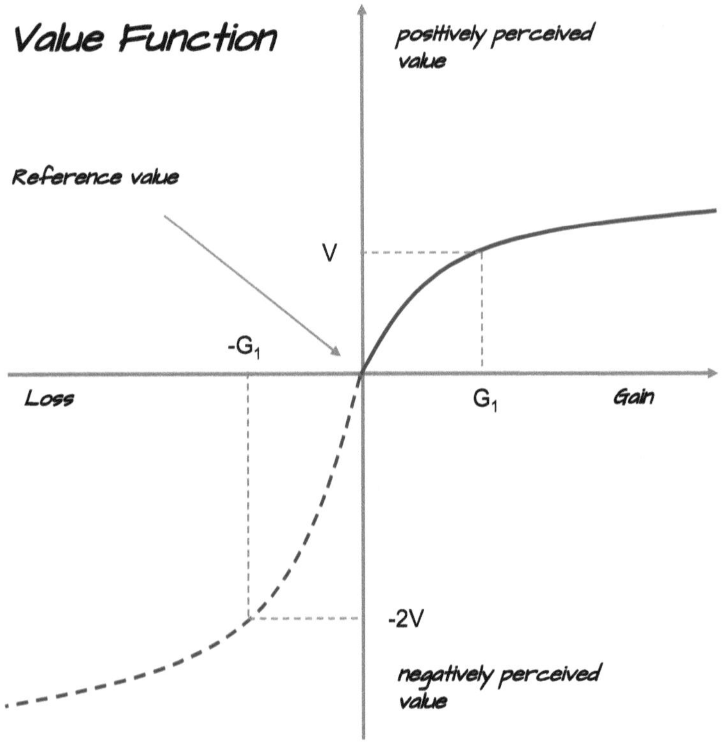


**Fig. 1** Value function from prospect theory

principle of application for such procedures and thus to also show their limitations.

Predictive modeling is generally understood as a set of tools consisting of methods and techniques from classical statistics and the field of machine learning. In simplified terms, these support the extraction of generally valid patterns from historical (customer) data for the prediction of events. If we expand the predictive modeling term somewhat to customer analytics in general, its methods and algorithms can be divided into two fundamentally different classes: *supervised* and *unsupervised learning* methods.

Machine learning is a subfield of artificial intelligence, which focuses on the development of algorithms for systematic and automatable searches of patterns in data.

In supervised learning methods, the dependent target variable or function is known. Translated into the CRM context, this means historical customer data has sample data points identifying the behavior that is to be predicted. Typical use cases for supervised learning methods include the following examples:

- Predicting the termination of a bank account or contract;
- Predicting the risk of failures;
- Detecting card misuse for credit or debit cards;
- Identifying cross-selling and upselling opportunities.

Typical supervised learning methods include logistic regression methods, neural networks, random forest, support vector machines, and deep learning.

In contrast to supervised learning, unsupervised learning methods identify general structures in the data. Unsupervised learning attempts to transform and group datasets such that the most homogeneous areas possible are identified. In the CRM context, this means finding instances in historical customer data in which customers exhibit similar behavior. The critical point here is to define what is meant by similar behavior. For example, customers ordering similar products or exhibiting similar preferences. This is where specific domain knowledge enters the model-building process. Typical use cases for unsupervised learning methods include the development of behavior-based customer segmentation, and the identification of unusual customer behavior, such as attempts at insurance fraud and money laundering transactions. Typical methods of unsupervised learning include cluster analysis methods like kNN (k-nearest neighbors algorithm) and SOM (self-organizing map).

In order to be comprehensive in regard to the CRM context, it is worth mentioning that another category of promising machine learning approaches has come into focus in recent years: *reinforcement learning*—or when linked to deep learning algorithms, *deep reinforcement learning*. Reinforcement learning (RL) is a machine learning approach for modeling stochastic decision-making problems without any prior labeling of the data with respect to the target event. Based on trial and error, the RL algorithm learns about the environment through interaction and associated feedback in terms of reward. It learns an optimal decision-making strategy, step by step, to maximize the aggregate reward. Put simply, the RL algorithm mimics, to a certain degree, the human learning process. For an in-depth look at this promising category of machine learning algorithms, please refer to the very good introductory book by Sutton and Barto (1998).

The second part of this section outlines a basic supervised learning procedure for building a prediction model.

The procedure is as follows: In the customer database, customers who have in the past exhibited the behavior to be predicted are marked accordingly. The technical term for this is *data labeling*. This information is recorded as a so-called *target variable*, such as whether a customer has cancelled their contract—yes or no. Then, for a representative data sample of customers with and without the observed behavior to be modeled (based on historical customer data), the so-called prognostic features are calculated.

The optimal situation is that both customer classes are equally distributed in the data sample. In practice, however, this is rarely the case. To solve this problem, appropriate procedures, such as so-called *oversampling*, generate the desired equal distribution through (stratified) sampling methods.

Examples of features include:

- Revenue in the last year;
- Number of call center contacts;
- Number of days since last purchase.

Together, the features form the *signature* or *footprint* of the customer. The technical term for this is the *customer signature*. Domain knowledge also flows into this feature formation. Close collaboration between the data scientists and the business department is highly recommended here, if not absolutely necessary.

Figure 2 shows the table generated in this process, with one data row per customer. Supervised learning methods are now applied to learn a map from the explanatory or independent variables (features) to the dependent variable (target), which differentiates as much as possible between the individual classes of the target variable to achieve the best possible discriminatory power.

To build a model that works in the real world with the highest possible prediction accuracy, the following approach has proven itself in practice. The dataset generated using the procedure described above is divided into three datasets—training, test, and validation—using a randomized splitting method.

Usually, stratified datasets are generated. This means, for example, that each dataset has the same ratio between event and non-event.

The training and test datasets are used, respectively, to develop and train the model. The validation dataset is used to validate the prediction accuracy measured in the training. If there are large deviations, it means the model does not generalize well enough and the forecasts must be interpreted and used with extreme caution.

This is the basic and recommended procedure to develop a prediction model. If only a few customer data are available, applying more advanced procedures such as k-fold cross-validation is highly recommended. Figure 3 illustrates a summary of the procedure.

The temporal aspect completes the explanation of how to develop a scoring model. In summary, Fig. 4 schematically represents the basic procedure for using historical data to forecast future events.

To illustrate the procedure with a concrete example, let's try to predict the termination of a service contract. In principle, we may only use data prior to the termination date for modeling (no future information). In practice, however, we usually go back a little further in history, so that the time interval between the termination date and a possible prior action to prevent the termination, like a direct email campaign or an outbound call, can also be considered.

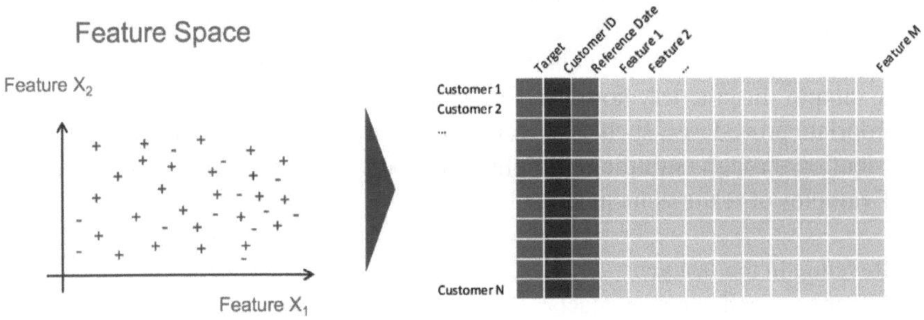


**Fig. 2** Customer signature

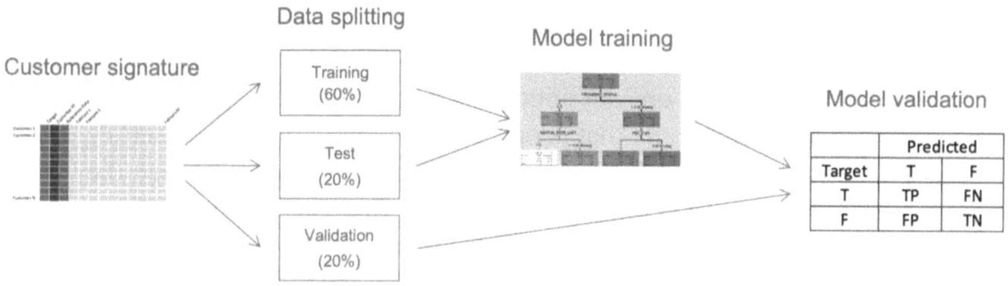


**Fig. 3** Procedure for developing a forecasting model

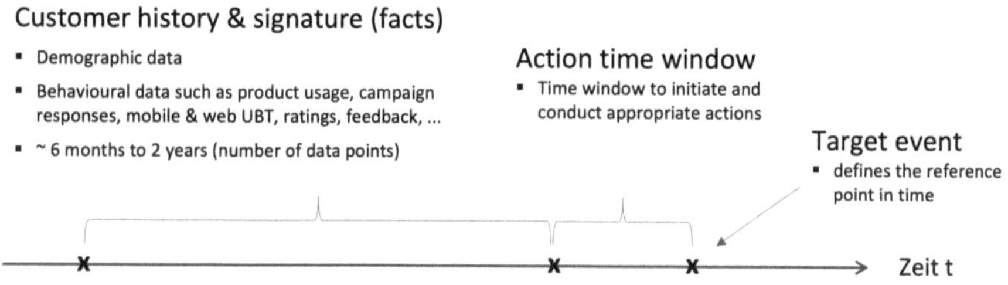


**Fig. 4** Procedure for modeling future events based on historical customer data

The process model presented here shows how a functioning prediction model can be developed, but also the limitations of this methodology. Basically, such models only work if customers behave similarly over time. This precondition is usually fulfilled quite well. The second precondition is that the event to be modeled has been observable in the past and that its data has been recorded. This second precondition thus implies that new events, such as the behavior of customers in response to a price change or the introduction of a new product, can only be predicted to a limited extent using this method. In these cases, it's possible for individual cases to use the "trick" of proxy events, i.e., a past event that is at least similar to the event being modeled.

The next section describes a method that slightly untangles the limitations of predictive modeling.

## 4 Prescriptive Modeling: Understanding and Controlling Customer Behavior

How can insights and methods from behavioral economics be integrated into the CRM framework, linked with a predictive analytics toolbox, and thus used to improve the prediction of customer behavior?

An initially obvious approach is the systematic evaluation, as well as design, of customer interactions along the customer journey according to behavioral economics criteria.

A classic example is to consciously determine the sequence of selection options, or the use of predefined default values or settings. For example, a conscious decision regarding an opt-in or opt-out option. Numerous experiments and field studies have demonstrated empirically that people tend to choose the default setting or preselected option, even though it has been set arbitrarily and even though they could choose an alternative option with minimal effort. See the articles by Dinner et al. (2011) and Johnson and Goldstein (2003). This anomaly is also known as the default effect.

The default effect is a cognitive bias that shows an excessive preference for an option whereby an actor need not make an active decision.

Another applicable example is the targeted integration of gamification into customer communication. Extensive literature describes how to optimally implement this approach. In addition to customer communication, gamification can also be integrated into the internal CRM application so that employees, such as call center agents or sales staff, can more readily accept the technical CRM application in particular and the CRM approach in general. Sufficient acceptance cannot be underestimated and is a significant factor in the success or failure of a CRM initiative.

Another possible and exciting approach to explore in more detail aims to incorporate a behavioral economics viewpoint and mindset into the development of (predictive) scoring models that predicts customer behavior. First, let's briefly outline the idea. When using predictive modeling techniques, practical applications generally model or try to predict a very concrete event, like the cancellation of a service by the consumer. The idea now is to raise the modeling to the next level of abstraction and model not the specific, observed customer behavior, but the *psychological* behavioral drivers underlying the observed behavior. Psychological drivers of behavior, in this context, include constructs like *perceived usefulness*, *social influence*, and *habit*.

This approach is illustrated by a concrete behavioral model. A highly simplified version of the Integrated Behavior Model (IBM) is used as a conceptual framework, i.e., a thought model. This model has been developed by Icek Ajzen and Martin Fishbein (2009). Figure 5 shows the simplified IBM.

The essential aspect to apply concretely is that the model tries to establish a causal relationship between the observed behavior and the behavior drivers. This model can be operationalized, for example, by using a survey in combination with choice experiments, or by linking the survey to the observed behavior. Once the relevant behavioral drivers and the strength of their influence have been identified, they can be specifically strengthened through targeted marketing or by highlighting product features.

By using such an approach, future scenarios such as a planned price adjustment can also be simulated. If the experimental data is linked to internal CRM data, optimal communication strategies can be developed for individual customer segments.

Particular experiments can be combined with simulation techniques such as agent-based modeling to simulate and test different scenarios. Agent-based modeling (ABM) is a special method of computer-based modeling and simulation that maps individual preferences and behavior in decision-making processes. In the

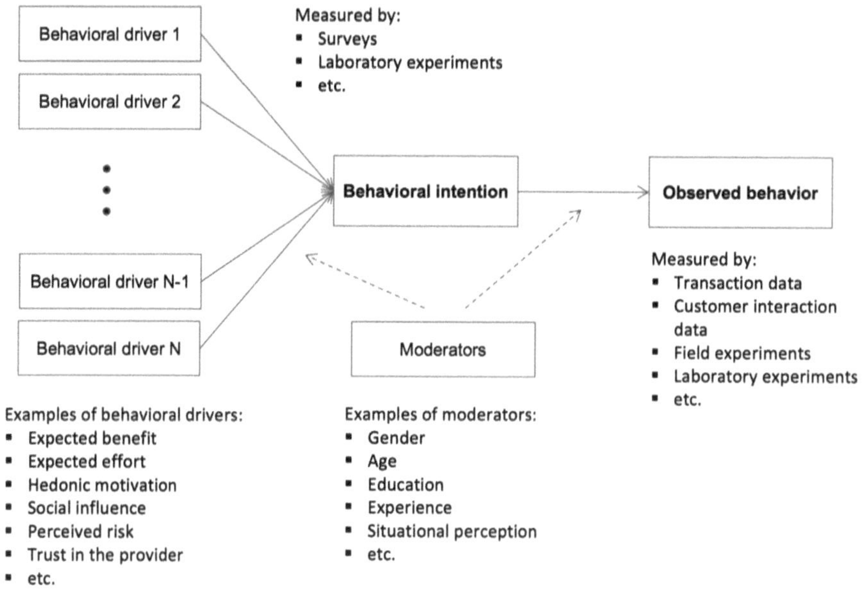


**Fig. 5** Behavior model based on Ajzen and Fishbein's Integrated Behavior Model (IBM)

CRM context, this means the method can simulate the influence of the end customer's decision on the acceptance and use of a new product or service, through to positive and negative communication by word-of-mouth and social networks. The simulation can be adjusted according to choice experiments, or even field experiments, that measure relevant parameters. This offers a cost-effective way to test and optimize different scenarios with respect to the desired effect.

In summary, it is possible to model scenarios that cannot be implemented with historical customer data alone by combining insights and experimental methods from behavioral economics with predictive modeling techniques. This approach is still in its infancy, but has immense potential. However, we should see this approach extending, rather than replacing, predictive modeling.

## References

Dinner I, Johnson EJ, Goldstein DG, Liu K (2011) Partitioning default effects: why people choose not to choose. J Exp Psychol Appl 17(4):332

Fehr E, Schmidt KM (1999) A theory of fairness, competition, and cooperation. Q J Econ 3(114):817–868

Fishbein M, & Ajzen I. (2009). Predicting and changing behavior: The reasoned action approach. Psychology press.

Johnson EJ, Goldstein D (2003) Medicine. Do defaults save lives? Science 302(5649):1338–1339

Kahneman D, Tversky A (1979) Prospect theory: an analysis of decision under risk. Econometrica 47:263–291

Kahneman D, Tversky A (2000) Choices, values, and frames. Cambridge University Press, Cambridge

Kahneman D, Knetsch JL, Thaler RH (1991) Anomalies: the endowment effect, loss aversion, and status quo bias. J Econ Perspect 5(1):193–206

Morgan RM, Hunt SD (1994) The commitment-trust theory of relationship marketing. J Mark:20–38

Morgenstern O, Von Neumann J (1953) Theory of games and economic behavior. Princeton University Press, Princeton, NJ

Sutton RS, Barto AG (1998) Introduction to reinforcement learning, vol 135. MIT Press, Cambridge

Thaler R (1980) Toward a positive theory of consumer choice. J Econ Behav Organ 1(1):39–60

Tversky A, Kahneman D (1974) Judgment under uncertainty: Heuristics and biases. Science 185(4157):1124–1131

Tversky A, Kahneman D (1981) The framing of decision and the psychology of choice. Science 211(418)

**Herbert Bucheli**, PhD, heads the Data Science department and is a member of the management team at Viseca Payment Services SA. He has been involved in the practical application of Machine Learning and AI methods in the extended CRM context for over 20 years. Additionally, Herbert Bucheli dedicates himself to academic research that links Behavioral Economics with AI and Machine Learning approaches, with a focus on the acceptance of new technologies by end users.

# Correction to: Trigger-Based Marketing: Tiki-Taka for Digital Customer Relationship Management

Frank M. Hannich and Marcel Hüttermann

**Correction to:**

**Chapter 15 in: S. Kirchem et al. (eds.), *CRM Goes Digital*, Management for Professionals, https://doi.org/10.1007/978-3-658-45798-3_15**

The original version of the chapter was inadvertently published with an incorrect author sequence "Marcel Hüttermann as the first author and Frank M. Hannich as the second author" due to a publisher's mistake.

We have rectified this error, and the correct sequence of authors is now as follows: Frank M. Hannich as the first author and Marcel Hüttermann as the second author.

The updated version of this chapter can be found at https://doi.org/10.1007/978-3-658-45798-3_15

F. M. Hannich (✉) · M. Hüttermann
ZHAW School of Management and Law, Winterthur, Switzerland
e-mail: hanf@zhaw.ch; huet@zhaw.ch


S. Kirchem et al. (eds.), *CRM Goes Digital*, Management for Professionals, https://doi.org/10.1007/978-3-658-45798-3_23

MIX
Papier aus verantwortungsvollen Quellen
Paper from responsible sources
FSC® C105338

If you have any concerns about our products,
you can contact us on
**ProductSafety@springernature.com**

In case Publisher is established outside the EU,
the EU authorized representative is:
**Springer Nature Customer Service Center GmbH**
**Europaplatz 3, 69115 Heidelberg, Germany**

Printed by Libri Plureos GmbH
in Hamburg, Germany